The Essentials of Human Resources Administration in Education

Ronald W. Rebore
Saint Louis University

Boston Columbus Indianapolis New York San Francisco Upper Saddle River
Amsterdam Cape Town Dubai London Madrid Milan Munich Paris Montreal Toronto
Delhi Mexico City São Paulo Sydney Hong Kong Seoul Singapore Taipei Tokyo

Vice President and Editor in Chief: Jeffery W. Johnston
Senior Acquisitions Editor: Meredith D. Fossel
Editorial Assistant: Nancy Holstein
Vice President, Director of Marketing: Margaret Waples
Senior Marketing Manager: Christopher Barry
Senior Managing Editor: Pamela D. Bennett
Production Editor: Kerry J. Rubadue
Project Manager: Susan Hannahs
Senior Art Director: Jayne Conte
Cover Designer: Suzanne Behnke
Cover Art: Fotolia
Full-Service Project Management: Karpagam Jagadeesan/PreMediaGlobal
Composition: PreMediaGlobal
Text and Cover Printer/Bindery: Courier/Stoughton
Text Font: 10/12 Times

Credits and acknowledgments borrowed from other sources and reproduced, with permission, in this textbook appear on the appropriate page within the text.

Library of Congress Cataloging-in-Publication Data
Rebore, Ronald W.
The essentials of human resources administration in education / Ronald W. Rebore.
p. cm.
Includes bibliographical references and index.
ISBN-13: 978-0-13-700853-7
ISBN-10: 0-13-700853-8
1. School personnel management. 2. School management and organization.
3. Educational leadership. I. Title.
LB2831.5.R37 2012
371.2'01—dc22

2010038330

10 9 8 7 6 5 4 3 2 1

www.pearsonhighered.com

ISBN 10: 0-13-700853-8
ISBN 13: 978-0-13-700853-7

I dedicate this book to my wife, Sandy,
in this our fortieth year of marriage.

BRIEF CONTENTS

CONTENTS

PREFACE

The evolving culture of our contemporary society continues to have an ongoing and profound effect upon the practice of human resources administration in schools and school districts.

An example of this evolving culture is set forth in the section in each chapter on how technology has affected all the various dimensions of human resources administration. The use of technology has enriched the human resources function in virtually every public school and school district. Technology not only impacts central office administration, but also every level of instruction and learning.

Legislation continues to have an impact on human resources management. The U.S. Congress enacted the Americans with Disabilities Act of 1990, which is the most comprehensive legislation ever passed protecting the rights of individuals with disabilities. Furthermore, the Civil Rights Act of 1991 has the potential of costing violators punitive damages through the decisions of jury trials. In 1993, the U.S. Congress also passed the Family and Medical Leave Act, which gives eligible employees the right to leave employment under certain circumstances. Testing for alcohol and controlled substances is now mandated for particular occupations, such as school bus drivers, by the Omnibus Transportation Employee Testing Act of 1991. The Health Insurance Portability and Accountability Act of 1996 assured employees that they, their spouses, and their dependents cannot be denied health insurance coverage because of an illness. In 2002, the No Child Left Behind Act ushered in the most extensive changes in federal law concerning public school education in forty years. The American Recovery & Reinvestment Act of 2009 has set aside billions of dollars for education that will be most beneficial to those public schools and school districts, which have been adversely impacted by the economic downturn.

Beginning in 2001 military reservist and National Guard units have been mobilized into active duty as a consequence of the September 11th terrorist attacks on the United States and the wars in Afghanistan and Iraq. These situations have prompted most human resources administrators to create policies and procedures that address school districts' responsibilities to those employees who have been called up for duty in the armed services.

Sexual harassment in the workplace has gained the attention of school district personnel across the nation as the media have presented coverage of the consequences of this inappropriate and illegal behavior. In addition, the phenomenon of collaborative bargaining as an alternative to the traditional model of negotiations has also become more prevalent in school districts.

Health risks in the workplace, an issue that is related to the ever-increasing cost of workers' compensation, are seriously affecting school district budgets. Likewise, the costs of fringe benefits continue to rise, prompting managed health care as an alternative to traditional medical and hospital insurance programs.

The ethical responsibilities of human resources administrators have become a national concern over the honesty of employees in all levels of business, government, religion, and public education. The underlying root cause of the "reform" movement is the level of accountability or lack thereof in public schools. Taxpayers in general and parents in particular believe that they are not receiving their proper entitlement. A large number of tax levy elections continue to fail because of this perception. The problem of accountability is a "people" problem and, thus, is a human resources administration problem. An important response to this lack of accountability is to make transparent all of the financial transactions of the school district. Such transparency enhances accountability, which ensures equality of opportunity in all human resources policies and procedures.

It is evident that school district administration parallels that of corporations and other organizations in U.S. society. Fiscal management, curriculum development, physical plant management, employee supervision, and human resources administration have become specialties that require educationally sophisticated administrators. This text contains a section in every chapter that sets forth how the material in the chapter can be applied to small and medium-sized school districts, and further describes the impact that Generation Y teachers and administrators have on specific aspects of the human resources administration function. The Essentials of Human Resources Administration in Education book should be of interest to three categories of individuals: first, professors of educational administration who have the instructional responsibility of teaching courses in school human resources administration; second, practicing central office administrators and building principals who want to become more familiar with the field of human resources management; and school board members and superintendents who may be searching for a model in order to establish a central office, human resources administrative position.

Chapter 1 establishes the rationale and organizational structure that support effective human resource administration. Chapters 2 through 5 are concerned with the acquisition of personnel, and Chapters 6 through 9 deal with personnel retention. Each of these chapters addresses a major dimension of the entire human resources management function and identifies the processes, procedures, and techniques necessary to carry out these dimensions. Finally, Chapter 10 considers the legal, ethical, and policy implications of human resources administration.

This book is a spin off from my graduate-level textbook, *Human Resources Administration in Education: A Management Approach,* which is in its 9th edition. The textbook has been and continues to be used in a significant number of universities throughout the United States. Furthermore, it has been translated into Chinese and is used to prepare educational leaders in that country.

For those looking for brief coverage of this topic, *The Essentials of Human Resources Administration in Education* should be a welcome resource.

At this point, I would like to sincerely thank my colleagues teaching at universities and their students who reviewed *The Essentials of Human Resources Administration in Education* and made valuable suggestions for its improvement. I continue to incorporate as many of their suggestions as possible. I particularly want to thank the reviewers of this edition: Judith Docekal, Loyola University; Gary Hoban, National University; K. Fritz Leifeste, Angelo State University; Michael J. Lovett, White Bear Lake School District; James K. Martin, University of Minnesota; George E. Pawlas, University of Central Florida; Max Skidmore, University of Georgia; and Linda Sloat, University of Illinois at Urbana-Champaign. Additionally, I extend my sincere gratitude to Ms. Patricia Polster, my graduate assistant, for her expert and diligent help with this book and also with my other publications.

R. W. R.

CHAPTER

1

The Organizational Structure of Human Resources Administration

FOCUS SCENARIO

You are the assistant superintendent for human resources in a school district with two elementary schools, one middle school, and one high school. There is one other assistant superintendent who is responsible for curriculum development. The human resources department consists of just yourself and a secretary. The department has been functioning only in the areas of personnel recruitment and selection. Given the fact that no additional personnel will be added to the department, you have decided that the human resources function must become a shared responsibility with other administrators, teachers, and staff members in the district. The school district has 100 professional employees, which includes building level administrators, teachers, counselor, media specialists, and others. There are 30 support personnel, which include secretaries, bus drivers, maintenance workers, and the housekeeping staff. There are approximately 2000 students in the school district.

The major issue facing the school district is the lack of financial resources. Over the last five years, the district has tried to increase the tax levy through two referendums, both of which failed. In addition, the district has been experiencing an influx of migrant workers (because of a newly established furniture factory) that has necessitated the opening of additional classrooms and the need to hire additional language arts teachers who can instruct the children of migrant workers in English as their second language.

The superintendent and the Board of Education are particularly concerned that you are able to help the district meet the requirements of the No Child Left Behind (NCLB) Act, and that you are capable of fulfilling the human resources function from a values-based approach. The former assistant superintendent was terminated from the school district because he falsified certain documents that alleged the district's compliance with NCLB.

THE ADMINISTRATIVE PROCESS

Administration is an indispensable component of all institutions in organized society; yet, it is often taken for granted. The need for administration has been evident whenever there was a task to be performed by two or more people. Many ancient records of significant events describe administrative activities. Building the pyramids, supervising medieval feudal domains, and governing colonies in distant hemispheres have demanded a degree of administrative skill and understanding of the administrative process.

Our understanding of the nature of administration has evolved over time. The earliest concepts centered on the action model. Administrators were those who took charge of an activity and accomplished a task. The formal study of administration is a recent phenomenon that has found its most fertile climate in the business world, where much study is devoted to the effective execution of managerial leadership.

The need for the formal study of administration in public education grew out of the increased complexity of urban school districts. The illusion that anyone with a good general education could become an effective administrator was quickly shattered during the urbanization period.

Administration is the social process of managing human, financial, and material resources toward the fulfillment of a mission. The school administrator fulfills these requisites by developing and establishing administrative processes, procedures, and techniques that harness human, financial, and material energies. The importance of administrative leadership stems from its potential for converting these energies within an organization into the fulfillment of educational objectives. This definition of administration views it as an executive activity, distinct from policy making. Administration is primarily concerned with the implementation, not the making, of policy. More specifically, the administration of a district is responsible for carrying out the policies of the board of education.

The systems approach to administration has gained steadily in popularity ever since President Lyndon B. Johnson mandated its implementation in federal agencies, and the outcry for accountability in the public sector advanced its use. In the systems approach, the school is viewed as a network of interrelated subsystems. Emphasis is given to formulating short- and long-range objectives that can be translated into operational activities, which are implemented and evaluated.

The approach followed in this book focuses on human resources administration as a function. Thus, administration is viewed as an all-encompassing process composed of various functions. Three of the most critical functions in a school system are human resources administration, instructional programs administration, and support services administration. Support services here include transportation, food service, and financial administration. Each of these functions has goals that are implemented through administrative processes, procedures, and techniques, which are collectively referred to as management. This book, of course, centers on the human resources function and its management.

Functions are carried out by administrators within a given organizational framework. The remaining portion of this section delineates and clarifies the role of the superintendent of schools and major central office administrators.

The Organization of the Central Office

Historically and, in most states, by statutory mandate, school boards have delegated the responsibility for implementing policies to a chief executive officer—the superintendent of schools. The superintendent assumes full control of all operations. As school districts grow in size and complexity, it becomes necessary to develop specialized functions, and the central office staff comes into being. However, all employees, professional and other, ultimately report to the superintendent and are subordinate to him or her. The superintendent is the only employee who deals with the board of education on a regular and direct basis.

The superintendent's role can be described in terms of the three major roles incorporated into this one position.

Chief Advisor

The superintendent is the main consultant and advisor to the school board on all matters concerning the school district. The superintendent is expected to contribute to the school board's deliberations by furnishing reports, information, and recommendations, both upon request of the board and upon self-directed initiative. A list of the superintendent's duties and functions as the school board's chief advisor includes the following:

- Formulate and recommend human resources policies necessary for the efficient functioning of the school staff.
- Provide information to the school board on vital matters pertaining to the school system.
- Prepare and submit a preliminary budget to the school board.
- Recommend all candidates for employment. (The school board may reject specific recommended candidates, but all personnel should be employed only upon the superintendent's recommendation.)
- Submit an annual report to the school board on the operations of the school system.

Executive Officer

Once a policy decision has been established by the board of education, it becomes the responsibility of the executive officer of the board and the district's staff to execute that decision. The administration should implement board policies via rules and regulations. As the chief executive officer of the district, the superintendent sets the tone for the entire system. In performing this function, the duties and responsibilities of the superintendent are to:

- Carry out policies and regulations established by the school board. (In matters not specifically covered by board policies, the superintendent should take appropriate action and report the action to the board no later than the next meeting.)
- Prepare regulations and instruct school employees as may be necessary to make effective the policies of the school board.
- Direct all purchases and expenditures in accordance with the policies of the school board.
- Formulate and administer a program of supervision for the schools.
- Develop a program of maintenance and improvement or expansion of buildings and site.

Educational Leader

The superintendent's educational leadership role should be exercised not only with other professional educators within the district but also with regional, state, and national professional educators, organizations, and agencies. As the educational leader within the community, the superintendent will be called upon to keep the public informed as to the activities, achievements, needs, and directions of the school system. The superintendent should also keep the members of the board informed of new trends in education and their implications for the local district. A leadership role must also be assumed among the staff members of the school district. Without the support and understanding of the employees, the goals and objectives set by the district cannot be achieved.[1]

An ongoing reality in school administration, particularly in the superintendency, is the administrative team approach to central office and building level management. In most districts, the administrative team is a group of administrators that oversee certain responsibilities of the superintendent of schools. Each administrator usually has the title of deputy, associate, or assistant superintendent. In most school districts, personnel having the title of director or coordinator are not members of the administrative team, but rather are support personnel to the team.

Formal designation of membership on the administrative team is appointment to the superintendent's cabinet, which is a strategy-planning and decision-making body. The heads of human resources administration, instructional programs administration, and support services administration are typically included in the cabinet. This formal organization of the superintendent's cabinet is not meant to imply that the superintendent should confine the "team" effort only to the highest levels of school-district administration. Rather, the establishment of a cabinet is an attempt to share the strategy-planning process with key administrators. The issues and problems facing school districts are so far-reaching today that the superintendent must have continual and effective counsel in making decisions.

Because there is a need in all school districts to identify various echelons in the administrative organization, it is recommended that the title of director or coordinator be attached to administrative positions reporting to an assistant superintendent in charge of a particular function.

HUMAN RESOURCES ADMINISTRATION

The Human Resources Function

In every school district, people must be recruited, selected, placed, evaluated, and compensated, whether by a central human resources office or by various administrators within the school district.

The goals of the human resources function are basically the same in all school systems. They are to hire, retain, develop, and motivate personnel in order to achieve the objectives of the school district, to assist individual members of the staff to reach the highest possible levels of achievement, and to maximize the career development of personnel. These goals must be implemented through the following dimensions of the human resources function:

- *Human resources planning*. Establishing a master plan of long- and short-range human resources requirements is a necessary ingredient in the school district's curricular and fiscal planning processes.
- *Recruitment.* Quality personnel, of course, are essential for the delivery of effective educational services to children, youth, and adults.
- *Selection.* The long- and short-range human resources requirements are implemented through selection techniques and processes.
- *Placement and induction*. Through appropriate planning, new personnel and the school district accommodate each other's goals.
- *Staff development*. Development programs help personnel meet school district objectives and also provide individuals with the opportunity for personal and professional growth.
- *Performance evaluation*. Processes and techniques for evaluation help the individual grow professionally and help the school district attain its objectives.
- *Compensation*. Establishing programs that compensate quality performance helps to motivate personnel.
- *Collective negotiations*. The negotiating process gives personnel an opportunity to participate in matters that affect their professional and personal welfare.

Unfortunately, many school districts still see the human resources function only as the hiring of competent teachers. These eight dimensions of the human resources function listed above are not discrete, isolated entities, but rather, integral aspects of the same function. Each of the next eight chapters of this book addresses one of these dimensions. Administrative processes, procedures, and techniques for accomplishing the human resources function are reviewed. Also, major issues that significantly influence the administration of human resources are addressed in these chapters.

RESPONSIBILITIES OF HUMAN RESOURCES SPECIALISTS

There are six human resources specialists that are found in very large school districts. Of course, smaller and medium-sized school districts will not need more than the services of an assistant superintendent who has the entire human resources administrative responsibility. However, the tasks that he or she will perform are the same as the specialists listed below.

Responsibilities of the Assistant Superintendent for Human Resources:

- He or she supervises the director of employee relations, the director of staff development, the director of employee benefits, and the director of risk management.
- The assistant superintendent for human resources is directly responsible for establishing administrative processes and procedures for human resources planning, recruitment of staff, selection of personnel, placement and induction of personnel, staff evaluation and compensation programs.

Responsibilities of the Director of Employee Relations:

- He or she is responsible for managing the school district's employee relations program.
- This includes formulating, recommending, and administering the school district's employee relations policies and managing the collective negotiations process.
- In preparing for the negotiations process, the director of employee relations will develop negotiations strategies for management, prepare proposals and counterproposals, analyze and evaluate employee proposals, and advise management accordingly.
- He or she will be knowledgeable about state laws and court decisions relevant to collective negotiations.
- He or she will secure input from all administrative personnel prior to developing management's proposals.
- In at-the-table negotiations, the director of employee relations shall serve as the chief negotiator for the school district, direct the school district's negotiations team, and keep administrative personnel informed during negotiations.
- The director will draft negotiated agreements reached with unions, and maintain records of proposals and counterproposals presented by all parties during negotiations.
- He or she will administer the negotiated agreement, advise management on the interpretation of adopted agreements, and manage all grievances filed by the unions.

Responsibilities of the Director of Staff Development:

- The director of staff development is responsible for the management of the school district's staff development program that includes the establishment, formulation, recommendation, and administration of the school district's staff development policies.
- He or she shall establish and implement ongoing needs assessment with all administrators, teachers, and other staff members concerning the content of staff development programs and the delivery model for the programs.

Responsibilities of the Director of Affirmative Action:

- The director of affirmative action is responsible for formulating, recommending, and administering the school district's affirmative action policies.
- He or she is responsible for investigating affirmative action problems and suggesting solutions to the superintendent of schools.
- Using school district data, the director reviews the qualifications of all employees, with particular emphasis on minorities, women, older workers, and people with disabilities as the data relate to fair employment practices.
- He or she develops and updates goals and timetables for correcting identifiable deficiencies.
- The director advises the superintendent on recruitment of minorities, women, older workers, and people with disabilities for those positions in which the district may be falling short of the district's affirmative action goals.
- He or she assumes the role of compliance officer and makes all contacts with state and federal agencies.
- The director reviews all job announcements, job descriptions, and selection criteria to ensure compliance with affirmative action requirements.
- He or she investigates formal complaints of alleged discrimination relating to fair employment practices, and recommends corrective measures to the superintendent.
- The director maintains liaison with local, state, and federal agencies and with organizations concerned with promoting fair employment practices.

Responsibilities of the Director of Employee Benefits:

- The director of employee benefits is responsible for formulating, recommending, and managing the employee benefits policies.
- He or she shall establish and implement ongoing monitoring and assessment of the cost effectiveness of the benefits programs.
- The director shall establish and chair the employee benefits committee which is charged with reviewing employee benefits, making suggestions for improving benefits, making suggestions for containing costs, reviewing specifications for bidding benefits insurance, reviewing the analysis of bids, and annually making recommendations to the superintendent of schools.
- He or she conducts an annual survey of employee perceptions concerning the scope and effectiveness of the benefits program.
- The director serves as the liaison between the district and those companies providing health care and related insurance.
- He or she develops informational materials for employees about the district's benefits program.
- The director plans and implements the workers' compensation program.

Responsibilities of the Director of Risk Management:

- The director of risk management is responsible for administering the school district's risk management program, which includes formulating the school district's risk management policies as well as establishing effective two-way communication between the district's organizational levels.
- He or she shall establish and chair the employee safety and security committee, which is charged with reviewing safety and security processes and procedures, making suggestions

for improving safety and security rules and procedures, reviewing specifications for bidding risk management services and equipment, and reviewing the analysis of bids.
- The director develops, implements, and evaluates an annual safety and security audit.
- He or she develops informational materials concerning safety and security on the job and provides safety and security education and training to employees.
- The director develops an annual safety and security report for the assistant superintendent for human resources that contains recommendations for improving the school district's safety and security program.
- He or she investigates, assesses, and manages safety and security crisis events.

Many school districts have seen the need in recent times to delegate a major share of the human resources function to a specialized central office unit. In this type of organization, an assistant superintendent for human resources (or director of human resources) administers the human resources function and aids the superintendent in solving personnel problems. Human resources administrator is usually a staff position that exists to service line administrators. Line positions include the assistant superintendents for secondary education and elementary education, administrators of certain support services, and building principals. These administrators have been granted authority to make decisions in the supervisory process as it relates to staff, faculty, and students.

The human resources function has an impact upon the continual staffing of positions, which in turn directly affects the quality of educational programs, but it also has a significant effect upon the budget. Approximately 80 percent of all school district expenditures are for salaries and benefits. Inefficiency in the human resources function can potentially cost the taxpayer unnecessarily large sums of money.

Boards of education and administrators are seldom fully aware of the pervasive effect their personnel decisions have on the planning process. Every position within a school system generates a series of decisions as to the type of work to be performed, the qualities needed for its proper performance, and its economic value. A variety of actions are required for the proper recruiting, selecting, inducting, developing, and evaluating of personnel. Policies and procedures also must be established regarding academic freedom, tenure, health, grievances, leaves of absences, and retirement. In all but the very smallest districts, the movement of personnel in and out of a school district requires the attention of human resources specialists.

The number of strikes by public school teachers has remained relatively constant over the last ten years. Salaries, fringe benefits, and working conditions constitute the major issues that may lead to an impasse at the table and result in a strike. Education, however, is a relative newcomer to the negotiations process.

Collective negotiation is traditionally a human resources function and correctly belongs under the jurisdiction of the assistant superintendent for human resources. Because of the magnitude of the issues involved with this process, most school districts should consider establishing the position of director of employee relations.

The knowledge explosion and the constantly changing social milieu have also produced a major issue in the area of human resources administration. In the past, staff development was viewed primarily from the in-service training model, which concentrated on providing a few workshops on instructional materials. The last quarter century, however, has ushered in federal legislation and litigation that have more clearly defined the rights of racial minorities, women, students, older workers, and those with disabilities. This, coupled with the deluge of new instructional technologies, the differing attitudes of the new professionals entering teaching, and the changing values of our society as manifested by parents and students, has created a need for an ongoing staff development program for administrators and teachers alike. This function is so specialized that, like collective negotiations, it also requires the attention of a human resources specialist, the director of staff development.

The avalanche of federal legislation and litigation concerning human rights has made it necessary to establish a central office administrative position, usually entitled director of affirmative action. Most federal legislation contains an equal opportunity clause, which in turn dictates the organization of a detailed program for carrying out the intent of the law in all phases of the human resources function. This organized program is more commonly called *affirmative action*. Chapter 2 of this book presents a complete explanation of all major civil rights legislation and the concept of affirmative action. A unique feature of this administrative position in the organizational structure of a school district is the fact that the director of affirmative action usually reports directly to the superintendent of schools. This provides integrity in the school district's compliance with civil rights legislation because the director is thus protected from the influences of other administrators.

The escalating cost of health care is an issue facing every school district that provides health care and related benefits to employees. Most school districts have undertaken drastic measures in an attempt to control costs, which has led to what is commonly referred to as *managed care*. Along with the many innovations underway is the need to hire human resources staff members who not only have experience, but also academic credentials in health care management. Further, the rising cost of workers' compensation reinforces the need to hire human resources staff members who also have experience with and understand of the nuances of risk management. Most school districts use the title director of employee benefits to designate the staff member who is responsible for managing the employee benefits and workers' compensation programs. This administrator, of course, reports to the assistant superintendent for human resources.

Contemporary society is fraught with risks to personal security and safety. This has been graphically embedded in the consciousness of all Americans because of the enormous loss of life in schools over the last decade due to student violence perpetrated against other students, teachers, staff members, and administrators. People from outside the school community have also entered school buildings and committed violent acts against students and employees. In addition, there is the ever-present risk of injury to students and employees because of accidents stemming from school facilities and equipment. Finally, there is the risk that arises from the potential breach of confidentiality in relation to student and employee records. Safety and security audits, rules, and procedures must be developed in order to ensure, as much as possible, a risk-free environment for both students and employees. This has prompted school districts to create the position of director of risk management.

LEADERSHIP THEORY FOR HUMAN RESOURCES ADMINISTRATION

There are three major reasons why transcendental leadership is an appropriate theory for human resources administrators. First, human resources administration operates within a milieu that is very complex, ambiguous, and stressful. Second, like other educational administrators, human resources administrators are required to perform their responsibilities even though they may not have job security. Finally, boards of education continue to cross the line between governance and administration.

In addition, superintendents, principals, other administrators, and human resources administrators are often criticized or blamed for the following: poor performance of students on standardized tests, substandard teacher performance, outdated curricula, student violence, and a lack of financial stewardship. Although some of these criticisms are legitimate in some schools and school districts, they do not accurately represent the general condition. In spite of such criticism and difficulties, a major influence in the lives of most administrators, including human resources administrators, is the search for meaning that goes beyond the paycheck and prestige that comes from being a superintendent, principal, or human resources administrator. This search for meaning may be identified in a very concise way as the transcendent dimension of leadership.

In this context, transcendence means a way of life dedicated to leadership within and on behalf of the academic community and profession rather than simply finding an administrative position in order to make a living. Obviously, making a living is an important consideration for everyone. However, without a sense of transcendence, administrators may concentrate on the performance of tasks and fail to reflect on their overall reasons for being educational leaders.

Accepting the transcendence of leadership requires a person to undertake a lifelong process of discerning how he or she can be of service to the academic community and profession while carrying out the tasks and responsibilities of his or her leadership position within a given school or school district. This sense of service is difficult to sustain unless a person has an agenda to follow. Operating from such a theoretical base ensures that a person will develop and maintain effective job performance. In this context, such an agenda consists of the elements in a transcendental model of leadership.

Because administrators in general and human resources administrators in particular are concerned with human growth and development, they are generally more open to the cultural differences that exist between human beings and institutions. The basic premise of transcendental leadership is that a person acts from the totality of who he or she is as a human being. Most administrators are generally aware that their decisions are influenced by more than just the immediately recognizable circumstances and that the effects of their decisions can go beyond the present situation.

Transcendental leadership has two components. First, there are six elements that pertain to dispositions individual human resources administrators should possess to be centered on human growth and development. Second, there are ten focuses that establish a transcendental culture in a school district. Such a culture is organizationally supportive of human growth and development.

The Elements of Transcendental Leadership

Operationalization is a process that includes various elements that are activated to guarantee that a theory is properly practiced. Many different theories have similar elements, but it is the combination of elements and the disposition of the person using the theory that makes it effective. There are six elements that make up transcendental leadership theory. The elements of this theory can be applied specifically to human resources administrators:

1. *Utilize reflection on practice*. The first element takes into account the importance of practice as the phenomenon upon which theory and foundational values are based. Everything begins with practice. Knowing and understanding what is occurring in human resources administration practice is the only way to evaluate effective leadership. Leadership cannot be a top-down phenomenon, but rather must begin with the processes and practices of human resources administration. This includes knowing and understanding the attitudes, emotions, and opinions of all stakeholders.
2. *Practice the principle of subsidiarity*. This element has a unique history in that it originated in social ethics and social economics. The principle of subsidiarity states that decisions should be made at the lowest possible level in a given school district. There is no question about the

relevance of allowing administrators to do their jobs without interference but with monitoring from others. There is also no question about the firsthand knowledge and experience that respective administrators have, which makes them eminently more qualified than others to handle specific issues and problems. Thus, the performance evaluation process must be implemented by first-line supervisors, with support from the human resources department. The human resources function cannot be operationalized without input and assistance from other members of the school district community, as will be demonstrated in subsequent chapters of this book.

3. *Act from a political base.* The third element refers to the human phenomenon whereby people try to manage the impact that their actions and decisions will have on the actions and decisions of others and on institutions. In human resources administration, the conceptualization of what constitutes a political base can be understood in a primary tension, the rights of government versus the rights of the individual. The role and function of administrators is to ensure that the rights of individual students, parents, teachers, staff members, and others are not in conflict with the rights of the local, state, and national governments. For example, there is a certain amount of tension between the right of the United States Congress to pass the Omnibus Transportation Employee Testing Act of 1991 and the right of employees to due process in the workplace.
4. *Act from a sense of duty and responsibility.* It is not easy to know one's duty and responsibility. For human resources administrators, it can be difficult and, at times, ambiguous. In the most sweeping context, people have responsibilities to themselves and their families, friends, neighbors, and colleagues in addition to their employing school district, community, state, and nation. Finally, human resources administrators have a duty and responsibility to their profession. The issue is how to balance all of their various duties and responsibilities. At times these duties and responsibilities come into conflict with each other. Reflection and common sense are the primary tools that will help administrators find the balance that is required at a given time.
5. *Advocate for social justice.* Pluralism can produce conflict; conflict can lead to injustices. Thus, there is a need to know and understand some basic notions about justice. Justice is that guide which regulates how people live out their lives as members of a community. In contemporary society, everyone is a member, even if he or she tries to live as a hermit. Computer and satellite technology make it possible to locate virtually every person on the planet. There are no places where a person can hide and neglect his or her obligations to society. The choice to either live in society or to retreat from it by living a solitary life no longer exists. The very fact of being brings with it social obligations and the need for effective human relations. Justice is one of the most important aspects of human resources administration because the actions of an administrator can have both an immediate and long-term effect upon people and the person's school district. Unfairness in administering human resources policies and procedures can be masked through the details of management. Thus, a just and fair human resources administrator is critical to social justice.
6. *Formulate professional positions through discourse.* Reasoning is the basis of all discourse in that participants must agree to this rationality if it is to be effective. Participants should be free from external and internal coercion other than the force of the best argument, which supports the cooperative search for truth. Because of the limitations of time and space, it is necessary to institutionalize discourse; the topics to be discussed and the contributions of participants must be organized in terms of opening, adjournment, and resumption of discussion. Discourse can be effective only if it is applied to questions which can be dealt with through impartial judgment. This implies that the process will lead to an answer that is equally beneficial to all

stakeholders. This does not mean that discourse seeks to reach consensus but, rather, to generate convictions in the participants. Further, the degree to which a society, its institutions, its political culture, its traditions, and its everyday practices permit a noncoercive and nonauthoritarian form of discourse is a hallmark of rationality. Thus, human resources administrators cannot expect to find the best solution to problems or to formulate the best policies and procedures if they carry out these tasks without discourse with those who have a stake in the problem or with those who will be affected by the policies or procedures.[2]

TECHNOLOGY AND THE ORGANIZATIONAL DIMENSIONS OF HUMAN RESOURCES ADMINISTRATION

The impact of technology upon the daily lives of people cannot be overestimated. It is a phenomenon that has changed the way people think and act, not only in their homes but also in the workplace. Virtually every school district in the United States is dealing with the use of technology in relation to the instructional program and in central office administration.

When applied to the school district human resources function, technology has many benefits, including:

- *Cost-effectiveness.* Fewer people are required to perform certain human resources responsibilities
- *Efficiency.* Processes and procedures can be computerized
- *Engagement.* Employees themselves can access services more quickly
- *Job enhancement.* Human resources department staff members can concentrate on planning and development rather than on routine tasks
- *Assessment.* Information available in databases can be quickly and easily organized into management reports

The entire field of computer technology has progressed through three phases that began in the 1950s and 1960s with large mainframe computers. With accelerated momentum, minicomputers and personal computers were developed and interconnected through privately owned networks. The 1990s through to the present time has experienced the emmergence of the Internet and the World Wide Web. Excitingly, the future will most likely see the merging of information databases with communication that utilizes nanotechnology, biotechnology, and genomics. Thus, it is imperative for educational administrators to continue their study and dialogue about the potential of technology on the human resources function. In fact, being proactive in visioning both the benefits and cautions of emerging technology should constitute a segment of every educational administrator's responsibility. It would be a professional failing for human resources administrators to neglect becoming the designers of the future when that is exactly what we are meant to do as educators.[3]

TECHNOLOGY AND ROUTINE HUMAN RESOURCES PROCEDURES

Initial Entry and Change of Personnel Information

Most school-district employees would like to have more control over routine human resources procedures, which is easily accomplished through technology. Human resources departments have enhanced the level of service to employees by eliminating paper intensive work through technology, which also tends to reduce errors. Self-service workflow technology also gives employees access to their ongoing status and allows them to have a quality assurance check on their status and benefits. Employees can thus have easy and reliable access to pay stub information: gross pay, deductions, year-to-date accumulations, and tax withholding data.

One of the easiest services to upgrade by using technology in school districts is benefits enrollment. Medical, dental, and life insurance plan enrollment can be accomplished through an interactive voice response telephone system. This technology utilizes a text-to-speech approach whereby the system voices the caller's current status and then prompts him or her to make a selection from a series of options. This type of self-service application is commonly referred to as a kiosk system, which is a standalone center that prompts users when data are entered. There are basically two types of kiosks: typing key words or using touch-screen technology.

This can also be accomplished through the Internet and an intranet system, which is the application of Web technology to the administrative computer network of a school district. Of course, changes in status in addition to initial enrollment also can be accomplished through this same technology. A change of primary care physician, the listing of a new dependent, and a change of beneficiary are common applications of self-service technology. Interactive voice response and Internet technology also provide a convenient way for retirees who continue to participate in district programs to make changes in their status without coming into the school district's central office or without sending in paperwork that is susceptible to keying error.

In utilizing these technologies, an employee of a school district can initiate a change in his or her home address, notify the human resources department about a newly earned degree, or initiate a change in marital status. In an automated workflow system, these types of changes can be programmed to activate other processes. Thus, a change in marital status might activate a request for additional information concerning name change or beneficiary election. Another example of this type of event-based processing is as follows: When a new teacher is hired and his or her human resources data file is created, event-based processing triggers the system to create a payroll file and enroll him or her in all standard employee benefits programs. The system then sends a message to the staff development department, which in turn enrolls the new employee in the school district's orientation program. In the case of a newly hired administrator, the system also sends a message to the information systems department in order to set up a system security identification number. The workflow capabilities of technology are limited only by the imagination and design of human resources administrators.

The potential of workflow is promising particularly in relation to carrying out teacher and staff member performance evaluations online. A workflow analytical system could activate a series of considerations that a supervisor should keep in mind given the evaluation of an employee. For example, if an elementary school teacher is having difficulty teaching a newly adopted mathematics curriculum, a prompt might suggest a series of actions that the principal could consider, including asking the teacher to enroll in a workshop on the new mathematics curriculum being conducted by the publisher of the mathematics materials. The prompt could even include the time and date that the professional development department of the school district has scheduled the workshop. Further, it is possible to design the performance evaluation online system in order to analyze the pattern that emerges in how the principal has evaluated the teachers in his or her school.

Of course, it is possible to incorporate security features into self-service programs. For example, an employee can be required to use a personal identification number to transact business, and Internet security features can be utilized to encrypt the information that employees enter and establish a secure connection to the Web site.

Request and Utilization of Forms

Forms are constantly being requested by employees for personal needs and by other members of various departments within a school district to carry out ordinary human resources business. Insurance claim forms are an often requested personal need form, while school building and department personnel are constantly in need of authorization-to-hire forms and performance evaluation documents. Requesting such forms and documents through an interactive voice response system, the Internet, or intranet saves valuable time for human resources personnel. In addition, printing such forms and documents from a Web site saves the time and energy needed to deliver hard copies.

Task Performance

However, the most important way to save time and energy, in addition to eliminating paperwork, is to perform the task by directly using interactive voice response, Internet, or intranet technology. This is accomplished in a way that is similar to the use of these technologies for benefits enrollment. An authorization-to-hire form, for example, can be completed by a principal or the head of a school district department by using an identification number or password along with other security methods. It is important for all employees to understand that identification numbers and passwords constitute the same authority and responsibility as a signature. Thus, the safeguarding of identification numbers and passwords is a serious professional responsibility.

Performance evaluation is another example of how the Internet or intranet can be utilized to save time and energy, and reduce paperwork. Filling out a form online and storing it in the school district's database is much more efficient than completing a form and keeping it in a file cabinet. Depending upon the level of security, the performance evaluation information can be more confidential and secure in the school district's database. It is just as effective, possibly more efficient, and ultimately more cost-effective to download the performance evaluation to a disk that can be given to the employee and utilized as an ongoing record of his or her performance. The principal or department supervisor and the employee can sign the identification sticker that is placed on the disk as an indication that the contents have been explained to the employee. An employee response can be recorded on the disk, downloaded, and a copy given to the principal who, in turn, can follow the ordinary procedure of response and appeal. The difference is that the district's database and a disk become the record, rather than traditional paper forms.

Posting Job Opportunities

The use of interactive voice response, the Internet, and intranet are excellent avenues for providing both employees and other people interested in working for the school district with information about available positions. These types of postings can provide the school district with more effective linkage to the best qualified people. Further, these technologies not only provide easily accessed information about job requirements and timely notification of job vacancies, but also can become the avenues for potential employees to apply for positions.

The use of these technologies can enhance the affirmative action efforts of a given school district by reaching people who do not live in the school district community or who do not have access to the daily newspapers where job vacancies are posted. This helps to recruit people with disabilities, minorities, older workers, and women.

Online Recruitment and Selection

A computerized application process allows principals and department administrators to enter the competencies that are appropriate for a vacant position. The system then searches the database for a match between the competencies and the skills of available applicants. Creating the applicant pool can take place through the Internet. For example, a person interested in working for a certain school district could consult the Web page for that school district which, in turn, could direct the person to an online application.

If a resume is mailed by a potential candidate to a school district, it can be entered into a database and reformatted so that it will be available to principals and department directors. Optical Character Recognition (OCR) capabilities allow human resources administrators and staff members to categorize individuals according to desired competencies. In addition, background screening results can be entered online along with other candidate information, providing an ongoing status check for principals and department directors seeking to fill vacancies. Initial screen of qualifications for a position can be handled through a front end interactive voice response system setting forth qualifications for position vacancies.

After the board of education votes to hire a candidate, a human resources data file can be created to prompt the delivery of a job description that includes expected competencies and performance criteria upon which the newly hired person's performance will be evaluated.

Online Staff Development and Training Programs

Staff development and training programs can be developed and provided to employees through videos and online technology. Further, such programs can be interactive; an employee can be led through a series of exercises with immediate feedback concerning his or her mastering of the information or skill. Although this will not replace other methods of delivering staff development and training programs, most are suited to this approach.[4]

Relational Database Reporting

The development of human resources reports once consisted of printed lists that were sorted and subtotaled according to a desired category, such as date of employment by department or job level. Human resources staff members once had to expend an enormous number of work hours taking data and reformatting them into usable information for the superintendent of schools, assistant superintendents, department heads, and principals. Software is now available that can immediately produce reports from data that have been entered into a database. For example, superintendents and other administrators can now view onscreen data in graphical formats that show turnover statistics in special education. They can also click and drag fields of information into reports or use software to create reports.

In addition, reports can be extracted into word processing software and spreadsheet formats. With the advent of email in most school districts, reports can be easily transferred to the offices of numerous administrators. An example is a monthly summary report that sets forth the status of those making claims as members of a self-insured school district medical insurance program. When employees, their dependent children, their spouses, or physicians send in a claim for medical services, the claim is entered into a database from which summary reports can be generated. In an actual report, the designation employee, spouse, and dependent would be accompanied by the employee's social security number or with the name of the person who made the claim.[5]

With the new technologies, human resources administrators and staff members can assume the role of internal consultants who are engaged in critical planning in order to meet the goals and objectives of a given school district. They are freed from routine tasks in order to be more involved in solving problems and addressing human resources issues.

HUMAN RESOURCES ADMINISTRATION COMPUTER HARDWARE AND SOFTWARE

Categories of Software Applications

The amount of software that is available to human resources departments in school districts is constantly increasing, especially because the human resources function is very easily adapted to technology. More importantly, the effective use of technology can free up significant financial resources that then can be allocated to the instructional program. The following nine areas within human resources administration were identified through a review of the Supplement section found in every issue of the journal, *Workforce,* during 2008, and software is available for each application:

1. *Attendance systems.* For support positions such as bus driver, cafeteria worker, and custodian, these programs eliminate the time clocks and timecards used in some large school districts. Using software for telephones, magnetic strip cards, and personal computers, the number of hours worked by employees can be electronically generated and sent to the payroll department.
2. *Compensation planning systems.* Such systems provide a structured data-based approach to planning teacher and staff member salary and benefits programs. This type of software is relatively new to school districts. However, it can provide the kind of analysis that will enhance the collective negotiations process, especially since a planning system makes it possible to identify compensation trends in large school districts.
3. *Competency management systems.* Superintendents and human resources administrators can use these kinds of programs to identify teacher and staff member educational levels, certifications, and special skills. Based on the human resources needs of the school district, such software also can help human resources staff members identify staff development needs.
4. *Decision support systems.* When an administrator needs or desires to generate data summaries and reports, these types of systems provide the analytical capability to reframe information in such a way that decision making becomes more data driven.
5. *Human resources management systems.* These programs constitute the central storage for records and for processing transactions—such as workflow—that can be initiated through self-service events.
6. *Payroll management systems.* These types of programs manage the entire payroll process including salary/benefits requirements and governmental regulations, including tax deductions.
7. *Recruitment and selection management systems.* Through these types of software, the superintendent of schools, principals, other administrators, and human resources staff members can search databases in order to find applicants who have specific education, certification, and skills. These systems also allow an administrator to monitor the status of applicants and even to mine the Internet for potential job applicants.
8. *Retirement management systems.* Using the Internet, intranet, or interactive voice response software, retirees can transact business with the human resources department and can receive information or have their questions answered.

9. *Staff development management systems.* Such systems retain information about the specific staff development programs and activities that employees attend, and also identify the special skills acquired by teachers and staff members who attended them. Further, software is available that allows individuals to access learning and training through personal computers and through distance learning, which is very important in providing staff development in schools so that teachers and staff members do not need to travel to a central office. Also, employees can have access to expert knowledge that would not be available to large groups of teachers and staff members on a given occasion. Providing staff development via the Internet and intranet allows people to acquire new knowledge and to learn new skills independent of time and location.

IMPLICATIONS FOR SMALL AND MEDIUM-SIZED SCHOOL DISTRICTS

All of the positions set forth in this chapter can be collapsed into the responsibilities of the superintendent of schools in small and medium-sized school districts. The superintendent can then delegate some of his or her responsibilities to an assistant superintendent or director. For example, an assistant superintendent may be responsible for transportation, food service, facilities, and the budgeting process. Further, building principals may assume the human resources responsibilities of advertising, and selecting the staff members and teachers who will be working in his or her school. A coordinator can be given the responsibilities of administering staff development programs, of directing special education, and developing curriculum. All of these responsibilities can be rather fluid from year to year depending on upcoming issues such as a bond issue election. In this situation, the assistant superintendent may be providing the superintendent with assistance in working with architects, construction managers, or bonding attorneys in preparing for the bond issue election. The bottom line is that the superintendent is ultimately responsible for all these functions and may need to delegate some of them to fewer central office or building level administrators.

A further implication for small and medium-sized school districts can be gleaned from the six major human resources specialists, which include responsibilities for overall human resources administration, employee relations, staff development, affirmative action, employee benefits, and risk management. Once again, all of these human resources responsibilities are ultimately the responsibility of the superintendent of schools. He or she may not have other central office administrators to whom he or she can delegate some of the human resources responsibilities. This is particularly true in relation to overall human resources administration, employee relations, affirmative action, employee benefits, and risk management. Staff development may be delegated to a building principal, but the others are usually not within the competency of building administrators. An insurance consultant or agent can assist with risk management, and the health insurance provider can assist with benefits management. An attorney can help with affirmative action to a certain degree, but the superintendent is probably the only person in a small or medium-sized school district who can assume the responsibilities of employee relations and certain dimensions of affirmative action. Once again, it is the superintendent who has the ultimate responsibility.

THE IMPACT OF GENERATION Y ON HUMAN RESOURCES ADMINISTRATION

Each generation has a unique set of characteristics; this is the same with the generation of new teachers and administrators that most school districts are attempting to recruit, hire, and retain. The purpose for including a section on Generation Y is to establish a perspective that will be helpful to human resources administrators, principals, and superintendents as they initiate the human resources functions. What follows are generalizations, and thus, may not apply to a given person. All the chapters in this book, except for Chapter 10, contain a section on how Generation Y impacts the specific content that is ascribed in those chapters.

For example, one of the most important characteristics of Generation Y is the desire to trust in authority. Baby Boomers, as a generalization, had little admiration for authority and government. What Generation Y employees want from their leaders is behavior that can be admired, which leads to trust. It is difficult to ask people to trust in principals and superintendents just on blind faith supported merely by the title of their leadership position. Admired behavior is a powerful force that can transform a school or school district into a true learning community where all employees feel appreciated and know that they can count on the good intention of administrators when they make decisions that affect their careers.

Another characteristic of Generation Y is value that they place in education. This characteristic has even been reflected in the popular media particularly in tandem with the economic crisis facing the United States and, indeed, all world markets. For some time, people have placed a significant amount of social and economic self worth on what they owned in terms of property and in terms of investment portfolios. However, now there is a shift that economists refer to as *human capital*. It is the value that a person has in relation to making a living that is based on his or her work ethic, skills, and education. How these human assets are utilized in getting a job constitutes a kind of capital that will not be easily diminished. Of course, there are fewer jobs, but the competition for the remaining jobs will be fierce and the winners will probably be those with the most human capital. This is the way that Generation Y looks upon their future economic stability. They value salary and fringe benefits along with wanting to get ahead in a shorter period of time as they seek out purposeful employment.[6]

Quick Review of Essentials

Administration is the process of managing human, financial, and material resources to accomplish an educational mission formulated as policies by the board of education. Therefore, administration is an executive rather than a policy-making activity. Its various functions include human resources administration, instructional programs administration, and support services administration. Each of these functions has objectives that are implemented through administrative processes, procedures, and techniques.

Functions are performed by administrators within a given organizational structure. The superintendent, as the chief executive officer of the school board, has full control of all school operations. These operations are so complex that his or her efforts must be amplified by a central-office administrative team. This team is usually composed of assistant superintendents who administer the major functions of the school system. These assistant superintendents form a cabinet that helps the superintendent formulate strategies and shares in the decision-making process. Directors and coordinators perform administrative tasks that support the major functions of the district. They report directly to assistant superintendents.

Every school system performs a human resources function, whether accomplished by a central-office unit or assigned to various administrators within the system. The goals of the human resources function are to achieve the objectives of the school district and to help individual staff members maximize their potentials and develop their professional careers. These goals are implemented through human resource planning, recruitment, selection, placement and induction, staff development, performance evaluation, compensation, and collective negotiations.

All but the very smallest school districts should delegate the human resources function to an assistant superintendent. The complexity of this function in our schools and the great impact it has on total school operations necessitate the hiring of this personnel specialist.

Collective negotiation has also created a need in most school districts for another specialist, the director of employee relations, who reports to the assistant superintendent for human resources and who is charged with managing the negotiations process.

The knowledge explosion, increased federal legislation and litigation, and the changing attitudes of parents, students, and educators have necessitated an ongoing staff development program for administrators and teachers. Like collective negotiation, this area is so specialized that most districts should consider establishing the position of director of staff development, who also reports to the assistant superintendent for human resources.

The avalanche of federal legislation and litigation also has mandated the creation of a central-office administrative position, director of affirmative action. All federal legislation requires that a detailed compliance program be established under the direction of an administrator who will be free from the influence of other administrators. Thus, the director of affirmative action should report directly to the superintendent of schools.

The escalating cost of health care, the need to implement managed care, and the rising cost of workers' compensation has reinforced the need for school districts to establish the position of director of employee benefits. The administrator reports to the assistant superintendent for human resources.

Like the rest of society, schools are places of potential risk to students and employees. The risks range from personal violence to accidents to loss of confidentiality. Safety and security audits, rules, and procedures must be developed in order to ensure a risk-free environment for both students and employees. Because of this need, school districts have created the position of director of risk management.

The basic premise of transcendental leadership is that a person acts from the totality of who he or she is as a human being. Most administrators are generally aware that their decisions are influenced by more than just the immediate circumstances and that the effects of their decisions can go beyond the present situation.

The impact of computer technology cannot be overestimated in all aspects of educational administration. When this technology is applied to the human resources function, it produces many benefits that include cost-effectiveness, efficiency, assessment of school district operations, and engagement of employees. In human resources administration, computer technology is being used for initial entry and changes in personnel information, request and utilization of forms, task performance, posting job opportunities, online recruitment and selection of personnel, online staff development and training, and relational database reporting. Computer software applications are available for every dimension of the human resources function.

Selected Further Readings

American Association of School Administrators (AASA), www.aasa.org (as of 2009).

American Association of School Personnel Administrators (ASSPA), www.aaspa.org (as of 2009).

International Society for Technology Education (ISTA), www.iste.org/navigationmenut/professional development (as of 2009).

National School Boards Association, www.nsba.org (as of 2009).

Society for Human Resources Management (SHRM), www.shrm.org (as of 2009).

The Human Resource Planning Society (HRPS), www.hrps.org (as of 2009).

CHAPTER

2

Human Resources Planning

FOCUS SCENARIO

You are the recently employed director of affirmative action in a suburban school district with approximately 5,000 students. This is a new position in the district that has been prompted by a series of complaints, some of which have been made to the Equal Employment Opportunity Commission (EEOC), that the school district has a systemic record of discrimination. Thus, the school district is being investigated by the Justice Department because of a series of complaints by applicants for teaching positions that the school district discriminated in the hiring of African Americans, particularly for administrator positions. Also, there is a complaint that has been filed with EEOC alleging that the school district discriminates against females in promotion to administrative positions. These complaints have been further exacerbated by another complaint to EEOC stating that the school district does not take the necessary steps to protect females from sexual harassment.

The board of education and the superintendent of schools? is concerned about the potential harm that such complaints could bring to the district because the district had been engaged in a voluntary desegregation settlement with neighboring school districts. The status of the civil rights case had been declared unitary.

The board of education and superintendent are looking to you for direction on how to investigate and plan to correct the discrimination, if it is true. Both the board and superintendent were under the impression that such discrimination had been eliminated when the district was involved in the voluntary desegregation program because of the many policies and procedures that were instituted at that time.

PLANNING

Planning is a process common to all human experience. Before embarking on a journey an individual must understand where he or she is, know where he or she wants to go, and decide how best to get there. In an elementary form, this exemplifies the essence of the process even as it is applied in educational organizations.

Through the process of human resource planning, a school district ensures that it has the right number of people, with the right skills, in the right place, and at the right time, and that these people are capable of effectively carrying out those tasks that will aid the organization in achieving its objectives. If a school district is to achieve its objectives, it needs financial resources, physical resources, and people. Too often the people are taken for granted, and yet they are the force that directly affects the main objective of a school district—to educate children. Human resources planning thus translates the organization's objectives into people requirements.

In some school districts, long- and short-range objectives are couched in ambiguous language and often known only by certain central-office administrators. This makes it difficult to involve building principals in the hiring process when unexpected vacancies occur, when replacements are needed because of natural attrition, or when new programs must be staffed.

From an organizational perspective, human resources planning is a process that analyzes the strengths, weaknesses, and opportunities, which could impact having the best possible teachers, administrators, and staff members educating the students of a given school district.[1]

ASSESSING HUMAN RESOURCES NEEDS

The process of assessing human resources needs has four aspects. First, human resources inventories must be developed to analyze the various tasks necessary to meet the school district's objectives; these tasks are then matched against the skills of current employees. Second, enrollment projections must be developed for a five-year period. The extreme mobility of the American population has made this aspect increasingly important over the past 25 years. Third, the overall objectives of the school district must be reviewed within the context of changing needs. At a time when school district budgets are tight, all but the wealthiest districts must establish priorities in meeting objectives. Fourth, human resources inventories, enrollment projections, and school district's objectives must be organized into a human resources forecast, which becomes the mandate of the human resources department.

Implementing this human resource mandate becomes more complex, however, when viewed in the light of compliance with federal legislation or because of staff reductions due to decreasing enrollment or decreases in revenue brought about by the downturn in the economy. These issues have had such a tremendous impact on the human resources function.

Human resources planning is sometimes understood only within the confines of the instructional program. However, for every two teachers there is usually one classified employee. The contemporary school district employs not only teachers and administrators but also cooks, custodians, maintenance personnel, secretaries, computer programmers, telephone switchboard operators, warehouse personnel, distribution truck drivers, and other specialists who are often considered by the average citizen to be employed only in the private business sector.

Human Resources Inventories

Human resources planning begins with the development of a profile indicating the status of current human resources. This profile is generated through forms completed by employees, verified by supervisors, and finally, sent to the human resources department. This form should include name of employee, age, date employed with the school district, sex, job title, place of employment within the district, education and training along with the dates when completed, special skills, and, for instructional personnel, certification.

A human resources profile for each job classification is then developed from the forms completed by the employees. The profile lists all relevant information for each job classification. From a planning perspective, this information is valuable not only in determining what skills are available but also in developing new instructional programs and support services. The human resources profile also helps administrators as they carry out other human resources tasks such as recruitment and staff development. For example, the length of time since an individual received his training or education helps the director of staff development plan appropriate programs.

The profile also provides crucial information for identifying weaknesses in the school district's ability to meet its objectives. For example, reviewing data under the "date employed" section will help the administration analyze such problems as staff turnover and job dissatisfaction. The "age of employee" information helps administrators formulate strategies for recruitment by identifying those individuals approaching retirement age. Accurate data are essential to every aspect of the human resources process and human resources profiles are an effective method of presenting such information.

Enrollment Prediction

Because educational institutions are service organizations, enrollment prediction is an essential aspect of human resources planning. Unless a school system makes an effort to predict declines or increases in the number of students to be served, it may unexpectedly experience half-filled classrooms and a surplus of teachers or overcrowded classrooms and a shortage of teachers.

The major question to be answered by an enrollment prediction is, "How many children are expected to attend a particular school over the next five to ten years?" Many methods can be used to forecast enrollments; among the most popular is the "percentage of retention" or "cohort-survival" technique. This method is predicated on birth rates and the historical retention of students. However, there are other indicators that highlight enrollment trends before the statistical time required by the former technique has elapsed. Such indicators identify social, financial, and residential factors for critical analysis of a school and community.

The following indicators are qualitative in nature because they are based on observations rather than on statistical analysis.[2]

- *The number of children in elementary school classes.* The use of alternative spaces as classrooms, such as the cafeteria, gymnasium, or auditorium stage, is an obvious indicator that the enrollment is increasing. A decline in student numbers in certain grade levels could indicate overall decreasing enrollments. Thus, it is important to analyze a decline of even a few children if it occurs in certain grade levels. For example, a trend may be developing when enrollments in the primary grades drop from 30 to 25 students, especially if this drop represents fewer students than those enrolled in grades four and five.
- *A persistent trend in elementary school enrollment over a three-year period.* Of course, there may be minor increases and decreases in enrollment over short periods of time. This may be due to outside factors such as the building of a new home subdivision or the demolition of homes because of a highway expansion project. Discounting such major factors, trends in enrollment increase or decrease must call for a larger-scale investigation.
- *Feedback from realtors.* The true insiders concerning the effects of housing on enrollments are realtors. Establishing ongoing communications with real estate firms in the community is of vital importance to enrollment prediction.

Reviewing School District Objectives

The future objectives of a school district determine future human resources needs. The number and mix of employees are determined by the types of services called for by organizational objectives. Establishing objectives is the prerogative of the board of education. The board, however, must rely upon the advice of the school administration as it establishes objectives that will best meet the educational needs of the community.

The review of current objectives in light of future educational needs is a cooperative task. In a district operating under the organizational structure presented in Chapter 1, the assistant superintendents for secondary education, elementary education, and instructional services would have the primary responsibility for determining future objectives. The assistant superintendent for human resources would develop a human resources forecast to meet the projected objectives developed by the three other assistant superintendents. The assistant superintendent for administrative services would then translate the objectives and human resources needs into a fiscal plan. The superintendent of schools is charged with prioritizing the objectives and recommending them to the school board for approval.

This review of objectives is not a one-time task but is rather a continual process. The objectives, however, should be established for at least a five-year period and if the need occurs, could be revised into a new five-year plan each year. Thus, a set of objectives is always in effect for a set period of time.

Human Resources Forecasting

When the objectives have been reviewed and an overall human resources forecast has been established, a more explicit projection of future human resources needs must be developed. This responsibility can be initiated through utilizing the expertise of the teachers, administrators, and staff members of the school district. They have a vested interest in the future of the school district and have insights that can be developed only through the experience of doing the jobs they occupy. In a sense, they are the experts.[3]

Of course, a human resources administrator can provide a historical comparison with past trends that will serve as benchmarks for future needs. Analyzing the responsibilities of current teachers, administrators, and staff members will provide a reality check that can be correlated with benchmark data in order to develop the forecast. The human resources inventories on current employees can also provide important and valuable information concerning the age, sex, education, certification, and types of positions within the school district.

THE SUPPLY OF HUMAN RESOURCES An increase in a school system's supply of human resources can come from two sources, newly hired employees and individuals returning from absences such as maternity, military, and sabbatical leaves. Both types of increases are relatively easy to incorporate into a human resources forecast because hiring is controlled and leaves are usually for set periods of time.

Decreases in a school system's supply of human resources, however, are more difficult to predict. Deaths, voluntary resignations, and dismissals are unpredictable except in the broadest sense, as through statistical averaging. However, some decreases, such as sabbatical leaves, can be controlled; and others, such as retirements, are easier to predict.

The available labor force has a significant effect on human resources forecasting. Graduates from high schools, colleges, and universities continually replenish the supply of labor necessary to carry out the mandate of public education. Educational organizations have experienced a decrease in the number of applicants for mathematics and science teaching positions because of the higher wages and advancement opportunities available in private business and industry.

A major source of employees other than recent graduates includes older individuals, particularly women reentering the work force and seeking full-time or part-time employment, either to supplement family income or, in many cases, to provide the primary income for the family. Divorce rates and the high cost of living are key factors contributing to the number of women reentering the labor force.

MATCHING NEEDS WITH SUPPLY A final activity in human resources forecasting is to match the school district's future human resources needs with current supply. This will pinpoint shortages, highlight areas of potential overstaffing, and identify the number of individuals who must be recruited from the labor force to satisfy future needs. In the final analysis, human resources planning ensures that we have the right number and mix of people to meet the school district's future needs as determined by its future objectives.

REDUCTION IN FORCE

Declining enrollments and the need to balance budgets because of the recent downturn in the economy have particular significance in the human resources planning process and have caused the initiation in some districts of a procedure commonly referred to as reduction in force, or RIF. Employees are usually placed on involuntary leave according to a seniority system, which follows the principle of "last in, first out." Retained employees may be transferred within the school system to balance a particular staff or faculty. Such changes are certain to create anxiety among individuals who have become accustomed to the atmosphere and procedures of a particular school. Because many school districts have hired minorities only within the last decade, the use of seniority-based reduction procedures usually means that minority employees are among the first to go. Court-mandated desegregation and the legislative demand for affirmative action call for the introduction of alternatives to RIF, whenever possible, in such school districts.

Alternatives to Reduction in Force

Two of the most successful alternatives to RIF have been early retirement incentive programs and retaining individuals for positions that will become vacant through attrition or will be created because of program development. Teacher negotiations have centered in recent years on the job security issue, and many contracts now call for teachers in excess areas to be transferred to other positions, hired as permanent substitutes, or retrained for new assignments at school district expense.

The Role of the Principal

A key person in human resources planning is the building principal. He or she is usually the first to spot dwindling enrollments. The principal, of course, can provide the central-office staff with up-to-date and projected enrollment figures, with projected maintenance and capital improvement costs, and with projected staffing needs.

The principal also has front-line contact with staff members, students, and parents. Therefore, he or she should be responsible for preparing teachers for possible job loss and for easing the concerns of parents and students. To perform these tasks effectively, the principal must become an integral part of the human resources planning process—being relied upon for data and input. In like manner, he or she must be constantly kept informed of central-office decisions before such decisions are announced to the staff and public.

FEDERAL INFLUENCES ON HUMAN RESOURCES PLANNING

A hallmark of our contemporary American society is the avalanche of federal legislation and court decisions delineating and more clearly defining civil rights. The term *civil rights* is somewhat misunderstood and is most often applied to the constitutional rights of racial minority groups. However, it correctly refers to those constitutional and legislative rights that are inalienable and applicable to *all* citizens. The human resources forecast should provide direction for the recruitment and selection processes. In so doing, this forecast must not violate the civil rights of job applicants or lead the school district into an indefensible position.

What follows is an explanation of major federal legislation, executive orders, and court decisions that should provide direction in the implementation phase of a human resources forecast. It is not meant to be exhaustive because the legislative and judicial processes are organic in nature; therefore, modifications and change will undoubtedly occur. The underlying concept of equality, however, has timeless application.

As prelude to this information, the important concepts of social justice and affirmative action must be clearly understood because they are requirements incorporated or implied in civil rights legislation and executive orders.

Social Justice and Human Resources Administration

The notion of civil rights emanates from the concept of social justice and, thus, it is important to briefly explain how social justice is embedded in the practice of human resources administration.[4] Justice is a guide that regulates how people live out their lives as members of various societies. The idea of justice implies that someone or a group of people can be treated fairly or unfairly. The content of justice is often referred to as entitlement and from this perspective people have claims that are properly due to them.

Because they are human beings, all people have an entitlement to be respected. Not only people but also governments and institutions must afford others this respect, which entails personal integrity, liberty, and equality of opportunity. Thus, human resources planning, recruitment, selection, placement and induction, staff development, performance evaluation, compensation, and collective negotiations policies and procedures have a foundation in social justice.

There are also various types of justice. Distributive justice refers to the responsibility of society to the individual, legal justice refers to the responsibility of each person to society, and commutative justice refers to the responsibility that exists between individuals. All three types are found in human resources administration. For example, the school district as a society has a responsibility to be racially and ethnically unbiased in the recruitment and selection of teachers. Teachers have a responsibility to provide truthful information on employment applications and human resources administrators have a responsibility to process applications for employment in a timely manner.

The notion of justice also has another dimension, restitution. It is recognized that unjustly depriving someone of an entitlement does not nullify the responsibility, but rather requires the implementation of the entitlement in addition to restoring what was withheld. This is easily verified by the actions of the Equal Employment Opportunity Commission (EEOC) that has rendered decisions against school districts for being biased against minorities and women. Some of the decisions by EEOC required school districts to hire the people filing the complaints.

A THEORY OF JUSTICE John Rawls was an American political philosopher who had formulated a theory of justice around the notion of fairness. The influence of Rawls has been extensive and he is considered to be a major defender of the social contract theory that can be found in the philosophical writings of Immanuel Kant, John Locke, and Jean-Jacques Rousseau. Rawls's basic premise is that the best principles of justice for the basic structure of any society are those that would be the object of an original agreement in the establishment of a society, which are derived by free rational persons as an initial position of equality.[5]

In all Western societies the original agreements were initially derived through many different means, some of which were violent. In fact, the murky remnants of the past are only maintained in a given society's collective consciousness. Of course, the original conflicts were eventually reduced to writing and have come down to us through time as constitutions. Nevertheless, in subsocieties there is the possibility to observe and even participate in formulating an agreement. The human resources policy formulation process used by boards of education and the administrative formulation of human resources procedures are examples of how original agreements live on in contemporary society. They should be the agreements of equality. Of course, it is true that state and federal laws and governmental agency regulations have established the boundaries within which policies and procedures are formulated. However, the manner in which boards of education, superintendents, and human resources administrators establish and interpret policies and procedures can violate the principle of fairness. This is seen in the human resources function particularly in regards to affirmative action and equal employment opportunity.

Furthermore, like all other institutions, school districts go through periods of time when it is necessary to reevaluate policies and procedures for the purpose of renewal and reform. As the process of reevaluation is carried out, there arises the opportunity to examine the policies and procedures of a given school district using the notion of fairness as a criterion.

Rawls set forth two principles that he believes people should choose as a means of implementing the notion of fairness. Rawls's first principle states that each person is to have an equal right to a system of liberties that is compatible with a similar system of liberties available to all people. The concept of system, of course, is an essential component of this principle because it establishes that the exercise of one liberty may be, and probably is, dependent upon other liberties. Further, Rawls states that the principles of justice are to be ranked and gives the example that liberty can be restricted only for the sake of liberty. Thus, administrative internship programs that are limited to minorities and women because of their under-representation in the administrative ranks of a given school district are justifiable based on this principle.

Rawls's second principle asserts that social and economic inequalities must benefit not only the least advantaged, but also everyone and that equal opportunity to secure offices and positions must be open to all. This principle of justice must also be ranked so that the principle of efficiency does not occupy the position of first priority. Affirmative action and equal opportunity in employment legislation and court decisions help to secure this principle along with legislation and case law that ensures equal opportunity to seek election to the board of education. The following federal laws, which are set forth later in this chapter, are examples of how this second principle has been operationalized in our American society:

- The Civil Rights Act of 1964 as amended
- Title V of the Rehabilitation Act of 1973
- The Americans with Disabilities Act of 1990

The principle of just savings must be invoked when considering how inequities can benefit the least advantaged. Therefore, a board of education that needs to raise the level of teachers' salaries because the assistant superintendent for human resources is finding it difficult to recruit and hire quality teachers, may place before the voters a tax levy referendum that will increase the amount of property taxes each property owner will pay in future years. Such an increase in taxation will benefit not only the present generation of students, but also future generations.

The application of the second principle through this example demonstrates that the present generation of taxpayers will bear the burden of higher taxes in order to enhance the opportunities of other generations. If there is a lack of quality teachers, the educational programs will continue to deteriorate and ultimately, the cost will be much higher in the future to bring the programs back to the appropriate level. In addition, competitive salaries will have increased to the point where it will be necessary to significantly increase the amount of taxes in order to attract the caliber of teachers required by the educational needs of the students. Consequently, future generations are saved from becoming the least advantaged through the present and immediate future generation of taxpayers.

In the United States, these principles of justice are embodied in certain documents that were the cornerstones on which the nation was founded. In addition to the Constitution of the United States, the Bill of Rights and the Declaration of Independence contain the principles concerning justice that are set forth in this chapter.[6]

AFFIRMATIVE ACTION

Definition

"There can be justice for none if there is not justice for all," captures the intent of civil rights legislation. Affirmative action programs are detailed, result-oriented programs, which, when carried out in good faith, result in compliance with the equal opportunity clauses found in most legislation and executive orders.[7] Affirmative action, therefore, is not a law within itself but rather an objective reached by following a set of guidelines that ensure compliance with legislation and executive orders. Thus, an organization does not violate affirmative action; it violates the law.

A Brief History of Affirmative Action

Although the term *affirmative action* is of recent origin, the concept of an employer taking specific steps to utilize fully and to treat equally minority groups can be traced to President Franklin D. Roosevelt's Executive Order 8802, issued in June 1941. This executive order, which had the force of law, established a policy of equal employment opportunity in regard to defense contracts. President Roosevelt issued a new order in 1943 extending the order to all government contractors and for the first time, mandating that all contracts contain a clause specifically forbidding discrimination.

In 1953, President Dwight D. Eisenhower issued Executive Order 10479, which established the Government Contract Compliance Committee. This committee received complaints of discrimination against government contractors, but had no power to enforce its guidelines. The period of voluntary compliance ended in 1961 when President John F. Kennedy issued Executive Order 10925. This order established the President's Committee on Equal Employment Opportunity and gave it the authority to make and enforce its own rules by imposing sanctions and penalties against non-complying contractors. Government contractors were required to have nondiscrimination clauses covering race, color, creed, and national origin.

In September 1965, President Lyndon B. Johnson issued the very important Executive Order 11246, which gave the secretary of labor jurisdiction over contract compliance and created the Office of Federal Contract Compliance, which replaced the Committee on Equal Employment Opportunity. Every federal contract was required to have a seven-point equal opportunity clause, by which a contractor agreed not to discriminate against anyone in hiring and during employment on the basis of race, color, creed, or national origin. Further, the contractor also had to agree in writing to take affirmative action measures in hiring. President Johnson's Executive Order 11375 in 1967 amended Executive Order 11246 by adding sex and religion to the list of protected categories.

The secretary of labor issued Chapter 60 of Title 41 of the Code of Federal Regulations for the purpose of implementing Executive Order 11375. The secretary delegated enforcement authority to the Office of Federal Contract Compliance (OFCC), which reports to the assistant secretary of the Employment Standards Administration. The Office of Federal Contract Compliance provides leadership in the area of nondiscrimination by government contractors and also coordinates matters relating to Title VII of the 1964 Civil Rights Act, as amended, with the Equal Employment Opportunity Commission (EEOC) and the Department of Justice.

The EEOC was established by Title VII of the 1964 Civil Rights Act to investigate alleged discrimination based on race, color, religion, sex, or national origin. The EEOC was greatly strengthened in 1972 by the passage of the Equal Employment Opportunity Act. It extended coverage to all private employers of 15 or more persons, all educational institutions, all state and local governments, public and private employment agencies, labor unions with 15 or more members, and joint labor-management committees for apprenticeships and training. This Act also gave the Commission the power to bring litigation against an organization that engages in discriminatory practices.

Equal Employment Opportunity Commission (EEOC)

A major failing of many school administrators is their lack of understanding about the Equal Employment Opportunity Commission (EEOC) and its influence on human resources administration. From time to time, this five-member commission has established affirmative action guidelines that, if adopted by school districts, can minimize liability when claims of discrimination occur. To further aid employers, on December 11, 1978, the EEOC adopted additional guidelines that can be used to avoid liability for claims of "reverse discrimination" that result from affirmative action that provides employment opportunities for women and racial and ethnic minorities. The following compilation from several sources will provide a framework for affirmative action compliance.

Eight steps have emerged from federal guidelines.[8] First, each board of education should issue a written policy covering equal employment opportunity and affirmative action to be enforced by its chief executive officer, the superintendent. Commitments that should be included in the policy are a determination to recruit, hire, and promote for all job classifications without regard to race, creed, national origins, sex, or age (except where sex or age is a *bona fide* occupational qualification); a determination to base decisions concerning employment solely on individual qualifications as related to the requirements of the position; and a determination to ensure that all human resources matters such as compensation, benefits, transfers, layoffs, returns from layoffs, and continuing education will be administered without regard to race, creed, national origin, sex, or age.

Second, the superintendent should appoint a top level official to be directly responsible for implementing the program. This official usually has the title director of affirmative action. He or she should be responsible for developing policy statements and affirmative action programs. In addition, he or she should initiate internal and external communications, assist other administrators in the identification of problem areas, design and implement auditing and reporting systems, serve as a liaison between the district and enforcement agencies, and keep the superintendent informed of the latest developments in the area of equal opportunities.

Third, a school district should disseminate information about its affirmative action program both internally and externally. The board policy should be publicized through all internal channels, such as at meetings and on bulletin boards. External dissemination might take the form of brochures advertising the district; written notification to recruitment sources; clauses in purchase orders, leases, contracts; and written notification to minority organizations, community agencies, and community leaders.

Step four begins with a survey and analysis of minority and female employees by school and job classification. The percentage and number of minority and female employees currently employed in each major job classification should be compared to their presence in the relevant labor market—that is, the area in which you can reasonably expect to recruit. This will determine *underutilization*, defined as having fewer minorities or women in a particular job category or school than could be reasonably expected; and *concentration*, defined as more of a particular group in a job category or school than would reasonably be expected. A survey also should be conducted to identify those females and minorities who have the credentials to handle other jobs. Such employees can be transferred to these positions, if necessary.

With this information, the school district's administration should proceed to step five, developing measurable and remedial goals on a timetable. Once long-range goals have been established, specific and numerical targets can be developed for the hiring, training, transferring, and promoting of personnel to reach goals within the established time frame. During this step, the causes of underutilization should be identified.

Step six calls for developing and implementing specific programs to eliminate discriminatory barriers. This is the heart of an affirmative action program and must be discussed under several subheadings, which will be further expanded in subsequent chapters of this book. Everyone involved in every aspect of the hiring process must be trained to use objective standards that support affirmative action goals. Recruitment procedures for each job category must be analyzed and reviewed to identify and eliminate discriminatory barriers. Recruitment procedures should include contacting educational institutions and community action organizations that represent minorities.

Reviewing the selection process to ensure that job requirements and hiring practices contribute to the attainment of affirmative action goals is a vital part of step six. This includes making certain that job qualifications and selection standards do not screen out minorities, unless the qualifications can be significantly related to job performance and no alternate nondiscriminatory standards can be developed. Upward-mobility systems such as promotions, transfers, and continuing education play an important role in fulfilling step six. Through careful record keeping, existing barriers may be identified and specific remedial programs initiated. These programs might include providing training for targeted minorities and women who are currently qualified for upward mobility and more extensive training for those who are not yet qualified.

Wage and salary structures, benefits, and conditions of employment are other areas of investigation. Title VII of the 1964 Civil Rights Act and the Equal Pay Act require fiscal parity for jobs of equal skill and responsibility. All fringe benefits such as medical, hospital, and life insurance must be equally applied to personnel performing similar functions. Even in instances where states had "protective laws" barring women from hard or dangerous work, the courts generally found that the equal employment requirements of Title VII superseded these state laws. Courts have also barred compulsory maternity leave and the discharge of pregnant teachers.

Under affirmative action guidelines, the criteria for deciding when a person will be terminated, demoted, disciplined, laid off, or recalled should be the same for all employees. Seemingly neutral practices should be reexamined to see if they have a disparate effect on minority groups. Special considerations, such as job transfers and career counseling, should be given to minorities who have been laid off because of legitimate seniority systems.

Step seven is to establish internal auditing and reporting systems to monitor and evaluate progress in meeting the goals of the affirmative action program. Quarterly reports based on the data already outlined should be available to all administrators, enabling them to see how the program is working and where improvement is needed. The issue of keeping records on current employees and applicants by gender, race, or national origin is a very sensitive issue. Such record keeping has been used in the past as a discriminatory device, and some states have outlawed the practice. However, in certain litigation these records have been used as evidence of discriminatory practices. The data could even be demanded by enforcement agencies, and it is necessary for affirmative action record keeping. The EEOC suggests that such information be coded and kept separate from personnel files.[9]

Developing supportive district and community programs is the last step in an affirmative action program. This may include developing support services for recruiting minority and female employees and encouraging current employees to further their education in order to qualify for promotions.

The EEOC Administrative Process

Alleged discrimination charges can be filed with any of EEOC's district offices. The following outlines the administrative process involved with an allegation of employment discrimination.[10]

THE CHARGE OF DISCRIMINATION. A charge can be filed by any person, by others on behalf of that person, or by any of the EEOC commissioners. This charge must be filed within 180 days from when the alleged discriminatory act occurred. In those states that have an employment discrimination law, the time may be extended to 300 days. EEOC must first refer the charge to the appropriate state agency. The Equal Employment Opportunity Commission begins its investigation after the state agency concludes its procedures or after 60 days from the date of referral by EEOC to the state agency, whichever occurs first.

Some discriminatory practices are considered to be *continuing violations*. A failure to promote because of a discriminatory system of promotions is an example of a continuing violation because it occurs each day the practice is followed. However, when an individual is denied employment because of discrimination, this constitutes a specific violation that occurred on a particular date. A continuing violation arises over a lengthy period of time. The time limit for filing a charge involving a continuing violation is 180 days after the cessation of the discriminatory practice. Therefore, as long as a practice continues, there is no time limit for filing a charge.

If an individual is subject to a collective bargaining agreement and believes that he or she has been discriminated against, he or she may follow the grievance procedures set out in the master contract. This procedure does not alter the time period during which a charge must be filed.

INVESTIGATION OF THE DISCRIMINATION CHARGE. It usually takes 18 months after a charge is filed for an investigation to begin. The EEOC will demand broad access to an employer's records. An employer may object to the subpoena of records on the following grounds: the information is privileged, the compilation of information would be excessively burdensome, or the information sought is irrelevant to the charges.

THE DETERMINATION. When the investigation has been completed, the EEOC will make a determination concerning the discrimination charges. This determination will take one of two forms: *reasonable cause*, which means that the charge is meritorious and both parties (employer and charging party) are invited to conciliate the case; or *no cause*, which means that the charge has no merit. If the charging party continues to believe that discrimination occurred, the court system is the next avenue of recourse.

THE PROCESS OF CONCILIATION. This process begins when the employer or his authorized representative meets with the staff of EEOC at one of the district offices to explore methods of conciliation. The four usual methods employed are listed here:

1. The employer and charging party may agree to a *conciliation agreement*. The terms of this agreement are designed to eliminate the discriminatory practice and may include provisions such as back pay, reinstatement of the charging party if he or she was terminated, and

establishing goals and a timetable for hiring and promoting minorities. EEOC negotiates thousands of conciliation agreements each year, recovering millions of dollars for employees who have experienced discrimination.

2. With the concurrence of EEOC, the employer may extend an offer to the charging party. If the charging party rejects the offer, EEOC issues a *right to sue* notice, which gives the charging party 90 days to bring legal action against the employer.
3. The employer and charging party may agree to a settlement for a single individual. However, if the investigation by EEOC reveals a discriminatory practice against a class of persons such as females or persons with disabilities and if the employer along with EEOC is unable to reach an agreement on a class determination, such is considered a *failure of conciliation*, and the case is referred to the litigation division of the Equal Employment Opportunity Commission.
4. If the employer, charging party, and EEOC are unable to reach an agreement, this also is considered a *failure of conciliation*, and referral is made to the litigation division.

THE LITIGATION DIVISION. When conciliation fails, the litigation division evaluates the case to determine if there is a significant legal issue involved or if the case could have a significant impact on systematic patterns of discrimination. If one or both of these conditions exist, EEOC will most likely bring a lawsuit against the alleged discriminating employer.

The vast majority of lawsuits filed in federal courts, however, are instigated by private individuals pursuing their claims of discrimination or are class action suits filed by a group of citizens. The prerequisites to filing an individual claim of discrimination in federal court are: the charge was filed first with EEOC within the required time, EEOC issues a *right to sue* letter, and the charging party filed suit within 90 days from receipt of the letter.

A *right to sue* letter is usually issued by EEOC under three circumstances: (1) when a charge of discrimination is determined to have a *no cause* status by EEOC, which allows the charging party to appeal through the courts; (2) when the litigation division of EEOC rejects a case for legal action; (3) when EEOC enters into a conciliation agreement with an employer that does not include the charging party's claim.

If a federal court rules in favor of the charging party, it may grant any award it deems equitable. Injunctive remedies, on the other hand, require an employer to do something such as modifying a promotional policy that does not follow affirmative action guidelines and discriminates against minorities. In an individual case of discrimination when back pay is involved, the court may award back pay to the discriminate for a period of up to two years prior to the date when the charge was filed with EEOC.

BONA FIDE *OCCUPATIONAL QUALIFICATION.* Discrimination by sex, religion, or national origin is allowed by the Equal Employment Opportunity Act under one condition, stated in the law as follows:

> Notwithstanding any other provision of this title, (1) it shall not be an unlawful employment practice for an employer to hire and employ employees, for an employment agency to classify, or refer for employment any individual, for a labor organization to classify its membership or to classify or refer for employment any individual, or for an employer, labor organization, or joint labor management committee controlling apprenticeship or other training or retraining programs to admit or employ any individual in any such program, on the basis of his religion, sex, or national origin in

> those certain instances where religion, sex, or national origin is a *bona fide* occupational qualification reasonably necessary to the normal operation of that particular business or enterprise, and (2) it shall not be an unlawful employment practice for a school, college, university, or other educational institution or institution of learning to hire and employ employees of a particular religion if such school, college, university, or other educational institution or institution of learning is, in whole or in substantial part, owned, supported, controlled, or managed by a particular religion or by a particular religious corporation, association, or society, or if the curriculum of such school, college, university, or other educational institution or institution of learning is directed toward the propagation of a particular religion.[11]

Therefore, a school district's personnel administrator has the right to specify a female for the position of swimming instructor when part of the job description includes supervising the locker room used by female students. In like manner, a Lutheran school official may hire only those applicants who profess the Lutheran creed because the mission of the school is to propagate that particular faith.

In certain school districts the national origin of teachers is extremely important. If in a particular school district over 30 percent of its student population has Spanish surnames, being of Hispanic origin could be a *bona fide* job qualification for certain teaching positions in that school system.

JUDICIAL REVIEW OF AFFIRMATIVE ACTION Court decisions have further modified affirmative action regulations. Although the courts will continue to refine the interpretation of the Civil Rights Act and the Equal Employment Opportunity Act, certain basic conclusions have emerged and provide direction to school districts in their efforts to construct and implement an affirmative action program.[12]

- Discrimination has been broadly defined, in most cases including a class of individuals rather than a single person. Where discrimination has been found by the courts to exist, remediation must be applied to all members of the class to which the individual complainant belongs.
- It is not the intent but rather the consequences of employment practices that determine if discrimination exists.
- Even when an employment practice is neutral in text and impartially administered, if it has a disparaging effect upon members of a protected class (those groups covered by a law) or if it perpetuates the effects of prior discriminatory practices, it constitutes unlawful discrimination.
- Statistics that show a disproportionate number of minorities or females in a job classification relative to their presence in the work force constitutes evidence of discriminatory practices. When such statistics exist, the employer must show that this is not the result of overt or institutional discrimination.
- For an employer to justify any practice or policy that creates a disparaging effect on a protected class, a "compelling business necessity" must be demonstrated. The courts have interpreted this in a very narrow sense to mean that no alternative nondiscriminatory practice can achieve the required result.
- Court-ordered remedies not only open the doors to equal employment opportunity, but also require employers to "make whole" and "restore the rightful economic status" of all those in the affected class. In practice, courts have ordered fundamental changes in almost every aspect of employment.

Two U.S. Supreme Court decisions from the late 1970s have had an indirect effect upon affirmative action programs in school districts. The first case, *Regents of the University of California* v. *Bakke*, was decided in 1978 and dealt with admission quotas to a medical school. The second, *United Steelworkers* v. *Brian F. Weber*, also decided in 1979, dealt with a voluntary race-conscious affirmative action plan in private industry. Both cases addressed the issue of reverse discrimination.

In June 2003, two U.S. Supreme Court rulings addressed a fundamental legal question that is at the heart of the affirmative action issue. The question concerned whether or not the U.S. Constitution permits affirmative action policies. The answer to the question is a resounding "yes." In *Grutter* v. *Bollinger*, the Supreme Court upheld a Michigan law school's admissions policies stating that the school had a compelling interest in enrolling a racially and ethnically diverse student body because such diversity provides a significant educational benefit. However, even though the Court upheld the importance of affirmative action in *Gratz* v. *Bollinger*, it ruled that Michigan's undergraduate admissions practice placed too much emphasis on race in assessing applicants. The University used a point system that automatically gave substantial bonuses to members of certain minority groups.[13] The implications of these two rulings for human resources administrators are that affirmative action policy is constitutionally assured, but the practices that implement affirmative action must be defensible.

FEDERAL LEGISLATION

Civil Rights Act, 1991

The passage of this civil rights legislation, along with the Americans with Disabilities Act of 1990, set school districts on a new path during the 1990s. This has been particularly true with regards to the Civil Rights Act of 1991. The law extends punitive damages and jury trials for the first time to employees who have been discriminated against because of their race, national origin, sex, disability, or religion. Thus, the school district must be vigilant in adhering not only to the provisions of this act but also the spirit of the legislation that prompted its enactment.[14]

There have been two significant procedural changes. First, the law allows compensatory and punitive damages. Prior to passage of this law and with few exceptions, plaintiffs could receive remedies limited to lost pay and benefits, reinstatement, and attorney fees. After passage, plaintiffs can receive "compensatory damages," for emotional pain, inconvenience, and mental anguish. Furthermore, if the plaintiff can prove that the employer acted with "malice" or with "reckless indifference," he or she may be awarded punitive damages. The customary remedies of receiving lost pay and benefits, reinstatement, and attorney fees are still available in addition to compensatory and punitive damages.

The major consideration for superintendents, assistant superintendents, and school board members has been that they can be named as codefendants in an action brought against a school district under the Civil Rights Act of 1991. The reason for this is that punitive damages cannot be levied against a school district because it is a governmental agency, but punitive damages can be levied against individuals such as administrators and school board members.

The limits on the amount of compensatory and punitive damages have been established as follows:

- Plaintiffs may be awarded damages up to $50,000 if the school district has at least 15 but not more than 99 employees.
- Plaintiffs may be awarded damages up to $100,000 if the school district has between 100 and 200 employees.

- Plaintiffs may be awarded damages up to $200,000 if the school district has between 200 and 500 employees.
- Plaintiffs may be awarded damages up to $300,000 if the school district has more than 500 employees.

There are two exceptions to these limits. For age discrimination the limit is twice the amount of lost pay and benefits, and for race discrimination there is no limit. There is another liability for a school district that has not been available in the past in relation to damages. A plaintiff who prevails may also recover the cost of expert witness fees.

The second significant procedural change involves the right of a complainant to receive a jury trial in an employment discrimination case in which compensatory and/or punitive damages are being sought. Jury trials were seldom allowed in employment discrimination cases prior to this law. The major consideration concerning this issue is not only the unpredictability of juries, but also the perceived bias of juries against employers.

Because of this law, there is also a significant substantive change in the way in which the school human resources function is managed. The Civil Rights Act of 1991 overruled several U.S. Supreme Court decisions that appeared to be pro-employer. School districts are now charged with the burden of proof when a seemingly neutral act has resulted in discrimination against an employee from a protected class.

Equality for People with Disabilities

Title V of the Rehabilitation Act of 1973 contains five sections, four relating to affirmative action for individuals with disabilities and one dealing with voluntary actions, remedial actions, and evaluation criteria for compliance with the law. The congressional intent of the Rehabilitation Act is identical to the intent of other civil rights legislation, such as the Civil Rights Act (covering discrimination based on race, sex, religion, or national origin) and Title IX of the Educational Amendments (covering discrimination based on sex). However, the U.S. Department of Health, Education, and Welfare (HEW) emphasized in the Federal Register promulgating the Rehabilitation Act that it contains a fundamental difference:

> The premise of both Title VII (Civil Rights Act) and Title IX (Educational Amendments) is that there is no inherent difference of equalities between the general public and the persons protected by these statutes and, therefore, there should be no differential treatment in the administration of federal programs. Section 504 (Rehabilitation Act), on the other hand is far more complex. Handicapped persons may require different treatment in order to be afforded equal access, and identical treatment may, in fact, constitute discrimination. The problem of establishing general rules as to when different treatment is prohibited or required is compounded by the diversity of existing handicaps and the differing degree to which particular persons may be affected.[15]

Subpart B of Section 504 of the Rehabilitation Act specifically refers to employment practices. It prohibits recipients of federal financial assistance from discriminating against qualified individuals with disabilities in recruitment, hiring, compensation, job assignment/classification, and fringe benefits. Employers are further required to provide reasonable work environment accommodations for qualified applicants or employees with disabilities unless they can demonstrate that such accommodations would impose an undue hardship. The law applies to all state, intermediate, and local educational agencies. Finally, any agency that receives assistance under the Individuals with Disabilities Act must take positive steps to employ and promote qualified persons with disabilities into programs assisted under this Act.

REASONABLE ACCOMMODATION The requirement that employers make "reasonable accommodations" in the work environment for applicants and employees with disabilities has created a great deal of confusion. Reasonable accommodations include providing employee facilities that are readily accessible to and usable by persons with disabilities; and taking action such as restructuring jobs, modifying work schedules, modifying and/or acquiring special equipment or devices, and providing readers.

In order to determine whether an accommodation imposes an undue hardship on an employer, the following factors should be considered: first, the size of the agency or company with respect to the number of employees; second, the number and type of facilities available; third, the size of the employer's budget; fourth, the composition of the work force; and finally, the nature and type of accommodation needed. If an employer believes that reasonable accommodations would impose a hardship, the burden of proof rests with the employer.

EMPLOYMENT CRITERIA The U.S. Department of Health and Human Services (formerly HEW), in concert with the guidelines on selection procedures developed by the Equal Employment Opportunity Commission, prohibits the use of any employment test or other criteria that screens out or discriminates against persons with disabilities unless the test or selection criteria is proven to be job-related. Therefore, in selecting and administering tests to an applicant or employee with a disability, the test results must accurately reflect the individual's job skills or other factors the test purports to measure rather than the person's impaired sensory, manual, or speaking skills, except when these skills are required for successful job performance.

The term *test* includes measures of general intelligence, mental ability, learning ability, specific intellectual ability, mechanical and clerical aptitudes, dexterity and coordination, knowledge, proficiency, attitudes, personality, and temperament. Formal techniques of assessing job suitability that yield qualifying criteria include specific personal history and background data, specific educational or work history, scored interviews, and scored application forms.

School district administrators must realize that they may be called on to present evidence concerning the validity and reliability of the testing procedures they use in selection and promotion processes. Casual techniques, of course, are very difficult to defend.

PREEMPLOYMENT INQUIRIES Subpart B of Section 504 of the Rehabilitation Act specifies that recipients of federal financial assistance should take (a) remedial action to correct past discrimination, (b) voluntary action to overcome the limited participation of individuals with disabilities, and (c) affirmative action to employ people with disabilities. An employer may use preemployment inquiries to determine progress in complying with the Rehabilitation Act. Subpart B also contains the following provision: An employer must state on all preemployment written questionnaires or, if no written questionnaire is used, must tell applicants that preemployment information is being requested for the purpose of implementing remedial, voluntary, or affirmative action programs; the employer must state that the information is being requested on a voluntary basis, that it will be kept confidential, and that refusal to provide such information will not subject the applicant or employee to any adverse treatment.

Nothing in Subpart B prohibits an employer from making employment conditional on the results of a medical examination prior to the assumption of duties by a person with disabilities. However, this condition can be applied only if all entering employees are required to have a medical examination and only if the results of such examinations are used in accordance with appropriate remedial, voluntary, and affirmative action programs. The medical information collected must be maintained on separate forms from other employment data and must be accorded the same confidentiality as medical records. This information may be used by supervisors and managers to determine the restrictions in the duties of employees with disabilities and to determine necessary accommodations. First aid and safety personnel may also use this information when emergencies occur. Finally, government officials may have access to such information when investigating an employer's compliance with the Rehabilitation Act.

ORGANIZATIONAL ACTION REQUIRED Although Subpart B of Section 504 does not require school districts to develop an affirmative action program for those with disabilities, it does require three types of organizational activities: remedial action, voluntary action, and self-evaluation. The Office of Civil Rights investigates allegations of discrimination by school districts against people with disabilities and the director of the office can require remedial action if discrimination is confirmed against persons with disabilities who are currently employed, who are no longer employed in the district but were when the discrimination occurred, or who would have been employed in the district had the discrimination not occurred.

In addition, school districts may take voluntary measures to alleviate discrimination. Such measures usually begin with the construction of a self-evaluation procedure. Paragraph 87.4 of the Federal Register outlines the self-evaluation requirements as follows:

> Within one year of the effective date of publishing Section 504 regulations (May 4, 1977), local school districts must: (a) evaluate, with the assistance of handicapped individuals and organizations, current district policies and practices that do not meet Section 504 requirements, (b) modify such district policies and practices, and (c) take appropriate remedial steps to eliminate the effects of any discrimination that resulted from adherence to such policies and practices.
>
> Furthermore, a local school district that employs fifteen or more persons must, for at least three years following completion of the self-evaluation, maintain on file and make available for public inspection: (a) a list of the interested individuals consulted, (b) a description of areas examined and any problems identified, and (c) a description of any modifications made and of any remedial steps taken.[16]

Table 2.1 schematically presents the necessary components for planning, conducting, and analyzing a self-evaluation procedure.

Table 2.1 Conceptual Components for a School District Evaluation Model

- The board of education develops a policy protecting the rights of individuals with disabilities.
- The superintendent of schools establishes objectives with a timetable for implementing the policy.
- The superintendent of schools appoints an administrator to monitor the progress towards implementation and ongoing compliance.
- The administrator develops an evaluation process to measure the progress towards implementation and compliance with the policy.
- The administrator creates a staff development program to inform teachers, administrators, and staff members concerning the implementation and compliance with the policy.
- The administrator makes a yearly report to the board of education on implementation and compliance with the policy.

The Americans with Disabilities Act (ADA), 1990

President George H. W. Bush signed into law the Americans with Disabilities Act (ADA) on July 26, 1990. This has been the most comprehensive legislation ever passed protecting the rights of individuals with disabilities. From a practical perspective, the Americans with Disabilities Act (ADA) is an extension of the Rehabilitation Act of 1973. This extension pertains to the private sector and to those local and state governmental agencies that receive no federal monies. Because almost every school district in the nation receives some federal financial assistance, either directly or indirectly, which is the threshold requiring adherence to the Rehabilitation Act, school districts in compliance with the Rehabilitation Act have little difficulty complying with the ADA.[17]

There are five titles to ADA. All of them except Title IV have some impact upon school districts. Title IV pertains to telecommunications companies.

TITLE I This title regulates employment practices and took effect on July 26, 1992 for school districts.

TITLE II All services, programs, and activities of state and local governmental agencies are subject to Title II even if they are provided by a contractor. This title took effect on January 26, 1992 and includes all activities involving all public contact as part of ongoing operations. Thus, classroom instruction and pupil transportation are affected. Even though Title II includes employment practices, the Department of Justice has decided that Equal Employment Opportunity regulations governing Title I are sufficient for Title II.

TITLE III This title also took effect on January 26, 1992. It pertains to public accommodations and applies only to the private sector. School districts are not covered by Title III as such. However, if a school district contracts with a private company, for example, to provide pupil transportation or food service, the district must ensure that the private company is operating in compliance with Title III. This compliance issue is usually set forth as a section in the contract between the district and the company providing the service.

TITLE IV This title took effect on July 26, 1993, and requires telecommunication companies to provide telecommunication relay services for people with hearing or speech disabilities.

TITLE V This title contains a number of provisions. The most important for school districts involves the relationship of ADA to other laws. It states, for example, that the "highest standard" applies whether that standard is ADA, the Rehabilitation Act, a state law, or even a local ordinance. It also prohibits retaliation against persons seeking redress under the ADA and allows the court to award attorney fees to the prevailing parties.

JURISDICTION AND SCOPE OF ADA Under the jurisdiction of the Equal Employment Opportunity Commission, the ADA covered all school districts with 25 or more employees after July 26, 1992, and all districts with 15 or more employees after July 26, 1994. However, under the jurisdiction of the Department of Justice, discrimination is prohibited by school districts regardless of the number of employees after January 26, 1992.

Because both the Department of Justice and the Equal Employment Opportunity Commission have been given jurisdiction for the enforcement of ADA, coordination between these two agencies is necessary. Further, because the Department of Labor has jurisdiction in cases involving discrimination and affirmative action under the Rehabilitation Act of 1973, coordination between this agency and the Department of Justice and the Equal Employment Opportunity Commission is not only necessary, but also critical.

Under ADA it is unlawful to discriminate in all human resources functions, including:

- recruitment
- selection
- promotion
- training
- staff development
- rewards including direct and indirect compensation
- reduction in force
- termination
- placement
- leave
- voluntary fringe benefits

THOSE PROTECTED BY ADA Title I sets forth who is qualified to be protected by ADA. Essentially, under ADA a person is disabled if he or she has a physical or mental impairment that substantially limits a major life activity. ADA also protects individuals who have a record of a substantially limiting impairment, and people who are regarded as having a substantially limiting impairment.

The terms *physical or mental impairment* in this definition include cerebral palsy, muscular dystrophy, multiple sclerosis, AIDS, HIV infection, emotional illness, drug addiction, alcoholism, dyslexia, etc. However, such conditions as a person's height, weight, or muscle tone, if these are within normal ranges, do not qualify under these terms. Further, the color of hair or eyes, being pregnant, or having served a sentence in prison are not examples of a physical or mental impairment. When determining if a person has a protected disability, the decision must be made without regard to mitigating measures such as medication and assistive or prosthetic devices.

The term *major life activity* means an activity that an average person can perform with little or no difficulty. Thus, hearing, seeing, speaking, breathing, performing manual tasks, walking, caring for oneself, learning, or working are major life activities. The Equal Employment Opportunity Commission takes into account three factors when determining if a disability substantially limits these major types of life activities: (1) the nature and severity of the impairment; (2) its duration or expected duration; (3) the actual or expected permanent long-term impact resulting from it. Thus, a broken limb, influenza, or a tonsillectomy are not considered disabilities.[18]

The term *record of impairment* refers to a disability for which an individual no longer receives treatment. Therefore, people who have a history of heart disease, mental illness, drug disease, or alcoholism are also protected by this law. The term *regarded as impaired* is meant to indicate those individuals who are not physically or mentally impaired but who are regarded as impaired and about whom there is concern regarding productivity, safety, liability, attendance, accommodation, workers' compensation, or acceptance by other employees.

In March 1995, the Equal Employment Opportunity Commission issued an interpretation of the Americans with Disabilities Act setting forth that the law protects people from employment discrimination who are healthy but who carry abnormal genes. More and more people are taking advantage of new genetic tests that can identify a person's predisposition to illnesses such as

Alzheimer's disease, heart disease, and certain types of cancer. This information allows individuals to access preventive measures and early treatment; it is also helpful in predicting what disease genes can be passed on to their children. If the results of these tests are known by potential employers, some of them might discriminate against those applicants who carry abnormal genes, in order to avoid future lost days from work and higher employer-paid health care premiums.

THE SELECTION PROCESS UNDER ADA An applicant for a position in a school district who is also protected by ADA must otherwise qualify for the job. The term otherwise qualify means that the applicant can perform the essential functions of the job with or without reasonable accommodation. Therefore, the applicant must satisfy job requirements for educational background, employment experience, skills, licenses, and other qualification standards that are job-related. Further, the person must be able to perform those tasks that are essential to the job either with or without reasonable accommodation. The school district can still hire the best qualified applicant and it does not impose any affirmative action obligations.

Determining what are essential functions is critical to not discriminating against a qualified candidate who has a disability under ADA. This determination about essential functions must be made before carrying out certain processes of the human resources function. This is certainly true in relation to initiating the selection process which includes developing a job description and advertising the position. A number of factors should be considered in determining if the function is essential:

- The actual work experience of present and/or past employees in the job
- The time needed to perform a function
- The terms of a collective bargaining agreement
- The consequences of not requiring that an employee perform a function
- The degree of expertise or skill required to perform the function
- The number of other employees available to perform the function or among whom the performance of the function can be distributed
- Whether the reason the position exists is to perform that function[19]

Reasonable accommodation may be defined as any change or adjustment to the job or the work environment which will permit a qualified person with a disability to participate in the selection process, to perform the essential functions of a job, and to enjoy benefits and privileges of employment equal to those enjoyed by employees without disabilities. Therefore, reasonable accommodation may include:

- Acquiring or modifying equipment or devices
- Job restructuring
- Part-time or modified work schedules
- Adjusting or modifying examinations, training materials, or policies
- Providing readers and interpreters
- Making the workplace readily accessible to and usable to people with disabilities.[20]

The reasonable accommodation requirement also applies to employees who become disabled after employment with the district. All of the above with the addition of reassignment to another position must be considered for the employee who becomes disabled.

In determining what accommodations may be necessary, the Equal Employment Opportunity Commission recommends the following approach. First, determine the essential functions of the job. Second, consult with the individual who has the disability in order to determine the individual's precise limitations and how they may be overcome. Third, also with the individual's assistance, identify potential accommodations and assess their effectiveness. Fourth, after considering the preferences of the individual with the disability, implement the accommodation most appropriate for the individual and the employer. It is important to understand that ADA does not require selection of the best accommodation as long as the accommodation selected provides an equal opportunity to perform the job. Examples of equipment which may be a reasonable accommodation include telecommunications devices, special computer software to enlarge or convert print documents to spoken words, telephone headsets, speaker phones, and adaptive light switches.

UNDUE HARDSHIP It is not necessary to provide a reasonable accommodation if this would cause an undue hardship on the school district. This means that the accommodation would be unduly costly, extensive, substantial, disruptive, or would fundamentally alter the nature of operation of the school district. Factors that can be considered in making this determination of undue hardship are the cost of the accommodation, the size of the school district, the financial resources of the district, and the nature or structure of the district's operations.

If a particular accommodation would be an undue hardship, the school district staff must try to identify another accommodation which will not pose a hardship. Further, if the hardship is caused by the lack of financial resources, the school district must attempt to find funding from an outside source such as a vocational rehabilitation agency. The applicant or employee must also be given the opportunity to provide the accommodation or pay for a portion of the accommodation that constitutes an undue hardship.[21]

ACCESSIBILITY Title II contains the provisions of ADA relating to accessibility. ADA required school districts to conduct a self-evaluation by January 26, 1993. Most school districts have a self-evaluation on file which complied with Section 504 of the Rehabilitation Act of 1973. Thus, the school district should have included in that evaluation only those policies and practices that were not covered in the previous self-evaluation. The self-evaluation should provide an opportunity for input from interested individuals, from individuals with disabilities, and from organizations representing people with disabilities. Each school district is to maintain a file that is open to inspection by the public that includes the names of the interested persons consulted, a description of the areas examined, the problems identified, and a description of any modifications made.[22]

School districts also must maintain on file a transition plan open to inspection by the public that sets forth the structural changes to facilities that were to be undertaken in order to achieve program accessibility. This should include a time schedule for taking corrective action and the name of the school district official responsible for implementing the plan. ADA also required school districts to appoint a staff member responsible for investigating complaints regarding noncompliance and a procedure for the prompt and equitable resolution of complaints.

DAMAGES FOR NONCOMPLIANCE WITH ADA Hiring, reinstatement, back pay, and injunctive relief are some of the remedies that are possible under ADA. The list has been expanded by the Civil Rights Act of 1991 to include damages such as future pecuniary losses, inconvenience, mental anguish, and emotional pain subject to specific dollar limitations. Punitive damages may not be awarded against a school district under ADA.[23]

AIDS and Discrimination

There is no topic or issue that has focused the attention and concern of so many people recently as the disease of AIDS (Acquired Immune Deficiency Syndrome). Without going into a long discussion of the medical aspects of the disease, it is sufficient here to state that the disease can be transmitted to others and that it is always fatal.[24]

The hysteria over this disease caused Dr. C. Everett Koop, the surgeon general when the syndrome was first publicized, to send an explanatory brochure to all the households in the United States. All health officials are in agreement about the manner in which the disease may be transmitted. Sexual contact with an infected person and the sharing of drug needles or syringes are the most common ways that the disease is transmitted. Health officials are also in agreement that the disease cannot be transmitted by casual contact with an infected person. In fact, ordinary and casual contact between family members where a member had AIDS verified that the disease cannot be transmitted this way.

The hysteria continues to exist, however, and has caused concern in the workplace, which has resulted in discriminatory practices by some individuals, companies, agencies, and organizations. A significant development occurred in 1987 that was helpful in dealing with discrimination against people infected with the AIDS virus. In *School Board of Nassau v. Arline*, the U.S. Supreme Court ruled that an infectious disease could constitute a disability under Section 504 of the Rehabilitation Act of 1973. In this case, the infectious disease was tuberculosis. However, in that same year a federal district circuit court of appeals in California applied the Arline decision to a case involving an Orange County teacher with AIDS. The court ordered the school district to reinstate the teacher to his previous duties.

A further development occurred in 1988, when the U.S. Justice Department reversed its earlier position on AIDS and declared that fear of contagion by itself does not permit federal agencies and federally assisted employers to fire or discriminate against workers infected with the virus. This legal opinion is binding on school boards, federal agencies, government contractors, managers of federally subsidized housing projects, and other organizations receiving federal contracts or financial assistance. The opinion emphasized that each situation must be determined on a case-by-case basis in order to decide if an infected person poses a direct threat to the health of others in the workplace.

The Rehabilitation Act of 1973 requires an employer to make "reasonable accommodations" for people with disabilities, which now includes AIDS. The accommodations must be made if the person with AIDS can still perform the essential requirements of his or her job. If an employer can demonstrate that making such accommodations would pose an undue hardship, then the company, agency, or organization can be excused. However, the regulations governing undue hardship are very stringent. A situation in which the reasonable accommodation regulation probably would not apply is in the case of a school bus driver who has advanced symptoms of the disease. The effects of AIDS on the central nervous system would preclude that person from continuing to drive a school bus.

It is extremely important to protect the privacy of individuals who have AIDS. Medical information on employees is confidential. This fact is clearly set forth in *Gammel* v. *United States* (1984). In this case, the U.S. government wanted to review the medical records of a federal employee, Mr. Gammel. The United States contended that Gammel was a potential health risk to the general public and reviewing his medical records would provide the necessary information in order to suitably assign him where he would not be a threat to the public. Gammel's attorney argued that the Fourteenth Amendment of the U.S. Constitution protects the privacy rights of citizens and the release of medical information would violate this Amendment unless there was proof that a clear and present danger to public safety, in fact, existed. The U.S. government failed to establish such proof and therefore, the federal district court ruled in favor of Gammel.

Therefore, if the personnel records of public school districts contain medical information about employees, these records are confidential. The only reason for revealing the contents of such records would be the existence of a clear and present danger to public health or safety.

There is also an area of concern in relation to the rights of coworkers of AIDS-infected employees. This issue has been addressed in a private sector federal court case, *Whirlpool* v. *Marshall* (1988). The case reaffirmed that the best available medical information does not consider casual contact with an AIDS infected person to be a health risk. The contact in schools between staff members and, in fact, between staff members and students can be classified as casual and thus, there is no risk of contracting AIDS. School district human resources policies and procedures must reflect this position.

In summary, case law clearly upholds the employment and privacy rights of persons with AIDS, with ARC, and with an HIV positive test. Further, case law upholds these same rights for persons suspected of being infected. It is imperative that the assistant superintendent for human resources ensure that discrimination does not occur in school district practices against persons with AIDS or with the above-mentioned AIDS-related conditions. A potential area for serious discrimination exists in life, medical, and hospitalization insurance programs.

Vietnam Era Veterans Readjustment Assistance Act

The Vietnam Era Veterans Readjustment Assistance Act was passed by Congress in 1974. School districts receiving $10,000 or more in federal funds must take affirmative action to hire veterans with disabilities of all wars, and all veterans of the Vietnam era. This Act defines a veteran with a disability as a person who has a 30 percent or more disability rating from the Veterans Administration, or who was discharged or released from active duty for a service-connected disability.[25]

Mobilization of Military Reserves and National Guard into Active Duty

On August 22, 1990, President George H.W. Bush ordered the mobilization of U.S. military reserves and National Guard units into active duty. This was the first mobilization in 20 years and activated approximately 40,000 troops. This mobilization, of course, was necessary in order to support the forthcoming war in the Persian Gulf against Iraq. The war was named Desert Storm.[26]

When the employee enters active military service, he or she is immediately covered by the military health care system. Dependents of the employee are eligible to be covered by the Civilian Health and Medical Program of the Uniformed Services (formerly CHAMPUS, now called TRICARE) under certain conditions. The most significant condition is the length of time that the employee will be on active duty. If the mobilization is for less than 390 days, dependents cannot be enrolled in TRICARE. However, if the mobilization is extended, TRICARE coverage will begin on the 31st day of active duty. If the mobilization is for more than 30 days at the outset, coverage begins from the first day of active duty. Dependents must receive health care from military health facilities or receive permission to go to a civilian facility.

Reservists and National Guard members are covered under the provisions of the Veteran's Reemployment Act of 1940, which also was amended in 1986. This Act obliges the school district to give reservists and National Guard members time off from their civilian jobs to participate in military training and active duty. Also, the Act protects them from termination and discrimination because of their military obligations. Further, the reservist or National Guard member is covered by an "escalator principle" which means that he or she will continue to accrue seniority, fringe benefits, and salary increases. Thus, if other employees in the same job category as the reservist or National Guard member received an increase in salary and/or additional fringe benefits, he or she will receive the same salary increase and/or fringe benefits when he or she returns to work. However, if there was a reduction in fringe benefits or salary for all the members of the job category, the same reductions will apply to the reservist or National Guard member upon his or her return.

Upon his or her release from military training or active duty, the reservist or National Guard member has 90 days to apply for reinstatement into his or her prior held position. If the prior held position is not available, he or she must be offered a position of like status or the job that is nearest in duties to the one he or she left. In regard to health care benefits, the employer cannot impose a preexisting exclusion or waiting period before reinsuring the reservist or National Guard member.

The Omnibus Transportation Employee Testing Act, 1991

On October 28, 1991, President Bush signed the Omnibus Transportation Employee Testing Act into law, which required the Secretary of Transportation to promulgate regulations for alcohol and controlled substances testing for persons in safety-sensitive positions including motor carriers. Implementation for districts with 50 or more employees was done in 1994. For districts with fewer than 50 employees, implementation began in early 1995.[27]

Regulations have been established that require school bus drivers and drivers of private motor carriers of passengers to submit to controlled-substance testing. Other regulations require school districts to conduct preemployment, post accident, random, reasonable suspicion, and return-to-duty testing. School districts must publish the board of education policy concerning this law and must publish implementation procedures which should include the action that the school district will take if a bus driver is found to be in violation of this law.

School districts must also develop procedures for the collection, shipment, and accessioning of urine specimens. The Department of Transportation requires urine samples to be analyzed by laboratories certified by the Department of Health and Human Services' National Institute on Drug Abuse. Laboratories are required to report the analysis to a medical review officer who contacts the bus driver concerning the results of the testing and who reports the results to the school district. Of course, these reports are confidential. The school district administrator responsible for determining if a reasonable suspicion exists to require a bus driver to undergo testing must receive at least 60 minutes of training on the physical, behavioral, speech, and performance indicators of probable controlled substance abuse. Finally, a bus driver who has violated this law must receive information from the school district concerning resources that are available for helping the bus driver with his or her drug abuse problem.

Family and Medical Leave Act, 1993

President Bill Clinton signed into law the Family and Medical Leave Act (P.L. 103–3) on February 5, 1993. The fundamental purpose of this Act is to provide eligible employees, as defined by section 3(e) of the Fair Labor Standards Act, with the right to take 12 weeks of unpaid leave per year in connection with certain circumstances.[28]

An employee may invoke this law in conjunction with the following:

- The birth and first-year care of a child. This includes paternity leave.
- The adoption or foster parent placement of a child. The entitlement ends when the child reaches age one or the twelve-week period ends.
- The illness of an employee's spouse, child, or parent. This includes a step-child, foster child, a child over eighteen years of age incapable of self care, and a step-parent.

- The employee's own illness. This means a serious health condition that may result from not only illness but also injury, impairment, physical or mental condition. This may involve inpatient care or any incapacity requiring absence from work for more than three days and which involves continuing treatment by a health care provider. Also, this refers to any treatment for prenatal care.

The law became effective on August 5, 1993. However, in those school districts that have a collective bargaining agreement with one or more bargaining units, the law became effective upon the termination of the master contract or on February 5, 1994, whichever occurred earlier. Because this is a labor law, the U.S. Department of Labor is the federal agency responsible for the development of implementation regulations.

All employees of private elementary and secondary schools and all employees of public school districts are covered by this law. In business and industry, a company must employ 50 or more people to be subject to the mandates of the law. Eligibility under this law means that an employee must have worked for the school district at least 12 months. The employment may have been consecutive or nonconsecutive. Also, the employee must have worked at least 1,250 hours during the year preceding the leave. Thus, many part-time employees are not eligible. There is also an exemption which could apply to the superintendent of schools and many other administrators. This exemption allows a board of education to deny the request for leave of an employee whose salary falls within the highest 10 percent category. The reason for the exclusion is that the absence of such an employee may cause substantial and grievous economic injury to the school district.

A school district may use a number of methods to calculate the 12-month period during which 12 weeks of leave may be requested. For example, the district policy may be the calendar year, 12 months forward from the date that an employee returned from a leave, or any fixed 12-month period. When both spouses are employees of the same school district, the combined amount of leave for birth, adoption, and family illness may be limited to 12 weeks. Obviously, this restriction does not apply to personal illness.

There are special regulations pertaining to "intermittent leave," "reduced leave schedule," and "leave near the end of an academic term." This provision applies to teachers and does not include teacher assistants and aides unless their principal job is actual teaching. Counselors, psychologists, curriculum specialists, and support staff such as cafeteria, maintenance, and transportation employees are not covered by the special regulations.

Thus, a teacher may take intermittent leave, which means a period of time from one hour to several weeks. A person being treated with chemotherapy is an example of such a situation. However, if a teacher will be absent more than 20 percent of the total number of working days during the period of the leave which is considered a reduced leave schedule, a school district may require the teacher to take leave for a particular duration which must not be longer than the duration of the treatment. An alternative approach for a school district is to transfer the teacher to a different assignment on a temporary basis. The teacher must receive equivalent pay and benefits. For example, a school district could assign the teacher to a full-time substitute teacher position.

In regards to leave near the end of an academic year, a school district may require a teacher to continue on leave until the end of the term if the leave begins more than five weeks, but continues into three weeks before the end of the term. Further, the school district may require the teacher to continue leave until the end of the term unless the leave is for the teacher's own serious health condition under two circumstances: (1) if the leave begins with five or fewer weeks before the end of the semester but lasts for more than two weeks and ends during the two-week period before the end of the term; (2) if the leave begins during the three-week period before the end of the semester and will last for more than five days.

If the employee has prior knowledge about the need for a leave, he or she is required to give 30 days verbal or written notice. When the employee does not have prior knowledge about the need for a leave, notice must be given as soon as is practicable, which may be interpreted as two working days. The school district may require the employee to first use accrued paid leave such as sick, personal, or vacation leave. The district must continue to pay health plan premiums for the employee during the period of leave and this period must be treated as continued service for purposes of vesting and eligibility to participate in retirement plans. However, the employee is not entitled to accrue additional benefits during the period of unpaid leave, such as additional paid sick leave.

The school district may require certification from the employee's health care provider or the family member's health care provider concerning the date when the condition began, its duration, the necessity for leave, and the employee's inability to perform his or her job functions. A second opinion from a health care provider can be required by the school district at its own expense; and a third opinion can be obtained on the same condition with this opinion binding.

Upon return from leave, an employee is entitled to the same position or an equivalent position as when leave commenced, with the same salary, benefits, and working conditions. The district may require a certification from the employee's health care provider stating that the employee is able to resume work. School districts must inform employees about the provisions of this Act. Also, policies and procedures for invoking this Act must be in writing and be provided to the employee prior to taking leave in order for the district to enforce the Act.

Complaints by employees can be initiated with the U.S. Department of Labor. The Department may conduct an administrative investigation or may file suit in court. Thus, federal record keeping requirements and investigations will be consistent with the Fair Labor Standards Act. The statute of limitations is two years, except in cases where willful violation is alleged, which carries a three-year limitation. A school district that violates this law may be subject to the following damages: (1) lost wages and benefits; (2) all other costs other than wages that an employee may have incurred as a result of the violation. The other costs usually include attorney and witness fees, but could also include, as an example, reimbursement for professional nursing care up to a sum equal to 12 weeks of wages if the employee's leave was denied.

Equality for Women

The French writer Stendhal (Marie-Henri Beyle) believed that granting women equality would be the surest sign of civilization and would double the intellectual power of the human race. Although he wrote over one hundred years ago, equality for women continues to be a significant issue in our society.[29]

In educational organizations the question of equal employment opportunity for women traditionally applies to a specific job classification—administration. It is clear to all observers that women are well represented in teaching, custodial, food service, and bus driving positions. Skilled trade positions (carpenters, electricians, and plumbers) in most school districts, however, are dominated by males, as are industrial arts teaching positions. In such situations, the norms of affirmative action previously outlined in this chapter are applicable. The critical issue, however, is the need to have women better represented in administrative ranks.

Why are there so few female administrators? Many researchers have put forth various theories. One such study argues that the causes are increased salary levels for teachers, which attracted more men, who were subsequently promoted to administrative positions; entry of male veterans into education after World War II and the Korean War, which also led to their eventual entry into administration; the executive image projected for administrators in the 1950s and 1960s, which attracted more men.

The legal mandate of equal employment opportunity for women emanates primarily from two federal laws: Title IX of the Education Amendments of 1972, which prohibits sex discrimination in educational programs or activities, including employment, when the school district is receiving federal financial assistance; and, of course, Title VII of the Civil Rights Act of 1964, as amended in 1972, which prohibits discrimination on the basis of sex as well as religion, national origin, race, or color.

In February 1992, the U.S. Supreme Court issued a unanimous opinion in connection with a lawsuit, *Franklin* v. *Gwinnett County Public Schools*, which upheld unlimited punitive and compensatory damages for victims of gender discrimination under Title IX of the Education Amendments of 1972. This is a landmark decision. Prior to this a female employee who believed that she had been discriminated against could seek only back pay in addition to the injunctive and declaratory relief otherwise available.

In November 2004, the U.S. Supreme Court ruled in *Jackson* v. *Birmingham Board of Education*, No. 02-1672, which advocates and whistle-blowers, along with victims, may sue under Title IX of the Education Amendments of 1972. The case involved a physical education teacher in the Birmingham, Alabama, School District who also coached the high school girls' basketball team. He was fired from his coaching position after he complained that the female basketball players were being discriminated against because of their gender. The coach sued the Board of Education in 2001. The trial court threw out the suit stating that Title IX did not apply in that case. The U.S. Court of Appeals for the Eleventh Circuit upheld that decision, but the U.S. Supreme Court overturned the lower courts' rulings.[30]

This is a significant ruling for human resources administrators because it is an extension of the prevailing attitude that retaliation for reporting violations of legal mandates will not be tolerated by the courts and federal agencies. For example, this ruling is certainly in consort with the guidelines of the United States Equal Employment Opportunity Commission (EEOC) that oppose retaliation in the administration of Title VII of the Civil Rights Act. EEOC guidelines prohibit the firing, demotion, harassment, and other forms of retaliation against individuals who file a charge of discrimination, participate in a discrimination proceeding, or otherwise oppose discrimination. The Supreme Court ruling, however, forges a new dimension in that it gives the same protection against retaliation to advocates and whistle blowers.[31]

POTENTIAL AREAS OF EMPLOYMENT DISCRIMINATION CONCERNING WOMEN As a general rule, school districts—and all employers—are prohibited from establishing job qualifications that are derived from female stereotyping. The courts have uniformly required employers to prove that any sex restriction is indeed a *bona fide* occupational qualification.

Some of the most common forms of discrimination against females in the industrial/business community are even less defensible in educational organizations. For example, females have been denied employment because of height and weight limitations. In such situations, a woman who is capable of performing the job-related tasks has clearly established case law precedent to bring the employer to court. However, it still occurs that an exceptionally talented woman may not be hired for an administrative position because she is a "nice and petite" person who does not measure up to the image of a strong leader.

The Equal Employment Opportunity Commission prohibits discrimination against women for the following reasons: because of their marital status, because they are pregnant, because they are not the principal wage earner in a family, or because they have preschool age children.

The preferences of customers and clientele are not *bona fide* occupational qualifications. Thus, the preference of parents and even students for male principals and administrators in a given school district does not permit the district to discriminate against females seeking administrative positions.

MATERNITY AS A PARTICULAR FORM OF DISCRIMINATION On October 31, 1978, President Jimmy Carter signed into law a pregnancy disability amendment (PL 95-555) to Title VII of the Civil Rights Act of 1964. The law had the effect of eliminating unequal treatment for pregnant women in all employment-related situations. The EEOC issued guidelines for implementing this law, indicating that it is discriminatory for an employer to refuse to hire, train, assign, or promote a woman solely because she is pregnant; to require maternity leave for a predetermined time period; to dismiss a woman because she is pregnant; to deny reemployment to a woman who has been on maternity leave; to deny seniority credit to a woman who has been on maternity leave; and to deny disability or medical benefits to a woman for disability or illness unrelated to but occurring during pregnancy, childbirth, or recovery from childbirth.[32]

RECRUITMENT AND SELECTION To ensure that discrimination against women does not occur in employment, as a first step, the school district's leadership should review recruitment and selection procedures. The following specific actions will minimize the potential for discriminating:

- Use women as recruiters and interviewers.
- Develop a list of women for potential promotion from within the school district.
- Encourage female employees to apply for available administrative positions.
- When recruiting outside the school district, contact such organizations as the American Association of University Women (AAUW), the National Council of Administrative Women in Education (NCAWE), the National Organization for Women (NOW), and minority employment agencies for referrals.
- Include female representatives on selection committees.
- Remove such title designations as Mr., Mrs., Miss, and Ms. from application forms.
- When interviewing female applicants, ask only questions that are related to the abilities needed for job performance.
- Review and evaluate the entire selection process to assure that job descriptions, selection criteria, and data-gathering instruments (such as paper-pencil tests and job applications) are job-related and do not screen out women.

PROMOTION AND TRAINING Positive steps also must be taken to overcome patterns of inequality that have become traditional in some school districts. Among the most effective procedures are the following:

- Publicize all promotional opportunities.
- Seek out capable women and assign them administrative tasks when possible, giving them the experience to move into administrative positions.
- Examine procedures for promotion to eliminate all facets except those that present a fair assessment of the employee's ability and record.
- Recommend women for administrative internship and in-service programs.

Sexual Harassment

In 1980, the Equal Employment Opportunity Commission declared sexual harassment to be a violation of Title VII of the Civil Rights Act of 1964.[35] Basically there are two types of sexual harassment, quid pro quo discrimination and hostile environment discrimination. The first type is obvious. *Quid pro quo* discrimination occurs when an employment or personnel decision is based upon an applicant's or employee's submission to or rejection of unwelcome sexual conduct. Thus, a *quid pro quo* personnel decision occurs when employment opportunities or fringe benefits are granted because of an employee's submission to the employer's or the supervisor's sexual advances.[33]

Hostile environment discrimination occurs when unwelcome sexual conduct interferes with the employee's job performance. The standard for deciding environmental discrimination is if the sexual conduct substantially affected the job performance of a reasonable person. Factors to consider in investigating hostile environment discrimination are: was the conduct physical, verbal, or both; the frequency of the conduct; the position of the harasser, coworker, or supervisors; if other employees were involved in the conduct; if there was more than one person against whom the conduct was directed; and was the conduct hostile or patently hostile. It is also important to investigate if the sexual conduct was unwelcome. Did the person alleging sexual harassment indicate by his or her conduct that the sexual advances were unwelcome? In making this determination, the timing of the protest and whether a prior consensual relationship existed with the alleged harasser are significant factors.

School districts are liable for the actions of their administrators and supervisors when these individuals act as the "agent" for the school district at the time of the harassment. For *quid pro quo* discrimination, the administrator or supervisor is always acting as the agent of the school district. For hostile environment discrimination, the school district is liable if the district knew or should have known of the sexual harassment of the supervisor.

For coworkers who sexually harass their colleagues, the school district is liable if the agents, administrators and supervisors, knew or should have known about the harassment. When sexual conduct becomes known, the appropriate administrator or supervisor must act to remedy the situation. It is also the responsibility of the administrators and supervisors to take appropriate action to protect employees in the workplace against sexual harassment by non-employees. This responsibility is present when school district agents knew or should have known about the harassment.

In order for a school district to demonstrate to employees and the general public that sexual harassment will not be tolerated, the board of education should adopt a policy prohibiting such conduct and administrative procedures should be developed to effectively deal with allegations. Further, all employees should be required to participate in a staff development program about the issue of sexual harassment.

The board of education policy should set forth the commitment of the school district to deal with sexual harassment in an expeditious and effective manner. Administrative procedures to implement the policy should set forth the complaint process and should include the filling out of a complaint form which must be signed by the complainant. The appropriate human resources administrator should inform all the parties of their rights. Both the complaint and the investigation should be kept confidential. The procedures also should contain a timeline for completion of the investigation. The policy and procedures must be communicated to all staff members.

A staff development program about sexual harassment for all employees should contain the following components: an explanation of the board policy and administrative procedures; specific examples of sexual harassment; myths about sexual harassment; the distinction between welcome, consensual, and illegal sexual harassment. Administrator and supervisor staff development should include the above but also should stress the importance of protecting the complainant against retaliation.

POLICY OF NONDISCRIMINATION ON THE BASIS OF SEX Good intentions by school administrators to remedy past practices of discrimination against women and to prevent future practices are not sufficient. The only defensible course of action is for the superintendent of schools to recommend a policy for adoption by the board of education. This would complement the school district's affirmative action policy and would provide the assurance required by law. The American Association of School Administrators has published a sample policy which is intended to be a guide for local boards of education in their policy formulation efforts.

The Equal Pay Act

The U.S. Congress enacted in 1963 the Equal Pay Act, which requires employers to pay males and females the same salary or wage for equal work. This Act is part of the Fair Labor Standards Act and protects employees who work for an employer engaged in an enterprise affected by interstate commerce. The interpretation of interstate commerce was broadly defined by the court in *Usery* v. *Columbia University*, 568 F. 2d 953 (2d Cir. 1977). In addition, the interpretation of equal work has been broadly defined to mean substantially equal and thus, strict equality of jobs is not required. Thus, this Act requires equal pay for jobs that demand equal skill, effort, and responsibility, and that are carried out under similar working conditions. However, if salaries or wages are contingent upon a seniority system, a merit system, a system that measures pay by production quantity or quality, or factors other than sex, this Act does not apply.[34]

An example of a court case involving the Equal Pay Act is *EEOC* v. *Madison Community Unit School District Number 12*, 818 F. 2d 577 (7th Cir. 1987). In this case, a female who coached girls' track and tennis was paid substantially less than the males who coached the boys' track and tennis at the same school. In addition, a female assistant coach of the girls' basketball team was paid less than a male assistant coach of the boys' track team; still another female coach was paid less for coaching girls' basketball, softball, and volleyball than male coaching boys' basketball, baseball, and soccer. Finally, an assistant coach of the girls' track team was paid less than the assistant coach of the boys' track team.

The Equal Employment Opportunity Commission filed a lawsuit against the school district, stating that the inequities violated the Equal Pay Act. The U.S. District Court ruled in favor of the EEOC but the school district appealed to the U.S. Court of Appeals, Seventh Circuit. This Court affirmed the district court's decision in the following situations: boys' and girls' track, boys' and girls' tennis, boys' baseball and girls' softball. However, the Court of Appeals reversed the district court's decision in comparing boys' soccer to girls' volleyball, boys' soccer to girls' basketball, and boys' track to girls' basketball. The Court stated that these situations did not require equal skill, effort, and responsibility.[35]

There is another aspect to the equal pay issue. When a school district has a performance-based evaluation system that is used to determine the salaries and wages of employees, the Equal Pay Act does not apply. However, in all organizations employees tend to compare their salaries and wages with those of coworkers and to compare how productive these coworkers are in comparison with themselves. The effects of this situation for school administration can be serious. It is a situation that will only fester if it is ignored. The best approach is to reemphasize the relationship between performance and reward; it is also important to reiterate that the performance-based evaluation process is the vehicle for determining the level of performance and the amount of reward.

Obviously, if a school district does not have an effective evaluation process, a merit-based reward program cannot be initiated. Performance and reward are two aspects of the same process—they go hand in hand.

Equality by Age

The Age Discrimination in Employment Act of 1967, as amended, is taking on ever-increasing importance for human resources administrators. This Act was passed by Congress to promote the employment of the older worker based upon ability rather than age by prohibiting arbitrary discrimination. Also, under this Act the Department of Labor has consistently sponsored informational and educational programs on the needs and abilities of the older worker. The "Statement of Findings and Purpose" in the Age Discrimination in Employment Act sets forth a rationale for its passage that is a true reflection of current societal trends towards older workers:[36]

Sec. 2. (a) The Congress hereby finds and declares that

(1) in the face of rising productivity and affluence, older workers find themselves disadvantaged in their efforts to retain employment, and especially to regain employment when displaced from jobs;
(2) the setting of arbitrary age limits regardless of potential for job performance has become a common practice, and certain otherwise desirable practices may work to the disadvantage of older persons;
(3) the incidence of unemployment, especially long-term unemployment with resultant deterioration of skill, morale, and employer acceptability is, relative to the younger ages, high among older workers; their numbers are great and growing; and their employment problems grave;
(4) the existence in industries affecting commerce of arbitrary discrimination in employment burdens commerce and the free flow of goods in commerce.

PROVISIONS OF THE AGE DISCRIMINATION IN EMPLOYMENT ACT The law protects individuals who are at least 40 years of age but less than 70. It applies to private employers of 20 or more persons. The law also applies to employment agencies and labor organizations having 25 or more members in an industry affecting interstate commerce. The law does not apply to elected officials or their appointees.

In January 2000 by a five-to-four decision, the U.S. Supreme Court held that Congress did not have the authority under the Fourteenth Amendment to the U.S. Constitution to extend this act to states and their political subdivision. Thus, at this writing it appears that public school districts cannot be sued in federal court under the Age Discrimination in Employment Act. However, there are age discrimination statutes in almost every state that can be invoked by job applicants and employees of school districts who believe that they have been discriminated against because of age. Thus, state compliance agencies and the state courts can provide remedies to age discrimination.

It is against the law for an employer to refuse to hire or otherwise discriminate against any person as to compensation, terms, conditions, or privileges of employment because of age; to limit, segregate, or classify employees so as to deprive any individual of employment opportunities or adversely affect that individual's status as an employee because of age. It is against the law for an employment agency to refuse to refer for employment or otherwise discriminate against an individual because of age, or to classify and refer anyone for employment on the basis of age. It is against the law for a labor union to discriminate against anyone because of age by excluding or expelling that person from membership; to limit, segregate, or classify its members on the basis of age; to refuse to refer anyone for employment so as to result in a deprivation or limitation of employment opportunity or otherwise adversely affect an individual's status as an employee because of age; or to cause or attempt to cause an employer to discriminate against an individual because of age.

Furthermore, the provisions of the Age Discrimination in Employment Act prohibit an employer, employment agency, or labor union from discriminating against a person for opposing a practice that is unlawful because of this Act, discriminating against a person making a charge, assisting or participating in any investigation, proceeding, or litigation under this Act; publishing a notice of an employment vacancy that indicates a preference, limitation, or specification based on age.

EXCEPTIONS TO THE AGE DISCRIMINATION IN EMPLOYMENT ACT The prohibitions of this Act do not apply if age is a *bona fide* occupational qualification reasonably necessary to the normal performance of a given task. Therefore, test pilot positions might be filled with individuals no older than 45, because accurate and quick reflexes are necessary to the safe flying of experimental aircraft. However, it would be difficult to justify age as a *bona fide* occupational qualification in education institutions.

The prohibitions of the Age Discrimination in Employment Act do not apply when an individual is discharged or disciplined for good cause, and when the terms of a new or existing employee seniority or benefits program differentiates by reason of age. However, no employee benefits plan can be used as an excuse for failing to hire an individual because of age.

ENFORCEMENT OF THE AGE DISCRIMINATION IN EMPLOYMENT ACT The administration of this Act passed from the Department of Labor to the Equal Employment Opportunity Commission on July 1, 1979. At that time the average number of complaints had reached 5,000 annually. The EEOC can conduct investigations, issue rules and regulations to administer the law, and enforce the provisions of the law through the courts when voluntary compliance cannot be obtained.

Other Legislation

This section has dealt with four major federal influences on the human resources planning process. Although affirmative action and the legislation on equality for people with disabilities, women, and individuals by age represent central trends in human resources administration, these are by no means the only federal considerations that affect human resources processes.

The following laws enacted by Congress constitute a significant part of the national public employment policy that directly and indirectly affects the employment policies of public and private educational institutions. They should be studied by all human resources administrators:

1883 Pendleton Act (Civil Service Commission)

1931 Davis-Bacon Act

1932 Anti-Injunction Act

1935 National Labor Relations Act

1935 Social Security Act

1936 Walsh-Healey Public Contracts Act

1938 Fair Labor Standards Act

1947 Labor-Management Relations Act

1959 Labor-Management Reporting and Disclosure Act

1962 Work House Act

1967 Reemployment of Veterans Act

1968 Garnishment Provisions, Consumer Credit Protection Act

1974 Employee Retirement Income Security Act

1986 Immigration Reform and Control Act

1990 Immigration Act

In addition, it must be kept in mind that various states and cities have enacted statutes and ordinances that also exert significant influence on human resources administration.

Finally, this chapter includes three appendices: (A) Steps in Developing an Affirmative Action Program; (B) Summary Facts Concerning Job Discrimination; and (C) Steps in Filing a Charge of Job Discrimination. These appendices provide summary data that further clarify how federal legislation impinges on human resources management.

TECHNOLOGY AND HUMAN RESOURCES PLANNING

The Internet is a most valuable resource in providing immediate access to original federal documents such as guidelines from the Equal Employment Opportunity Commission on the responsibilities of employers. Further, it is helpful to read certain sections of specific federal laws such as the Family and Medical Leave Act of 1993 or the EEOC declaration on sexual harassment. Nothing substitutes for the original documents, which are now readily available to every administrator who has access to the Internet.

The planning process can be easily engaged through computer software programs that convert population and student data into an enrollment projection. Likewise, simple statistical programs can be helpful in developing a human resources forecast. Further, there is available software programs commonly referred to as *human resource management system programs* (HRMS), which provide easy and immediate access to human resources information. Such information can include academic degrees, teaching or administrative experience, licensure, and special skills such as athletic coaching and program sponsorship. The newer software is user-friendly and can be linked to other school district information systems.

IMPLICATIONS FOR SMALL AND MEDIUM-SIZED SCHOOL DISTRICTS

The obvious implications for small and medium-sized school districts begin with the fact that all federal guidelines and laws are mandatory for every school district. There is no excuse for violations. Thus, it is incumbent on superintendents, principals, and all other administrators to know and understand the guidelines and laws. The size of the school district will not be a reasonable defense for noncompliance.

The real issue revolves around how school districts will promulgate and implement the guidelines and laws. No administrator will have the time neither to investigate changes in existing guidelines and laws nor to become acquainted with new guidelines and laws. Thus, the usual approach that superintendents take is to hire a human resources consultant or attorney who will be able to keep the school district personnel up to date on federal guidelines and laws. This is also the reason why it is important for school administrators to become members of local, state, and national professional associations such as the American Association of School Administrators (AASA), National Association of Secondary School Principals (NASSP), and National Association of Elementary School Principals (NAESP) because such organizations act as a clearinghouse for legal responsibilities of educational administrators. Likewise, it is important for school board members to be current in their understanding of federal guidelines and laws, which is also facilitated by membership in the National School Boards Association (NSBA). All of these organizations have state affiliates and there are many local organizations of educational administrators where such issues are discussed.

There is a considerable amount of latitude in how small and medium-sized school districts deal with the planning process and particularly with enrollment projections. Because of size it is easy to keep basic statistics on teacher, administrator, and staff turnover; and likewise, it is easy to know population trends in such districts. Communication from and with teachers, administrators, staff members, parents, business leaders, and public officials is often direct and touches upon issues that affect the planning process and enrollment projections.

The coordination of planning, enrollment projecting, and compliance with federal guidelines and laws typically will be the responsibility of the superintendent of schools, but also may become the responsibility of another central office administrator such as an assistant superintendent or may be divided up among a number of administrators. For example, building principals may be responsible for enrollment projections in their respective attendance areas. A curriculum coordinator may be responsible for having the right number of teachers with the appropriate state licensure. The superintendent may take the lead in working with the school district's attorney or federal compliance issues. The administrator with staff development responsibilities may be the person who organizes continuing education on federal compliance for teachers, administrators, and staff members. When all else is not possible, the superintendent of schools has all of these responsibilities.

THE IMPACT OF GENERATION Y ON HUMAN RESOURCES PLANNING

It is obvious to most people that Generation Y teachers and principals are seriously and intensely involved in communicating by electronic means, which include cell phones, iPods, text messages, email, and Web sites. Further, such communication is carried out asynchronously, meaning that they are not tied to real time in their endeavor to communicate. The communication is instantaneous and dialogue can continue to whatever extent that the people desire through chat rooms. Of course, the danger in relying solely upon electronic communication is that it is *not* tied to real time, which tends to isolate those using these types of communication. That may seem difficult to understand since there is a flurry of communication taking place, but if we only communicate electronically and not in-person, we may eventually know more information, but not understand the person or persons with whom we are communicating.

Electronic communication does not permit a holistic approach to communication that values verbal and non-verbal communication, which often reveals the true intention of the person with whom we are communicating, and the realms of emotions and feelings. Teachers and principals certainly need to communicate with children and colleagues in all areas: electronic writing, verbal, and nonverbal.

In the human resources planning process, it is possible for administrators to communicate important information to all employees using electronic devices. This is especially useful in notifying teachers, administrators, and staff members about legislation and policies that affect certain categories of employees or everyone in general. Thus. a change in a school district maternity policy and procedures could be communicated to employees through electronic means. The information will certainly reach Generation Y employees, but may not reach those from other generations. Thus, it should not be the only means of communication.[37]

Quick Review of Essentials

Planning is a process common to all human experience. It encompasses an understanding of the present condition, future objectives, and methods for reaching these objectives.

Human resources planning as a process in human resources management is undertaken to ensure that a school district has the right number of people, with the right skills, in the right place, and at the right time.

The first step in the human resources planning process is to assess human resources needs, which includes the following four aspects: (1) developing human resources inventories, (2) developing a five-year enrollment projection, (3) developing school district objectives, and (4) developing a human resources forecast.

Two of the most pressing problems facing school districts are human resources planning and increasing and decreasing pupil enrollments, and because of faculty and staff layoffs due to decreases in school district revenue. Two of the most successful alternatives to reduction in a workforce have been early retirement incentive programs and the retraining of individuals for positions that become vacant through attrition or are created through program development.

A hallmark of our contemporary American society is the avalanche of federal legislation and court decisions, which in turn has had a definite influence on the human resources planning process. Incorporated or implied in all civil rights legislation are the important concepts of social justice and affirmative action.

Justice is a guide that regulates how people live out their lives as members of a given society. The substance of justice is entitlement that refers to those rights to which individuals and groups of people have a claim. The responsibility of society to the individual is called distributive justice. The responsibility of each person to society is termed legal justice. Commutative justice involves the responsibility that exists between individuals. Justice also involves restitution that is the right of a person to have an entitlement restored.

John Rawls was a contemporary political philosopher who described his theory of justice in terms of fairness. His basic premise is that the best principles of justice for the basic structure of any society are those that would be the object of an original agreement in the establishment of a society. Rawls elucidated two principles that he believes people should choose to implement the notion of fairness. The first principle asserts that each person is to have an equal right to a system of liberties that is compatible with a similar system of liberties available to all people. The second principle asserts that social and economic inequalities must benefit the least advantaged and that equal opportunity to secure offices and position must be open to all. In explaining how present inequities may benefit the least advantaged, Rawls developed the principle of just savings.

Affirmative action is not a law within itself, but rather an objective reached by following a set of guidelines that ensure compliance with legislation and executive orders. The Equal Employment Opportunity Commission (EEOC) was established by Title VII of the Civil Rights Act to investigate alleged discrimination in employment practices based on race, color, religion, sex, or national origin. This five-member commission has also established, from time to time, affirmative action guidelines. Alleged discrimination charges can be filed with any of EEOC's district offices. The administrative process includes an individual's filing of a charge, investigation of the charge, determination of the charge, and the process of conciliation.

Limited discrimination is allowed by the Equal Employment Opportunity Act under one condition: when there is a *bona fide* occupational qualification mandating the employing of an individual of a particular sex, religious affiliation, or national origin.

Therefore, a school district human resources administrator has the right to employ a female rather than a male for the position of swimming instructor when the job description includes supervising the locker room used by female students.

The Civil Rights Act of 1991 is landmark legislation because it extends punitive damages and jury trials for the first time to employees who have been discriminated against because of their race, national origin, gender, disability, or religion.

The Rehabilitation Act of 1973 prohibits recipients of federal financial assistance from discriminating against qualified individuals with disabilities in recruitment, hiring, compensation, job assignment/classification, and in those fringe benefits provided. Employers are further required to provide reasonable accommodations for qualified employees with disabilities. The Vietnam Era Veterans Readjustment Assistance Act of 1974 requires affirmative action to hire veterans with disabilities of all wars and all veterans of the Vietnam era.

The Americans with Disabilities Act (ADA) of 1990 is also landmark legislation because it is the most comprehensive legislation ever passed protecting the rights of individuals with disabilities. There are five titles to ADA, and all of them except Title IV have some impact upon school districts.

On August 22, 1990, President George H.W. Bush ordered the mobilization of U.S. military reserves and National Guard units into active duty. This triggered several issues concerning the health care of dependents and the reentry of reservists and members of the National Guard into the workplace.

On October 28, 1991, President George Bush signed into law the Omnibus Transportation Employee Testing Act, which required the Secretary of Transportation to promulgate regulations for alcohol and controlled substances testing for persons in safety-sensitive positions including school bus drivers.

President Bill Clinton signed into law the Family and Medical Leave Act on February 5, 1993. The fundamental purpose of this act is to provide eligible employees with the right to take unpaid leave in connection with certain circumstances.

Equality in employment opportunity for women is a central issue in human resources management. The legal mandate of equal opportunity for women emanates primarily from two federal laws: Title IX of the Education Amendments of 1972, which prohibits sex discrimination in educational programs or activities, including employment, when the school district is receiving federal financial assistance; and, of course, Title VII of the Civil Rights Act of 1964, as amended in 1972. In addition, President Jimmy Carter in 1978 signed into law a pregnancy disability amendment to the Civil Rights Act. This law had the effect of eliminating unequal treatment of pregnant women in all employment-related situations.

Since 1980, the Equal Employment Opportunity Commission has considered sexual harassment to be a violation of Title VII of the Civil Rights Act of 1964. The issue of sexual harassment in the workplace has gained national attention and will continue to be a concern in school districts across the nation.

The Equal Pay Act of 1963 requires employers to pay males and females the same salary or wage for equal work.

The Age Discrimination in Employment Act of 1967, as amended, promotes the employment of the older worker by prohibiting arbitrary discrimination based on age.

Because of their importance, only major federal influences in the human resources planning process have been presented in this chapter in detail. However, human resources administrators must also become familiar with all legislation that protects employment opportunity rights.

Selected Further Readings

Age Discrimination in Employment Act of 1967. www.eeoc.gov/policy/adea.html (as of 2009).

Civilian Health and Medical Program of the Uniformed Services, TRICARE. www.tricare.mil/ (as of 2009).

Civil Rights Act of 1991. www.eeoc.gov/policy/cra91.html (as of 2009).

Department of Justice. www.usdoj.gov (as of 2009).

Department of Labor. www.dol.gov (as of 2009).

Title IX of the Education Amendments of 1972. www.usdoj.gov/crt/cor/coord/titleixstat.php (as of 2009).

Equal Pay Act of 1963. www.eeoc.gov/policy/epa.html (as of 2009).

Family and Medical Leave Act of 1993. www.dol.gov/esa/whd/fmla/ (as of 2009).

Federal Equal Employment Opportunity Act of 1972. www.eeoc.gov/abouteeoc/35th/thelaw/eeo_1972.html (as of 2009).

Federal Equal Employment Opportunities Commission. www.eeoc.gov (as of 2009).

Human Rights Campaign, *Statewide Anti-Discrimination Laws and Policies*. www.hrc.org (as of 2009).

Omnibus Transportation Employee Testing Act of 1991. www.dot.gov/ost/dapc/ (as of 2009).

Pregnancy Disability Amendment of Title VII, Civil Rights Act of 1964. www.eeoc.gov/types/pregnancy.html (as of 2009).

Rehabilitation Act of 1973, Title V. www.eeoc.gov/policy/rehab.html (as of 2009).

Sexual Harassment, Equal Employment Opportunity Commission. www.eeoc.gov/types/sexual_harassment.html (as of 2009).

Society for Human Resource Management (SHRM). www.shrm.org (as of 2009).

The Americans with Disabilities Act of 1990. www.eeoc.gov/policy/ada.html (as of 2009).

Vietnam Era Veterans Readjustment Assistance Act of 1974. www.dol.gov/compliance/laws/comp-vevraa.htm (as of 2009).

APPENDIX A

Steps in Developing an Affirmative Action Program*

- Establish a strong company policy and commitment.
- Assign responsibility and authority for the program to a top company official.
- Analyze present work force to identify jobs, departments, and units where minorities and females are underutilized.
- Set specific, measurable, attainable hiring and promotion goals, with target dates, in each area of underutilization.
- Make every manager and supervisor responsible and accountable for helping to meet these goals.
- Reevaluate job descriptions and hiring criteria to assure that they reflect actual job needs.
- Find minorities and females who qualify or who can become qualified to fulfill goals.
- Review and revise all employment procedures to assure that they do not have a discriminatory effect and that they help attain the goals.
- Focus on getting minorities and females into upward mobility and relevant training pipelines especially where they have not had previous access.
- Develop systems to monitor and measure progress on a continued basis. If results are not satisfactory in meeting goals, find out why, and make necessary changes.

*Source: www.eeoc.gov/federal/eeomd715.html Federal Equal Employment Opportunity Commission, Affirmative Action and Equal Employment (as of 2009).

■ ■ ■

APPENDIX B

Summary Facts Concerning Job Discrimination*

Title VII of the 1964 Civil Rights Act, as amended, provides that an individual cannot be denied a job or fair treatment on a job because of:

- Race
- Color

- Religion
- Sex
- National origin

The Act established the Equal Employment Opportunity Commission (EEOC) to ensure that these rights are protected. If an individual believes that he or she has been discriminated against in the workplace by any of the groups listed here, he or she may file a charge of discrimination with the EEOC.

- Private employer of 15 or more persons
- State and local government
- Public and private educational institutions
- Public and private employment agencies
- Labor unions with fifteen or more members
- Joint labor-management committees for apprenticeship and training programs

Also a charge may be filed by another person or by a group if the person alleging the discrimination gives his or her permission to these other parties.

The EEOC does not cover discrimination because of:

- Citizenship
- Political affiliation
- Sexual orientation

It also does not cover job discrimination by federal government agencies, government-owned corporations, Native American tribes, or by small private employers with fewer than 15 workers.

If a person wishes to file a charge of job discrimination, he or she must do so promptly—within 180 days from the time the discrimination took place.

An employer is prohibited by law from harassing or bothering an individual in any unfair manner because he or she filed a charge, assisted in an investigation, or opposed unlawful employment practices.

*Source: www.eeoc.gov/policy/vii.html Federal Equal Employment Opportunity Commission, Title VII of the 1964 Civil Rights Act, as amended (as of 2009).

■ ■ ■

APPENDIX C

Steps in Filing a Charge of Job Discrimination*

To file a charge of job discrimination, an individual must:

- Visit the nearest EEOC District Office or mail in a "Charge of Discrimination" form. If a form cannot be obtained, a written statement may be sent identifying all parties and clearly describing what act(s) of discrimination took place.
- Be interviewed by an intake officer of the commission at the district office or be interviewed by telephone if an in-person interview is impossible.
- Provide information, including records and names of witnesses to the discrimination.
- Swear or affirm, under oath, to the charge of discrimination, or make a declaration under penalty of perjury.

As the charging party, an individual must:

- Cooperate with the commission
- Attend fact-finding conferences and other meetings when scheduled
- Inform the commission of changes in his or her address, telephone number, and other such information
- Contact the commission if he or she wishes to withdraw the charge.

After a charge is filed:

- The employer, union, employment agency, or labor-management committee named in the charge will be notified.
- In many states, the charge may be referred for remedy to a state or local fair employment practices agency for 60 days (120 days if the agency is new).
- The commission may require the person making the charge to attend a fact-finding conference in order to establish facts, define issues, and determine a basis for negotiating a settlement.
- If settlement efforts are unsuccessful, the commission may investigate to determine the merits of the charge.
- After the investigation, the commission will issue a letter of determination on the merits of the charge.

*Source: www.eeoc.gov/facts/howtofil.html Federal Equal Employment Opportunity Commission, Filing a Charge of Job Discrimination (as of 2009).

■ ■ ■

CHAPTER

3

Recruitment

FOCUS SCENARIO

You are the assistant superintendent for human resources in a school district that is experiencing a shortage of qualified teachers and other support employees. You have scheduled a meeting with the administrative staff, the teacher organization leaders, and the support staff organization leaders in order to elicit their assistance in recruiting applicants and also to help them understand why recruitment needs to be more proactive.

After conducting informal telephone interviews with very qualified candidates who did not accept your offer of employment or who dropped out of the selection process, it is clear that the school district has a number of obstacles to overcome. First, the school district has a reputation that militates against hiring the best candidates. The reputation is one of a district that offers students an outdated curriculum with inadequate support services. Further, the district appears to lack support from the community because of the failure of a bond issue referendum to build an addition to the middle school.

The accountability of the administration was called into question by the local newspaper when a teacher was dismissed from the district for incompetence. She was also the teacher who publicly criticized the administration and the board of education for misuse of school district funds because some classroom teachers were using outdated textbooks and instructional materials. Further, the district was cited in the newspaper for not having an effective technology instructional program while the superintendent of schools was provided with a district-owned automobile and was given an annuity in addition to board paid medical and hospital insurance for his wife and children.

Applicants stated that other school districts in the same vicinity had higher salaries and better fringe benefits. These, along with the other issues, seem to be the reasons why the school district has been unable to hire those applicants who were the first choice of the administrators and teachers who were involved in the selection process.

After the human resources planning process identifies current and future staffing needs, the next step is to recruit personnel. In the 1970s, many U.S. school districts experienced a rather dramatic decrease in pupil enrollment. This phenomenon forced districts to lay off large numbers of teachers, which affected the number of college students entering schools of education. Young people interested in teaching anticipated a rather dismal job market upon completion of their education and thus changed their career goals. This situation was compounded by the large number of teachers who retired in the 1980s and by the many teacher defections to the business community.

The current situation is not radically different in terms of teacher turnover and the shortage of teachers in certain areas such as special education, the sciences, mathematics, and foreign languages. This is particularly true in rural school districts. The National Center for Educational Statistics has issued three reports that must be analyzed and considered in tandem in order to fully understand the future recruitment demands. The first report was issued in 2005 about the mobility of the teaching workforce. During the 1999–2000 school years, 580,000 teachers were new hires, which is approximately 17 percent of the workforce. The second report issued in 2008 indicates that there will be a need to increase the teaching workforce by 28 percent in 2017. However, the most significant report for this presentation focuses on teacher career choices. This longitudinal study sets forth that as of 2003 approximately 87 percent of prior graduates reported that they were no longer teaching.[1] The implications for the recruitment process indicate that competition will be fierce for the best and brightest candidates for teaching positions in general.

There is a particular concern in urban school districts where African American, Hispanic, and Native American student populations continue to grow yearly. Demographers predict that this trend will continue to gain momentum. There is no corresponding increase in the percent of minority teachers and, in fact, the trend signals a decline in African American and Hispanic teachers and administrators.[2]

However, for human resources administrators, the issue of diversity is a much broader issue. The United States continues to be a nation of immigrants, but the immigrants no longer come from Western Europe. Although there is a definite influx of immigrants from Eastern Europe, the most significant number of immigrants come from Asia and the Americas. Of course, this has changed the composition of the population in the United States, not only ethnically but also religiously. Although the United States is still a nation of Christians and Jews, it is also a nation of Muslims, Hindus, and Confucians.

Obviously, the population is also composed of citizens from the traditional categories of age, disability, gender, illness, and lifestyles. Thus, one of the most important issues facing many human resources administrators is recruiting teachers, staff members, and administrators from underrepresented categories. This is a necessity for two reasons. First, it is crucial to have teachers, staff members, and administrators who are ethnically representative of the community in which the schools are located. Second, all children should be exposed to teachers, staff members, and administrators who are representative of the larger population in the United States. Obviously this situation places an immediate and long-term responsibility upon human resources administrators to develop strategies for recruiting minority employees.[3]

Therefore, the recruitment process has never been more important to school districts as they search for the best people available to help achieve the mission of each district, educating children and young people. This is the major thrust of every recruitment program—not to hire just to fill a position, but rather to acquire the number and type of people necessary for the present and future success of the school district. Affirmative action requirements, future staffing needs, and dual certification are issues that impinge upon recruitment programs. It is a mistake to assume that the correct mix of people will be available to fill vacancies without making a concerted effort to find the most qualified individuals to fill specific human resource needs.

Recruitment as a process also entails discovering potential applicants for anticipated vacancies. This perspective on the recruitment process depends to a great extent on the size of the school district. An urban or metropolitan school district engages, of course, in recruiting potential applicants more often than smaller suburban districts. Many other variables influence the extent of recruiting activities. First, the employment conditions in a community where the school district is located affect recruitment. For example, the existence of a university with a school of education located near the district often ensures sufficient applicants for entry-level teaching positions. In like manner, the labor pool in a metropolitan area has many skilled carpenters, electricians, and plumbers.

A second set of variables affecting recruitment include working conditions, salary levels, and fringe benefits provided by a school district. These affect employee turnover and, therefore, the need to engage in recruitment activities. Districts experiencing a rapid increase in pupil population, and hence a need for increased staff, look upon recruitment as a major human resources priority.

Finally, even school districts experiencing decreasing enrollment and reduction in the workforce may need to engage in recruitment activities from time to time, because certain vacancies require special skills that current employees lack. The sciences, special education, and foreign languages are cases in point. A school district may find that teachers who are already employed and scheduled to be placed on involuntary leave cannot be transferred to fill a vacancy in industrial arts because they lack the required certification.

Recruitment, therefore, should be common to all school districts. The idea of "stealing" proven employees from another company has become an acceptable practice, considered perfectly legitimate if no coercion or illegal pressures are brought to bear upon a potential employee. Talent and skills are scarce commodities. School districts are ethically bound to find the most talented and skilled people available to achieve their mandate of educating children. In practice, this requires them to develop employment conditions, salary levels, and benefits that will attract the best applicants while remaining within the fiscal constraints of the school district.

The practice of overtly contacting and recruiting individuals who meet a given set of job requirements and encouraging them to become applicants should be emulated by school districts. It is recruitment in its purest form. Many state departments of elementary and secondary education have recognized the need to assist school districts that are having difficulties finding and hiring qualified teachers. Thus, the phenomenon of alternative certification programs has emerged in many states. Usually these are programs at colleges and universities that provide individuals who have bachelor's degrees with the opportunity to obtain certification as teachers in a relatively short period of time. Of course, the curriculum varies in the different colleges and universities. However, the emphasis is on the essentials of pedagogy and adapting a person's life skills and academic knowledge to the instructional process.

For example, such programs would help a retired accountant adapt his or her knowledge into lesson plans to teach high school accounting. Of course, considerable attention would also be afforded to understanding adolescent and educational psychology. Obviously, the target populations for these programs are retired people and those seeking a second or third career.

ISSUES THAT IMPACT RECRUITMENT

Affirmative Action

Many school districts make a practice of promoting already hired employees into supervisory or administrative positions. For example, a school bus driver could advance to dispatcher and on from there to route supervisor and eventually, become director of transportation. A classroom teacher may become a department chairperson and, if certificated as an administrator, become an assistant principal, with eventual promotion into the principalship. This is, of course, a legitimate practice with many advantages for building morale within the school district.[4]

Employees who recognize that the district provides them with an opportunity to advance their careers through promotion to positions of greater responsibility are more likely to make a long-term commitment to the school district. In like manner, employees should also be made aware of the link between job performance and promotion. This places a responsibility on the administration to develop procedures that ensure promotion opportunities for those who have demonstrated on the job that they are capable of handling higher-level tasks. The appraisal process is the vehicle for documenting the quality of such performance.

Chapter 2 presented in detail the affirmative action and equal employment opportunity requirements mandated by various civil rights legislation. This legislation basically prohibits discrimination in recruitment because of race, age, disability, military service, color, religion, sex, pregnancy, and national origin. The concept of equality in opportunity, however, must eventuate in a set of recruitment procedures.

Internal promotion as a practice does not nullify affirmative action requirements. The only exceptions to such requirements are those situations in which sex, not being disabled, etc., constitutes *bona fide* occupational qualifications. Thus, a school district may discriminate against a teacher's aide who has an orthopedic disability by promoting another aide to a gymnastics teaching position when the ability to demonstrate routines is part of the job description.

Except for *bona fide* occupational qualifications, a district must establish promotion procedures that clearly do not discriminate against minorities and protected groups of employees. A district can demonstrate equal opportunity by advertising promotional opportunities, establishing promotion criteria, and offering equal access to career advancement training programs. No position should be filled without giving all qualified employees an opportunity to apply. This may be accomplished by publishing promotion opportunities on bulletin boards or in a district publication such as a newsletter. Whatever the method, it must be clear that all qualified employees have been informed of the opening and have been given an opportunity to apply.

Promotion criteria should include the level of current job performance, qualifications and skills, and job knowledge. Affirmative action does not require the promoting of unqualified employees; it does require that all qualified individuals be given an equal opportunity. Finally, minority employees, those with disabilities, and other employees should be encouraged to participate in educational and training programs that will enhance their knowledge and skills, thus providing them with the qualifications necessary to apply for promotions.

The size of a school district usually determines not only the extent of internal recruitment for promotion, but also the extent of external recruitment. In a small school district it may happen that no one currently employed is qualified for an administrative or supervisory opening. Thus, external recruitment is the only available avenue for filling the vacancy.

Affirmative action and equal employment opportunity must be a major consideration in developing and implementing recruitment practices and procedures. The days should be gone when a person can be hired simply because he or she is someone's friend or relative. Physical appearance and the interviewer's hunch are also no longer acceptable criteria for hiring or promoting an individual.

The Public Image and Policies of the School District

A second possible constraint on recruiting candidates for a position emanates from the school district itself. Prospective candidates may not be interested in pursuing a job opportunity in a particular school district because of that district's image in the community. For example, a district that offers an inferior curriculum, that is understaffed, or that lacks support services will find it difficult to attract the best people in education.

The policies of the board of education and the administrative processes and procedures of the district are also important considerations to most candidates. These are the criteria by which the quality of the work environment may be measured. If, for example, a school district lacks a well-defined and effective appraisal process, the prospective candidate will have little confidence in the district's ability to evaluate adequately his or her future performance, which in turn may affect his or her salary increases.

The Position to Be Filled

A third constraint in recruiting for a position centers on the attractiveness of the job itself. A position that is viewed as anxiety-laden or that lacks promotion potential may not interest the best people.

The most common situation that falls within this category is the succession problem. Following either a very successful person or a person who was a failure will be difficult. If the person who previously held the position was exceptionally capable, a successor may find the expectations of the school board, parents, students, and even colleagues to be beyond anyone's capabilities. Following someone who failed in a position will probably be easier. However, the responsibilities of the job may have been neglected to the point where chaos and disorganization reign. A person brought in to restore order may make other employees anxious if they have become accustomed to a lack of supervision.

Salary and Fringe Benefits

The best people for a job will become candidates only if the financial compensation is in keeping with the responsibilities of the position. Education is a service enterprise and, as such, the major priority must be attracting highly qualified employees. Recruiters may need to negotiate compensation with candidates. This practice helps to attract highly qualified individuals for less desirable positions. In school districts, the salary for a position is usually fixed on a salary schedule, and the fringe benefits are universally applied to all employees in a certain category. This makes the recruitment of highly skilled candidates a very difficult task, particularly if the job is undesirable or if the district has a poor image.

The exceptions to this rule are the central-office administrative positions at the superintendent and assistant superintendent levels. In recruiting candidates for such positions, both salary and fringe benefits are usually negotiable.

CAREER CHOICES AND RECRUITMENT

Although the focus of human resources administration is on organizational practices, in recruitment it is important to understand those factors that influence the career choices of prospective candidates. First, people have different interests, abilities, and personalities that, nevertheless, will qualify each person for many different occupations. In fact, experience verifies that an individual will probably change his or her entire occupational field at least three times during his or her working lifetime. When recruiting people for a particular position, the recruiter should understand how ability, interest, and personality interface in various occupations. For example, the successful high school journalism teacher may be a good candidate for the position of public relations director. Both occupations require the ability to communicate ideas, an interest in writing, and a person capable of relating to others on a professional level. There are also links between guidance counseling and human resources administration, as well as between the principalship and central-office administration. The essence of this observation is that the recruitment of candidates for a particular position must not be limited only to individuals who already perform similar tasks.[5]

Second, occupational preferences, competencies, and the self-image of people will change with time and experience, making personal adjustment a continuous process. It is, therefore, unwise to assume that current employees are probably not interested in changing occupations within the organization. An internal search for potential applicants often reveals that many employees are interested in alternative positions.

Third, both life and work satisfaction depend upon how well an individual can utilize his or her abilities and find adequate outlets for his or her interests, personality traits, and values. A high turnover of people in a certain position should clue a human resources administrator to reevaluate the responsibilities of the position to ascertain the accuracy of the job description. This reevaluation should then provide a clearer profile of the type of individual who will be successful in the job. It is obviously important to link the interest, abilities, and personality traits of potential candidates to how such individual characteristics will be challenged in the position. For example, a particular middle school principalship located in an urban ghetto may require a self-motivated individual who feels comfortable with a constant demand to handle students who are chronic behavioral problems, while at the same time supervising a highly unionized teaching staff. Not every applicant will have the personal characteristics necessary to be successful in this situation.

Fourth, the process of occupational choice is influenced by employment variables such as salary, fringe benefits, location, opportunity for advancement, and the nature of the work to be performed. The importance of these variables will differ from one applicant to the next. In recruitment, it is important from the very start to present this information to every candidate in an extremely clear format. Sometimes, people are so intent on finding an alternative to their present employment that they initially tend to overlook these variables. However, when an employment offer is made, these factors become very apparent, which may result in a refusal by the candidate after a search that has cost the school district considerable time and money.

Finally, career choices are compromises between personal characteristics, such as interests and abilities, and external factors, such as the type of work to be performed. The effectiveness of this compromise is tested out through role playing, whether this is in fantasy, simulation, or in the actual work environment. The emergence of assessment centers gives testimony to this principle. Assessment centers set up career paths for already-hired employees. At such a center, the capabilities of an employee are matched with the requirements of various positions within the school district. A career path is then planned that will allow the employee to experience various levels of responsibility in different locations. As he or she demonstrates success at each level, the employee is advanced to a higher level along the path. Thus, an individual who has been hired as a maintenance supervisor may be promoted, after an assessment, to assistant director of maintenance, and then, eventually, promoted to director.

The implication is that job success is the only true measure of how effective the recruitment process has been. This implication is often overlooked, and many school districts never evaluate their recruitment procedures through a follow-up study on the success of those who were hired.

METHODS OF RECRUITMENT

It can be demonstrated from experience that certain recruiting methods produce the best candidates for particular job vacancies. Consequently, before initiating the recruitment process, each job vacancy should be analyzed to ascertain what method will be most effective. For example, an advertisement for a business manager's position appearing in the classified section of *School Business Affairs* will most likely reach individuals with the required qualifications. An advertisement in a local newspaper will probably produce few, if any, qualified candidates. In like manner, a recruiter who visits students at a four-year teacher education college in search of candidates for a high school principal's position requiring a minimum of a master's degree in educational administration is looking in the wrong place.[6]

Internal Search

Some school districts find it advantageous to train their own employees for all positions beyond the lowest level. As mentioned, promotion from within has definite advantages, particularly in creating high morale among employees. The second and most obvious benefit to promoting from within is that supervisors have greater knowledge about a person already on the payroll than about an unknown applicant. The selection process discussed in the following chapter helps to minimize the danger of making the wrong choice. However, firsthand information about an employee's performance is the best basis upon which that person can be promoted.

Many school districts have not traditionally promoted from within because of the minimal number of job categories available. Classroom teachers, principals, cooks, custodians, bus drivers, and a superintendent of schools continue to constitute the breadth of differentiation in staffing in rural and very small suburban school districts.

School districts located in metropolitan areas offer such a multitude of services that promotion from within is a possibility even for teaching positions. Teacher aides and substitute teachers can be promoted into full-time teaching positions when vacancies occur. Similarly, most large school districts have some classroom teachers who are qualified to become principals. The same situation occurs in support areas such as transportation, food service, and maintenance. Theoretically, a cook can be promoted into a commodities purchasing position and on to director of food services.

There are a few disadvantages to rigidly following a system of promoting from within. First, mediocre personnel in the school district may be promoted while excellent individuals in the community are not considered. Second, affirmative action requirements may dictate searching for personnel outside the organization. Finally, there is the possible danger of "inbreeding." New ideas and methods are not only a welcomed change; they are absolutely necessary when the personnel in a school district appear content with the status quo. The observations and performance evaluations of supervisors and principals are sources of information available to human resources administrators as they analyze a promotion-from-within policy.

It is a standard operating procedure in many school districts to post job vacancies on bulletin boards, in newsletters, or in special publications issued from the human resources office. This allows current employees to apply for positions or to notify friends, relatives, and associates about vacancies. The assumption here is that current employees should not be overlooked, but that a policy limiting all promotions to those presently employed is not the most beneficial approach for a school district.

Large urban school districts are using an approach unique to school districts. Many of these districts are having difficulty recruiting teachers particularly in science and mathematics. They are offering to pay a portion of the costs for staff members to acquire a college degree in order to hire them to fill teacher vacancies. Teacher assistants have been targeted as a group of staff members who are more likely to take advantage of this kind of program.

Referrals

Current employees are perhaps the best source of referrals when a vacancy occurs. There are a number of reasons for this observation. The most significant reason is that employees will not usually recommend someone unless they believe that the referred person will do a good job, since their reputations as recommenders are at stake. A quality control on referrals from current employees is the job performance of the recommender and his or her satisfaction with the school district as a whole. A recommendation from an employee with inferior performance or from an employee who is constantly complaining about the policies and procedures of the district should be carefully reviewed.

The employee recommending a friend may also confuse friendship with potential job success. It is not uncommon for people to want friends in the workplace, both for social and economic reasons. An employee, for example, may want to share a ride to work with a friend who lives in the same neighborhood.

Referrals from teachers and principals, however, often reflect professional rather than social contact. Membership in professional organizations such as the National Association of Secondary School Principals or the National Education Association is one way in which people become acquainted with the competencies of colleagues. Consequently, such referrals may be more credible than referrals based only on social contact.

A school district should establish a policy and procedures that encourage employees to recommend people for job vacancies. A common practice is for the employee to provide the human resources department with the name or names of potential candidates. The human resources department can then send letters to the referred individuals, stating that they have been recommended to become candidates and inviting them to submit an application for the job. It should be noted that the invitation is extended to become a candidate; a human resources administrator must be very careful not to give the referred person the impression that the job is being offered.

Employment Agencies

Employment agencies fall into two categories: public or state agencies and private agencies. For all practical purposes, teachers and administrators have made limited use of employment agencies in their searching for professional positions. This is not the case for support personnel such as custodians, bus drivers, and cafeteria workers.

A public employment service was established in 1933 as a federal-state partnership. It was created not only to help individuals find suitable employment, but also to help employers find qualified workers. All fifty states have a state employment service agency, with branch offices strategically located throughout each state. The U.S. Training and Employment Service supervises these agencies. The agencies provide services to those receiving unemployment benefits; benefits are available only to people who are registered with the state employment agency. Although state employment agencies are happy to list individuals with extensive training and highly developed skills, most people with such qualifications go to private agencies. Nevertheless, it is foolish for a school district not to list all vacancies with the appropriate state employment service agency because of the possibility that the right employee may be registered. The financial outlay for such a listing is negligible, requiring nothing more than the cost of postage.

Private employment agencies, of course, charge a fee for their services. This fee may be charged to either the employer or employee, or shared by both. The fee arrangement is usually dictated by the supply-and-demand principle. When applicants are abundant, potential employees are usually required to absorb the fee. When applicants are scarce, the employers pay the fee.

Another major difference between public and private employment agencies is in the scope of services provided. Private agencies not only advertise and screen applicants for a job. but also provide a guarantee against unsatisfactory performance for a specified period of time, usually six to twelve months. If a particular employee does not work out, the agency will place the employee elsewhere and find the company another employee without a fee.

Some private employment agencies specialize in helping to fill executive positions, a practice commonly referred to as "head-hunting." Through nationwide contacts and through extensive investigation of each potential executive's credentials, these agencies are able to recommend candidates for executive management positions, usually in private business and industry. They charge a rather high fee for this service, usually a percentage of the executive's first-year salary.

Although most school districts do not engage the services of private employment agencies in searching for potential candidates to fill school executive positions, a growing trend in this direction can be seen, particularly in relation to the position of superintendent of schools. This trend is reflected in the consulting services offered by the American School Board Association and such state organizations as the Illinois Association of School Boards. These associations offer basically the same type of services as the private employment agencies in searching for school superintendents. The fee, however, is not as high as that charged by the private agencies, usually ranging between $5,000 and $25,000, depending upon the time and expenses incurred during the search. Furthermore, in recent years private consulting firms have begun to specialize in the recruitment of potential candidates for vacant superintendencies. Like other private agencies, they have nationwide contacts, advertise the position, and screen potential candidates.

This is certainly a healthy trend in education, but it carries with it a potential danger. Associations and private consulting agencies may develop a list of favored candidates who are continually recommended for positions; in turn, it could become difficult for even qualified individuals to "break into" the inner circle of favored candidates.

Colleges and Universities

Most colleges and universities offer placement services not only to recent graduates, but also to former graduates. The most important service available in these placement departments is the maintaining of a personal file containing references, transcripts, and other pertinent documents. Thus, each time an individual leaves a position, he or she may request his or her supervisor and other colleagues to send letters of reference to his or her placement service. This, in turn, will alleviate the burden of requesting former employers and colleagues to write reference letters each time an application is made for a different job. The placement service simply duplicates the references and sends them to prospective employers on the request of the graduate.

In terms of recruiting, listing vacancies with college and university placement services will not only reach recent graduates, but also individuals with extensive experience who still use the service as a receptacle for employment references. Because teachers and administrators seeking jobs in school districts seldom use private or public employment agencies, college and university placement services are the best sources for finding potential candidates for professional positions.

Most college and university placement services also sponsor job fairs at which human resources administrators can meet potential teachers. It is an opportunity for recruiters to highlight the positive aspects of their school districts in order to attract quality applicants. Some school districts that are having a difficult time recruiting teachers, may be given the authority by their respective boards of education to make a job offer to qualified candidates at these events.

Professional Organizations

Many professional organizations and labor unions provide limited placement services for their members. These organizations either publish a roster of job vacancies or notify individual members concerning potential jobs. They usually list job vacancies in the classified section of their publications. However, having a classified section advertising jobs in a professional publication is common only to those organizations representing a specialty in educational administration. Professional education administration organizations include the American Association of School Personnel Administrators (AASPA), Association for Supervision and Curriculum Development (ASCD), Association of School Business Officials (ASBO), Council of Educational Facility Planners International (CEFPI), National Association of Elementary School Principals (NAESP), National Association of Pupil Personnel Administrators (NAPPA), National Association of Secondary School Principals (NASSP), National School Boards Association (NSBA), and National School Public Relations Association (NSPRA).

The American Association of School Administrators (AASA) is an exception. It publishes a listing of vacancies nationwide covering the following categories: the superintendency, the assistant superintendency, central-office positions, administrative positions in higher education, and professorships of educational administration.

Other Sources for Recruitment

There are two other avenues for obtaining potential job applicants: unsolicited or walk-in applicants and minority media resources. Although affirmative action requirements usually dictate advertising most positions, the walk-in applicant can be a good candidate. Most unsolicited applicants contact the school district either by mail, by telephone, by email, or in person. It is important to inform such individuals of the potential for employment with the district and to present them with an application to be completed. If a vacancy occurs that fits an applicant's qualifications, that individual should then be contacted and invited to activate his or her application by written notification.

Every metropolitan area has minority populations that are serviced by media resources that can be used in recruiting minorities. For example, in the southwestern United States, there are many local radio stations that are directed to the Mexican American population. Advertising vacancies on these radio stations can be a valuable method of recruiting.

ADVERTISING POSITION VACANCIES

When a school district wishes to communicate that it has a vacancy, it usually develops a formal advertisement. This advertisement can be used to implement the various methods of recruitment.

The Content and Style of an Advertisement

The content of an advertisement is determined by the job description and criteria that will be used in selecting the most qualified candidate for the position. The procedures used in determining and writing job descriptions, along with the method of developing selection criteria will be addressed in Chapter 4.

To be effective, an advertisement must accurately reflect the major responsibilities of the position and the minimum qualifications to become a candidate. This is no easy task, because the advertisement must also be brief if it is to appear in a newspaper, newsletter, or professional publication.

School districts usually identify their districts and list factual rather than personal requirements; these are desirable practices. Candidates should know the name and location of the educational organization, since this may determine the level of interest they have in the position and, in turn, may limit the number of applicants to those who are seriously interested in the job. Personal requirements for a job are better evaluated through the selection process. Individuals are seldom good judges of their personal qualifications, and many could be falsely encouraged or discouraged from applying for a position if personal qualifications are listed in the advertisement. The practice of giving information about the organization and listing the job title first effectively attracts the attention of those individuals who are most qualified for the position.

Recruitment Brochures

Appendix A at the end of this chapter contains samples of a special type of advertisement—the recruitment brochure. These brochures are usually mailed to individuals who have indicated an interest in an advertised position. The brochure provides potential candidates with extensive information, enabling them to better ascertain if they wish to apply for the job and if they possess the minimum requirements. The recruitment brochure is obviously more extensive in content and scope than the normal advertisement.

The format for such brochures will vary, but certain information is usually provided. The most important information to communicate includes the announcement of the vacancy, the procedure for applying, a description of the qualifications that the successful candidate must possess, information about the community served by the school or school district, and data about the school and/or school district, which normally includes financial, personnel, and curriculum information.

Brochures are certainly a valuable recruitment tool and should be used as much as possible for all vacancies in a school district. A general information brochure containing data about the community and school district could be used when recruiting for teachers and support personnel. The tailored, special-position brochure could be reserved for executive educational positions. This approach would help to hold down the cost of printing a special brochure for the more commonly occurring vacancies in a school district.

TECHNOLOGY AND RECRUITMENT

Both job seekers and human resources departments in school districts have discovered the benefits of Internet recruiting. It has transformed the recruiting process. It is very possible that in the not too distant future, newspaper job advertisements, positing job positions in profession journals, the use of recruitment brochures, and all other print media will be replaced by the Internet.

School districts are designing home Web sites that provide potential employees access to information about school districts, such as salary and fringe benefits information, student-teacher ratios, financial solvency, employee turnover, student discipline, a mission statement, and so on. Some school districts have also learned the advantage of designing a Web site that includes an online response form, which allows potential candidates to complete a résumé page and submit it. With other school districts, a potential employee can access information about the application process and even send a resume via email directly to a school district.

Of course, there are school districts experiencing financial and other difficulties that will prevent them from recruiting through the Internet. For example, a district with substandard salaries and fringe benefits probably will not provide such information which, in turn, will discourage seasoned job seekers from considering school districts that neglect to include such information.

When a school district has an unexpected vacancy, recruiting on the Internet could provide a pool of applicants in the shortest period of time. In addition, there are companies and organizations that provide their members with a job-posting site on the Internet. This allows a job seeker to post a copy of his or her résumé on the Web site and allows school district recruiters to search the résumé bank on a daily or weekly basis in order to find suitable candidates for job vacancies. This is a compelling reason to use this recruitment tool. The greatest advantage, however, to recruiting through the Internet is the ability to reach as many potential applicants as possible in the most cost-effective manner. If this method gains acceptance among job seekers, it could reduce postage costs and may even eventuate in a reduction in the number of staff members needed to manage the recruitment process in school districts.

There is another trend that has taken hold, which is used by the most aggressive job seekers. It is commonly referred to as *websumes*. Teachers and administrators develop their own Web sites that could include not only a résumé, but also supporting documents, and in some cases, even a video. This allows a job seeker to introduce himself or herself in a very positive way, which could attract the attention of school district administrators and even members of the board of education.

There is also a relatively new approach that is being used by companies and is commonly referred to as social network recruiting, which could be utilized by school districts. It is a modification of the long-standing networking approach that has always existed in some form or fashion. People make social contacts with other people in order to form a network that will be supportive when they are searching for a different place to work. Now there are companies that provide networking services. An interested person registers with a networking company, supplying his or her name, location, and employment status. Networking companies provide privacy and usually pledge not to sell personal information to a third party.

Thus, an individual adds his or her name to an enormous list that can be accessed to find contacts by zip code, job, and even place of employment. The objective is to find other people who live and work in places and organizations that interest you. Some companies allow human resources administrators to place job postings on the network, and even to transmit applications and other job-related information through email. The people who are networked can also direct employment information to each other. The effectiveness of this type of recruiting and job searching is not conclusive. However, no one disputes the large number of people who are members of Internet-based social networks that function for other purposes, such as finding a compatible significant other. It is a trend that all human resources administrators should be cautiously investigating.

Thus, the potential of technology in human resources recruitment could help school districts find and hire the most qualified and creative candidates in the shortest amount of time and in the most cost effective manner.

IMPLICATIONS FOR SMALL AND MEDIUM-SIZED SCHOOL DISTRICTS

Recruitment has become a more necessary function due to the shortage of teachers in certain areas such as special education, mathematics, and the sciences. In addition, speech pathologists, physical therapists, school psychologists, and counselors are in short supply in certain locations.

Furthermore, federal laws and policies require superintendents and other administrators to search for and to hire the most qualified candidates regardless of the position vacancy.

In many school districts, there is no designated human resources administrator. Rather, a central office administrator is responsible for multiple functions including the human resources function. Of course, in a small school district, the superintendent of schools performs the human resources function. However, regardless of the individual size of the school district or the staffing of the human resources function, the following elements of the recruitment function are necessary:

- Each school district should have a Web site that sets forth in the most positive manner the benefits of becoming an administrator, teacher, or staff member in the district.
- The application process should be as easy as possible for potential candidates. Applying online is quickly becoming an expectation for job seekers.
- In this context it is understood that many administrators may not have the expertise to develop a district Web site, but hiring a firm to design the Web site is worth the advantages of such an approach to recruitment.
- The traditional methods of recruitment set forth in this chapter do require time and commitment on the part of the administration of the school district. However, overburdened superintendents and other administrators can be assisted in carrying out this function by teachers and other staff members who can be compensated for the extra workload. All school employees have a vested interest in recruiting excellent colleagues because the students and all employees are affected by the quality of those who are hired.

THE IMPACT OF GENERATION Y ON RECRUITMENT

Generation Y teachers and administrators want to be convinced rather than informed about the benefits of becoming an employee in a given school district. Thus. principals, superintendents, and other administrators must use various techniques employed by marketing firms to convince Generation Y teachers and administrators that it is a good opportunity to accept employment in their school district. As a consequence of this characteristic, the school district needs to conceptualize recruitment as marketing rather than advertising.

Research indicates that Generation Y teachers and administrators want their work experience to be enjoyable, but also accept that it will be demanding and challenging. Furthermore, Generation Y teachers and administrators look upon their work experience as a career or vocation and definitely do not consider it as just a job. This perspective is important because they see themselves as doing something that is worthwhile, that has value to themselves, other, and society in general.[7]

Other research points out that Generation Y teachers and administrators are also searching for security and stability in the work experience.[8] Thus, they are looking for a school district that is financially solvent and, if not growing in population, then at least stable.

It is interesting to note that approximately 25 percent of Generation Y consults their parents or others before accepting a position. Another implication for recruiting Generation Y teachers and administrators is the extensive use they make of school districts' Web sites in order to gather information about the district, which will influence their decision to search for a position in the district that meets their needs and desires. In general, approximately 75 percent of Generation Y will study the Web site of the company or school district that they are interested in.[9]

Quick Review of Essentials

After the human resources planning process identifies current and future staffing needs, the next step is to recruit qualified personnel. However, certain constraints on recruitment must be taken into consideration. Affirmative action requirements, public image and policies of a school district, responsibilities of positions in education, and salary and fringe benefits offered in certain school districts have an influence on how a district will implement the recruitment process.

To carry out a recruitment program effectively, human resources administrators must have a good understanding of vocational development theory. The following principles are common to many theories and can be used to formulate recruitment strategies. First, people have different interests, abilities, and personalities, which will qualify them for a number of occupations. Second, the occupational preferences, competencies, and the self-image of people will change with time and experience, making personal adjustment a continuous process. Third, both life and work satisfaction depend upon how well individuals can utilize their abilities and find outlets for their interests, personality traits, and values. Fourth, the process of occupational choice is influenced by employment variables such as salary, fringe benefits, location, opportunity for advancement, and the nature of the work to be performed. Finally, vocational development is essentially a compromise between personal characteristics such as interests and abilities, and external factors such as the type of work to be performed.

Experience shows that certain recruiting methods produce the best applicants for particular job vacancies. Therefore, before initiating the recruitment process, administrators should analyze each job vacancy to ascertain what method will be most effective. The most common methods include internal search, referrals, contacting employment agencies, advertising vacancies with college and university placement services or job fairs, advertising on the Internet, advertising in newspapers and in the publications of professional organizations, following up on unsolicited applications, and contacting community organizations that promote the interests of minority groups.

When a school district wishes to communicate that it has a vacancy, it usually produces a formal advertisement. The content of an advertisement is dictated by the job description and criteria to be used in selecting the most qualified candidate for the position. An effective advertisement must accurately reflect the major responsibilities of the position and the minimum qualifications an individual must possess to become a candidate for the job.

In terms of content and style, the most effective advertisement will include the title of the position, information about the school district, information on how to apply, and desired qualifications for candidates. Listing subjective qualifications and using "blind ads" are generally not appropriate. It is also more effective for a school district to place only a few vacancies in a given advertisement and, when possible, to advertise each position by itself.

A special type of advertisement is the recruitment brochure. Its purpose is to provide potential candidates with enough information to allow them to determine if they wish to apply for the job and if they possess the necessary requirements. The brochure should include the announcement of the vacancy, the procedure for applying, a description of the qualifications that the successful candidate must possess, information about the community served by the school or school district, and financial, personnel, and curricular data about the school and/or school district.

General information brochures containing data about the community and school district could be used when recruiting teachers and support personnel. The more extensive brochure is commonly reserved for recruiting school executives. The cost of printing such brochures for each vacancy would be prohibitive.

Selected Further Readings

Equal Employment Opportunity commission (EEOC). www.eeoc.gov (as of 2009).

Hoerr, Thomas R., "Finding the Right Teachers, *Educational Leadership* (May 2006), 94.

Lahey, Joanna N., "Age, Women, and Hiring: An Experimental Study," *The Journal of Human Resources*, XLIII, no. 1 (2008), 30–56.

National Center for Educational Statistics, "Digest of Educational Statistics," 2001. http://nces.ed.gov/pubs2002/digest2001/

Newton, Mary Rose, "Does Recruitment Message Content Normalize the Superintendency as Male? *Educational Administration Quarterly*, 42, no. 4 (October 2006), 551–577.

Ordanini, Andreas and Silvestri Giacomo, "Recruitment and Selection Services: Efficiency and Competitive Reasons in the Outsourcing of HR Practices," *The International Journal of Human Resource Management,* 19, no. 2 (February 2008), 372–391.

Reeves, Douglas, "New Ways to Hire Educators," *Educational Leadership* (May 2007), 83–84.

Taylor, Scott, "Acquaintance, Meritocracy, and Critical Realism: Researching Recruitment and Selection Processes in Smaller and Growth Organizations," *Human Resource Management Review*, 16 (2006), 478–489.

Winter, Paul A. and Samuel H. Melloy, "Teacher Recruitment in a School Reform State: Factors That Influence Applicant Attraction to Teaching Vacancies," *Educational Administration Quarterly*, 41, no. 2 (April 2005), 349–372.

APPENDIX A

Principal of Thomas Jefferson High School

The Community

Goodville is primarily a suburban residential community with easy access to the metropolitan area, as well as to all major shopping centers. Parochial schools, both elementary and secondary, are located within the school district's boundaries. There are many active parent organizations working on behalf of the students, all of which foster a close relationship between the schools and the parents in the community. The Chamber of Commerce functions as a viable catalyst for the business community. The Goodville School District has one of the highest tax bases in the county.

The Principal

The Goodville School District is seeking qualified applicants for the position of principal for Thomas Jefferson High School. The following qualifications and leadership abilities will be taken into consideration in the selection process:

- Good interpersonal relations skills
- Skill in all types of communications
- Ability to generate support and enthusiasm among students, faculty, and the community for the total educational program, including extracurricular activities
- Proven ability to formulate and implement both short- and long-range objectives
- Experience in the evaluation process of both staff and programs
- Certification as a secondary school administrator
- Classroom teaching experience for five years
- Educational administrative experience for three years

The School District

The Goodville School District was organized in 1875. Education in Goodville encompasses the entire community. Starting with the preschooler, ages 3–5, there are tuition-sponsored programs in early childhood education. Evening courses are offered to adults in a continuing education program.

The total district enrollment is about 5,500 students. There are four elementary schools, one middle school, and one high school. The district employs approximately 300 professional educators and 100 support employees.

The Board of Education is composed of six members, each elected for a three-year term. The district's budget is $40 million and the average per pupil expenditure is approximately $7,000.

The High School

Thomas Jefferson High School has an enrollment of 2,000 students and a staff of 98 full- and part-time certificated professionals. The school is fully accredited by the North Central Association of Colleges and Secondary Schools.

Approximately 68 percent of the graduating class goes on to college. This requires a comprehensive offering of courses, which currently numbers approximately 150.

The High School campus is located on a twenty-four acre site. Built in several stages, the school was completed in 1972, when a major addition provided much-needed classrooms and expanded physical education and drama facilities.

The Staff

"Experienced and highly qualified" best describes the high school faculty.Approximately 65 percent have more than 15 years teaching experience; 60 percent have taught 15 years or more in the high school; 75 percent of the faculty members have a master's degree or higher.

Salaries are paid according to placement on an adopted schedule that recognizes experience and education. Fringe benefits include a unique plan for staff sick leave, personal leave, major medical insurance, dental insurance, term life insurance, and excellent retirement benefits. Administrators with a twelve-month contract receive one month's vacation.

Contact the Human Resources Department of the Goodville School District for an application package.

■ ■ ■

CHAPTER

4

Selection

FOCUS SCENARIO

Parents and the school district's professional teacher association have complained to the superintendent of schools and the board of education that the human resources department has failed to hire the best and the brightest for teaching positions in the district. You are the newly hired assistant superintendent for human resources. The community that is served by the school district is very affluent and most of the parents are well-educated with at least a bachelor's degree, but many of the parents have graduate or professional degrees.

Additional problems are present in the selection process. It has been the practice in the school district for the assistant superintendent of human resources to be the primary person making the decision on who should be hired. He often carried out this function without input from other administrators or teachers in the district. Job descriptions seem to be outdated, and there have been no selection criteria except the professional opinion of the assistant superintendent.

Some administrative positions have been filled without the public advertising of the positions. The assistant superintendent selected candidates. The application process is also flawed, and the application forms are outdated and appear to have no effect upon the selection of employees.

Finally, two people had been hired for positions without adequate background checks that resulted in their termination because they had lied on their applications. The teacher hired had been terminated from another school district for drinking alcohol at school and a bus driver had been convicted of child abuse. Thus, the board of education and the superintendent of schools hired you for the position because of your experience in human resources administration, and they expect you to develop defensible and effective human relations selection procedures.

The objective of the selection process is to hire individuals who will have the potential to be successful on the job in relation to the formal performance evaluation process of the school district. Self-evident as this purpose may appear, its implementation requires a rather thorough process. The cost of selecting employees is a major expenditure for most school districts. If the process does not produce effective employees, the cost to the district is often incalculable because of inadequate performance, the expense connected with the termination process, and the expense involved in hiring new employees.

The minimum cost in hiring any new employee has been calculated at $1,000; it can cost more than $25,000 to hire a superintendent of schools. In selecting an individual for most positions in a school district, the costs include advertising the position; printing and mailing applications; and personnel time required to review applications, interview candidates, and check references. This presupposes that many routine tasks, such as writing job descriptions and establishing proper selection criteria, have already been accomplished. Training and orienting new employees are additional costs directly related to the hiring process but often overlooked. Therefore, selecting individuals with the potential to meet the performance evaluation criteria and who will remain with the school district for a reasonable period of time is an extremely important human resources process. It is not only significant in fulfilling the district's mandate to educate children, but also affecting the financial condition of the school district.

Human resources planning is necessary for school districts, and all other organizations, in order to achieve their goals and objectives by having the right number of people, with the right skills, in the right place, and at the right time. Adequate human, financial, and physical resources constitute the three requisites for organizational success. However, organizational success is synonymous with organizational change. School districts must meet the ever-changing educational needs and expectations of parents and students in order to be successful.

It is important for human resources administrators to understand the current research on organizational change that has proven to be helpful not only to schools and school districts, but also to many business enterprises. School districts have much in common with other organizations, and many of the principles concerning change are applicable across all organizations. For example, two fundamental principles apply to school districts and all other organizations: stakeholders and vision.

First, all internal stakeholders constitute the organization. Thus, the board of education, superintendent, central-office administrators, principals, and all other employees are, in the aggregate, the school district. Buildings and financial and other material resources are not the school district. Rather, the board, administrators, teachers, and staff members use these resources to fulfill their responsibilities and the mission of education.

Second, all organizations are driven by a vision. The board of education, superintendent, other administrators, teachers, and staff members usually operationalize the vision through the establishment of goals and objectives. The vision of a school district will certainly revolve around the intellectual, emotional, physical, and ethical development of students. Of course, all stakeholders should be engaged in the establishment of a school district's vision, which means that parents, students, and other members of the community, along with the board and staff, must be engaged in public discourse.

The implications for human resources administration are obvious. The planning process requires the school district to be focused on a vision that addresses the signs of the times along with operational goals and objectives. The steps in the selection process that follow must support these directives. This is particularly important in relation to the selection criteria, which must incorporate indicators that reflect the vision, goals, and objectives of the school district. Such an approach will ensure the hiring of administrators, teachers, and staff members who are capable and willing to implement the directives.

A selection decision may result in four possible outcomes: two are correct decisions and two are errors. The correct decisions occur when the individual hired proves to be successful on the job or when a rejected applicant would have performed inadequately if hired. In both instances, the selection process has met the objective of hiring the most appropriate candidate. The process has failed when a rejected candidate could have performed successfully on the job or when the individual hired performs inadequately. Thus, embedded in the selection process must be predictors of success, which are usually identified through the performance evaluation.

However, the steps presented below have the reliability and validity of experience that makes them invaluable in making reasoned employment decisions. With this in mind, it behooves human resources administrators, and in small and medium-sized school districts, the superintendent of schools, to analyze the effects of the performance evaluation process in light of the selection process.[1]

The selection process, therefore, should be implemented through a series of activities that will minimize the chances of hiring individuals who are inadequate performers.

STEPS IN THE SELECTION PROCESS

Write the Job Description

A written job description is the end product of a process that is commonly referred to as "job analysis." This process gathers information about the position: what an employee does; why he or she performs certain tasks; how he or she does the job; what skills, education, or training are required to perform the job; the relationship the job has to other jobs; what physical demands and environmental conditions affect the job. A number of recognized techniques can be used in job analysis. These include:

1. *Observation.* For example, a human resources administrator or building principal would directly observe a teacher, secretary, or other employee as he or she is performing his or her job.
2. *Individual interviews.* In like manner, a human resources administrator or director of maintenance would engage a custodian in an interview and analyze results (perhaps from a number of such interviews) in order to create a job description.
3. *Group interviews.* When a school district uses a search committee approach, the committee might interview a building principal before developing the job description for the principalship.
4. *Job questionnaire.* Some school districts have developed job questionnaires which substitute for the interview technique in developing job descriptions.
5. *Consulting.* In a very large school district, it might be more efficient to hire a human resources consulting firm to develop categorical job descriptions for teachers, administrators, and staff member positions.
6. *Supervisor analysis.* Of course, it is always helpful to consult with the supervisors of employees before writing job descriptions such as the assistant superintendent for secondary education, a building principal, the director of transportation, or the superintendent of schools.
7. *Diary method.* For a central office position, it is probably more effective for an assistant superintendent to keep a diary of his or her daily activities for a given period of time.[2]

The seven methods described above are not meant to be used in isolation from each other. They are complementary techniques that will result in a superior job analysis if used in combination with each other. Of course, all the techniques listed are appropriate for conducting a job analysis that will lead to the development of job descriptions. However, certain techniques are more appropriate to particular classifications of jobs. The first three methods would probably be more effective in analyzing the jobs of classified employees. Techniques four, five, and seven would be beneficial in analyzing the tasks common to professional positions. Number six would always be helpful in analyzing professional jobs.

The job analysis is, as previously mentioned, the vehicle for obtaining the necessary data to write a job description. The job description is an outline providing specific details concerning a job and the minimum qualifications necessary to perform it successfully. No one format for writing a job description can be universally acclaimed as most effective in each and every circumstance. However, certain elements should be common to most job descriptions. These include the title of the job, duties that must be performed, the authority and responsibilities accompanying the job, and specific qualifications necessary to successful performance of the job.

Exhibit 4.1 provides two sample job descriptions that are models of a particular style appropriate for school district positions. Note that the titles for these two positions are very specific. The first is a job description for a middle school principal; and the second, for a high school biology teacher.

EXHIBIT 4.1

Job Descriptions

Job Description for a Middle School Principal

Job Summary

The middle school principal is responsible for the maintenance and continuation of a sound instructional program within his or her school building. This includes using leadership and communication skills in dealing with teachers, counselors, and other professional staff members, and with classified personnel, in order to develop a climate that promotes quality educational practices.

Organizational Relationships

The middle school principal has a line relationship with the assistant superintendent for secondary education. He or she is directly responsible to the assistant superintendent for secondary education. The middle school principal also has a line relationship with the building staff, which includes the assistant principal, teachers, counselors, librarian, and all other certificated and classified personnel within the building complex.

Organizational Tasks

The middle school principal is responsible for establishing administrative processes and procedures in the middle school for the following areas: staff development, curriculum planning, scheduling and grading, budget development, building and grounds maintenance, classroom instruction, consulting with individual pupils, parents, and staff members. He or she is also responsible for other duties assigned by the assistant superintendent for secondary education and is directly responsible for supervising and evaluating the assistant principal, teachers, counselors, librarian, educational specialists, secretaries, and custodians within the building complex.

Job Qualifications

The middle school principal should possess the following educational and professional qualifications:

- A master's degree in educational administration
- A state middle school principal's certificate
- Minimum of five years experience as a classroom teacher
- Minimum of two years experience as an assistant principal

Job Description for a High School Biology Teacher

Teaching Responsibilities

The high school biology teacher is responsible for teaching five periods of Biology I per school day with one non-instructional period for planning, grading papers, and individual conferences with parents and students. Teaching biology includes following the general curricular program established by the science department and approved by the building principal. He or she is responsible directly to the building principal.

Professional Responsibilities

The high school biology teacher is responsible for promoting an effective instructional program in the classroom. He or she accepts responsibility for the academic success of students by evaluating the strengths and weaknesses of the curricular program and instructional materials; helping develop, implement, and evaluate new ideas, methods, and techniques for teaching biology; assisting in departmental budget preparation to ensure the appropriateness of instructional supplies; recognizing that each student is an individual with different needs and abilities; utilizing a variety of instructional techniques; serving on textbook committees; maintaining effective discipline and high academic standards; accepting constructive criticism; and recognizing the need for continuous self-evaluation. In addition, the teacher is expected to keep up-to-date on biology research findings by participating in local and state science associations.

Required Qualifications

The high school biology teacher should possess the following minimum educational and professional qualifications:

- A bachelor's degree with a major or minor in biological science
- A State Secondary School Teaching Certificate in high school biology

Each description begins with a summary of the job, outlining the overall responsibilities of the position. This is followed by a detailed explanation of specific job tasks and the relationship of the job to other positions in the organizational structure of the school district. At a time when legal rights and responsibilities are being emphasized by parents and employees, organizational relationships are extremely important and must be clearly explained to prospective employees. Finally, minimum job qualifications are listed as an integral part of the job description.

Job descriptions should be updated from time to time because working conditions change with advances in technology and education. But it is absolutely critical to perform a job analysis and to revise the job description for a position each time it becomes vacant. This will affect the establishment of the selection criteria and will ensure that the individual being hired properly understands the responsibilities and duties of the job.

There is another important reason to diligently develop an accurate and complete job description. If a person is hired for a position and ultimately does not fulfill the job requirements in a satisfactory manner that ultimately results in his or her termination, the job description is the normative criteria for the responsibilities that were not fulfilled in an acceptable manner.

Establish the Selection Criteria

The second step in the selection procedure is to establish the criteria against which the candidates will be evaluated to determine who will be offered the job. Selection criteria are very different from the job description, in that the selection criteria delineate those ideal characteristics that, if possessed by an individual to the fullest extent possible, would ensure the successful performance of the job. Obviously, no one person will possess all the characteristics to their fullest extent, and not all characteristics have equal importance in determining who the best candidate is.

The use of selection criteria also can become a method for quantifying the expert opinions of those who will interview candidates. Without criteria, each interviewer is left to his or her own discretion in determining if an individual will be able to perform the job.

Quantifying the opinions of interviewers also provides data to show that the best candidate was offered the position, thus demonstrating that the school district is an affirmative action and equal opportunity employer. The candidate with the highest score should be offered the position first; if he or she does not accept, then the candidate receiving the next highest score should be offered the position, and so on.

It is a generally accepted practice for the human resources department to assume the responsibilities for organizing and conducting job analyses, for writing job descriptions, and for establishing the selection criteria used in filling a vacancy. The timing for writing the job description and for developing the selection criteria is extremely important. Both tasks should be performed before a job vacancy is advertised and before applications are received, not only because the advertisement should be based on the description, but also because it will demonstrate that the criteria were not prepared to favor a particular applicant.

Exhibit 4.2 presents a sample of three sets of selection criteria, one for a high school English teacher and a second for a sixth-grade elementary school teacher; the third presents

EXHIBIT 4.2

Selection Criteria For An Elementary Grade Teaching Position

On a scale of 1 to 5 with 5 being the highest, rate the degree to which each candidate meets the following criteria.

Academic Criteria:

- Has appropriate college or university degrees
- Has earned a grade point average in all degree programs that meets the standards of the school district
- Has demonstrated during an interview that he or she possesses a working knowledge of the content and skills required of the position
- Has demonstrated during an interview that he or she possesses the knowledge and skills that are compatible with the school district's curriculum

Personal Criteria:

- Indicates in an interview that he or she has communication skills that are required to interact with colleagues, parents, and students
- Demonstrates in an interview that he or she possesses attitudes that will promote positive relationships with colleagues, parents, and students
- Dresses in a manner that meets the standards of the school district

Experiential Criteria:

- Has successful and relevant past teaching or student teaching experience
- If the candidate has prior teaching experience, he or she demonstrated an interest in ongoing professional improvement
- Demonstrated in prior teaching or student teaching experience a positive attitude towards professional performance evaluations

general criteria for an elementary school teacher in a self-contained classroom. Each criteria instrument has been constructed in such a way that particular characteristics may be rated and a final score obtained. The significant difference between the first two instruments and the third is the weighting that is designated on the general criteria instrument. The compatibility of an applicant's educational philosophy with the school district's policies and curriculum is of primary importance, as indicated on this third instrument. Professional preparation is second, personal characteristics third, and experiences the least important. The assumption underlying this third selection instrument is that an individual will best meet the needs of the school district if he or she has the proper attitude and philosophy. Experience will enrich an individual's performance, but philosophy is necessary to direct the benefits obtained by the experience. In like manner, an individual will grow in the job if his or her educational values are in harmony with those of the school district.

Note too that this third instrument is less specific in describing desirable characteristics and leaves the interviewer with more discretion in making a judgment about the candidate's qualifications. For example, an individual with a Ph.D. in early childhood education may not be the most desirable candidate for a first-grade self-contained classroom position. That applicant may be more effective in a laboratory school attached to a university in which aspiring teachers observe instructional techniques. In this latter situation, the candidate with a Ph.D. would likely receive the maximum number of points in the "professional preparation" category.

The first two criteria instruments, for a high school English teacher and sixth-grade teacher, are rather detailed and more traditional in style and content. Each is divided into categories, delineating academic, personal, and experiential qualifications.

This method of evaluating candidates places a responsibility on each interviewer to make a discriminatory judgment concerning the qualifications of each individual. The interview itself will not be the only source of information used to fill out the selection criteria instrument. The application, placement papers, transcripts, and letters of reference also will be used by the interviewers in determining an individual's qualifications for the job.

Each interviewer will sign and return to the human resources department a selection criteria instrument for each person interviewed. The human resources department is then responsible for compiling the results.

Write the Job Vacancy Announcement and Advertise the Position

Chapter 3 describes in detail the nuances of writing a job vacancy advertisement. The advertisement should be viewed as an integral part of the selection process. It is based upon the job description and should provide potential candidates with sufficient information to make a decision on whether to apply for the position. Consequently, an advertisement must clearly identify the job title, major responsibilities of the job, the name and location of the school district, how to apply for the job, and the minimum qualifications to become a candidate.

It is the responsibility of the human resources department to write the advertisement and to publish it according to the recruitment policy of the school district. In providing information about how to apply for a position, the advertisement should include a deadline for receiving applications. It is a common practice to allow a two-week period for receiving applications for classified and teaching jobs. A month is the usual time period allotted to receiving applications for school executive positions. Of course, each individual situation will dictate the length of time allotted for the receiving of applications and may deviate from these usual time periods.

A common mistake made by some school administrators and inexperienced human resources administrators is not providing sufficient time to effectively implement the selection process. A hurried process may place the school district in an indefensible position in terms of affirmative action requirements and, in addition, may result in the hiring of the wrong person. In an average-sized school district, with a human resources department or at least one central-office human resources administrator, two months will be a comfortable time period to carry out the selection process. This period begins with the publication of an advertisement and extends through to the time when a job offer is made.

Receive Applications

A central-office staff member, usually a secretary, should be assigned to receive all the applications for a given job vacancy. As the applications are received, they should be dated and placed in a designated file folder. This will provide integrity to the process, and also will provide a method of monitoring the incoming applications for a particular vacancy.

Many applicants will request their college or university placement offices to send their transcripts and letters of reference to the school district. These documents must also be dated and attached to the appropriate applications.

After the deadline for receiving applications has been reached, a master list should be compiled with the names, addresses, and telephone numbers of those who have applied. The master list also should include by title the other documents that have been received in support of each application, such as transcripts and letters of reference. The entire folder of applications, support documents, and the master list can then be assigned and given to a human resources administrator, who will perform the initial screening of the applications.

Keeping applicants informed during the selection process will help to cut down on the number of inquiries that are normally received in the human resources department. One very effective method is to send a postcard to each applicant stating that his or her application has been received and listing a date by which individuals will be selected for interviews. It is also important to notify immediately those who sent in applications after the deadline that they will not be considered for the position. A common practice is to accept those applications postmarked on the day of the deadline.

Some school districts and many colleges and universities have initiated the practice of receiving applications until the position is filled. Under this procedure individuals who sent their applications to the school district by the deadline are given first consideration. If a suitable candidate is not identified, then those individuals who sent their applications to the district before a later designated date are considered, and so on until a suitable candidate is offered and accepts the position. This is an acceptable practice which can encourage qualified individuals to apply for positions even though they did not know about the positions in a timely manner.

At this point, a procedure can be initiated that will help in evaluating the effectiveness of the school district's affirmative action program. The master list of applicants should be given to the administrator responsible for monitoring the affirmative action program. He or she can then send a letter to all those who have made application, asking them to identify if they belong to one or more minority groups listed on an enclosed form, and requesting them to mail the form back to the school district. Because the purpose of the selection process is to hire the best candidate, it is important to state in this letter that filling out the form will have no bearing upon who is hired for the position. Consequently, the form should not be signed by the applicant and should not be sent to the human resources department, but rather to the affirmative action officer.

Select the Candidates to be Interviewed

Screening the applications is the fifth step in the selection process. It is initiated to identify those applicants who are to be interviewed for the position. The application form should contain a statement requesting the applicant to have his or her placement papers, transcripts, and letters of reference sent to the human resources department. These documents, along with the application form, will provide the human resources administrator with sufficient information to evaluate each person against the selection criteria and against the minimum education and certification requirements.

The number of applicants to be interviewed will depend upon the number of people who apply and on the nature of the position to be filled. If only five people apply for a vacancy and if each person meets the minimum qualifications, all five can be interviewed. This, of course, is not the norm except for those very few job classifications in which there is a shortage of qualified individuals, such as the field of special education. On the average, between three and five applicants are selected to be interviewed for classified and teaching positions. For school executive positions, the average number interviewed is between five and ten applicants.

Interview the Candidates

Interviewing candidates is a responsibility shared between the human resources department and other school district employees. The individuals who will participate in the interviewing process will be determined by the position to be filled. It is important to include not only those who will supervise the new employee, but also others who have expert knowledge about the duties to be performed by the successful candidate. For example, candidates for a high school biology teaching position should be interviewed by the high school principal, the chairperson of the biology department, a biology teacher, a human resources administrator, and the assistant superintendent for secondary education. In like manner, candidates for an elementary principal position should be interviewed by the superintendent of schools, the assistant superintendent for elementary education, an elementary school principal, and a human resources administrator.

This same process is also useful in hiring classified employees. Applicants for a custodial position can be interviewed by the head custodian in a building, the director of maintenance and custodial services, a custodian, and a human resources administrator.

Members of the interviewing committee will need assistance in learning the strategies of credentials evaluation and interviewing. A method that will hold down expenses and make maximum use of the skills learned through a staff development program is to select a group of teachers, department chairpersons, classified employees, and building principals who will participate in the selection process for a year's time. Each year a different group of employees can be selected and trained to participate in evaluating credentials and interviewing applicants.

How these individuals are selected to participate in the hiring process will depend upon the size of the school district. Seniority in the school district, of course, in one of the most defensible methods for selecting participants, but it is also imperative to have individuals who represent all job categories and teaching disciplines. Thus, a maintenance staff member, bus driver, cafeteria worker, elementary school art teacher, mathematics teacher, science teacher, social studies teacher, and so on, will be needed and should be available.

Released time from work is the most effective way to involve staff members. Substitute teachers and temporary classified employees will be needed to fill in for individuals who will be interviewing candidates and evaluating credentials during the working day. The average turnover of employees during a year's period of time is usually between 5 and 10 percent. This means that a given employee will participate in the selection process only on particular occasions, probably no more than ten working days a year.

Some school executives, such as assistant superintendents, will be more involved in the process because of their line authority to so many categories of employees. The assistant superintendent for elementary education, for example, will interview candidates for all elementary teaching and administrative vacancies. Of course, the immediate supervisor for the position to be filled is always a member of the committee.

DEFINITION OF AN INTERVIEW Most interviews are structured around a conversational motif between individuals who have a related objective. In this situation, the objective of the candidate is to obtain a job, and the objective of the school district official or officials is to hire the best candidate for the position. The essence of all interviews is communication, which is particularly important for teaching and other professional educator positions.[3] However, there are certain dimensions to every interview that distinguish it from an ordinary conversation. The job interview has a definite purpose and format; there is a beginning, middle, and conclusion.

TYPES OF INTERVIEWS There are two basic types of interviews: the standardized interview and the open-ended interview. The standardized interview is conducted by asking a set of questions established to help ensure that the responses of the candidates can be readily compared. It is most effective in the initial interviewing of all candidates. The open-ended interview encourages the candidate to talk freely and at length about topics introduced by the interviewer to suit the occasion. This type of interview is very helpful in the selection of administrators. The interviewer is attempting to learn as much as possible about the candidate's professional opinions and attitudes.

Some school districts have moved away from conducting in-person interviews because of cost and time commitment. In those districts, the candidate pool is interviewed by telephone; after which, there is a decision on which candidates are finalists for a given position. The finalists are then interviewed in person. The opinion of many interviewers is that telephone interviews are just as effective as in-person interviews.[4]

ROLE OF THE INTERVIEWER The interviewer has extremely important responsibilities. Not only does he or she direct the interview by asking questions, but also he or she must record the respondent's answers and present the respondent with a favorable image of the school district. Through the interview process, the interviewer must evaluate and come to a conclusion about the suitability of each candidate. A selection criteria instrument will be used to quantify the observations of the interviewer, but ultimately the observations are subjective interpretations.

Interviews are usually more effective if they are conducted in a pleasant environment. This will help put the candidate at ease and will facilitate the kind of verbal exchange that gives the interviewer the most information about each candidate. The interviewer should find a place to conduct the interview that will give the candidate the best information about where he or she will work. Thus, a classroom is an excellent place to interview a candidate for a teaching position.[5] In like manner, the bus garage is the best place to interview a bus driver candidate, and a school building is the best place to interview a housekeeping candidate. Of course, the interviewer must be very careful to present a demeanor that is accepting to such a degree that candidates feel free to answer questions without hesitation and with the understanding that there are no wrong answers.[6]

There is also a pitfall that some interviewers encounter when they unintentionally identify with the candidate. For example, this could occur when both the interviewer and candidate are certificated mathematics teachers, are from the same city, or have the same hobby.[7]

LEGAL IMPLICATIONS OF INTERVIEWING Federal legislation and court decisions have had a significant impact upon the types of questions that legally may be asked in an interview. For example, it was once common practice to ask a candidate if he or she had ever been arrested or spent time in jail. Because of a court case, *Gregory* v. *Litton Systems, Inc.*, school districts are now permitted to ask only about a candidate's record of criminal conviction. The following are common inquiries that have legal implications: age, race, ethnicity, religion, life styles, marital, and family status.[8]

THE ART OF QUESTIONING The success of the entire interviewing process rests on the interviewer's skill in asking questions. It is a skill that is acquired through experience. However, a well-planned interview with a pre-established set of questions can be extremely useful to even the most experienced interviewer, and it is a necessity in the standardized interview.

GROUP INTERVIEWING Some school districts prefer group interviewing, in which a number of staff members who are scheduled to interview a candidate jointly perform this task. Group interviewing can be very effective, and it certainly cuts down upon the amount of time spent on this process. The dynamics described in this chapter are also applicable to the group interviewing method. However, to be effective, one staff member must serve as the group leader and take responsibility for directing the interview.

Check References and Credentials

CREDENTIALS Checking references and credentials, the seventh step in the selection process, has profound implications. A candidate's "credentials" include such items as a college or university transcript, administrator or teacher certification document, and a physician's verification of health. Transcripts and health verifications should not be accepted if they are presented to the human resources department by the applicant; rather, they should be mailed directly to the school district by the respective college or university and physician. It is important to inform a candidate that his or her file is not complete until these documents are received.

It is common and accepted practice to request the health verification from a candidate only if he or she is chosen for the position. However, a contract or formal employment should not be initiated until the health verification has been received in the human resources department. It is best to state on the application form that a health examination will be required as a condition of employment if a job offer is made.

An administrator or teacher certification document is usually issued by a state department of education and given directly to the individual. Although the candidate presents the certification document to the human resources department, it is still necessary to contact the issuing state in order to ascertain if the certification remains valid. When a certification is revoked, the actual document is not always returned by the individual to the state department of education.

If a person is applying for a teaching or administrative position in a state where he or she is not currently certificated, he or she is responsible for obtaining written verification from the state department of education that he or she has the qualifications to receive certification. For such positions, a contract should never be offered to a candidate in the absence of a certification document or verification letter.

LETTERS OF REFERENCE Letters of reference are the most vulnerable part of this process. A human resources administrator must write, telephone, or contact in person those individuals who have sent in reference letters supporting an applicant. The application form should state that a minimum of three reference letters are required; they should be mailed directly to the human resources department; and they must include a reference letter from the applicant's current or last immediate supervisor.

Evaluating reference letters is a very difficult task. There are three basic types of references. The first is the glowing letter, affirming in detail that the candidate is an excellent employee with tremendous potential. The second is the letter indicating that the applicant's performance has been inferior and that he or she would be the wrong person for the job. The third is the reference letter telling very little about the applicant and couched in vague language. However, reference letters often have hidden messages, and understanding the significance of these references requires the talent of a human resources administrator who is skilled in detecting discrepancies between the candidate's credentials, his or her interview performance, and the reference letters. Consider, for example, the candidate who performs rather poorly in the interview and has unimpressive credentials, but who has an excellent letter of reference from his immediate supervisor. This could be an individual who is not performing satisfactorily in his or her present position and whose supervisor would be happy to see him or her find another job.

Obviously, it is the responsibility of a human resources administrator to verify the reference letters of the candidates who have been interviewed. It is impossible and unnecessary to check every reference for each candidate. However, it would be very difficult to choose the best candidate from those interviewed without reference verification.

There is another issue that significantly impacts the reference verification process in our litigious society: the fear of being sued for giving a truthful but negative reference. Of course, this is an important consideration for the hiring school district and for the districts where candidates were employed. Some states have passed legislation that protects employers from being sued for providing a negative reference if it was truthful and given in good faith. Also, if an employee gives his or her former employer written permission to provide a reference to potential employers, and even if such information is negative but held to be privileged and confidential, the employer has protection in potential litigation.[9]

CRIMINAL-BACKGROUND INVESTIGATION The risk of hiring a person who has a criminal record has created much concern for human resources administrators. School districts have been sensitized to this possibility because of the news media notoriety given to educators who have been convicted of child molestation. This is probably the ultimate nightmare of every school administrator.

Criminal-background investigations are time-consuming and expensive, in addition to being controversial. The National Education Association has taken a position in opposition to fingerprinting as a condition of employment. The often heard criticism is that fingerprinting is an insult to teachers and their profession. However, many school districts require the fingerprinting of potential employees as part of a background investigation conducted through law enforcement agencies.

Conducting criminal-background investigations and the extent of such investigations should not be dependent upon the discretion of the interviewing human resources administrator, and should be initiated regardless of state statutes. The extent of the investigation is usually limited in most school districts to checking with the local and state police in order to ascertain if the potential employee has been convicted of a crime. If he or she is a teacher, it is also possible to check with the Teacher Identification Clearinghouse (TIC), which is maintained by the National Association of State Directors of Teacher Education and Certification (NASDTEC). This nationwide clearinghouse has a database of all teachers who have been denied certification and whose certification has been revoked or suspended for moral reasons. The data are available only to states that have joined the Clearinghouse. Individual school districts can neither join the Clearinghouse nor directly obtain information from it. Only states may join.

Those states that are members agree to list, by name, any known alias, date of birth, and social security number of those persons from whom certification has been withdrawn or withheld in the last 15 years. The individual state certification officials are responsible for finding out why the action was taken.

A school district wishing to check the fingerprints of an applicant against the files of the FBI can do this only if the state in which the school district is located has passed legislation authorizing this type of investigation. This legislation must also have the approval of the U.S. Attorney General's Office. Even then, the request must be processed by a law enforcement agency such as the state police. Finally, all states have sex offender's registration laws, which are available to school district administrators. Thus, it is good human resources administration practice to conduct criminal-background investigations. In fact, if the wrong person is hired because a criminal-background investigation was not conducted, the liability of the school district for the wrongs committed by this person could be staggering.

As a final note to the issue of background checks in general and criminal background checks in particular, small to medium-sized school districts with limited personnel may find it advantageous and cost-effective to hire a third party company that conducts background checks. In some situations building principals, an assistant superintendent, or the superintendent may spend an enormous amount of time conducting an investigation that may take away from his or her regular duties. Because small and medium-sized school districts will probably not be hiring a large number of teachers and other staff members, the cost of outsourcing the background checking may be relatively insignificant.[10]

UNLAWFUL EMPLOYMENT OF ALIENS In 1986, the U.S. Congress passed the Immigration Reform and Control Act, which makes it unlawful to knowingly hire an unauthorized alien, to continue the employment of one who becomes an unauthorized alien, or to hire any individual without first verifying his or her employability and identity.

Select the Best Candidate

The human resources administrator responsible for implementing the selection process for a particular vacancy must organize all relevant data in such a manner that a choice may be made by the superintendent of schools. The data should include the rank ordering by scores against the selection criteria of those candidates who were interviewed, verified credentials and reference letters, and the application forms.

The superintendent then selects the candidate who appears best qualified. If this selection process is utilized, this will usually be the candidate who scored the highest against the selection criteria.

Implement the Job Offer and Acceptance

PROFESSIONAL POSITIONS The superintendent of schools may wish to interview the candidate he or she selects for a position or may wish to interview the top two, three, or five candidates before making a final choice. When the final decision has been made, the selected candidate must be offered the job in a formal manner. If this individual accepts the offer, a contract must be approved by the board of education and signed by the finalist. Usually, a board of education will require the superintendent to make a recommendation of employment and will want an explanation of why this particular person was selected.

CLASSIFIED POSITIONS The superintendent also may want to interview candidates for classified positions, but in most cases will accept the recommendation of the human resources department to hire the candidate with the highest score in relation to the selection criteria. The superintendent may make the job offer himself or delegate this to a human resources administrator. Once the candidate accepts the offer, employment may commence at a mutually acceptable time.

NOTIFYING THE UNSUCCESSFUL CANDIDATES The final step in the selection process is to notify all applicants that the position has been filled. This is initiated only after the offer of employment has been accepted by the selected candidate, since there may be a need to offer the position to another candidate if the first candidate refuses the offer. Good public relations also dictates that all applicants be notified when the job has been filled; they have expended some time and money in applying for the position.

PRINCIPLES OF CONSTRUCTING APPLICATION FORMS

The first task in applying for a position is filling out an application form, an often tedious task enjoyed by very few people. There are two major reasons why most people dislike these forms. First, some forms require information that seems irrelevant, and second, some forms allot too little space for filling in the required information.

Application forms are constructed in one of two basic formats. The first style emphasizes detailed and extensive factual information about the individual; little or no attention is given to the person's attitudes, opinions, and values. Conversely, the second style emphasizes the applicant's attitudes, opinions, and values and asks for less factual information.

All application forms must contain an affirmative action and equal employment opportunity statement in order to notify potential applicants and the school district community that the district is, and will continue to be. in compliance with federal and state laws governing employment. There is also a legal necessity to include a falsification statement that sets forth the fact that a person's employment with the school district can be terminated if he or she deliberately provides false or incorrect information on the application form.

Appendix C provides examples of both styles, which are composites of the forms used by a variety of school districts. The application for a teaching position and the one for a classified job are samples of the factual information style. A third application form, one for a high school principal's position, is a sample of the second, less factual, style.

These samples also demonstrate the types of style commonly used for particular positions. The style is dictated by the kind of information the district needs to elicit from the applicants. For teaching and classified positions, factual information about the applicants' personal characteristics, their work experience, their professional preparation, and supportive data such as references help the personnel department determine who should be interviewed. For school executive positions, the minimum requirements are highly specialized and thus can be requested on an application in a relatively limited space. Applicants to be interviewed are best selected by evaluating a set of responses that give some indication of each person's attitudes, opinions, and values.

Contents of the Application Form

The basic principle in constructing application forms is to only ask for information you need to know. Most information requested on applications falls under one of the following headings: personal data, education and professional preparation, experience, and references. Exhibit 4.3 lists information that is inappropriate on an application form either because it is irrelevant or because it is illegal under civil rights and labor legislation.

The physical layout of the application form should give an individual sufficient space to answer the questions and to provide the requested information. The kinds of information requested should also be grouped under headings to provide continuity. This helps the human resources department in analyzing the applications, and helps the individual providing the data.

EXHIBIT 4.3

Information Irrelevant or Inappropriate For Application Forms

- Maiden name
- Marital status
- Name of spouse
- Occupation of spouse
- Number and age of children
- If applicant owns a home or rents
- Religion
- National origin
- Race
- Arrest record—conviction is appropriate
- If the applicant has an automobile and a driver's license—unless this is a bona fide occupational qualification
- Height and weight—unless these are *bona fide* occupational qualifications

Employment Tests

Intelligence, aptitude, ability, and interest tests can provide valuable data when selecting classified employees. Legal rulings, however, have significantly limited their use because tests must be clearly job related to justify their administration. Aptitude and ability tests are easiest to justify and can be used successfully for most classified jobs. In fact, it would be inappropriate to hire a person to train as a school bus mechanic who did not possess mechanical aptitude. In like manner, an applicant for a secretarial position could be a test to measure the person's computer skills. It should be remembered that testing has definite limitations and the results must be interpreted in relation to the interview, references, and other employment documents.

TECHNOLOGY AND SELECTION

The following section on how small and medium-sized school districts can implement the steps in the selection process can be significantly enhanced though the use of technology. For example, the school district's Web site can contain a link to an online application process that can be transmitted electronically directly to the school district and even to the person who has been designated to receive the applications such as a building principal where a teaching vacancy exists. All communications with candidates can occur through email, and because the applications are in electronic form, they can be sent to members of the search committee. Checking references and credentials along with conducting a background review can, in part or whole, be electronically carried out. Further, credentials such as transcripts and teaching certifications can be scanned into a database and electronically stored for review by the search committee and ultimately, comprise a permanent file for the successful candidate. In fact, every aspect of the selection process including writing the job description, establishing the selection criteria, advertising the position, and those mentioned above can be electronically developed, stored, and utilized when necessary in the present or future.

Not only can cybertechnology enhance the selection process in small and medium-sized school districts, but also it is often necessary in very large school districts because the number of applicants for a position may number in the hundreds. Effective and efficient administration of all human resources functions requires technology.

IMPLICATIONS FOR SMALL AND MEDIUM-SIZED SCHOOL DISTRICTS

There is no doubt that all school districts should follow the steps in the selection process because they fulfill two major objectives. First, all state and federal equal opportunity and affirmative action laws require a defensible process that clearly demonstrates compliance with those laws. Secondly, the steps demonstrate that a school district has utilized a process for hiring the best candidates for teaching and other positions. With a small central office staff that may even be just the superintendent of schools, it will be necessary for teachers, principals, and other employees to be responsible for certain dimensions of the process.

Thus, writing the job and establishing the selection criteria may become the responsibility of faculty members. Advertising the position and receiving the applications may be the responsibility of the principal for the school where the vacancy exists. As an example for a teaching position, a search committee composed of teachers, the principal, and the superintendent may select the candidates to be interviewed, conduct the interview, and make a recommendation to the board of education. The superintendent should validate the person's credentials, contact the references, and conduct a background review. Of course, the superintendent should make the job offer, and the principal could notify the unsuccessful candidates. This approach also has the secondary effect of solidifying the professional relationship between administrators, teachers, and other staff members.

THE IMPACT OF GENERATION Y ON SELECTION

Generation Y is also different from other current generations in the degree to which they develop their career paths. At some point in their careers, other generations of teachers and administrators come to a decision in their professional experience concerning what they want to accomplish, usually in a linear fashion. For example, a teacher might decide to become an assistant principal and may leave his or her present teaching position to obtain that desired position in another school district. In order to prepare for this career, he or she might decide to obtain a master's degree in school administration. Generation Y teachers and administrators tend to be more focused on balancing the demands of their professional and personal life experiences. If and when that sense of balance diminishes, they then search for alternative positions that could provide the personal fulfillment that they have lost. It is an inward search rather than a strict career path that propels Generation Y.[11]

Thus the same inner passion also affects Generation Y administrators who might be searching for a superintendent's position. Of course, Generation Y teachers and administrators searing for personal fulfillment will certainly come to realize that, like their counterparts, they must also obtain the credentials of a master's degree and/or a doctorate in school leadership or administration in order to make themselves available to new opportunities. In this respect, Generation Y wants to achieve the next level of professional responsibilities much quicker than prior generations. It is fair to state that Generation Y wants to work in a school district that provides opportunities for both professional and personal growth.[12]

Quick Review of Essentials

The objective of the selection process is to hire individuals who have the potential to be successful on the job in relation to the performance evaluation process of the school district. Individual success is measured against organizational success, which is synonymous with "organizational change." Because of the evolutionary nature of human needs, school districts must continually involve stakeholders in crafting their vision. Further, the cost of the selection process is a major expenditure for most school districts, which includes advertising the position, printing and mailing applications, and human resources costs for interviewing candidates and checking references. The selection process should be implemented through a series of steps that will minimize the chances of hiring individuals who are inadequate performers. These steps are as follows:

1. *Writing the job description.* The job description is the end product of another process known as the "job analysis." This process gathers information about each job through

observations, interviews, questionnaires, consulting, and the diary method. The job description outlines specific details of a position and establishes the minimum qualifications needed to perform the job successfully.

2. *Establishing the selection criteria.* Criteria instruments delineate those ideal characteristics that, if possessed by an individual to the fullest extent possible, will ensure the successful performance of the job. The selection criteria instrument can be used also to quantify the expert opinion of those who will be interviewing candidates.
3. *Writing the job vacancy announcement and advertising the position.* The advertisement is based upon the job description and provides interested individuals with sufficient information to decide if they wish to apply for the position. The advertisement must clearly identify the job title, major responsibilities, name and location of the school district, application procedure, and the minimum job qualifications.
4. *Receiving applications.* A central-office staff member should be assigned to receive all applications for a given vacancy. As the applications are received, they should be dated and filed in a designated folder. This will provide integrity to the process and will establish a method of monitoring the progress toward filling the vacancy.
5. *Selecting the candidates to be interviewed.* The application form should contain a statement requesting the applicants to have their placement papers, transcripts, and letters of reference sent to the human resources department. The application should provide sufficient information to evaluate each person against the selection criteria and against the minimum requirements for the job. A selected group of applicants are then interviewed for the position.
6. *Interviewing the candidates.* Interviewing candidates is a responsibility shared by the human resources department and other school district employees. It is important to include not only those who will supervise the new employee, but also others who have expert knowledge about the duties which will be performed by the successful candidate. An interview is essentially a conversation between two or more individuals conducted to generate information about the candidate. Interviewing is a learned skill; it also has profound legal implications.
7. *Checking references and credentials.* "Credentials" refers to such items as a college or university transcript, teaching certification, and a physician's verification of health. These credentials along with letters of reference, whenever possible, should be sent directly to the human resources department by the issuing source.
8. *Selecting the best candidate.* The human resources administrator who is responsible for implementing the selection process for a particular vacancy must organize all relevant data in such a manner that a choice may be made by the superintendent of schools.
9. *Implementing the job offer and acceptance.* For professional positions, a contract must be approved by the board of education and signed by the finalist before this step is completed. For classified positions, once the candidate affirms that he or she will accept the offer, employment may commence at a mutually acceptable time.
10. *Notifying the unsuccessful candidates.* This step is initiated only after the offer of employment has been accepted by the candidate because there may be a need to offer the position to another individual if the first selected candidate refuses the offer.

The risk of hiring a person who has a criminal record has created much concern for human resources administrators over the past five years. Conducting criminal-background investigations and the extent of such investigations are usually dependent upon a mix of school district policy, state statutes, and the discretion of the interviewing human resources administrator. The extent of an investigation is usually limited in most school districts to checking with the local and state police in order to ascertain if the potential employee has been convicted of a crime. When the potential employee is a teacher, it is also possible to check with the Teacher Identification Clearinghouse, if the school district is in a state that is a member of this organization. A school district wishing to check the fingerprints of an applicant against the files of the FBI can only do this if the state in which the district is located has passed legislation authorizing this type of investigation.

The first task in applying for a position is filling out the application form. There are two basic formats used in constructing applications. The first format emphasizes detailed factual information; the second emphasizes the applicant's attitudes, opinions, and values.

The basic principle in constructing application forms is to only ask for information you need to know. The information requested on most applications falls under one of the following headings: personal data, education and professional preparation, experience, and references. The physical layout of the form should allot sufficient space for answering the questions and providing the requested information.

Aptitude and ability testing can be used successfully as part of the selection process for most classified jobs in school districts. In fact, they are necessary for some positions.

Selected Further Readings

Department of Justice. www.usdoj.gov, 2009.

Department of Labor. www.dol.gov, 2009.

Equal Employment Opportunity Commission (EEOC). www.eeoc.gov, 2009.

Gibson, Cathy Lee, *Mission-Driven Interviewing: Moving Beyond Behavior-Based Questions*. Huntington, CT: PTI Publishing, 2006.

Liu, Edward, and Susan Moore Johnson, "New Teachers' Experiences of Hiring: Late, Rushed, and Information-Poor," *Educational Administration Quarterly*, 42, no. 3 (2006), 324–360.

McDermid, Shelley M., and Andrea K. Wittenborn, "Lessons from Work-Life Research for Developing Human Resources," *Advances in Developing Human Resources*, 9, no. 4 (November 2007), 556–568.

Reiter-Palmon, Roni, Marcy Young, Jill Strange, Renae Manning, and Joseph James, "Occupationally-Specific Skills: Using Skills to Define and Understand Jobs and their Requirements," *Human Resources Management Review*, 16 (2006), 356–375.

Rothstein, Mitchell G., and Richard D. Goffin, "The Use of Personality Measures in Personnel Selection: What Does Current Research Support? *Human Resource Management Review*, 16(2006), 155–180.

Russo, Charles J., "Teacher Certification, Employment, and Contracts," *Reutter's the Law of Public Education*, 6th ed. New York: Foundation Press, 2006, pp. 476–564.

Society for Human Resource Management (SHRM). www.shrm.org (as of 2009).

Sullivan, Sherry E., and Lisa Mainiero, "Using the Kaleidoscope Career Model to Understand the Changing Patterns of Women's Careers: Designing HRD Programs that Attract and Retain Women," *Advances in Developing Human Resources*, 10, no. 1 (February 2008), 32–49.

CHAPTER

5

Placement and Induction

FOCUS SCENARIO

One of your responsibilities as the director of human resources is the placement and induction of administrators, teachers, and staff members. The school district has 250 teachers and approximately 125 support personnel. It is located in a rural area with a changing population. For years the European American population has been decreasing, but due to the recent opening of a manufacturing center, a significant number of Mexican immigrants now live in the school district. The culture of the community has changed and there is significant concern being voiced by the new residents about the lack of understanding of the Mexican culture by administrators, teachers, and support personnel. In fact, there are no Mexican Americans working as administrators or teachers in the district.

Furthermore, parents generally believe that first-year teachers lack the professional training to teach children from diverse backgrounds because their university pre-teaching experiences were with children from European American families. Also, there is a lack of curricular materials for children who have English as their second language. The parents of children in the district have voiced their aspirations for their children to the superintendent and the board of education on numerous occasions. However, the parents still believe that the board of education does not fully understand the cultural issues that they have raised because all the board members are of European American decent.

As director of human resources you have decided to develop a strategic plan that will address the processes and procedures for assigning staff, the induction of staff, and particularly, the mentoring of first-year teachers.

After a person has been hired, the next two processes involve placing that individual in an assignment and orientating him or her to the school community. Both of these processes are covered in this chapter because they are interrelated; both also are continual processes because some staff members will be reassigned each year and thus, will require a certain amount of induction. Placement and induction is not a one-time task, but rather an ongoing concern of the human resources department.

PLACEMENT

In all but the very smallest districts, a new employee should not be told that he or she has been hired only for a particular job in a specific school building. The selection process explicated in the previous chapter will result in the employment of an individual for a certain position. However, the employee must understand from the outset that the assignment can be changed, even immediately, if the administration deems such to be in the best interest of the school district.

This sample board of education placement policy clearly specifies the role of the superintendent in assigning all staff members to particular positions within the school system. The planning required in making assignments is very complicated, demanding the full-time attention of at least one human resources administrator in most metropolitan school districts. The human resources planning inventories described in Chapter 2 could provide the human resources department with valuable information for making assignments. Of course, it is to the advantage of the school district to make assignments that are in harmony with the wishes of the employees. A significant cause of low morale, particularly among teachers, is the assigning of individuals to schools, grade levels, and subject areas that they find undesirable. Using the staffing survey is one method of minimizing discontent over reassignments. The survey instrument can be very simple in construction and very easy to fill out.

The human resources department must also consider a number of circumstances in trying to fulfill the wishes of employees in making reassignments. Some of these circumstances include maternity leave, resignations, retirements, deaths, and terminations. In addition, the following

EXHIBIT 5.1

Placement Policy

The following sample placement policy specifies how placement could be handled by a school district:

> The placement of employees within the school system is the responsibility of the superintendent of schools. The superintendent may delegate the implementation of the placement process to other appropriate administrators, but he or she ultimately retains the responsibility for placement. In determining assignments, the wishes of the employee are taken into consideration if these do not conflict with the requirements of the district's programming, staff balancing, and the welfare of students. Other factors that will be taken into consideration in making assignments are educational preparation and training, certification, experience, working relationships, and seniority with the school system.
>
> A staffing survey form will be secured from each employee annually in January to assist in making assignment plans for the forthcoming school year.
>
> Professional staffing assignments will be announced by April 1st. Administrators affected by an assignment change will be notified of the change by the superintendent of schools. Teachers affected by a change in grade or subject assignment or a building transfer will be notified of the change by their respective building principals.
>
> Classified staffing assignments will be announced by May 1st and will become effective on July 1st. Supervisors and managers affected by an assignment change will be notified of the change by the superintendent of schools or his designated representative. Other employees affected by a change in assignment will be notified by their immediate supervisors.

variables must be taken into consideration: staff balancing, affirmative action requirements, the certification of professional employees, experience in an assignment, and working relationships.

For example, a teacher who is having difficulty accepting a certain principal's philosophy about how to handle children with behavioral problems might request reassignment to another school. The human resources department then would determine if another position is, or will become available that requires the certification qualifications of the teacher. Further, an analysis must be made to determine if such a reassignment would upset the balance in either school between experienced and inexperienced teachers, male and female teachers, and minority representation.

The welfare of students and implementation of the school district's instructional program are other important considerations in making reassignments. A biology teacher who is certificated also as a physical education teacher might be denied reassignment to the physical education department because of the scarcity in applicants for biology positions, or because he has taught only biology throughout his fifteen-year career as a teacher.

When there are a number of requests for reassignment, seniority is a defensible criterion in making decisions only after the other variables have been considered. Those employees with the most seniority in the school district should be given the first choice in assignments; involuntary reassignments should be given to those employees with the least seniority. Involuntary reassignments are sometimes necessary because of unexpected vacancies.

Placement Grievance Procedure

If an employee has a concern regarding a permanent or temporary change in assignment, the following procedure must be observed: (1) the employee should initiate an interview with the administrator who processed the assignment change. (2) If agreement is not reached at this point, the employee may initiate an interview with the superintendent of schools and formally request a review of the reassignment; should the employee continue to be dissatisfied, he or she may resign his or her position with the school district.

The due process presented in this grievance procedure identifies the superintendent of schools as the ultimate authority in reviewing assignments within the school district. A grievance procedure is necessary to effectively operate the district and highlights the fact that an individual is employed in the district and not in a particular school or position.

INDUCTION

Induction is the process designed to acquaint newly employed individuals with the community, the school district, and their colleagues. Reassigned employees need to be acquainted with their new school, program, and colleagues. Much of what this section covers are equally applicable to both newly employed and reassigned individuals. It is an administrative responsibility that is often neglected or loosely organized in many school districts. The industrial and business communities place a high priority on induction; they have recognized for many years the cause-and-effect relationship of this process to employee retention and job performance.

An effective induction program must have well-defined objectives that reflect the needs of new employees and the specific philosophy of the school system. Although the objectives of an induction program will vary among individual school districts, some universal objectives should be common to all programs:

- To make the employee feel welcome and secure
- To help the employee become a member of the "team"

- To inspire the employee towards excellence in performance
- To help the employee adjust to the work environment
- To provide information about the community, school systems, school building, faculty, and students
- To acquaint the individual with other employees with whom he or she will be associated
- To facilitate the opening of school each year

These objectives support the ultimate purpose of an induction program, to promote quality education for children. The employee who is able to adjust in a reasonable period of time to a new position helps to accomplish this purpose.

Once the overall purpose and specific objectives are defined, the subsequent steps include deciding upon the most effective method of implementation and the content of the program. Some school districts consider a one- or two-day orientation at the beginning of each school year to be sufficient. Other districts provide an ongoing induction program to orient new employees and reassigned employees. Certainly, an ongoing program is better able to meet the concerns of reassigned individuals in large school districts who will need information about their new school building, the faculty, the students, and the community it serves. The fallacy, as previously mentioned, is assuming that induction is a one-time task, only for new employees.

Induction programs fall into one of two major categories: informational and personal adjustment programs. Informational programs, in turn, are concerned with either initial data or updating information. Initial data consist primarily of information about the school system, the community it serves, and the particular school in which the employee will work. New employees, of course, are targeted for this type of program. Updating informational programs are geared to the employee who is reassigned; they concentrate on the particular school and community to which he or she has been reassigned.

Personal adjustment programs aim at helping the newly hired or reassigned employee interact with the principal, faculty, students, and parents of a particular school. With a classified employee, the emphasis should be on helping the individual interact with his or her supervisor and coworkers, as well as those administrators, faculty members, students, and parents with whom he or she will come into contact.

The following four sections of this chapter deal with the content and methods of four induction programs. The first is most effective in orienting individuals to the school system; the second helps orient individuals to the community served by the school system or particular school. The third is designed to orient employees to the school to which they are assigned; the fourth is geared to orienting the employees to the people with whom they must establish a relationship.

The School District

The human resources department is responsible for implementing this part of the induction program. The main thrust of this program is to convey an understanding of the school system's policies and services and to identify system wide personnel such as assistant superintendents, program directors, and coordinators.

All employees should receive a copy of the school board policies and a copy of the employee manuals that pertain to their specific job. They should be allowed time during the orientation sessions to become familiar with these policies and manuals. To be truly effective, the program should also give the employees the opportunity to ask clarifying questions about policies and procedures.

Of course, the policies of the school district should set forth the vision and mission of the district. It is always a good idea to begin an orientation session with the vision and mission statements. Because schools are service-rendering institutions, the vision and mission are people-driven. Thus, most statements are focused on providing the children with an opportunity to develop all dimensions of their potential to the fullest extent possible. Such development includes the intellectual, emotional, physical, ethical, and cultural aspects of education. Teachers, staff members, and administrators are usually interested in this type of presentation; it is why they chose education as their career. Such an approach adds significance to the more mundane aspects of employment orientation.

The employee benefits provided by the school district must be carefully explained to new employees. Major medical and hospitalization insurance applications, retirement forms, government payroll withholding forms, and other enrollment documents are generally explained to new employees at the earliest possible time during the orientation process. Most insurance programs require a new employee to enroll a spouse and dependents within 30 days after commencing employment. If a spouse or dependent is enrolled after that time, he or she is usually required to take a physical examination, and the insurance company may deny coverage because of a medical condition. For example, a newly employed female teacher who does not enroll her husband in a medical insurance program within the 30-day grace period may be denied coverage for him because he has a heart condition.

The most effective vehicle for conveying an understanding of policies, procedures, and services is the small-group seminar. In this format, five to ten employees are assigned to a human resources administrator who presents the material and instructs them about how to fill out all necessary forms. This is usually done within the first few days of employment. A meeting, breakfast, or luncheon could be held each year, during which the superintendent of schools, board members, and other central-office administrators and staff members are introduced to new employees. Such a special event is very effective in conveying to new employees their importance to the district.

The Community

Orientation to the community is also the responsibility of the human resources department. Employees should be presented with information about the economic, social, racial, cultural, ethnic, and religious makeup of the community. Specific topics to be covered should include occupations, customs, clubs and organizations, church denominations, museums, libraries, colleges or universities, and social services.

Orientation to the community usually begins during the selection process, particularly during the interview. Candidates are told about the community and questioned about how they would respond to its various publics if they were employed with the district. A very effective way to begin the orientation process after selection is with a tour of the community conducted by the human resources department or, perhaps, a member of the Chamber of Commerce. Other methods include introducing new employees at club or organization meetings and inviting representatives from community resource services, such as libraries or museums, to address the new employees about their programs.

Orientation to the community does not end with the initial program; rather, a continuous updating should be provided by the human resources department. For example, as community service resources are improved or changed, this information should be brought to the attention of school staff members.

The School Building and Program

The building principal has the responsibility for orienting new teachers to a particular school. First, and most important is introducing new teachers to all other employees, both professional and classified, who work in the building. Classified employees should be introduced by their immediate supervisors to both professional and other classified employees.

New employees must know, in detail, the layout of the building in which they will work. This is best accomplished by giving new employees a tour of the facility and, if it is a large school, presenting each person with a map. Explaining administrative procedures is also the responsibility of the building principal. It is essential for new teachers to know how to complete attendance forms, where to obtain supplies and materials, how to requisition audiovisual equipment, and how the school schedule operates. An initial conference with the building principal, an assistant principal, or a department chairperson is one method of explaining these procedures to new staff members.

Orientating the new teacher to the instructional program is the responsibility of the building principal. Like administrative procedures, this may be delegated to an assistant principal or a department chairperson. At times, explaining the instructional program might be a central-office task, especially when the school district has subject matter coordinators and a uniform curriculum in all the schools.

In some school districts a new teacher is assigned to an experienced teacher during the first year of employment. The new teacher will then have a definite person to call on when questions arise about the curriculum or building procedures. This has proven to be a successful technique because the experienced teacher does not pose a threat to the new teacher, whereas an administrator might.

Personal Adjustment

In line with the current research on the effectiveness of participatory decision making, establishing good working relationships among colleagues is viewed as most important if an organization is to achieve its objectives. In a service-rendering organization, such as a school district, that is even more crucial because good human relations are the basis for the effective delivery of services. Forming relationships with other staff members helps an employee to achieve satisfaction in his or her work. Nothing is less satisfying than being alienated from colleagues in an organization. The responsibility for helping a new employee form meaningful relationships with other staff members rests with the individual's immediate supervisor or, if the new employee is a teacher, with the building principal.

A highly effective orientation method for new employees is to organize activities that give them the opportunity to socialize with other staff members. Many schools make a practice of serving refreshments and allotting a certain amount of time for personal interaction either before or after meetings. Holiday parties or dinners are also an effective means of enabling employees to meet each other on a social level, which can provide staff members with new insights about each other.

Service on faculty, school, and district committees is another way for employees to become acquainted with each other while providing the district with valuable assistance in carrying out projects. Textbook selection committees, energy conservation committees, and principals' advisory committees are common in many school districts and have proven to be very successful.

Finally, it is important for professional staff members to become affiliated with local, state, and national teacher and administrator organizations. These organizations not only provide an avenue for exchanging ideas, but also are a source of current professional information. Their social activities certainly help the individual form relationships with professionals in other school districts.

Many new employees come from other nations or states or, at least, have lived beyond the immediate vicinity of the school district. Although it is not a part of the formal induction program, helping the new employee relocate is a valuable service that the human resources department can provide. Relocation can be facilitated by making initial contacts with real estate agents for new employees and by chauffeuring them around the area, pointing out aspects of neighborhoods reasonably close to their school and the district.

Evaluating the effectiveness of induction programs is an extremely important part of the induction process. Evaluation of the programs for professional employees is best accomplished by establishing an induction committee chaired by a human resources administrator and composed of teachers, principals, and supervisors. This committee should gather input from new teachers that can be used to make changes in the programs. This same procedure can be initiated to evaluate programs for classified employees, that is, by establishing a committee composed of classified staff members and supervisors to react to the suggestions and insights of new employees after their first year with the district.

THE INDUCTION OF FIRST-YEAR TEACHERS

Although other professions provide transitional assistance for new members (e.g., residents in medicine, interns in architecture, and associates in law), historically the education profession has ignored the support needs of its new recruits.[1]

Statistical information on the plight of new teachers indicates that nearly one-fourth of them will leave the profession after two years of service, and a staggering one-third will leave after three years. These data clearly indicate that the needs of new teachers are not being met by school districts. Possible remedies for this situation fall within the following categories:

- A school level systemic approach to mentoring
- Assistance in knowing and understanding the teacher's role and function
- Assistance in knowing and understanding school and school district policies and procedures
- Collegial encouragement and support[2]

School district and school building administrative policies can have a significant effect upon the induction of beginning teachers. The scope and sequence of such policies are most effective if they call for a multiple-year approach to the mentoring of new teachers. From this perspective, the administrators of school districts and individual schools assume the role of teacher educators.[3]

The National Association of Secondary School Principals (NASSP) initiated a project to study the induction of first-year teachers. The committee also developed a four-phase time period during which induction should occur. Phase I would begin during the summer months and would concentrate on orienting the new teachers to the school, school district, and community. Phase II, scheduled for the week before school opens, would emphasize procedures and identify support personnel. Phase III, during the first semester, would include daily meetings between a beginning teacher and a cooperating master teacher. They would review practical aspects of teaching, such as lesson planning, testing, grading, and disciplinary techniques. During the second semester, the final phase would emphasize a more theoretical approach to teaching. The new teacher would be encouraged to begin evaluating his or her performance and verbalizing his or her philosophy of education.

MENTORING AS AN INDUCTION STRATEGY FOR BEGINNING TEACHERS

The education reform movement, which formally began with the publication of *A Nation at Risk*, has resulted in the enactment, in over 16 states, of legislation calling for the inclusion of mentoring as an induction strategy for newly hired teachers. These states have mentoring programs that differ one from the other to some degree. However, the basic concept is the same in all of the programs, which is the pairing of an experienced teacher with a beginning teacher in order to provide the latter with support and encouragement.

The experienced teacher can act as a role model for the beginning teacher and through coaching, help the teacher develop his or her competencies, self-esteem, and sense of professionalism. In some school districts, the beginning teacher attends traditional orientation and induction programs. A mentor is assigned to each teacher, who then provides support throughout the entire year. In other school districts, beginning teachers are assigned to a group comprising other beginning teachers, the interaction of which is facilitated by a mentor.

It is important to clarify the role of the mentor to building principals and to the beginning teachers. This is especially true in relation to the issue of teacher evaluation. The mentor should not be an evaluator, but rather someone who assists. Teacher evaluation should be the responsibility only of administrators. The criteria for selecting mentors and the process for matching such mentors with beginning teachers are also important considerations. Research indicates that mentoring is successful when it functions through in-class coaching by experienced teachers from the same subject areas or grade levels as the beginning teachers.[4]

Other research sets forth the issues that confront beginning teachers and therefore, reveals the kinds of competencies that mentors must possess. This is extremely helpful information in the mentor selection process. Beginning teachers need assistance from mentors primarily in pedagogical methods and lesson planning, but beginning teachers also need help with learning how to handle time pressures, the ever growing amount of paperwork, and noninstructional meetings.[5]

Newly selected mentors usually require some type of staff development in order to acquire or enhance certain skills. For example, programs to enhance supervision and coaching techniques or programs that update the mentors on instructional strategies can be most helpful.

MENTORING AS AN INDUCTION STRATEGY FOR BEGINNING ADMINISTRATORS

Whereas mentoring programs for beginning teachers are commonplace, this is not the situation for beginning administrators. Usually, a beginning principal or superintendent may informally seek the opinions of more seasoned administrators whom he or she encounters through membership in administrator professional associations or at regional and state administrator meetings.

However, mentoring is typically recognized as an indispensable tool in professional development, and school districts tend to assign an experienced principal or other educational administrator as a mentor to beginning and less experienced administrators. Also, it is not uncommon for administrators to move freely along a line that begins with being a protégé and being a mentor on the opposite end. Both roles are sometimes fulfilled by the same person. This phenomenon is not surprising because change is a constant in leadership positions. Social, political, and economic factors constantly impinge upon the responsibilities of superintendents, principals, and all other educational administrators. The private business sector has experienced this phenomenon for many years and views the mentoring relationship as having the most influence on the practices of less experienced administrators. Furthermore, the emotional involvement of protégés and mentors can be intense.[6]

Research on the relationship between protégés and mentors seems to indicate that those leaders who were protégés were also the most effective mentors. Secondly, mentors were more enthusiastic about their role when they recognized positive leadership traits in protégés. Thirdly, mentors considered themselves as role models in the mentoring process. Finally, mentors learned their role as mentors from their mentors. Thus, mentoring was viewed as passing on the *wisdom of leadership*.[7]

There are ethical considerations in the mentoring process that revolve around three issues: cultural replication, access, and power. Mentoring can have a negative effect when the mentor is so influential that the protégé unquestionably accepts the mentors opinions and practices. A key objective in the mentoring process is for the mentor to encourage and direct the protégé to critically analyze situations and to use evidence and data when making decisions. In this context, the mentor is a support person and not the primary decision maker.[8]

Access to mentorship is a concern in school districts where there are few experienced women and minority administrators that can act as mentors for beginning women and minority administrators. Cross gender and ethnic mentoring is usually very effective. However, in some situations same gender or same ethnic mentoring might be more effective if that is the desire of the protégé or mentor.[9]

Of course, sometimes power issues occur, and it is not always on the side of the mentor. The underlying concern is the motive behind a power play. Strong differences of opinion on how a beginning administrator should address an issue or make a decision are not the problem. Rather, power issues demand attention of the superintendent when a protégé uses deception or exploits the mentor relationship. For example, an unscrupulous protégé may damage the reputation of an experienced administrator through lying about the counsel of his or her mentor.[10]

TECHNOLOGY AND PLACEMENT/INDUCTION

Using technology as a work tool and even for recreational and information purposes has become commonly place for most education professionals. Some teachers and administrators from more recent generations tend to be more intuitive about the use of technology, while others from previous generations have learned the basics and are proficient in using such technology in schools and school districts. Although beginning teachers and administrators may have the assistance of mentors and others who orientate them to the nuances of the school and school district, still they are on-their-own to a certain degree and could certainly benefit from technological support. In a sense, it breaks the isolation that sometimes occurs when beginning teachers and administrators are overwhelmed with the requirements of teaching and administering.

Some of the most valuable technological help can come from www.teachers.net. This is a Web site that serves approximately 50,000 teachers. It provides a forum where teachers can communicate about their pedagogy and other education topics in addition to job listings. Photos of classrooms and the sharing of lesson plans augment the chat rooms. The teachers subscribing to this Web site are not only from the United States, but also from around the world. The Teachers Network Web site, www.teachersnetwork.org, besides providing similar assistance as the former Web site, also boasts of a new teacher hotline through which expert advice can be received on education issues within 72 hours.

The New Teacher Center at the University of California at Santa Cruz, www.newteachercenter.org, is a valuable tool for those administrators and staff members who are responsible for managing induction programs. This Web site supports the development of innovative methods to induct beginning teachers and administrators. It also seeks to strengthen the relationship between school districts and the University. Specifically, the quality of mentoring is a focal point in the Center's Network of Researchers on Teacher Induction, where papers and presentations address topics that are related to induction. A school district can also share information, documents, and other materials that the administrators of the district use for the induction process.

California also has initiated a Beginning Teacher Support and Assessment Program, www.btsa.ca.gov, which is geared to first- and second-year teachers. The program helps teachers learn about effective methods of teaching and there is a frequently asked questions link. Furthermore, there is a link to program standards that can be used to assess the success of induction programs.

School districts that are having a difficult time hiring teachers can garner help from the National Teacher Recruitment Clearinghouse, which provides advice and assistance in not only enlarging the number of teacher applicants, but also how to retain those teachers after they are hired. The "Find and Keep Teachers" link provides important information on how to encourage young people to consider teaching as a career and provides opinions on how to retain teachers. Finally, the "Successful Teaching" link provides ways and means for helping new teachers transition from university teacher education programs into the dynamic world of teaching. The emphasis is on how to keep teachers motivated and growing professionally.

There are also international Web sites that provide information about effective induction programs in foreign countries that can have transference to education here in the United States. For example, WestEd Web site, www.wested.org, contains an article that presents effective programs in China, Japan, New Zealand, and Switzerland. The National College for School Leadership, www.ncsl.org.uk, is a Web site in England that supports beginning and experienced principals. There is also a "Research & Development" link on that Web site, which carries publications concerning issues of interest to U.S. administrators.[11]

IMPLICATIONS FOR SMALL AND MEDIUM-SIZED SCHOOL DISTRICTS

The process for placement of principals, other administrators, teachers, and staff members is the same in all school districts; it is the prerogative of the superintendent in consultation with the board of education. In the uncertain financial times that school districts are currently experiencing, teachers and administrators with dual or multiple certifications and experience will continue to be in demand. The process cannot be other than it is regardless of the size of the school district.

However, induction is a different process altogether and certainly is affected by the size of the school district. The expediential factor is part of the mix with the number of new hires that a school district experiences on a yearly basis. Some large school districts hire hundreds of teachers and other employees yearly while, in some districts, the overall percentage of new hires may be small. Thus, the turnover in a school district is an important factor more so than even the actual number of teachers and others who are employed. In small to medium-sized school districts, the number of new hires each year may be less than ten. For such a small number, the induction process may not require the assistance of a human resources administrator, and may become the responsibility of building principals and the superintendent of schools. Of course, managing the payroll forms and enrolling the new employee in such benefits as medical and hospitalization insurance can be handled by a business manager or the superintendent.

Induction takes on two main thrusts in small and medium-sized districts: the culture of the school community and the nuances of teaching or administering. The school community is comprised of the school and school district in addition to the community in which the students live. A school bus ride around the district can help the beginning teacher or administrator learn the economic status of the community from observation. Personal contact with students and their parents at a "meet the parents" event can help a new teacher or administrator understand the social and educational concerns and issues of parents.

The more difficult challenge resides in the instructional or administering process, which is more effectively learned in a mentoring relationship with an experienced teacher or administrator. Sometimes, it might be difficult to find a person who is willing or capable of being a mentor because of lack of experience or just being overworked. A possible solution to such a situation is for a number of small school districts to come together and support newly hired teachers and administrators as a group. Mentors can be effective even if they are not from the same districts as the beginning teachers or administrators. Since every school district will need to hire new teachers and administrators at some time in the future, being of assistance to another school district will ensure that assistance will be provided when it is necessary for the helping school district.

Mentoring can also be effective if a group of new teachers or administrator meet together in order to discuss responsibilities and issues. Thus, a group of three to five new teachers or administrators can learn from each other and can invite an experienced teacher or administrator to join in the discussions when possible.

THE IMPACT OF GENERATION Y ON PLACEMENT AND INDUCTION

Generation Y teachers, administrators, and staff members have a definite impact on the culture of school districts and individual schools. It is important for human resources administrators to recognize the importance of this fact in placing and inducting Generation Y employees. The effect, of course, is reciprocal. The culture of a given school and school district will have an effect on how Generation Y employees will view their own particular perspectives, and how they will need to adjust that perspective in working with teachers, administrators, and staff members from other generations.

Generation Y is certainly adventuresome, but in a manner that is somewhat different than other generations. They definitely enjoy collaboration to the degree that it involves continual involvement with other teachers and administrators. They want to know what other professionals know and think about the issues that arise during the performance of their responsibilities. In a sense, they prefer to have a work area that they share with other teachers rather that being isolated from them.[12]

Generation Y teachers and administrators also tend to look at the phenomenon of change in a different way. Rather than dealing with the consequences of change, they seek ways to precipitate change and often embrace change as something not only to be expected, but also as exciting as long as they see the value and worth in the change. Thus, new models for developing curricula and new curricular materials are often welcomed and present desired challenges to Generation Y teachers and principals. More fundamental to embracing change, Generation Y employees view themselves as being altered by the change and even enriched. To a degree, they conceptualize themselves as being reinvented rather than bothered by change.[13]

In placing Generation Y employees, it is important to capitalize upon these strengths while helping them learn how to engage others from different generations and to learn from each other. These characteristics can also be valuable insights on how to plan and implement induction programs that utilize the perspectives of Generation Y employees.

Quick Review of Essentials

After a person has been hired, the next two processes involve placing that individual in an assignment and orienting him or her to the school community. The placement of employees within the school system is the responsibility of the superintendent of schools. The planning required in making assignments is a very complicated task, demanding the full-time attention of at least one human resources administrator in most metropolitan-area school districts. It is to the advantage of the school district to make assignments that are in harmony with the wishes of the employees. A staffing survey is one method of systematically gathering information on the placement preferences of employees.

Other variables that the human resources department must take into consideration in making assignments include staff balancing, certification requirements, experience, and working relationships. However, the welfare of students and implementation of the school district's instructional program are the most important considerations. When there are a number of requests for reassignment, seniority is a defensible criteria after these other variables are considered. A due process should be established to give employees the opportunity to have an assignment reviewed by the appropriate administrator.

Induction is the process designed to acquaint newly employed individuals with the school system and with other staff members. It is also the process for acquainting reassigned employees with their new school, program, and colleagues. An effective induction program must have well-defined objectives that will help the employee to feel welcome and secure, to become a member of the "team," to be inspired towards excellence in performance, to adjust to the work environment, and to become familiar with the school community.

Induction programs fall into one of two major categories: informational and personal adjustment programs. Informational programs are concerned with providing either initial material or updated information. Initial data consist primarily of information about the school system, the community it serves, and the school where the new employee will work. Updated informational programs are geared to the employee who is reassigned; they concentrate on a particular school and community. Personal adjustment programs are designed to help the newly hired or reassigned employee interact with the other people for whom and with whom he or she will work.

To orient new employees effectively to the school district, policies and services must be thoroughly explained and system-wide personnel identified. Orientation to the community must convey the knowledge of the economic, social, cultural, ethnic, racial, and religious makeup of the community to employees. The occupations, customs, clubs and organizations, church denominations, museums, libraries, colleges and universities, and social services are also topics that should be covered in this program.

Orienting a new employee to a particular school begins with an introduction to the other staff members. A tour of the facility and an explanation of administrative procedures along with an orientation to the instructional program are also important aspects of this induction.

Personal adjustment orientation centers on encouraging new employees to establish working relationships with their colleagues. Organized activities such as faculty meetings, holiday parties or dinners, faculty and district committees, and membership in professional organizations provide new employees with the opportunity to establish desired relationships with other professionals.

Evaluating the effectiveness of the induction process is extremely important and will provide the necessary data for improving the process. An area of special concern centers on the induction of first-year teachers. Many potentially excellent teachers could be lost to the education profession because they were not properly inducted. A number of suggestions and models have been developed. They all recognize the importance of giving first-year teachers time to consult with colleagues and providing them with feedback concerning their performance. Many school districts have developed mentoring programs not only for beginning teachers, but also for entry-year administrators.

Selected Further Readings

Allen, Rick, "Supporting New Educators," *Educational Leadership* (May 2005), 96.

Cochran-Smith, M., and K. Fries, "Researching Teacher Education in Changing Times: Politics and Paradigms," in *Studying Teacher Education*, M. Cochran-Smith and K. Fries, eds., Mahwah, NJ: Lawrence Erlbaum, 2005, pp. 69–109.

Gilbert, Linda, "What Helps Beginning Teachers?" *Educational Leadership* (May 2005), 36–39.

Hezlett, Sarah A., and Sharon K. Gibson, "Linking Mentoring and Social Capital: Implications for Career and Organization Development," *Advances in Developing Human Resources*, 9, no. 3 (August 2007), 384–412.

Hezlett, Sarah A., and Sharon K. Gibson, "Mentoring and Human Resource Development: Where We Are and Where We Need to Go," *Advances in Developing Human Resources*, 7, no. 4 (November 2005), 446–469.

Hoerr, Thomas R., "Meeting New Teachers' Personal Needs," *Educational Leadership* (May 2005), 82, 84.

McCauley, Cynthia D., "The Mentoring Tool," *Advances in Developing Human Resources*, 7, no. 4 (November 2005), 443–445.

McDonald, Kimberly S. and Linda M. Hite, "Ethical Issues in Mentoring: The Role of HRD," *Advances in Developing Human Resources*, 7, no. 4 (November 2005), 569–582.

Rosser, Manda H., "Mentoring From the Top: CEO Perspectives," *Advances in Developing Human Resources*, 7, no. 4 (November 2005), 527–539.

Tillman, Linda C., "Mentoring New Teachers: Implications for Leadership Practice in an Urban School," *Educational Administration Quarterly*, 41, no. 4 (October 2005), 609–629.

Useem, Elizabeth and Ruth Curran Neild, "Supporting New Teachers in the City," *Educational Leadership* (May 2005), 44–47.

Wang, Jian and S. J. Odell, "An Alternative Conception of Mentor/Novice Relationships: Learning to Teach Reform-Minded Teaching as a Context," *Teaching & Teacher Education*, 23, no. 2 (2007), 473–489.

Wang, Jian, Sandra J. Odell, and Sharon A. Schwille, "Effects of Teacher Induction on Beginning Teachers' Teaching: A Critical Review of the Literature," *Journal of Teacher Education*, 59, no. 2 (March/April 2008), 132–152.

Wayne, Andres J., Peter Youngs, and Steve Fleischman, "Improving Teacher Induction," *Educational Leadership* (May 2005), 76–78.

CHAPTER

6

Staff Development

FOCUS SCENARIO

You are the director of staff development for a school district with approximately 500 teachers and 250 support personnel. Because of pressure from parent organizations, the state legislature has just mandated that 1 percent of the state aid that a school district receives must be used for teacher staff development. Thus, you have approximately $250,000 dollars to spend on staff development.

The school district is very stable. Parents and other citizens have been supportive of the district in terms of passing tax levy and bond issue referendums. The school district experienced significant growth in the 1950s and 1960s, but experienced a decrease in student population in the 1970s and 1980s. This was due to the fact that the houses in the school district had appreciated in value to the point that younger families with children could not afford to buy homes in the district, and the empty-nesters were not interested in leaving the district because their home mortgages were paid. This situation caused the school district to lose enrollment, and thus, the district was forced to lay off younger teachers. The administrators, teachers, and support personnel have become rather set in their ways and are in need of staff development programs that will help them to renew their enthusiasm and bring them up-to-date on current best practice in administering and teaching children. The local Teachers' Association has endorsed the need of the district to rethink its staff development commitment and programming. Furthermore, the administrators and teachers have a positive attitude towards this end and are ready and willing to participate in staff development.

Change is a constant occurrence in contemporary society. Instant communication channels, produced by technological advances, present students and educators with changes in politics, economics, science, and social status from every corner of the world. The mandate of public schools, of course, is to educate the children, adolescents, and young adults of our country in order to help them meet the challenges that tomorrow will bring because of these changes. As an organization, a school district needs well-qualified administrators, teachers, and support personnel to fulfill this mandate. As the positions and job requirements within a school district become more complex, the importance of staff development programs increases.

Staff development practices have undergone considerable change over the last two decades. Three trends that have contributed to this metamorphosis are (1) results-driven education, (2) the systems approach to school and school district organization, and (3) constructivism. As a practice, results-driven staff development is concerned with changing the behavior and attitudes of teachers, administrators, and staff members rather than being concerned with the number of participants in such programs. The systems approach to administration recognizes the interrelatedness of all components in a given school and ultimately, in a school district. Thus, an innovation in elementary school instructional techniques could have ramifications for the counseling program and for the curriculum committee in a school. Across the district, an innovation in an elementary school could affect the program in that district's middle school and eventually, the high school instructional program.

Finally, constructivism sets forth the premise that learners build knowledge structures in their minds. The implication for educators is that they can benefit from nontraditional methods of delivering professional development activities such as workshops and presentations when the activities arise from their daily professional responsibilities. Action research is a good example of how focusing a coherent purpose can build upon the constructivist's approach to staff development.[1]

It is literally impossible today for any individual to take on a job or enter a profession and remain in it for 40 or so years with his or her skills basically unchanged. Therefore, staff development is not only desirable, but also an activity to which each school system must commit human and fiscal resources if it is to maintain a skilled and knowledgeable staff.

Professional Learning Communities

As a dimension of the human resources function, staff development can be organized according to various structures. Currently, the most effective structure is the professional learning community. Such a structure has four major focuses:

1. Learning rather than teaching
2. Collaboration
3. Viewing all members of the community as learners
4. Self-accountability

The first focus, learning rather than teaching, is a departure from the traditional approach to educating students, which centers on the responsibility of schools and school districts to ensure effective teaching. When the focus is placed upon learning, teachers, administrators, and staff members tend to see their responsibilities in a different light. They begin to analyze the cultures of the school and school district in order to ascertain whether it supports student learning. Furthermore, teachers, administrators, and staff members begin to understand that effective school and school district cultures are founded on a commitment to learning that must be articulated to all stakeholders, which includes students and parents. It is important to keep in mind that the term *staff members* refers to guidance counselors, media specialists, special education teachers, assistant superintendents for instruction, human resources administrators, and all other professional and support members of the school and school district community.

Of course, this focus on learning that can be investigated through cultural analyses and commitment leads to the second focus, which is collaboration. Teachers, administrators, and staff members must collaboratively engage in discourse and investigate what students need to learn, how to assess what students have learned, and how to help students who are having difficulty learning. Collaboration also means that teachers, administrators, and staff members will recognize that every aspect of the learning process is subject to team efforts. For example, if a certain student is having difficulty learning, assisting the student is not the responsibility of only his or her classroom teacher. All members of the community who have related expertise will formulate a timely and required intervention plan to help the student. The usual format for collaboration is teaming, whereby a number of different teams of teachers, administrators, and staff members come together based on the expertise of the individual members in order to address common professional issues. Once formed, a given team may meet on a continual basis or only when necessary.

The third focus of professional learning communities empowers all members of the school and school district communities, not just students, to become learners. Of course, the most fundamental reality of this focus is the phenomenon of change. Thus, it is impossible for anyone to know all that he or she needs to know for all times in relation to his or her job. Consequently, parents, teachers, administrators, and staff members are constantly in need of acquiring new information, knowledge, skills, and attitudes. It is impossible to remain static in the dynamic environments of schools and school districts. This, of course, is the domain of staff development.

The final focus centers on self-accountability. The notion of professional learning communities rests on the ability of all members to self-actualize in a manner that contributes to the mission of their respective schools and school districts. For the human resources function, this means not only that professional staff development programs need to be organized and carried out in relation to the four focuses of the professional learning community, but also that the other human resources functions need to be geared towards these same focuses. The recruitment, selection, and performance evaluation functions are the most affected by the professional learning community approach. Thus, the concepts and processes set forth in this chapter constitute a professional learning community approach to human resources administration and, particularly, to professional staff development.[2]

Dimensions of the Learning Process

Because of the focus on professional learning communities, staff development activities for newly hired teachers, administrators, and staff members are sometimes met with misunderstandings about programming. Typically, some educators think of staff development activities as something that others bring to them in the form of presentations and information. However, in keeping with adult learning theory and effective programming experiences with professionals, development activities build upon the knowledge base and skills that educators already have. Thus, the participants must enhance the professional development activities through personal reflection and discussion with other colleagues. Furthermore, the learning community model requires collaboration and dialogue between the human resources administrator responsible for staff development and those educators for whom the staff development is targeted. Planning, delivery, and assessment of the programs are integral elements of this kind of collaboration.[3]

Staff development usually consists of learning through training and education. Of course, training is the process of learning a sequence of programmed tasks which constitute the job responsibilities of custodians, cooks, and maintenance personnel, which is usually learned on-the-job and consists of knowing best practice in performing certain tasks. Education is the process of helping teachers, administrators, and staff members acquire knowledge that will help them make discretionary decisions based on the evidence that confronts them in carrying out their job responsibilities. Education emphasizes acquiring sound reasoning processes rather than learning a body of serial facts. Education helps an employee develop a rational approach towards analyzing the relationship between variables and consequently understanding phenomena.

Teachers and administrators have job responsibilities that, in most respects, require education rather than training. Teachers and administrators usually do not perform programmed work. For example, an administrator can be trained in management techniques and procedures. However, an administrator cannot be trained to manage. Speaking about managers in the private sector, David A. DeCenszo and Stephen Robbins summarize the differences between training and education:

> "Successful employees prepared for positions of greater responsibility have analytical, human, conceptual, and specialized skills. They think and understand. Training *per se* cannot overcome an individual's inability to understand cause-and-effect relationships, to synthesize from experience, to visualize relationships, or to think logically. As a result, we suggest that employee development be predominantly an education process rather than a training process."[4]

In discussing the distinction between training and education, care must be taken not to assume that all job-related activities of a particular position are either trainable or educable. Teachers and administrators perform some activities that can be enhanced by training because these activities are capable of being programmed. Both teachers and administrators need good listening skills and interviewing skills; in today's technological society, they also need skills in using various types of computer software. However, understanding the instructional-learning process and being able to create a learning environment conducive to teaching goes beyond the scope of training and requires education.

This same distinction must also be applied to support personnel. An administrative assistant needs to develop and upgrade skills in using word-processing programs and in carrying out routine office procedures; these are trainable skills. However, this person is often called on to make decisions about setting up and prioritizing appointments for an administrator; this requires an understanding of the importance of each appointment relative to the responsibilities of that administrator. An effective administrative assistant should also have the ability to analyze inquiries and to refer them to the appropriate staff member. Acquiring such abilities goes beyond the scope of training and requires education.

To some, this distinction between training and education may seem to be only an academic exercise; however, it has very practical application. As will be demonstrated later in this chapter, it is extremely important to categorize and analyze the needs of employees in order to establish objectives for the various components of a staff development program. Understanding the type of learning required to meet these needs is essential to an effective program.

A staff development program centers on creating instructional-learning situations. Consequently, those charged with organizing such a program must know and understanding the psychological dimensions of learning. Numerous theories have been proposed about how learning occurs. This chapter will touch only on a few principals of learning that are related to staff development.

Learning is a change in human capability that can be retained and that is not simply ascribable to the process of growth. The manifestation of change as described in this definition is the behavior of the learner. The extent to which learning has occurred is measured by comparing those behaviors that were present before the individual was placed in the instructional-learning situation against those behaviors that can be demonstrated after the experience. The desired change is usually an increased skill or capability of more than momentary significance.

Those changes are brought about by certain aspects of the learning process. A stimulus is someone or something that initiates an action. An instructor will stimulate a learner by asking a question. The learner answering the question makes a response. If the instructor responds to the learner with, "that is a correct and appropriate answer," the learner is receiving reinforcement. Finally, if the learner perceives completion of the course of instruction as a means of obtaining a job, a promotion, a raise in salary, or some other desired goal, the learner is said to have motivation. Although this explanation of the four basic components of learning is rather simplistic, it does present the necessary conditions for learning to take place.

Considerations that impinge upon these aspects of the learning process are mentioned here because they are related to staff development planning. First, a certain amount of planning must precede the instructional learning situation to determine the most appropriate learning structure for the subject matter that will be taught. In learning, every new capability builds on a foundation established by previously learned capabilities. Planning specifies and orders these prerequisite capabilities in order that a learning objective can be reached. For example, a staff development workshop designed to help teachers construct metric system materials for classroom use should be preceded by a seminar explaining the metric system to teachers who are not proficient with the system.

Second, the environment of learning must be effectively managed. Those responsible for planning should ask themselves what is the most appropriate time and setting to carry out instruction. A comfortable and stimulating environment certainly enhances learning; and especially for adult learners, the instruction should take place at a time of day when they are not fatigued. This suggests that certain staff development seminars, workshops, or courses for teachers should be scheduled on days when school is not in session. This also implies that an effective staff development program should provide employees with released time from their regular duties so they can attend during the working day.

Third, instruction must have some practical application for the adult learner. Adults generally can learn more material in less time when they understand that the material can help them in their work. A school bus driver who attends a workshop on managing student behavior must be shown techniques that he or she can actually use with disruptive students.

Fourth, learning rarely takes place at a constant rate; rather, it fluctuates according to the difficulty of the subject matter or skill to be learned and the ability of the learner. Developing computer skills is a good example. During the first three months of instruction, the learner becomes familiar with the basic techniques. During the next three months, the individual develops speed, and learning accelerates. After six months of instruction, learning normally slows down because the individual has progressed to the point of technique refinement.[5]

CREATING A STAFF DEVELOPMENT PROGRAM

Experience has taught human resources administrators the folly of approaching staff development merely from the "Let's have a workshop" model. This traditional concept of what was and is still referred to in some school districts as "inservice training" has severe limitations, not only in scope, but also in effectiveness. Rather, the concept of "staff development" addresses the real needs of educational organizations. The evolution of this approach is mirrored in all of our societal institutions. In the past, changes were thrust upon the schools without giving teachers and administrators an opportunity to prepare for such changes. With the decline in pupil enrollments, there was a greater need for developing existing personnel resources to assume different positions created by change. Also, both the Elementary and Secondary Education Act of 1965 and the Education Professions Development Act of 1968 provided funding for staff development projects. These funds helped to forward the current interest in staff development.[6]

During the last decade, there has been a myriad of research on staff development. Most of this research has centered upon identifying those variables that produce effective staff development programs. As a consequence of this research, many models have been created. Some of the most often proposed in staff development literature are PET (Program for Effective Teaching); RPTIM (Readiness, Planning, Training, Implementation, Maintenance); CBAM (Concern-Based Adoption Model); and SDSI (Staff Development for School Improvement). A common thread connecting all these models is the goal of producing effective instruction through clinical supervision. As principals evaluate and supervise teachers in order to improve instruction, staff development programs become a vehicle through which teachers can enhance skills and remedy deficiencies.

Some employees perceive staff development activities as ineffective because they receive little support for implementing newly acquired skills and ideas. Other conditions that affect the success of a staff development program include lack of appropriate program organization and lack of supervision during implementation. Clearly, these conditions are symptomatic of a more fundamental problem, the lack of commitment. In any organization, this commitment must emanate from the highest level of responsibility down through the various levels of administration to the employees. In order to be effective, the board of education must support the program; the administration must organize and supervise the program; and the employees must participate in program planning.

In delineating the tasks to be performed by the various components of a school district, the board of education must set the stage by creating a positive climate for the program and by providing the necessary fiscal funding and appropriate policies for implementation. The central-office administration, through the director of staff development, is responsible for creating a master plan and for overall management and supervision of the program. Building principals and supervisors are responsible for identifying the knowledge, skills, and abilities that are needed to carry out the goals and objectives of the school district. Teachers and staff members are responsible for participating not only in program planning, but also in the programs. Consequently, the success of a staff development program depends upon the commitment of each individual within each level of the school district. Firestone et al. confirms the importance of commitment as follows:

> "The top leader in this district made improved literacy, and later mathematics, his top priority. After hiring and removing staff to get a team that shard his commitment, he began a long-term process of helping teachers develop a deeper understanding of subject areas and how to teach them. The professional development effort was part of a broader change program that became central to all decision making in the district, and it required constant protection from threats to resources and its coherence."[7]

Firestone et al. also promote the concept of local initiative and internal accountability particularly when a school district is using professional development to initiate and sustain reform efforts.[8]

Figure 6.1, a model for a staff development program, is a summary of the steps necessary for designing an effective program, which is elucidated in the following pages.

School District Goals and Objectives

Educational goals and objectives, taken in the broadest sense, are similar across the country. Schools are concerned about educating children in the basic skills and developing in them those cultural values that will perpetuate our American heritage. The genesis of a staff development program, therefore, originates from educational goals and objectives. When these goals and objectives are formulated into written policies of the board of education, a staff development

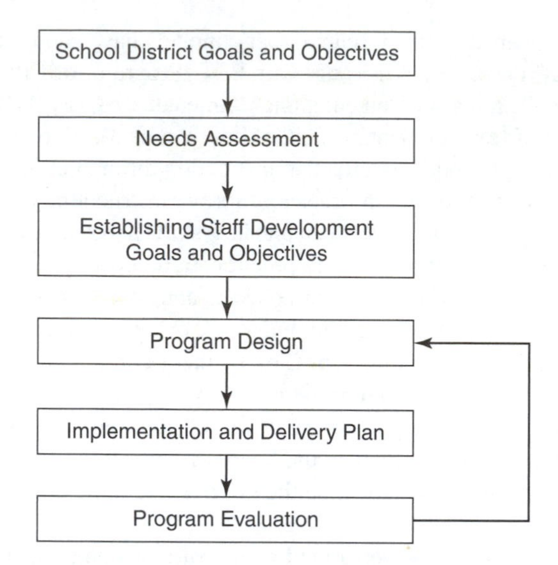

FIGURE 6.1 A Model for a Staff Development Program

program has the guidance necessary for integrating the individual goals of employees with those of the school district.

Needs Assessment

The primary purpose of a staff development program is to increase the knowledge and skills of employees and thereby, increase the potential of the school district to attain its goals and objectives. The process of assessing employee needs is essentially the process of determining the discrepancy between the existing and the needed competencies of the staff. This analysis also must consider projected human resource needs. Thus, a staff development program must be concerned not only with the abilities of individuals currently occupying positions, but also with the abilities individuals need to qualify for promotion to positions of more responsibility. The data obtained from the human resources inventories used in the human resources planning process, along with the data obtained from needs assessment techniques, provide the framework within which program goals and objectives can be established.[9]

Establishing Staff Development Goals and Objectives

Staff development goals and objectives continually change to meet the evolving needs of individual staff members and the school district. A predominantly European American suburban school district that begins to get an influx of Mexican American families might consider creating a program for the administrative, teaching, and support staffs on the impact that the mingling of these two distinctive cultures will have on the functioning of the school district. The purchase of new computer equipment will create a need to instruct the office staff on its most effective use.

These examples of changes that affect the operations of a school district should be more broadly formulated into goals and objectives. For example, a staff development goal involving integration might be stated as follows: to prepare the administration, teachers, and staff to effectively address the integration of Mexican American students into the school community. Objectives specifying this goal could be formulated as follows:

- To develop a sense of appreciation for cultural differences on the part of teachers, administrators, and staff members
- To develop strategies that will help students acquire an understanding of different cultural heritages

Such a goal with accompanying objectives provides direction to the next phase in creating a staff development program which is designing the program.

Program Design

Designing a program involves more than simply finding a university professor who is interested in giving a workshop on a particular topic. Broadly conceived, program design is a process of matching needs with available resources through an effective delivery method. Therefore, it is unproductive to assign or endorse an activity without considering how this activity helps to meet goals and objectives. Also, it is unproductive to consider only one method of delivering a staff development program. The National Education Association's Research Division lists the following methods used in program delivery: courses, institutes, conferences, workshops, staff meetings, committee work, professional reading, individual conferences, field trips, travel, camping, work experience, teacher exchanges, research, professional writing, professional association work, cultural experiences, visits, demonstrations, and community organization work.[10]

This is certainly not a listing of all the possibilities for designing a staff development program, and it is important to recognize that no one design will satisfy all. A variety of resource people will also enhance a staff development program. Among the most available and knowledgeable persons are teachers, senior staff members, college and university professors, professional consultants, journal authors, teacher organization representatives, and administrators.

Group-oriented design has proven to be an effective method for delivering staff development programs. Some are centered on behavior modification techniques in the instructional-learning environment. Individualized programs are another alternative to the traditional program design model. Such programs allow the individual maximum creativity in matching personal interests and needs to the goals and objectives of the school district. Teachers who engage in personalized activities usually improve their teaching skills. There are many different approaches to personalized activities that could include professional writing for journals, serving on school district curriculum research committees, attending conferences, making presentations at conferences, professional reading, professional development traveling, developing curriculum materials, becoming active in community relations events, and sponsoring student activities. Program design is an organic process that will continually change to meet the needs of individual staff members and the needs of the school district.

Implementation and Delivery Plan

A critical aspect in all staff development programs is the implementation and delivery phase. The very best of intentions and planning may fail unless attention is paid to providing employees with appropriate incentives to participate, to making satisfactory time arrangements, and to properly handling ordinary organizational problems.[11]

A common practice is to reimburse employees for tuition and fees incurred in attending workshops or taking courses. Many school districts also pay for substitutes in order to facilitate program arrangements. The research on staff development programs generally agrees that incentives should be provided. Other incentives could be reimbursement for attendance at professional conferences and for attending university courses, or advanced placement on the salary schedule. Although direct payment in the form of salary increments is a proven incentive, this study indicates that indirect financial aid is more influential in promoting participation in staff development programs.

Time is a valuable commodity to all employees and, thus, it is a key factor in organizing and encouraging employee participation in development programs. There is a growing trend to incorporate staff development programs as part of the working day or, at least, as an extension of the day. Some school districts set aside a number of afternoons each month for development programs; others bring courses and lectures directly to the schools. A variation of this approach is to release students by subject area so that the teachers in a given discipline can meet for an entire day. Whatever the arrangement for delivering a staff development program, experience indicates that the least effective time is after a full day of teaching or work. No teacher, administrator, or employee will be able to assimilate new ideas when fatigued.

A final consideration in administering a staff development program is providing the administrative mechanism to handle the ordinary problems that occur in all human interaction. For example, some teachers often are not certain about the objectives of the staff development program. Likewise, if a program is not structured in such a way that teachers readily recognize its relevance to their particular situation, they may see the program as a waste of time and energy. Staff development programs for large groups of teachers tend to hinder participation; and not having the best possible presenters creates a negative impression about the program. Finally, all teachers understand the need to evaluate all programs, which is even more important if they are staff development programs. When administrators do their best to deal with such problems effectively, employees will more readily participate and will be more satisfied with the development programs.

Program Evaluation

Effective evaluation is the final phase in a staff development program. Some school districts see this as a rather complicated task involving the multiple applications of statistics; others neglect it entirely. For most programs, a perception-based approach is both appropriate and effective. Participants are asked to rate the instructor or individual conducting the program, the content of the program, how the program was organized, and the time and place of the program presentation.[12]

When a particular program centers on skill or technique acquisition, it is appropriate to conduct a follow-up evaluation after the participants have had the opportunity to implement the techniques or use their new skills. The evaluations are then used in future program planning and also should provide the necessary data to improve the entire staff development program. The controlling effects of program evaluation are as follows:

1. The evaluation of staff development programs should attempt to ascertain if the participants acquired the intended knowledge and skills.
2. The evaluation should attempt to ascertain if the participants utilize their newly acquired knowledge and skills in fulfilling their responsibilities.
3. The evaluation should address the impact that the new knowledge and skills has had on student learning outcomes.[13]

Also, the director of staff development should evaluate the program to ascertain if it is helping to achieve the mandate of the school district as outlined in its goals and objectives. This is a much more complicated process than evaluating a specific course or workshop and must involve the perceptions of the board of education, superintendent of schools, other central-office administrators, and building administrators.

STAFF DEVELOPMENT FOR THE INSTRUCTIONAL STAFF

During the first few decades of this century, boards of education were concerned about encouraging teachers to earn a baccalaureate degree. This orientation changed in the 1970s to one that emphasized the remediation of teacher deficiencies. The current thrust is to provide teachers with the opportunity to maintain a favorable outlook on teaching and to improve their effectiveness in the classroom. At times, it is necessary for principals to recommend certain staff development programs to teachers who are not performing at the level established by the board of education. Therefore, performance appraisal and staff development are complementary aspects of effective supervision. A staff development program can offer the teacher opportunities to:[14]

1. *Update skills and knowledge in a subject area.* The knowledge explosion has created the need to reinterpret and restructure former knowledge. A teacher can no longer assume on the basis of past learning that he or she understands the nuances of a subject area.
2. *Keep abreast of societal demands.* Our society is continually changing. This has presented the teacher with a need to understand and interpret the new demands society is placing on all its institutions and on the school, in particular, and to become acquainted with research on the instructional process and on new methods of teaching. Like other professionals, teachers generally have good intentions of keeping up with the advances that are being made in their field. A shortage of available time often prevents them from carrying out this intention, and a staff development program can meet this need.
3. *Become acquainted with the advances in instructional materials and equipment.* The Internet and computer-assisted instruction are only a few of the many innovations that have potential for improving the quality of classroom instruction.

In the process of assessing teacher needs, the following sources of information can be of considerable help in designing a staff development program. First, the teacher needs assessment survey has been a very effective technique. Most surveys take the form of a checklist containing many areas of possible needs and interests (see Appendix). A second source of information is the community survey, which is administered to parents, usually through a school-based organization such as the Parent-Teacher Association. This survey may reveal parental concerns about a wide range of issues such as grading, student groupings, discipline, and drug use by students. Third, certification requirements vary from state to state and occasionally change. The director of staff development needs to keep all teachers and other certificated employees informed about requirements and should plan appropriate credit courses on both an off-campus and on-campus basis. The human resources master plan also will provide the director with information about the future needs of the district in relation to certain categories of certificated employees.

The final source of information is curricular research. Staff development programs can be planned to correlate with future curriculum changes. Research points to future skills and competencies that can be acquired and gradually introduced to ensure an even transition. The historic report, *A Nation at Risk*, published by the National Commission on Excellence in Education, was the impetus for many states to pass legislation centered on improving the quality of education. Much of this legislation calls for the establishment of professional development committees composed of teachers and other staff members who are responsible for assisting the administration in identifying the staff development needs of teachers. Along with the administration, these committees are also involved in the creation of staff development delivery systems.

STAFF DEVELOPMENT FOR SCHOOL PRINCIPALS

All administrators wonder from time to time about how they will be able to continue meeting the multiple challenges of their job, but school principals are particularly vulnerable because they are on the front line. James L. Olivero, a member of the Association of California School Administrators, wrote an article for the Bulletin of the American Association of School Administrators entitled "Reducing Battle Fatigue—or: Staff Development for School Principals," which significantly addresses this problem. Much of the material in this section was gleaned from this article.[15]

Types of Staff Development Programs

Many studies concerning the ever-changing role of the school principal have been conducted over the last 15 years. These studies have identified the following major areas as appropriate for development programs:

- *Instructional skills.* To effectively evaluate and supervise the instructional process, which includes providing curriculum leadership and securing instructional resources.
- *Management skills.* To establish job objectives and be able to assess the needs of the staff. To be able to identify problem areas and plan towards an effective solution. To be capable of unit budgeting and reviewing priorities in the efficient use of scarce resources.
- *Human relations abilities.* To establish an open, two-way system of communication between students, parents, teachers, and other members of the community. To develop a method of involving parents, students, and teachers in the school-based decision-making process. To create an atmosphere of trust in the school that encourages the staff and students to perform to the best of their abilities.
- *Political and cultural awareness.* To have the ability to identify the leaders within the community and to involve them in school-level decision making. To address with positive techniques the resolution of conflicts between the school and community. To work towards meeting the needs of all clients of the school through school programs.
- *Leadership skills.* Through a plan of self-development, to keep current with advances in the field of education. To share leadership skills with other professionals and with parents and the public.
- *Self-understanding.* To develop a plan of self-improvement through evaluation by the school-based public.

Programming for Principals

Two types of programming can meet the development needs of principals. The first is the traditional vehicle, which includes workshops, conferences, and seminars that usually focus on a single topic and attempt to transmit a given body of information on such issues as new legislation or drug abuse.

A growing number of school districts are taking a more personalized approach to staff development for principals. This second type of program emphasizes acquiring skills that either help principals with their job or enhance their personal development. Programs that emphasize the principal's job could include budget preparation, developing performance objectives, and initiating procedures to improve building maintenance. Programs that emphasize personal growth might address techniques for working with advisory groups, methods of communicating verbally and in writing, stress management, or time management.

Whatever an individual principal identifies as the area of personal need, a prerequisite for success is commitment. Therefore, it is advantageous to write down such personalized programs in a document that includes a personal needs assessment and a plan of action.

Future Directions for the Principal and Staff Development

Dramatic changes have occurred in our society over the last 10 years, and they, in turn, have created a new set of competencies that principals need to acquire. A great many principals today were educated before the emergence of such current trends as cultural pluralism, community involvement, program assessment, instruction-assisted technology, and the inclusion of students with disabilities. These trends, of course, are by no means the end, but rather just the beginning of even more dramatic changes taking place at an accelerated pace. We must be prepared to meet this ongoing challenge in staff development. Effective staff development for principals can be enhanced if the development programs are systematic, concrete, and relevant to the principal's job, including not only what the job is, but what the job should be. Thus, staff development opportunities should be:

- Ongoing and personalized
- Flexible and adaptable to change as the need arises
- Carried out when the participant is not fatigued because of work
- An integral part of the school district's policies and supported by adequate funds

STAFF DEVELOPMENT FOR CLASSIFIED EMPLOYEES

Employee development programs in some school districts are limited to teachers and administrators. Development programs for classified employees have just recently taken hold on a large scale throughout the United States.

Three methods of development are commonly used for classified employees: (1) on-the-job, (2) off-the-job, and (3) apprenticeship training. Because of the nature of their job responsibilities, classified employee development programs are aimed more at training than education. Nevertheless, there is a growing awareness that administrative assistants, custodians, bus drivers, and cafeteria workers will perform more efficiently if they are given the opportunity to participate in personal growth activities. Time management and human relations skills are important abilities for all school district employees, particularly with the current emphasis on community involvement in the schools.

Staff development has a definite orientation for classified employees. It is used not only to update skills, but also to introduce new employees to the requirements and tasks they will be responsible for performing. Classified employees who are promoted to supervisory positions, in most cases, will learn how to handle their new responsibilities through a staff development program. This is also a nuance of development programs for classified employees.

On-the-Job Training

Most training takes place on the job, and in all probability this method is an effective means of training. Besides being the easiest form of training to organize, it is also least costly to operate. Employees are placed in the actual work situation, which makes them feel immediately productive. They learn by doing, which is the most suitable training method for jobs that are difficult to simulate or that can be learned quickly by performance. A significant drawback to on-the-job training is the possibility of future low productivity, because in this setting an individual may never fully develop needed work-related skills when left to work alone.[16]

A modification of on-the-job training is job-instruction training, a more systematic approach to training. This highly effective method consists of the following steps: (1) preparing trainees by telling them about the job, (2) presenting information essential to performing the job, (3) having trainees demonstrate their understanding of the job, and (4) placing trainees in the job on their own and assigning a resource person to assist the trainees if they need help.

Off-the-Job Training

The term *off-the-job training* refers to various kinds of programs, such as lectures, seminars, workshops, case studies, programmed instruction, and simulations. The lecture method is best suited to conveying information such as procedures, methods, and rules. Contrary to common assumptions, lectures can be either highly structured or fairly informal, allowing for a considerable amount of two-way communication.[17]

In the last two decades, there has been an increase in the use of case studies, programmed instruction, and simulation exercises in training programs. The case study allows the employee to study a particular problem in depth. After analyzing the problem, the individual evaluates alternative courses of action and finally selects one that appears to provide the best potential for solving the problem.

Programmed instruction is a method that can be carried out through manuals and textbooks as well as teaching equipment. This approach condenses the material to be learned into a highly organized and logical sequence. The trainee responds to a question or set of circumstances and is provided with immediate feedback, telling the trainee if the response was right or wrong.

Simulations are the most expensive but also most effective method of training. The trainee is placed in an environment that nearly duplicates the actual work situation. This method has been widely used by airlines to train pilots and by schools in driver education classes. By using computer-enhanced instruction, it is possible to simulate a wide variety of job dimensions without risking mistakes in a real-life situation, which might be dangerous or very costly.

Assistant-to Training

The oldest form of training is the apprenticeship, which is commonly referred to as *assistant-to* positions. By this method, a trainee understudies a master worker for a given period of time or until the trainee acquires the necessary skills. Assistant-to positions are common in the skilled trades, but have seldom been used in staff development programs. However, the concept is applicable and is gaining in popularity in educational staff development.[18]

TEACHER CENTERS AND STAFF DEVELOPMENT

In the early 1980s, there were 90 teacher centers operating in the United States under the U.S. Department of Education's Teacher Center Program (Public Law 94-482). This legislation was a direct outgrowth of the strategy employed by the National Education Association in its efforts to help teachers gain more control over curricular innovations. Teacher centers had long existed throughout the world before their emergence in the United States. Although the orientation of such centers varied considerably, many had evolved as a mechanism to help teachers deal with change. With the proliferation of teacher-center literature, many different center models have been initiated in the United States. Many were cooperative endeavors that included centers established by local school districts along with universities. Some state-funded teacher centers also emerged, along with federally funded centers established under Title III of the Elementary and Secondary Education Act.[19]

The U.S. Congress, through the provisions of the Education Amendments of 1976 (PL 94-482, Section 153), funded the establishment of local teacher centers that operated in-service programs aimed at improving the classroom skills and techniques of teachers.

Essentially, a teacher center program is concerned with curriculum development and/or in-service education for elementary and secondary teachers carried out in one or more local education agencies. The Teacher Center Policy Board should be composed primarily of practicing elementary and secondary teachers from the area served. Other membership on a policy board may include administrators, board members, or representatives from institutions of higher education.

Teacher centers were founded on the premise that teachers are self-motivating professionals who are capable of determining their own needs and who, through the policies of the governing board, can best deliver a staff development program to meet these needs. Although the premise is undeniably true, there remain a number of concerns that must be outlined. First, federal funding for teacher centers no longer exists. Second, staff development is a need not only for teachers but also for all employees of a school district. Therefore, a board of education should assume the initial responsibility in providing fiscal resources to develop and administer such programs. Third, teacher centers are essentially delivery systems and should be funded with local and state funds if this is determined to be the most effective way to conduct a staff development program. Teachers, like all employees, must be involved in the entire staff development planning process if such programs are going to meet their needs. This is a normal procedure in all effective staff development programs.

Teacher centers have been a worthwhile innovation for those school districts that lacked an effective staff development program, but they should not be considered a panacea for all school districts. With commitment and proper local and state funding, most school districts are capable of providing adequate programs utilizing a more traditional model administered by a director of staff development.

TECHNOLOGY AND STAFF DEVELOPMENT

Educational administrators searching for information and opportunities to enhance their school districts' staff development programs can find no better online resources than what are available from the National Staff Development Council (www.nsdc.org) and the Association for Supervision and Curriculum Development (www.ascd.org).

The National Staff Development Council (NSCD) provides learning opportunities for individuals, custom designed services for school districts, newsletters, and blogs. The learning opportunities include the annual conference, specialized conferences and institutes. However, the cybertechnological services are centered on custom-designing opportunities that support the job responsibilities of staff development administrators and other administrators charged with staff development responsibilities. The Council will conduct online staff development audits in order to assist school districts as they establish professional development goals and institute programming. On-line coaching is also available for administrators and an effective instrument that administrators can use in setting goals is the Standards Assessment Inventory, which is a research tool that helps districts assess their present effectiveness in meeting well-established staff development standards. In addition, on-line purchasing of books and staff development materials are available. Thus, the staff development opportunities are a mixture of resources that support staff development administrators, superintendents of schools, principals, teachers, and staff members as they fulfill their professional responsibilities.

In like manner, the Association for Supervision and Curriculum Development (ASCD) is an equally important cybertechnological resource for administrators of staff development programs and for the individual development of administrators, teachers, and staff members. In addition to providing conferences and workshops for educators, the LEAP Institute sponsored by ASCD that brings together staff development administrators to present the educational need, concerns, and suggestions to Congress and other national agencies. Information is available on the Web site about national initiatives such as Healthy School Communities and Outstanding Young Educators. The ASCD store contains books, videos, newsletters, and other materials that can be purchased on-line.

There are a number of related Web site links that are helpful in specific ways. For example, www.ascd.org/professional_development.aspx contains information about on-site staff development consulting and on-line courses in such areas as classroom management and various dimensions of learning. Also, www.ascd.org/research_a_topic allows professional development administrators and other educations the opportunity to research specific topics such as neuroscience and what it can teach educators about learning.

IMPLICATIONS FOR SMALL AND MEDIUM-SIZED SCHOOL DISTRICTS

Because many school districts do not have a human resources department or even a human resources administrator, the responsibility for promoting, organizing, and implementing staff development programs falls to the superintendent of schools or building principals or both. Also, because the number of teachers, administrators, and staff members is relatively small in many school districts, the programming for staff development will be targeted to individuals rather than to groups of individuals.

Consequently, the most effective programming will be offered in tandem with the notion of the *learning community*. Thus, self-accountability and collaboration are usually characteristics of staff development programs in such school districts. Of course, the methods of delivery will be enhanced through technology. Furthermore, the model utilized by other professions, tailor-made programming, particularly accommodates teachers and administrators. Attendance at professional conferences and meetings are very important in general and are often staff development-types of experiences. In some areas, a number of school districts may come together for programs that address common concerns. Mentoring is also very appropriate to small and medium-sized school districts. The needs are generally the same throughout all schools and school districts. However, it is only the delivery models that are different, from group to individual design. Thus, the opportunities set forth in the previous section, technology and staff development, are very supportive of small and medium-sized school districts.

THE IMPACT OF GENERATION Y TEACHEERS AND ADMINISTRATORS ON STAFF DEVELOPMENT

Much of the research concerning Generation Y seems to indicate that they are keenly interested in staff development that centers on personal development. This is easily applicable to Generation Y teachers and administrators who are in the business of holistically educating all children. It is a resurgence based upon the premise that the core of a person's individual life is constantly in a state of flux, but purposefully tending towards becoming rather than regressing. This self-awareness of Generation Y teachers and administrators is evident in their lifestyles that appear to be geared towards becoming a well-balanced person capable of controlling their life aspirations. Thus, they are keenly aware of the need for staff development not only for their professional lives, but also for their personal lives.

In pursuing their professional careers, Generation Y also value the principal or superintendent who is willing and capable of coaching them in their professional careers. They want a principal or superintendent whom they can trust and who is an empathetic and genuine professional. They like continual feedback and are appreciative of the value that professional development can make in their professional careers.

Generation Y teachers and administrators are capable of multi-tasking, which means that they can do a good job teaching and mentoring students, engaging colleagues on committees and enjoy being a member of the learning community. They want to have an impact upon their students and colleagues. Thus, Generation Y teachers and administrators are not only appreciative, but also have expectations that a school district will provide them with development opportunities.[20]

Quick Review of Essentials

Change is a constant condition of our American way of life. Improved communications place changes in politics, economics, and science almost as soon as they occur before students and educators. School districts have a mandate to educate the youth of our country. To do so successfully, schools need well-qualified teachers, administrators, and support personnel. No employee will remain qualified in the face of accelerating change without some form of ongoing education and training. This is the impetus behind the recent emphasis on staff development programs.

As a dimension of the human resources function, staff development can be organized according to various structures. Currently, the most effective structure is probably the professional learning community. Such a structure has four major focuses: (1) learning rather than teaching, (2) collaboration, (3) viewing all members of the community as learners, and (4) self-accountability.

Adult learning usually consists of two processes: training and education. Training is designed to teach a sequence of programmed behaviors; education seeks to impart understanding and an ability to interpret knowledge. Both types of learning can occur in a staff development program depending on the objectives to be reached.

In all learning environments, four basic components must be present to ensure success: stimulus, response, reinforcement, and motivation.

Creating a staff development program consists of six separate but sequential processes: (1) establishing school district goals and objectives, which become the foundation of the program; (2) assessing the needs of the school district employees to determine if there is a discrepancy between the competencies of the staff and the requirements of the organization; (3) establishing staff development goals and objectives; (4) designing a program that will meet the staff development requirements; (5) implementing the designed plan in such a way that effective learning may occur; and (6) evaluating the program to ascertain if it is meeting its objectives, which in turn will affect future program design.

A staff development program for the instructional staff focuses upon updating subject area skills and knowledge in order to improve instruction; outlining societal demands and changes; presenting the findings of research on teaching methods and practices; and updating teachers on the advances in instructional materials and equipment.

In assessing the needs of teachers, four sources of information may be helpful: (1) the teacher needs assessment survey, (2) community surveys, (3) certification information, and (4) research and curricular studies.

In the last decade the school principalship has experienced multiple challenges brought on by such trends as cultural pluralism, community involvement, program assessment, instruction-assisted technology, and the inclusion of students with disabilities. A study conducted in California identified the following areas as appropriate for principal development programs: instructional skills, management skills, human relations abilities, political and cultural awareness, leadership skills, and self-understanding.

Besides the traditional models of staff development for principals, which include workshops and seminars, many school districts are taking a more personalized approach directed at helping principals acquire skills that relate simultaneously to their job and their personal development.

Staff development programs have been limited to the professional staff in many school districts. However, all employees can profit from development programs, and classified employees should have the opportunity to increase their skills and participate in personal growth activities. Newly hired and promoted classified employees can be inducted into the responsibilities of their positions through a staff development program. The three most commonly used methods are (1) on-the-job training, (2) off-the-job training, and (3) apprenticeship training.

An innovation in staff development programming was the emergence of teacher centers, which was a direct result of Public Law 94-482, Section 153. These federally funded centers were locally governed and operated and were aimed at improving the instructional techniques of teachers.

Selected Further Readings

Association for Supervision and Curriculum Development, 2009 (www.ascd.org).

Dall'Alba, Gloria and Jörgen Sandberg, "Unveiling Professional Development: A Critical Review of Stage Models," *Review of Educational Research*, 76, no. 3 (Fall 2006), 383–412.

Davis, E. A. and J. S. Krajcik, "Designing Educative Curriculum Materials to Promote Teacher Learning," *Educational Researcher*, 34, no. 3 (2005), 2–14.

Firestone, William A., Melinda M. Mangin, M. Cecilia Martinez, and Terrie Polovsky, "Leading Coherent Professional Development: A Comparison of Three Districts," *Educational Administration Quarterly*, 41, no. 3 (August 2005), 413–448.

Husby, Vicki R. *Individualizing Professional Development: A Framework for Meeting School and District Goals*. Thousand Oaks, California: Corwin Press, 2005.

Kirkpatrick, Donald L., and James D. Kirkpatrick. *Evaluating Training Programs: The Four Levels*, 3rd ed. San Francisco: Berrett-Koehler Publishers, 2006.

Lawless, Kimberly A., and James W. Pellegrino, "Professional Development in Integrating Technology into Teaching and Learning: Knowns, Unknowns, and Ways to Pursue Better Questions and Answers," *Review of Educational Research*, 77, no. 4 (2007), 575–614.

Martin, Vivien and Joyce Barlow, "Staff Development for a More Inclusive Curriculum," *Learning and Teaching in Higher Education*, 3 (2007–08), 3–19.

National Staff Development Council, 2009 (www.nsdc.org).

Penuel, William R., Barry J. Fishman, Ryoko Yamaguchi, and Lawrence P. Gallagher, "What Makes Professional Development Effective? Strategies that Foster Curriculum Implementation," *American Educational Research Journal*, 44, no. 4 (December 2007), 921–958.

Senge, Peter M. *The Fifth Discipline: The Art & Practice of the Learning Organization*. New York: Currency, 2006.

CHAPTER 7

Performance Evaluation

FOCUS SCENARIO

You are the assistant superintendent for human resources in a school district with approximately 500 teachers and 250 support personnel. This is the same school district that was described in the previous problem scenario. The school district is very stable. Parents and other citizens have been supportive of the district in terms of passing tax levy and bond issue referendums. The school district experienced significant growth in the 1950s and 1960s, but experienced a decrease in student population in the 1970s and 1980s. This was due to the fact that the houses in the district had appreciated in value to the point that younger families with children could not afford to buy homes in the district, and the empty-nesters did not have any interest in leaving the district because their home mortgages were paid.

This situation caused the school district to lose enrollment, and thus, the district was forced to lay off younger teachers. The administrators, teachers, and support personnel had become rather set in their ways and were in need of staff development programs that would help them renew their enthusiasm and bring them up-to-date on current best practice in administering and teaching children. The local Teachers' Association had endorsed the need of the district to rethink its staff development commitment and programming. Furthermore, the administrators and teachers had a positive attitude towards this end and were ready and willing to participate in staff development.

However, it became obvious to the board of education and the superintendent of schools that there were some teachers who were not interested in improving their instructional methodology, nor interested in learning best practice in updating the curriculum. Because of this situation, the board of education mandated the development of a new performance evaluation process that focused more directly on the learning instructional process from a learning community perspective. Also, the board of education mandated the review and updating of the employee termination process to focus upon the accountability of administrators to initiate more effective procedural due process procedures.

The evaluation of teacher performance is as old as the education profession. However, for the most part, only three stages of historical development in American education during this century were concerned with the formal evaluation of teachers. During the 1920s, the efforts were primarily centered on analyzing if a given teaching style correlated with the philosophy and psychology of William James or John Dewey. The second stage was more concerned with ascribing certain personality traits as being related to excellence in teaching. The final stage, which appeared in the 1960s and persisted through the 1970s, emphasized generic teaching behaviors that would be effective in all instructional settings. The research in this area coined such catch words as *structured* and *task-oriented* when speaking about the types of teacher behavior that produced effective student outcomes.

In 1976, the National Institute of Education, in a request for proposals, called for a new approach to the definition of effective teacher training. This signaled the growth of a movement to license teachers on the basis of competencies and performance rather than on the completion of a teacher education program at an accredited college or university. Obviously, such an approach is predicated on a preconceived notion of what constitutes effective teaching.

The last decade has ushered in a dramatic change in the entire concept of quality teaching that is centered on the relationship between teacher qualifications, teacher preparation, teaching performance, and educational outcomes.[1] In addition, an ongoing trend requires more accountability at all levels of performance. School board members are also subject to this trend towards accountability, which has developed to the point that school employees, parents, and even organizations support specific candidates in school board elections because of their dissatisfaction with the policies of particular board members.

The systems approach to management, which has been used extensively by industry and received a big boost in the early 1960s when Robert S. McNamara advocated its use in the U.S. Department of Defense, shifted the emphasis away from the traditional concept of teacher evaluation to the broader concept of employee evaluation management. Evaluation by objectives has become a touchstone. This implies that an employee can be effectively evaluated only within the context of attaining certain pre-established objectives. Establishing these objectives is part of the overall process of determining the organizational objectives of the school district.

Because of the integral relationship between all employees and because one employee's performance can affect the performance of other employees, all personnel should be evaluated. This begins with the evaluation of the superintendent of schools by the board of education and proceeds down through the chain of command, with each administrator evaluating those employees reporting to her or him. This process applies not only to the professional staff but also to classified employees, whose performance should be evaluated by their immediate supervisors.

It is important for all employees to recognize the positive nature of performance evaluation. Of the six reasons for evaluation given below, only number five could be interpreted as being negative. However, it is a positive reason because students are entitled to the best services possible. Thus, it is not the reasons that make performance evaluation a negative experience, but rather, in some school districts, it is the manner in which it is carried out. Procedural due process is an important element because it ensures fairness and the positive effects of performance evaluation.

This is the role that is played by teacher and labor unions; it is also the role of negotiated master contracts. Performance evaluation is always considered to be a management prerogative process. However, a master contract negotiated by a teacher or labor union will certainly include a clause on procedural due process that helps to protect employees' rights to fairness The following statements set forth the positive dimensions of performance evaluation.

1. Evaluation fosters the self-development of each employee.
2. Evaluation helps to identify a variety of tasks that an employee is capable of performing.
3. Evaluation helps to identify staff development needs.
4. Evaluation helps to improve performance.
5. Evaluation helps to determine if an employee should be retained in the school district and how large a salary increase he or she should be given.
6. Evaluation helps to determine the placement, transfer, or promotion of an employee.

Parents and taxpayers are demanding increased accountability in employee performance; employees also are demanding accountability in the evaluation methods and techniques used in their evaluations. Administrators and supervisors are being asked to defend their evaluations and the procedures they used in making them. Consequently, it is extremely important to develop a consistent benchmark in establishing an evaluation process.

The benchmark is the "job description" under which an individual was employed. Thus, employees are evaluated in relation to their job descriptions, which is the only defensible criterion against which performance should be measured.[2] Although this does not mean that a given job position will remain unchanged, it does imply that a revised job description may be needed if a job has undergone considerable modification.

A significant distinction must be made at this point to avoid confusion. This chapter is addressing the evaluation process from a central-office perspective with emphasis on the development of procedures, on the use of instruments and methods, and on the legal considerations of the process. It is not concerned with supervision as a task of the principal and other administrators. Supervision addresses the human interaction between teachers and administrators, an interaction that is required of the principal in fulfilling his or her role as the instructional leader within a particular school.

DEVELOPING A PERFORMANCE EVALUATION PROCESS

The ultimate goal of all school districts is to educate children and adolescents. How this is accomplished depends upon a multitude of subordinate goals and objectives. It is not only organizationally appropriate, but also legally wise for a school board to establish a policy statement on employee appraisal that will serve as one of these supportive goals. Such a policy gives direction to the various administrative divisions of the school district in their development of organizational objectives. A policy statement might read:

> Recognizing that quality education for the children and adolescents of this school district depends upon the level of teacher, administrator, and staff member performance, the board of education directs the superintendent of schools to develop and implement a process for employee evaluation.
>
> This process must address as its first priority the impartial and objective evaluation of individual employees, in relation to the requirements of their positions within the school district. A second priority is to analyze how these positions help to actualize and support the instructional goals and objectives of this school board.

Thus, organizational context is critical to the development and attainment of both school and school district goals.[3] The three major divisions in most school districts are human resources, instruction, and support services. Following the organizational structure outlined in Chapter 1, the assistant superintendents for human resources, administrative services, secondary education, elementary education, and instructional services must develop divisional objectives. In the human resources division, objectives might center on improving recruitment techniques, human resource planning methods, or interviewing procedures. The administrative services division could establish objectives in business management aimed at constructing a more effective investment schedule. The transportation component of this division might work on fuel-efficient bus routing, which would free up funds to improve other areas in the organization.

It is certainly obvious that this procedure of developing objectives may reach a level of refinement within a division that would reach down to component objectives developed by directors (director of federal programs, director of special education, director of pupil personnel services, and so on). This is a procedure that is followed in some school districts. However, individual school districts may not need this level of refinement and divisional objectives could be sufficient—the assumption being employed in this chapter.

After divisional objectives have been established by the appropriate assistant superintendents, all employees in that division are responsible for developing personal objectives that support the divisional objectives. An assistant superintendent for secondary education might see a need to be present more often in the schools to observe operations firsthand. This would constitute a personal objective to be accomplished over a given period of time. A high school teacher of U.S. history might develop an objective aimed at using more audiovisual techniques in lesson presentations. A custodian might attempt to reorganize the floor waxing schedule to make better use of work time when students are not in school. This constitutes an objective for the custodian.

The next step in the evaluation development process is to decide upon formal evaluation procedures. These procedures should be in written form and made available to the entire staff. A concern often voiced by employees is that they were not adequately informed about the evaluation process. Because evaluation procedures are applicable to all school district employees, a common practice is to incorporate them into the board of education policy manual that is distributed to all employees when they are hired. Other school districts have employee handbooks that outline working conditions and specify the procedures and forms used in the evaluation process.

Developing the actual procedures is a task that is best performed by involving employee representatives who both evaluate and will be evaluated. This committee approach produces a sense of involvement and accountability that will help to defend evaluation procedures in the face of possible criticism. It is appropriate to divide the employees of the school district into two groups, professional and classified, when organizing the evaluation development committees. The work situations of these two groups are significantly different and consequently may necessitate different evaluation procedures. It is more defensible to have committee members elected by the employees they represent than to have them appointed. If a school district's employees belong to unions or professional associations, it would be appropriate to have these organizations appoint representatives to serve on the committees.

The number of committee members will vary depending on the size of the school district, the number of employees represented, and the number of unions and associations active in the district. However, the most important consideration is that the committee be composed of an odd number of members such as three, five, seven, or nine, which will avoid the possibility of deadlocked decisions. Of course, the procedures will be tailored to the needs of the individual school district. However, the following questions should be addressed in every set of procedures:

- Who, by position, has the primary responsibility for making evaluations? (Examples: assistant superintendent for elementary education, principals, director of transportation, director of food service.)
- Who is evaluated by these designated positions? (Examples: assistant superintendent for secondary education evaluates secondary school principals; building principals evaluate teachers; director of maintenance evaluates carpenters.)

- In what settings will formal evaluations take place? (Examples: a teacher will be evaluated in the classroom when he or she is teaching a lesson; a principal will be evaluated in how he or she conducts a staff meeting.)
- On how many occasions will formal evaluations occur? (Examples: tenured teachers will be evaluated on one formal occasion each year; probationary teachers will be evaluated at a minimum on two formal occasions.)
- In what setting will the results of formal evaluations be communicated to the person evaluated? (Examples: in a conference immediately after the evaluation in the teacher's classroom; in a conference held in the principal's office at the end of each semester.)
- If an employee disagrees with his or her evaluation, what grievance procedure should be available? (Examples: written rebuttal may be attached to the evaluation form; appeal may be made to the superintendent.)
- What effect will evaluation have on salary increase? (Examples: a teacher with an excellent rating may receive a double step on the salary schedule; an employee may receive a merit increase in addition to a step increase on the salary schedule.)

The final step in the evaluation process is analysis of the results that have been obtained through employee evaluations to determine if division objectives are being met. If objectives have not been reached, and if they are still relevant to implementing the objectives and goals of the school board, the divisional objectives should be retargeted. This suggests that the employee objectives apparently did not support the divisional objectives and should be realigned to support them. If both the divisional and employee objectives have been realized, new objectives can be identified that will further the goals of the organization and the development of individual employees. Figure 7.1 is a schematic representation of the evaluation process.

There are a number of popular evaluation techniques that have not been addressed in this section, such as self-evaluation, peer evaluation, and student evaluation. These

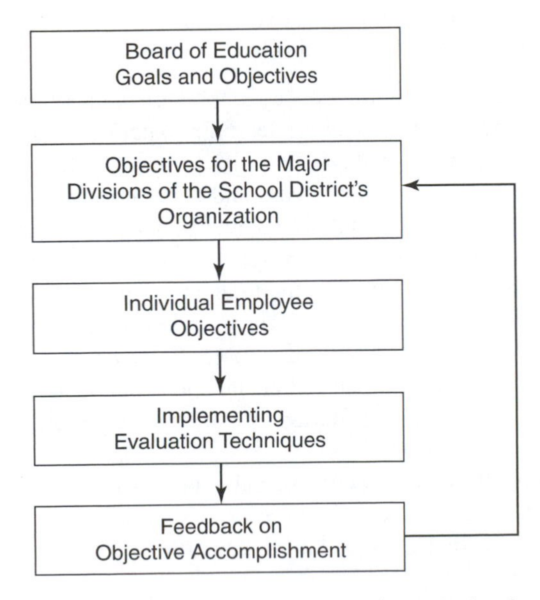

FIGURE 7.1 Model for Developing an Employee Evaluation Process

techniques are aimed more at personal growth and do not directly affect the evaluation process from a central-office perspective. They are referred to more properly as supervisory techniques.

THE CONSTRUCTION OF PERFORMANCE EVALUATION INSTRUMENTS

As with the development of evaluation procedures, evaluation instruments should be constructed by the committee process. Many management consulting firms have developed evaluation forms that are easily adapted to the requirements of a given school district. However, the construction of evaluation forms is not a difficult task, particularly with the many prototypes available for the asking from neighboring school districts.

The basic format of an evaluation instrument has certain theoretical overtones. Most authors recognize two basic categories: trait forms and result forms. In the trait approach, the employee is rated against a predetermined list of indicators in order to ascertain his or her level of performance. The results method compares the employee's performance against goals and objectives that were developed by the employee and agreed to by his or her supervisor. Using instructional assessment, the teachers and supervisor can document how the goals and objectives were reached.[4]

Many school districts are using standards that have been developed by several professional associations as guides in constructing performance-based evaluation instruments. The Interstate New Teacher Assessment and Support Consortium (INTASC) standards developed under the auspices of the Council of Chief State School Officers are currently considered to be best practice for licensure requirements in many states. INTASC standards are also compatible with the advanced certification standards of the new National Board for Professional Teaching Standards. These standards can be transformed into performance criteria.

Representatives from the teaching profession, colleges and universities, and representatives from a number of state educational agencies developed the INTASC standards. What follows are the ten core standards that INTASC considers essential for all teachers without regard to the subject or grade level that they teach:

1. The teacher understands the central concepts, tools of inquiry, and structures of the discipline(s) he or she teaches and can create learning experiences that make these aspects of subject matter meaningful for students.
2. The teacher understands how children learn and develop, and can provide learning opportunities that support their intellectual, social, and personal development.
3. The teacher understands how students differ in their approaches to learning and creates instructional opportunities that are adapted to diverse learners.
4. The teacher understands and uses a variety of instructional strategies to encourage students' development of critical thinking, problem solving, and performance skills.
5. The teacher uses an understanding of individual and group motivation and behavior to create a learning environment that encourages positive social interaction, active engagement in learning, and self-motivation.
6. The teacher uses knowledge of effective verbal, nonverbal, and media communication techniques to foster active inquiry, collaboration, and supportive interaction in the classroom.
7. The teacher plans instruction based on knowledge of subject matter, students, the community, and curriculum goals.

8. The teacher understands and uses formal and informal assessment strategies to evaluate and ensure the continuous intellectual, social, and physical development of the learner.
9. The teacher is a reflective practitioner who continually evaluates the effect of his or her choices and actions upon others (students, parents, and other professionals in the learning community) and who actively seeks out opportunities to grow professionally.
10. The teacher fosters relationships with school colleagues, parents, and agencies in the larger community to support students' learning and well-being.[5]

There are also standards for art education, elementary education, English language arts, foreign languages, mathematics, science, social studies, and special education. The developers of the INTASC standards also developed knowledge, dispositions, and performance indicators.[6]

The appendices to this chapter exhibit a number of trait instruments that have roots in standards, knowledge, dispositions, and performance similar to those developed by INTASC. The focus may be different given the specific issues and concerns of individual school districts and individual state agencies. This is as it should be, because standards and indicators are only guides that must be individualized by school districts and state agencies.

The State Board of Education and the Department of Public Instruction of North Carolina have adopted the INTASC standards for licensure, but have developed their own indicators. However, the construction of the indicators has been guided not only by the standards but also by the knowledge, dispositions, and performance indicators. Here, for example, are the North Carolina Key Indicators for the first INTASC standard:

The candidate:

- Demonstrates an understanding of the central concepts of his or her discipline
- Uses explanations and representations that link curriculum to prior learning
- Evaluates resources and curriculum materials for appropriateness to the curriculum and instructional delivery
- Engages students in interpreting ideas from a variety of perspectives
- Uses interdisciplinary approaches to teaching and learning
- Uses methods of inquiry that are central to the discipline[7]

This author believes that the most appropriate method of evaluating performance is to use a trait instrument to ascertain overall performance and to target objectives to specify needed improvement in performance. The results method also helps to ascertain if employee objectives are supporting divisional and school board objectives. Employee objectives can be developed easily if overall performance has been measured. Although the simultaneous use of trait instruments and objectives is not a common practice, the exclusive use of one or the other has never proven in experience to be superior. Appendices B, D, and E at the end of this chapter represent various trait formats that have wide use in educational organizations.

Job descriptions play an important role in constructing appraisal instruments and in the development of objectives. The job requirements of a position are the legal parameters within which evaluation must be confined. An employee performs job requirements to an acceptable, unacceptable, or superior level. To require an employee to assume responsibilities that are not within his or her job description and to evaluate how he or she carries out these responsibilities is poor management. The dismissal of an employee because he or she did not perform responsibilities omitted from the job description may not hold up in court.

EMPLOYEE DISCIPLINE

The term *discipline* is often used with a negative connotation. However, the term itself refers to a condition in an organization created by employees conducting themselves according to the rules and regulations of the organization and in a socially accepted manner. Most individuals are self-disciplined and have little difficulty in following rules and regulations. Also, fellow employees can exert significant pressure on people who violate socially accepted norms. Using inappropriate language is a typical example of conduct offensive to most people.

There are two areas of misconduct that call for some action on the part of management: excessive absence from work and inappropriate on-the-job behavior. *Absenteeism* has become a major issue costing literally millions of dollars. Many theories have been proposed for this change in work ethic. However, the cause is usually rooted in the person, who must take responsibility for his or her actions.

Inappropriate on-the-job behavior is meant to cover a variety of offenses such as carelessness, failure to use safety devices, fighting, and alcohol and drug abuse. There are a number of variables that affect the seriousness of absenteeism and inappropriate on-the job behavior. The administration must consider the nature of the problem, its duration and frequency, the employee's work history, and other extenuating factors. However, it is clear to all practicing administrators that a response must be made that will correct the problem.

The response of the administration to such problems must be corrective rather than punitive; and the action taken must be progressive if it is to withstand the test of "due process." For example, if a custodian is tardy for work two times within a given week, the custodial supervisor should give that custodian a verbal warning. If the custodian is late the following week, the supervisor should then present the custodian with a written warning. If the tardiness continues for a third week, the custodian should be suspended from work for a week without pay. If the inappropriate behavior continues after the suspension period, the supervisor must continue with progressive discipline involving demotion, a pay cut, and finally, dismissal.

In terminating the employment of a person, it is critical for the supervisor and a designated staff member from the human resources department to carefully review the documentation of the reasons for the termination with the school district's attorney for assurance that defensible and appropriate procedures were followed. In preparing for the meeting at which the employee will be informed that his or her employment with the school district is being terminated, the individual's supervisor and a human resources staff member should have completed all the necessary reports and documents along with obtaining the individual's final paycheck. It is always important to have two people present at the meeting who will be representing the school district, usually the person's supervisor and a staff member from the human resources department. This provides a witness to the proceedings which may be important in the event of a lawsuit filed against the school district by the fired employee. It may be helpful to role-play what will take place at the meeting, including the anticipated reaction of the person to be fired.

Selection of the time and place of the meeting is important because the objective is to conduct the meeting in the most pleasant way possible for the person being fired and in the least disruptive way possible to other employees. For example, Monday afternoon may be the most appropriate time to have the meeting because the fired person will be able to use the rest of the week to search for another job, whereas Friday afternoon might result in intensifying the person's anger during the weekend. Immediately after the meeting, district property should be returned and, after the individual collects his or her personal property, the dismissed person should be escorted out of the building by either the supervisor or the human resources staff member.

At the meeting, it is important to tell the person why he or she is being dismissed. Of course, the person is entitled to ask questions for clarification but it is not the time to defend the decision. However, during the meeting it is important to explain the school district's appeal process. This is also the time to discuss issues such as severance pay and legal benefits that are available to dismissed employees.[8]

In a school district with a collective-negotiated master agreement, such a progressive disciplinary process should be clearly outlined in the agreement. This type of disciplinary process is very effective with classified personnel such as custodians, cooks, and bus drivers, but it is not very useful with teachers and administrators. Therefore, the following section deals with the due process that is more appropriately applied to certificated staff members. Both processes, however, may lead to the same outcome, termination of employment. It is important to keep in mind that a progressive discipline process does not supersede the evaluation process. Rather, it is a method of dealing with problems that cannot wait to be dealt with through the normal evaluation process.

DEVELOPING TERMINATION PROCEDURES

A universally accepted purpose for evaluating an individual's performance is to make a determination concerning the desirability of retaining that person as an employee of the school district. A decision to dismiss an employee, of course, is extremely difficult to make because of the importance of employment to a person's welfare and also because of the effects such a decision has on the employee's dependents.

Employment counselors have seen the devastating financial and psychological effects that getting fired has on a person's life. In fact, the trauma usually centers on the individual's self-concept. Feelings of inadequacy, failure, self-contempt, and anger are common to people who have their employment terminated. Although most individuals are able to cope with such a situation, others never fully recover from such an experience. Consequently, it is not only good human resources management, but also a humane responsibility for school district administrators to develop termination procedures that are objective and fair, and that incorporate a due process that gives employees the opportunity to modify or defend their behavior. The Missouri State Statutes Governing Revocation of License, Contract Management, and Termination Procedures present a model that is being used here to explicate the nuances of due process and the grounds for terminating employment. Although the statutes pertain specifically to teachers, the concepts explained are applicable to other categories of employees.

Grounds for Terminating the Employment of Tenured Teachers

A tenured teacher may have his or her employment terminated for one or more of the following causes: physical or mental condition unfitting him or her to instruct or associate with children; immoral conduct; insubordination, inefficiency, or incompetency in the line of duty; willful or persistent violation of, or failure to obey, the state laws pertaining to schools; willful or persistent violation of the published policies and procedures of the school board; excessive or unreasonable absence from work; conviction of a felony or a crime involving moral turpitude.

The first cause listed must be understood within the context of the Rehabilitation Act of 1973. A disability does not constitute a physical condition that may in any way be construed as unfitting an individual from associating with children or students. In fact, the prevalent interpretation of the law is that an aide must be hired to assist an employee if the employee's disability interferes with the instruction or supervision of children. The only possible physical condition that would prevent an employee from associating with children is the contracting of a contagious disease. This would be a potential cause for dismissal only if the individual refused to get medical treatment and insisted on working while he or she was contagious. Emotional illness that produces dangerous or bizarre behavior is also a potential cause for dismissal if the employee refuses to receive medical treatment and insists on working while ill. In both cases, documentation from a physician is necessary to proceed with the termination process. Of course, the school district is responsible for all expenses incurred in securing the expert opinion of the physician.

Immoral conduct must be judged within the context of local standards, but also must be reasonable and consistent with recent court decisions. A number of significant court cases have been reviewed and form the foundation for the following principles that should be used in judging employee conduct. First, the health of the pupil-teacher relationship is the criterion for judging employee behavior. A teacher or other employee who establishes a relationship with a student that goes beyond friendship and is exhibited in some form of "dating" is unacceptable. Second, illegal sexual acts are cause for immediate suspension. If an employee is convicted of performing such an act, his employment with the district must be terminated. Suspension is a justifiable practice while investigating allegations of sexual misconduct, if the employee receives his or her salary during this period. Third, private nonconventional sexual lifestyles are not a cause for employee dismissal. For example, homosexuality or cohabitation outside of matrimony may be unacceptable to many people in the community, but they do not inherently affect an individual's performance in the workplace. These and other practices are displayed publicly on television and in other media, which to an extent has nullified their impact on students. Fourth, if an employee advocates nonconventional sexual lifestyles at school, the employee has placed himself or herself in a position where termination is possible, because such lifestyles are in direct conflict with local standards.

Insubordination in the line of duty is always a cause for dismissal. Although the interpretation of what constitutes insubordination may appear to be self-evident, insubordination has restricted application. Employees can be insubordinate only if they refuse to comply with a directive of their supervisor that is clearly within their job expertise. If a principal asks a teacher to supervise the children on the playground during the teacher's preparation time and the teacher refuses, the teacher is insubordinate because teachers have the job-related responsibility of supervising children. On the other hand, if the principal were to direct a custodian to supervise the children on the playground and he refused, the custodian would not be guilty of insubordination because this is not within his occupational expertise. Nor would it be insubordination if a teacher refused to fill in for the principal's secretary, who was absent from work because of illness. The teacher was not hired to perform secretarial functions and may refuse this directive. The manner in which an employee responds to a directive does not usually constitute insubordination if the employee performs the task. Thus, if a teacher responds in a sharp tone to the principal when assigned to playground duty, but obeys the directive, the teacher is not guilty of insubordination.

Inefficiency is relatively easy to document. It usually refers to the inability of an individual to manage those tasks that are integral to a job responsibility. A teacher who never takes class attendance or who cannot account for the equipment, books, or materials assigned to his or her class is obviously inefficient. A principal who is always late in turning in building budgets or other reports also falls into this category.

Incompetency is perhaps the most difficult cause to document in terminating an employee. It also is directly related to the formal evaluation process. If a tenured teacher is performing in an incompetent manner, it means that he or she is hindering the instructional-learning process. The evaluations made by the principal must clearly indicate that major deficiencies have been identified and that objectives to remedy these deficiencies have not been met.

Claiming willful or persistent violation of state school laws or board of education policies and procedures as a cause for termination presupposes that school district employees have been informed of these. An effective method of notifying employees about these laws, policies, and procedures is through the publication and distribution of a handbook or manual that clearly outlines the employee's responsibilities.

Excessive or unreasonable absence from work is a relative circumstance that can be substantiated only through a policy defining what is meant by excessive or unreasonable. Local school boards probably will rely on patterns of absences in making their determination. Five consecutive days per month over a year's span, for example, could be considered excessive if the employee is not suffering from a chronic physical condition that interferes with attendance at work.

Conviction of a felony is obviously a reason to terminate the employment of an individual. The conviction for a crime involving moral turpitude, however, requires some explanation. Prostitution is usually classified as a misdemeanor, but because it involves morally offensive conduct according to most community standards, it is a reason to terminate a tenured teacher. The selling of pornography or a conviction for the use or sale of drugs also falls within the definition of moral turpitude.

In 1989, Congress passed the Drug-Free Workplace Act, which gives employers the choice of rehabilitating or dismissing staff members working in federal grant programs who are convicted of drug abuse offenses in the workplace. This law and federal administrative regulations require school districts to maintain a drug-free work environment by explicitly prohibiting employees from manufacturing, distributing, dispensing, possessing, or using unlawful drugs in the workplace. In addition, schools must also provide a drug-free awareness program, which must include a description of the dangers of drug abuse, notification of the new requirements and penalties for violations, and information on available employee assistance programs. Employees must inform their supervisor within five days of a criminal conviction for a workplace drug crime. Job applicants must inform a potential employer of prior workplace drug conviction.

It is becoming common practice for school districts to give a second chance to persons convicted of a workplace drug offense by offering them the services of a drug rehabilitation program. This also points out the growing necessity of employee assistance programs as a voluntary fringe benefit for all employees. The Drug-free Workplace Act also gives school district administrators the right to require persons to be tested for drugs when there is reason to suspect that these individuals are using or are under the influence of drugs on school premises or at school functions.[9]

Notification of Charges against a Tenured Teacher

After a behavior has been identified that could result in the termination of an employee, the next step in a due process is notification. This is a formal procedure of serving the employee with written charges specifying the alleged grounds that, if not corrected, will eventuate in dismissal. It must be kept in mind that notification with an opportunity to correct behavior is applicable only to charges arising out of incompetency, inefficiency, or insubordination in the line of duty. Physical or mental conditions as described in the previous section, immoral conduct, violation of school laws or board of education policies and procedures, excessive absences, and conviction of a felony or crime involving moral turpitude require a hearing before termination of employment, but they obviously do not require a period of time to correct the behavior. The behavior has already gone beyond what is rectifiable in an educational setting. A hearing is required, however, to determine if the facts substantiate the allegation.

Notification of charges, which is an extremely formal process, must not be confused with evaluation procedures that permit an employee the right to disagree with a written evaluation. As a normal course of action, employees may attach a written rebuttal to the evaluation instrument, setting forth points of disagreement and including any documentation to support their position.

Time periods are an essential component of the notification process. Three time periods are specified in these statutes: (1) a 30-day period during which time the employee has an opportunity to modify behavior; (2) a 20-day period before a hearing is held, which allows the employee time to gather evidence supporting his or her position; and (3) a 10-day period after service of a hearing on the teacher during which time he or she must respond to the notification that he or she wishes to have the hearing. If the employee does not wish to have a hearing on the charges, the board of education may terminate his or her employment with the school district by a majority vote of the board members.

This statute also sets forth another common practice in termination proceedings. The teacher may be suspended with pay after notice of a hearing until the board of education makes a determination concerning the employment of the teacher.

Termination Hearing on Charges against a Tenured Teacher

This statute outlines a procedure that must be followed in conducting a hearing that might eventuate in the dismissal of a tenured teacher. Once again, these statutes present a model that is applicable to all termination proceedings:

1. The hearing shall be held in a public forum. There is a distinction between a public hearing and a hearing held in public. At a public hearing, those in attendance are usually allowed to address those conducting the hearing according to pre-established procedures; at a hearing held in a public forum, only those representing the party making the allegation and those representing the party against whom the allegation is made are allowed to speak and participate in the hearing.
2. Both parties may be represented by an attorney, who may cross-examine witnesses.
3. The testimony given at a hearing shall be under oath. Government agencies such as school districts are usually allowed the privilege of administering oaths in official proceedings. Normally, the president or secretary of the board of education is the official so empowered.
4. The board of education may subpoena witnesses and documentary evidence requested by the teacher. As with the power to administer oaths, school districts usually have subpoena rights and may limit the number of witnesses called on behalf of the teacher or school district administrators.
5. The proceedings at the hearing should be recorded by a stenographer employed by the school district. A tape recording of the hearing is usually acceptable in lieu of a stenographer. A transcript of the proceedings must be made available not only to the school board, but also to the teacher. The transcript of a hearing held in public should be open to public inspection.

6. Except for the fee paid to the attorney representing the teacher, all expenses for conducting the hearing should be paid by the school district.
7. The decision by the board of education should be reached within a pre-established time period to ensure fair treatment of the employee.

The board of education is exercising judicial authority in conducting the hearing and reaching a decision on the possible dismissal of a tenured teacher. This is a unique circumstance because the school board acts in two capacities: prosecution, in the sense that the charges are brought against the employee in the name of the school board; and judiciary, because the school board renders the decision. In this respect the board of education is reviewing its own action. Consequently, it is extremely important to demonstrate, as much as possible, impartiality in the hearing structure. The evidence should be presented by an attorney representing the building principal and other line administrators because these administrators have the responsibility for evaluating and reviewing employee performance.

The room should be arranged to clearly delineate the functions that will be exercised at the hearing. The board of education will occupy a central place in the room seated at a table. A second table with a chair could be set up perhaps ten to fifteen feet in front of and facing the board members where witnesses will give testimony. To either side of the board table and facing each other should be two tables: seated at one, the teacher and his or her attorney; and at the other, the appropriate administrator with the school district's attorney. Those in attendance should be seated in a manner that clearly indicates that they are observers and not participants in the proceedings.

Another mechanism sometimes used in lieu of a formal hearing when discussing the possible termination of an employee is an executive session board meeting. Most states have statutes permitting government bodies to hold such private meetings at which public attendance is excluded. If a teacher or any employee is confronted with documentary evidence that could possibly result in his or her termination and if that employee had been given notice that his or her behavior must be modified, it may be possible to invite the employee to discuss his or her lack of improvement at an executive session of the school board. If the employee resigns in the face of the documentation, the expense and potential embarrassment of a public hearing are avoided.

Figure 7.2, Evaluation of a Permanent Teacher, schematically represents the relationship between the statutes elucidated in this section concerning the termination of a tenured teacher.

Appeal by a Tenured Teacher to a Termination Decision Issued by the Board of Education

Because school districts are state government agencies, appeal from the decision of a school board is made to the state circuit court, which is the court of original jurisdiction in state civil and criminal matters. In most states this appeal must be made within a set period of time. All evidence, documentation, records, and the transcript of the hearing probably will be requested by the court. Of course, the employee has the right to appeal the decision of the circuit court, as in all civil cases, through to a court of appeals and Supreme Court if there is a justifiable reason.

Termination Procedures for Probationary Teachers

A distinction must be made from the very beginning of this section between terminating the employment of a probationary teacher and not renewing a probationary teacher's contract. In the latter situation no formal due process is necessary; the employer-employee relationship simply ceases to

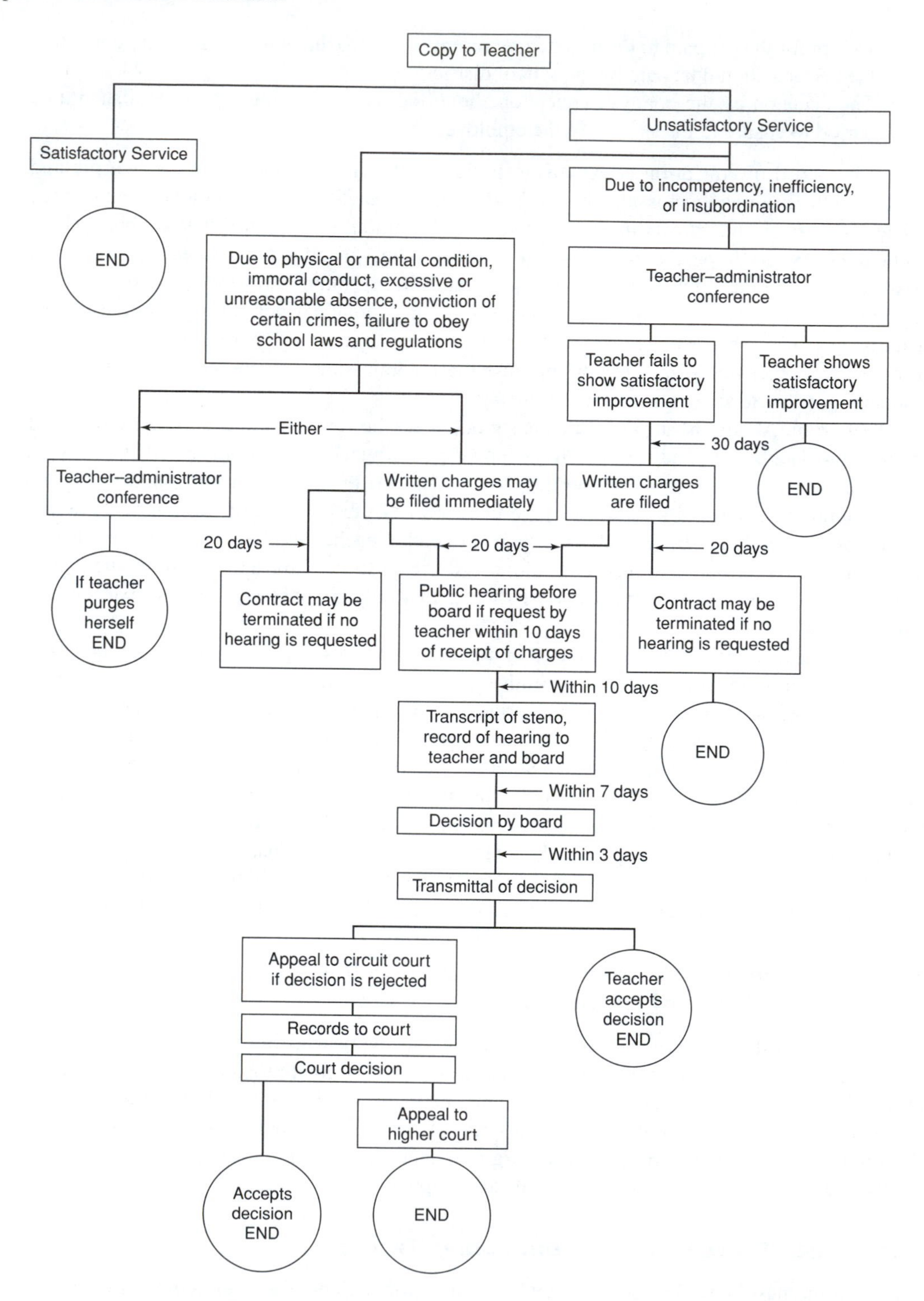

FIGURE 7.2 Evaluation of a Permanent Teacher

Source: Missouri State Department of Elementary and Secondary Education, www.dese.mo.gov (as of 2009).

exist with the expiration of the contract. This may occur if a probationary teacher is not performing at a level acceptable to the administration. A probationary teacher may have difficulty interacting with the students, staff, or parents in the school district or may be teaching at a minimal level. It is not only to the district's benefit but also to the teacher's benefit not to renew the contract, since the teacher might be more successful in another school district. Not renewing a contract presupposes that evaluations have been made by the teacher's principal, that deficiencies have been pointed out, and that advice and help have been offered on how to improve performance or correct the stated deficiencies. If such a process has occurred, nonrenewal of the teacher's contract is justified.

This statute refers to terminating the employment of a probationary teacher before his or her contract expires. As with all other school district employees, the teacher must be given a written statement setting forth the allegations along with a reasonable time period to correct deficiencies and improve performance. If such corrections or improvements are not made within the specified time, the employee may be dismissed by action of the board of education.

Grounds and Procedure for Revocation of a Teacher's License to Teach

A final formal procedure must be briefly alluded to when discussing termination procedures. A teacher's license to teach may be revoked if it can be proven that he or she has exhibited incompetency, cruelty, immorality, drunkenness, neglect of duty, or the annulling of a written contract with the board of education. As in the statute dealing with the termination of a tenured teacher, the reasons for revocation of a teacher's license have a very narrow interpretation.

Incompetency means that the teacher seriously hinders the instructional-learning process. A chronic mental illness or sociopathic behavior that has been diagnosed by a psychiatrist are examples of incompetency that could result in revocation of a teacher's license.

Cruelty refers not only to physical, but also to mental or emotional abuse of children. The conditions that constitute cruelty may be summarized as follows: Any act that is meant to injure or bring serious ridicule and embarrassment to a child is abusive and cruel.

Of course, immorality is an extremely sensitive accusation. For practical considerations, this cause is commonly interpreted to mean that an individual has been convicted of a serious sexual offense or a crime involving moral turpitude. The examples provided earlier in this chapter are applicable to immorality as a cause for revocation of a teacher's license.

Drunkenness as a cause for revocation of an individual's license is usually interpreted to mean that the employee is either intoxicated or drinks alcoholic beverages while working. This cause is further strengthened by the fact that drinking alcoholic beverages in a government building such as a school is a misdemeanor in most states. A complicating factor is how drunkenness relates to the issue of alcoholism. Because alcoholism is considered to be a disease by the medical profession, the same considerations should be afforded the alcoholic as are granted to other employees with a medical problem. These considerations usually involve granting sick leave to an employee receiving medical treatment or reassigning the employee to a position with limited responsibilities during treatment. If an employee is not a diagnosed alcoholic and if he or she persists in drinking alcoholic beverages at work or continuously arrives at school intoxicated, license revocation is in the best interest of a school district's clientele, the children.

Neglect of duty presupposes that an employee has been informed about the responsibilities that are integral to his or her position with the school district. This is usually accomplished through written job descriptions or in policy manuals and handbooks specifying these responsibilities. Neglect of duty as a cause for revoking a teacher's license requires that the teacher be given an opportunity to rectify his or her behavior. Thus, evaluations that set forth the employee's deficiencies are necessary to such a situation. It also must be remembered that revocation of license is extremely serious and the neglect of duty, in like manner, must be extremely serious and chronic. A teacher who leaves young children unattended on a field trip and who continues such irresponsible behavior after being informed of the danger by the principal has exhibited a lack of understanding that seriously affects his or her ability to supervise children. This is a reason not only to terminate the employment of the individual, but also to safeguard against this teacher's potential employment with another school district by proceeding to have his or her license revoked.

Annulling of a written contract with the board of education is an improperly worded statement in this statute. Annulment means that both parties have agreed to the dissolution of the contract and the governing board has formally approved the dissolution. As cause for revocation of license, however, this aspect of the statute refers to the breaking of a contract by a teacher. Sometimes a teacher or other employee is offered a position with another school district or in private business and industry. If that teacher neglects to request a contract annulment from the school board and assumes another position, the board of education may proceed to have his or her license revoked. Most school boards are not resistant to annulling a contract except in those cases when the education of the students would be seriously affected. A teacher who tenders a resignation the day before the opening of school in September may not receive a contract annulment until a suitable replacement is obtained.

It should be clearly understood that the board of education does not have the authority to revoke a license; rather, the board may follow a statutory procedure that could eventuate in the revocation of a teacher's license. The state board of education, which issues teaching licenses, has the sole authority to revoke them.

Finally, revocation of a teacher's license is usually irreversible unless the statutory procedures were neglected or the evidence was faulty. It is, therefore, a very serious matter that should be initiated only if the education or health and safety of children will be significantly jeopardized not only now, but also in future situations. Terminating the employment of an individual obviously removes him or her from injuring the children presently in his or her care. Revocation of license prevents the teacher from bringing such injury to children in another school district where he or she could be employed. A classic example involves the teacher who is convicted of child molestation and subsequently is fired from his position, but who manages to get hired in another school district and commits a similar crime because his or her license was not revoked.

Humane Considerations in the Termination Process

The procedures described in this section may appear to overemphasize the legal and negative side of the evaluation process. It is, however, an aspect of evaluation that is seldom addressed and that is extremely important. Confusion over appropriate and fair termination procedures could result in a school district being saddled with an employee who hinders the instructional-learning process or who, in fact, may place children in an unsafe situation.

The educational welfare of children is the primary responsibility of a school district. The hiring, retaining, developing, and terminating of personnel should be guided by this mandate. However, employees also have rights that must be taken into consideration when developing procedures and dealing with employee evaluation. Due process is one right that has long been a fundamental principle in English common law and is basic to the legal procedures of American democracy.[10]

Chapter 6, Staff Development, of this book makes the point that a legitimate objective of a staff development program is helping teachers and other employees to overcome deficiencies that affect their job performance. In like manner, Chapter 5, Placement and Induction, further provides guidelines for the transfer and placement of personnel to improve their performance. Humane human resources management presupposes that all alternatives have been exhausted in helping employees improve their performance or remove deficiencies before the process of termination is initiated.

TECHNOLOGY AND PERFORMANCE EVALUATION

The technological implications for performance evaluations can be divided into two different aspects. First, the performance evaluation of salaried and hourly waged employees, which tends to utilize a trait and factor approach. The school district human resources department or the superintendent develops a set of indicators, which are associated with the effective and efficient performance of certain tasks. For example, a school bus driver could be evaluated by a supervisor while he or she is driving the bus. A safety protocol could be devised that the driver follows by extending the stop sign when picking-up children and checking the bus at the end of the route for children who may not have departed the bus at their stop.

Using a personal digital assistantdevice (PDA) that contains the criteria and place to check that the criteria had been followed allows for consistence and ease of performance evaluation. The same approach can be used with cafeteria workers, custodians, clerks/secretaries, and maintenance workers. As another example, compliance with student safety and health standards are crucial issues in the evaluation of cafeteria workers and custodians. Other electronic devices and computers are efficient and effective tools in maintaining accurate and timely performance evaluation records. Such records are easy to access and analyze in terms of performance, which could indicate successful or unsuccessful staff development programming. For example, if there is a serious breach in protocol in terms of safety in the way cafeteria food is stored and prepared, the training program for cafeteria workers needs to be reviewed. This approach is analogous to the approach not only that is being used in businesses and corporations, but also in health care administration where computers are located in or around every patient's room and accessed in terms of patient care with such records as the distribution of medication.

Secondly, the performance evaluation of contracted personnel such as teachers and principals tends to function on a somewhat different level. The performance of tasks is not the main responsibility of the professionals, but rather the decision making process that involves taking into consideration a significant number of factors in making decisions. Thus, decisions about teaching methodology, student behavior management, curricular materials, and parental issues are not subject to the exclusive use of the trait and factor approach for teacher performance evaluation. Furthermore, principals make ongoing decisions about problems and issues that have more than one or a few possible solutions. Finding a solution sometimes requires a trial and error approach that ultimately may be considered *best practice* given a set of circumstances.

Computers and other electronic devices can be helpful in keeping accurate records of how teachers and principals address the various situations that occur in the human dynamics of working with students, parents, and colleagues. Software programs are also available that would allow a superintendent or principal to broadly categorize the behavior of those professionals whom they supervise. For example, the human relations skills of a teacher may be: effective, sometimes effective, or ineffective; may be effective with students but not with parents; or effective with students and parents but not with colleagues. Indicating the type of situation in which the human relations skills were observed could also be helpful in the future.

Certainly these electronic and computerized capabilities could be very important in the dismissal of a teacher or principal who was not able, through procedural due process, to learn new ways of handling human relations situations in an effective manner. Accurate and timely kept records could make the difference in the dismissal of ineffective teachers and administrators.

In consort with this approach, having performance evaluation policies and procedures on the school district's Web site provides the type of transparency that is often needed in the termination process. Through this approach there would be no questions that the teacher or principal knew what was expected of him or her. Finally, it is important for parents and citizens in general to know how all staff members will be evaluated in terms of polices and procedures.

IMPLICATIONS FOR SMALL AND MEDIUM-SIZED SCHOOL DISTRICTS

The size of the school district has no bearing on the reasons why performance evaluation of all employees is vitally important. Most of the literature deals with the performance evaluations of teacher and somewhat deals with the evaluation of administrators. However, there is a serious lack of information about the performance evaluation of secretaries, cooks, custodians, bus drivers, and maintenance personnel. The reasons are the same; performance evaluation is necessary to foster self development, to improve performance, to identify staff development needs, to create performance incentives, to decide on employee promotion and placement, and to develop termination processes and procedures. All of these dimensions of school and school district leadership are dependent on the quality of performance evaluation.

The organizational issues are the same including board of education policies that deal with performance evaluation, and the melding of personal and school or school district performance objectives. Thus, the processes and procedures are essentially the same in all school districts. It is also important to remember that the size of a school district does not necessary translate into more or less performance evaluations. For example, a small school district may have so few administrators that the number of teachers to be evaluated could be more that in a larger school district.

The process of performance evaluation, the development of standards, and the creation of evaluation instruments, of course, should be initiated in consort with representatives of the various employee classifications. The issue that some small or medium-sized school district might encounter is the time that is necessary to perform these elements of performance evaluation. Larger school districts undoubtedly have central-office administrators who can assist the superintendent of school and building principals with these necessary tasks. Also, there are a number of evaluation prototypes that can be adapted to a given school or school district. Neighboring schools and school districts are usually willing to share their performance materials and procedures, which could be of help to school districts with a limited number of administrators.

Termination procedures take a considerable amount of time to properly initiate. However, attorneys are available who can guide superintendents and principals through the difficulties of terminating employees who are not fulfilling their responsibilities and who have been given the necessary due process. State departments of education can also be consulted about legislation and guidelines for implementing the termination procedures. Once again the major difference between smaller and larger school district is fewer central-office administrators, who can provide support to the superintendent and principals.

IMPACT OF GENERATION Y TEACHERS AND ADMINISTRATORS ON PERFORMANCE EVALUATION

Generation Y teachers and administrators have reactions to events that require a response. For example, a teacher must require a certain amount of order in his or her classroom. Students who are constantly being disruptive to the instructional-learning process, or teachers who are performing at a less than adequate level require a response that may lead to an adjustment in behavior that is acceptable in terms of best practice. Rather than just teaching, Generation Y teachers and principals seem to want to search for ways not only to address the situation, but also to alter the situation that requires the reaction. In other words, they appear to be proactive in addressing issues in a policy manner.

In search for the answers to problems and issues, Generation Y teachers and administrators appear to be ready and willing to take a multi-disciplinary approach. They are not constrained by just education theory and practice, but willing to find solutions wherever they can be found.

Generation Y teachers and administrators are capable of multi-tasking, which means that they can do a good job teaching and mentoring students, engaging colleagues on committees and enjoy being a member of the learning community. They want to have an impact on their students and colleagues. In all of these endeavors, they are supportive of the merit pay concept because they believe that such a system motivates and rewards those who want to go beyond just the requirements of being a teacher or administrator.

Thus, in establishing performance evaluation policies and procedures, these characteristics of Generation Y teachers and administrators should be taken into account by superintendents and human resources administrators. The same criteria for performance is much more effective if it is culture-sensitive in terms of the expectations and values of the multiple generations of employees that are found in most school districts.[11]

Quick Review of Essentials

There are three historical stages of development in U.S. education during this century concerning the evaluation of teachers. In the 1920s, efforts were primarily centered on analyzing if a given teaching style correlated with the philosophy and psychology of William James and John Dewey. The second stage was concerned with ascribing certain personality traits as being related to excellence in teaching. In the 1960s, the final stage emphasized generic teaching behaviors. The last 20 years have ushered in a dramatic change in evaluation procedures. The traditional concept of teacher evaluation has been replaced by the broader concept of evaluation management. By this approach, an employee is evaluated within the context of attaining certain pre-established objectives.

The reasons that justify the establishment and implementation of an evaluation process for all school district employees include the following: to foster self-development, to identify a variety of tasks which an employee is capable of performing, to identify staff development needs, to improve employee performance, to determine if an employee should be retained and what his or her salary increase should be, and to help in the proper placement or promotion of an employee.

A significant aspect of an appraisal process is measuring an employee's performance against his or her job responsibilities as outlined in his or her job description. In developing an evaluation process, the board of education should establish a policy on employee evaluation that will give direction to the various divisions within a school district. These divisions are responsible for developing objectives aimed at implementing the goals of the school board. Each employee is then responsible for developing personal objectives that further the divisional objectives. Consequently, employee performance is measured against the degree to which each individual has attained his or her objectives. Feedback data is then available to analyze if divisional objectives have been reached. The actual evaluation procedures for implementing this process are best developed by involving representatives of the employees who will be evaluated.

Some school districts are using the standards developed by the Interstate New Teacher Assessment and Support Consortium (INTASC) as a guide in constructing performance-based evaluation instruments. In essence, the standards then become performance criteria. The ten INTASC core standards are considered necessary for all teachers.

As with the development of evaluation procedures, evaluation instruments are more appropriately constructed by the committee process. There are two basic categories of evaluation instruments: trait forms and result forms. The trait approach rates an employee against a predetermined list of traits to ascertain overall performance. The results approach involves comparing an employee's performance against objectives that were developed by the employee and agreed to by his or her supervisor. Using both types of instruments helps to identify areas where improvement is needed.

Termination procedures, an aspect of the evaluation process that is seldom addressed, are extremely important. Because getting fired has such a devastating effect upon the financial and emotional welfare of an individual, termination procedures must be fair and objective. Most states have statutory provisions outlining the due process that must be afforded teachers before termination. Such legislation, while applying to the professional staff, also provides a model for boards of education in establishing similar procedures for all employees. The educational welfare of students is the primary concern of a school district, but employees also have rights that must be taken into consideration when developing appraisal procedures and dealing with employee dismissal.

Selected Further Readings

Barkert, Cornelius I. and Claudette J. Searchwell, *Writing Year-End Teacher Improvement Plans-Right Now!!: The Principal's Time-Saving Reference Guide*, 2nd ed. Thousand Oaks, California: Corwin Press, 2008.

Dana, Nancy Fichtman, Diane Yendol-Hoppey, *The Reflective Educator's Guide to Classroom Research: Learning to Teach and Teaching to Learn through Practitioner Inquiry*, 2nd ed. Thousand Oaks, California: Corwin Press, 2009.

Hursh, David, *High-Stakes Testing and the Decline of Teaching and Learning: The Real Crisis in Education*. Lanham, MD: Rowman & Littlefield Publishing Group, 2008.

Kennedy, Mary M., "Contributions of Qualitative Research to Research on Teacher Qualifications,"*Educational Evaluation and Policy Analysis*, 30, no. 4 (December 2008), 344–368.

Love, Nancy, ed., *Using Data to Improve Learning for All: A Collaborative Inquiry Approach.* Thousand Oaks, California: Corwin Press, 2009.

Saginor, Nicole. *Diagnostic Classroom Observation: Moving Beyond Best Practice*. Thousand Oaks, California: Corwin Press, 2008.

Tobias, Sigmund and Thomas M. Duffy, eds., *Constructivist Theory Applied to Instruction: Success or Failure.* New York: Routledge Publishing, 2009.

CHAPTER

8

Compensation

FOCUS SCENARIO

You are the director of employee benefits in a school district that is experiencing a shortage of qualified teachers and other support employees. This is the same school district that was described in Chapter 3 of this book.

After conducting informal telephone interviews with very qualified candidates who did not accept the district's offer of employment or who dropped out of the selection process, it is clear that one of the reasons was that other school districts in the same vicinity have higher salaries and better fringe benefits. Furthermore, the reputation of the district that has been circulated within the larger education community gives the impression that the district does not value its employees. Also troubling is the fact that the district appears to lack support from the community because a bond issue referendum failed, which was needed to build an addition to the middle school.

The fiscal accountability of the administration was called into question by the local newspaper last year when the teachers were given only a 2 percent salary increase and the fringe benefits package for employees' dependents increased by 18 percent. Perhaps, the most damaging issue to the district's reputation (which also appeared in the newspaper) concerned the superintendent's contract, which provided him with a district-owned car, provided him with an annuity, and paid medical and hospital insurance for his wife and children.

The board of education has asked you to develop a plan of action that will address the entire compensation package offered to all employees, but with particular focus on teachers.

Before engaging in any activity, most of us consider the same question: *What will I get out of this?* Psychologists have recognized for a long time that satisfaction of needs is the motivation behind all actions. This satisfaction or reward might be money, a promotion, recognition, acceptance, receipt of information, or the feeling that comes from doing a good job.[1]

This self-interest motive often carries a negative connotation, yet it is a reality of life. People act in ways that they perceive to be in their own best interests. Whether a given act is truly in an individual's best interest is irrelevant; what counts is that he or she believes it to be so. Even if an action appears to be irrational such as a resignation because of a minor misunderstanding at work, to the individual resigning, the act may be totally in keeping with what he or she believes to be in his or her best interest.

From an administrative standpoint, managers can develop a unique compensation system if they understand what their employees believe to be in their best interest. Not all individuals value the same type of compensation. Consequently, a compensation program must be flexible enough to meet the expectations of individual employees. It is also necessary to structure a compensation program in such a way that people realize they are actng in their own best interest when they are acting in the best interest of the school district. This exemplifies the importance of compensation in a performance-based model, which utilizes incentives as the foundation of a compensation program. This is also an approach that minimizes the membership-based type of program, which increases compensation for teachers, administrators, and staff members because of seniority and credentials. The membership approach extends salary increases and fringe benefit improvement regardless of the level of an employee's performance. Thus, as a result of this model, several things become clear:

- Compensation must be linked to behaviors that the school system classifies as desirable.
- The employee should recognize that good job performance is compatible with self-interest.
- Employees should recognize that the compensation system also will satisfy their own needs.
- Administrators must analyze and interpret the needs of the employees.

The fourth statement above requires further explanation. In recommending that administrators analyze and interpret employees' needs, the major question that arises is how this can best be accomplished.

The most obvious way of learning about an individual's needs is to ask the person. However, some people do not always understand their own needs and self-interests; others find it difficult to put such needs into words. The most immediate way for an administrator to learn about employees' needs is to observe and develop an awareness of employee behaviors. Behavior is usually a stronger indicator than the verbal utterances of employees. Unfortunately, developing skill in interpreting behavior takes time and practice. The only reliable method of determining needs is through social scientific research aimed at determining patterns of needs, quantified and analyzed through statistical applications. A number of consulting firms are capable of providing this service, and some packaged programs are available that can be administered by staff employees.[2]

VARIABLES AFFECTING COMPENSATION

The main purpose for establishing a compensation policy is to attract and retain qualified employees who will provide the type of service expected by the public. It is essential that employees understand the compensation structure and have confidence in the objectivity by which the system is implemented. Five major variables must be taken into consideration by the administration in constructing and recommending a compensation policy to the board of education for approval: (1) performance, (2) effort, (3) seniority, (4) skills, and (5) job requirements. It is not important how appropriations are allocated for the compensation system; whether through board approval of the budget or collectively negotiated with employee unions, these variables are necessary to the policy.

Performance

The evaluation of performance is concerned with a basic question: *Did you get the job done?* Compensating individuals requires criteria that define performance. The task of constructing valid and reliable criteria for evaluating performance was treated in Chapter 7. The importance of using performance as a basis for compensating employees is critical to all effective compensation systems.

Effort

School districts have required teachers to consider the effort put forth by students as a determinant in evaluating student performance. Even if effort does not directly influence a grade, some method is usually employed to indicate whether a given student is putting forth his or her best effort. It is ironic, therefore, that school districts have long neglected using the degree of effort put forth by employees as a component in their compensation systems. Yet, without such an orientation, a school district will fall prey to compensating quantity rather than quality and the end rather than the means. Also, there are some situations in which an outcome is difficult to evaluate and effort becomes a primary determinant of compensation. Thus, not all curricular innovation programs turn out to be successful as measured by student-demonstrated learning through test scores or projects. However, the efforts that go into investigating, developing, and assessing the effectiveness of instructional programs can be significant. Because teaching and learning are human activities, there is no one way of delivering these activities for all times. Rather, research and development (R&D) demand a certain amount of risk-taking that will contribute to educators' understanding of the instructional/learning process, which effort should be rewarded.

This discussion is obviously concerned with a topic much debated in education: performance incentives. There is no one best method for rewarding performance with money; however, the following comments will help to clarify this issue. Compensation programs for teachers and administrators in school districts tend to be very parochial in scope and neglect some basic considerations for rewarding teachers who strive for excellence in performance. Indications that a school district is moving towards a performance-based, rather than a membership-based approach include paying teachers who demonstrate that their knowledge and skills contribute to improved student outcomes. Other indications are paying proven teachers to mentor less successful teachers and paying teachers more if they are willing to accept a difficult teaching assignment.[3]

In a more systematic way, a performance-based approach provides incentives within the following context:

- Entry-level teachers must also benefit from a performance incentive program by receiving all salaries as they begin their careers.
- School district citizens must be willing to provide the funding for a performance incentive program by raising their taxes, which can only occur if citizens recognize that the membership-based approach is no longer in place.
- Performance incentive programs must compensate those with the most needed skills.
- All teachers and administrators must recognize that those who work the hardest as measured by normative criteria receive the most compensation.
- Performance evaluation policies and procedures must be equitable and easily recognized as such by all employees.[4]

Seniority

Length of time in a particular position plays a significant role in compensation systems in the public sector. The civil service system of the United States is the best example of how seniority operates in a compensation program. The master salary schedule approach used by many school districts, incorporating channels for credentials and an incremental dollar amount for years of service, testifies to the influence of seniority in compensation systems. In business and industry, seniority has some impact on the compensation systems collectively bargained by unions. However, for management positions, seniority has little or no effect upon rewards.

The reason that seniority has been used by educational organizations to determine financial compensation is because it can be applied so easily. A principal may evaluate a given teacher's performance either higher or lower than another teacher's performance; but if both teachers perform within the limits of what is considered satisfactory, both will get the same salary increase if they both have served the same number of years in the school system. This relieves the principal from recommending to the superintendent different dollar-amount compensation for each teacher based on his or her evaluation of their performance. Nevertheless, seniority is a variable to be incorporated into a compensation system because the basic purpose of establishing a compensation policy is to attract and retain qualified employees. A compensation system is ineffective when its sole criterion for rewarding employees is seniority.

The necessity of retaining some form of seniority in a compensation plan that also rewards performance has led to the establishment of what is commonly referred to as "career ladders." Two of the more frequently discussed programs are the Charlotte-Mecklenburg Schools Career Development Plan and the Tennessee Better Schools Program. The objective of these two and most other programs is to encourage teachers to direct their careers along a path that will lead to refined skills and higher levels of responsibilities. For example, a person entering the education profession as an apprentice teacher must have met the following requirements:

a. Completed a teacher education program offered through an approved college or university
b. Attained a bachelor's degree
c. Successfully completed student teaching
d. Successfully passed the National Teacher's Examination

This apprentice teacher could progress to subsequent higher levels of designation such as "professional teacher," "senior teacher," and finally, "master teacher." The path to these levels requires additional education and the assuming of more and more responsibilities. For example, a master teacher could be expected to serve as a curriculum specialist, seminar presenter in a staff development program, or a resource person to apprentice teachers. Each level of attainment could be rewarded with perhaps a more lucrative salary schedule. A bonus upon attaining each successive level would be another method of rewarding those reaching such levels.

Skills

A common practice in organizations, particularly in the private sector, is allocating compensation based on the skills of employees. Those who possess the most advanced skills receive the highest compensation. When an individual is hired by an organization, his or her skill level is usually a major consideration in determining the amount of compensation to be received.

Competition, therefore, to hire individuals with certain skills becomes an element in the compensation package. The standard as to what constitutes a desirable skill is imposed from either the human resource requirements of the organization or from the occupational category itself. If the board of education has mandated having a community education program, individuals possessing the experience and educational qualifications necessary for implementing such a program have skills that will demand a quality compensation package.

Job Requirements

The complexity and responsibility of a job are often criteria by which compensation is distributed. A job that is difficult to perform because of stress, unpleasant working conditions, or level of responsibility must also offer higher compensation to attract capable individuals. A major determinant of job difficulty is the degree of discretion a job requires. The greater the discretion, the greater the need for good judgment and consequently, the greater the need for commensurate compensation.

Any good compensation system must recognize effort, seniority, skills, and job requirements; performance, however, must also be given a primary emphasis. Quality individuals are attracted to school districts that reward performance, which in turn, affects the quality of education offered by a school district.

TYPES OF COMPENSATION

If compensation is to motivate performance, employees must recognize the relationship between performance and compensation. Most school districts have traditionally used nonperformance criteria, such as seniority-based salary schedules, for allocating compensation. However, this chapter views compensation primarily as a payoff for performance. This concept is in keeping with the outcry for accountability and, if properly applied, might be the only realistic approach to improving the quality of education. For too long, teachers and other employees of school districts have been placed apart from the rest of humankind by taxpayers who believe that they should be more dedicated to service than concerned about making a living. Teachers and other public employees have fought this long-held belief by engaging in unionism and collective negotiations for wages and fringe benefits. A reasonable compensation system that recognizes quality performance and that is objectively administered could help remedy some of the dissatisfaction voiced by school district employees.[5]

The most obvious kinds of compensation are wages and fringe benefits. However, a truly effective compensation system must be multifaceted, incorporating both intrinsic and extrinsic aspects. Although modern school districts employ people in many different occupational categories, many of the possible rewards are applicable only to particular job positions. For example, teachers, administrators, bus drivers, and custodians would receive a salary; administrators, in addition, would have greater job discretion; and custodians could receive overtime pay.

In addition, rewarding performance and encouraging higher levels of performance must be fashioned into a comprehensive system that is ongoing and integral to the operation of the school district. Thus, Figure 8.1 has many functions; first and foremost, it demonstrates that compensation can be weaved into a complete system for both rewarding performance and creating organizational commitment that encourages improvement of performance.

Intrinsic compensation is a reward that the employee receives from doing the job itself. The employee's satisfaction on the job is usually increased by the following: participation in the policy-making process, greater job discretion, increased responsibility, and opportunities for professional development.

Extrinsic rewards are divided into direct and indirect compensation. The most common forms of direct compensation are salary, overtime pay, holiday pay, and merit pay for performance. Direct compensation is also the part of a compensation system that generates the most controversy and disgruntlement among employees. Industrial psychologists have long contended that rate of pay is not the most important determinant of job satisfaction. However, it is an indispensable part of every compensation package and, because of its importance, is treated at length under a separate title in this chapter.

Indirect compensation usually includes insurance programs, pay for time away from work, and services. There is a widespread attitude among human resources administrators who view indirect compensation as that which helps to retain individuals in an organization rather

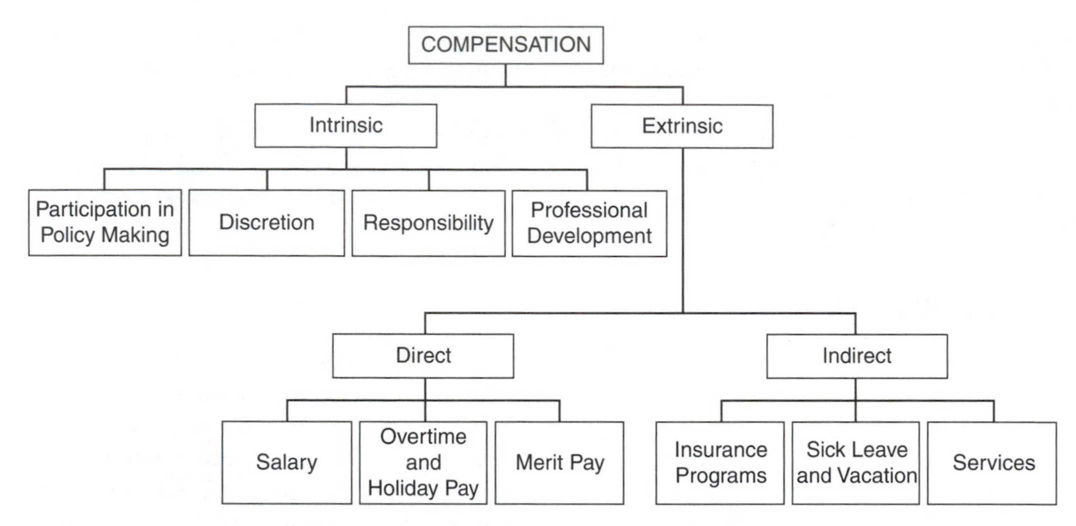

FIGURE 8.1 Structure of Compensation

than motivating them to greater performance. Direct compensation is considered the stimulus to better performance. Because of the complexity and importance of indirect compensation, more frequently referred to as fringe benefits, this also is treated under a separate heading in this chapter.

Nonfinancial rewards have begun to appear in some school districts. These rewards may either motivate an employee to greater performance or help to retain his or her services. The limits to the kind and extent of nonfinancial compensation are established only by the creativity of those responsible for establishing a compensation program. Nonfinancial compensation, however, is effective only if it meets the needs of specific employees. What one person considers desirable might seem superfluous to another. For example, a very status-conscious employee might be motivated by a job title, a reserved parking place, the services of a private secretary, or a paneled and carpeted office. Another individual might value working without close supervision that could both motivate performance and retain his or her services. The significant point is that organizations can use a variety of nonfinancial means as part of a total program and that these means may be more appreciated by certain individuals than direct or indirect forms of compensation.[6]

DIRECT COMPENSATION: SALARY AND WAGE ADMINISTRATION

The basic philosophy underlying pay systems in school districts is compensation for services rendered. However, the subjective nature of administrative judgments, of collectively bargained agreements, of state and federal pay guidelines, and of salary rates in the public and private sectors have a definite influence on actual wage programs. To ensure external and internal wage comparability, a school district must continually gather data on the wage and salary policies of other school districts and also of public and private employers in the community and region. Most organizations are cooperative in sharing information concerning salary programs because they too understand that their systems are influenced by others. Surveys by telephone and letter, governmental publications, and literature published by employee organizations and unions are also valuable resources in gathering information.

Because the principle of compensation for services rendered is somewhat elusive, the following policy should help a school district in developing a salary and wage policy aimed at fair treatment for all employees:

> The board of education recognizes the importance of creating a compensation plan for teachers, administrators, and staff members that is equitable and transparent in application to the various job categories in the school district. Thus, the board requires the on-going evaluation of every job category and individual position in order to determine a justifiable compensation for the skills and talents required to efficiently and effectively carry-out the responsibilities of the categories and positions.
>
> As a method of implementing the uniform administration of wages and benefits, all categories and positions in the school district will be arranged in a relative hierarchical order of responsibility with the position of most responsibility at the top. Thereby, a gradations system is created that will permit wage and benefit differentiation. Furthermore, the board is requiring the administration to develop a process whereby representatives of the teachers, administrators, and staff members can participate in establishing the gradation system of responsibility.
>
> The board of education further is requiring the superintendent of schools or his or her representative to advise the board on a yearly basis concerning the competitive worth of the compensation plan in relation to other school districts, public agencies, and private business within the state and local community.
>
> The primary focus of this compensation plan is the improvement of performance by teachers, administrators, and staff members. As such, this policy will be effective only if it is amalgamated with the school district's performance-based evaluation policy and procedures. Thus, the graduation of responsibility will be tempered by the quality of performance of each individual employee. In essence, the board of education is also establishing by this policy a performance-based incentive plan that rewards the quality of performance. Consequently, the superintendent of schools, along with the human resources administrator, are being required to establish a uniform and justifiable method of evaluating job performance in collaboration with the representatives of the teachers, administrators, and staff members.

Figure 8.1 presents an array of performance incentives that can be utilized to encourage all employees to strive for higher levels of performance. The key, of course, is demonstration by human resources administrators that there is a direct link between incentive rewards and the quality of performance.

The Effects of Salary on Motivation

An interesting question central to all pay systems is, *Does money stimulate an employee to put forth more effort?* The answer to this question is closely related to individual needs, because money in itself is rarely an end but rather a means to "purchasing an end." A $4,000 raise for an employee making $40,000 per year would help that individual maintain the standard of living in the face of ordinary inflation. That same raise would considerably improve the standard of living for an individual earning $20,000 per year, but it would have much less effect on the life style of someone earning $80,000 per year. From this perspective, money does have a potential to motivate if individuals are seeking to maintain or improve their standard of living. We rarely find a person who is not concerned when his or her life style deteriorates because salary increases have not been keeping pace with inflation.

Performance-based teacher evaluation along with performance-based pay incentives appear to have the most significant impact upon motivating teachers and administrators to strive for excellence in their teaching and administering. Performance pay without accompanying performance evaluation programs do not in themselves appear to motivate teachers and administrators because there is no structure within which to encourage excellence in performance.[7] This research suggests that money is important to employees, regardless of the job level in the organization or the amount of salary that the individual earns. In addition, money has a great deal of symbolic value in our society, even though it has varying degrees of importance to individuals having different backgrounds and experiences.

If money is to motivate an individual within an organization to greater performance, it must be very clear that such performance is indeed rewarded with more money. The behavior that is thus rewarded will be repeated, and the behaviors that are not rewarded with money will not be repeated. This, of course, is not the *modus operandi* of most school systems in the United States. The common position has been one of emphasizing intrinsic motivation. Teachers and other school district employees are expected to perform to the best of their abilities because of the importance of educating children and because of the status afforded to these individuals. The accountability movement, with taxpayers demanding a return on their dollar from school district employees by way of increased student performance, and the number of teacher strikes for higher wages should dispel the myth that the performance of any group of employees in any organization, public or private, is unaffected by money.

Furthermore, performance-based pay incentives for individual employees are more effective if the school district has clearly defined performance objectives. There are other issues related to group pay incentives. For example, if a group of teachers in a given school or department are singled out for their performance and offered pay incentives, the incentive program may become dysfunctional through the phenomenon of competition. Competition sometimes fosters corner-cutting and inflated values in addition to disparaging other employees.[8] A reasonable conclusion concerning the relationship of money to motivation is that money definitely affects performance under certain circumstances. Unfortunately, most school districts use a seniority-based salary schedule, which does not reward performance but rather rewards an individual's survival for another year.

However, developing monetary incentives is only limited by the creativity of the human resources department. For example, giving a double-step increase on the salary schedule to an outstanding teacher is a way of using a traditional salary schedule in an innovative way. Salary bonuses for exceptional performance, longevity pay for a certain number of years that outstanding teachers have committed to a school district, and signing bonuses to encourage excellent teachers to continue teaching in a school district are other examples of performance incentives.

Public Disclosure of Salaries

Because school districts are public agencies, salary schedules and budget information are disclosed not only to school district employees, but also to the general public and at times to the news media. However, many school districts consider the salaries of individual employees to be confidential. This situation brings up a number of concerns. First, in public agencies supported by tax money, the public would seem to have a right to know how tax money is being spent and for what. Second, secrecy regarding salaries sometimes leads to misperceptions, which in turn may lead to the dissatisfaction of employees with their pay.

An open salary policy may also affect management effectiveness. If pay information became common knowledge among employees, individuals could compare their salaries, and inequities in the pay system would soon become apparent. Of course, there also would be petty complaints and misperceived inequities. However, an open pay system would demonstrate that the administration has confidence in the management of the pay system and this may increase the trust individual employees have in the school district's administration. Although very few statistical data are available on the preferences of employees concerning an open salary policy, experience suggests that most Americans are sensitive about their wages and would probably prefer to have their salaries undisclosed.

The Equal Employment Opportunity Commission (EEOC) continues to receive cases alleging that women are being paid less than men for doing comparable work. This, of course, is contrary to the provisions of the Equal Pay Act of 1963 and Title VII of the Civil Rights Act of 1964.[9] In like manner, school districts receiving federal funds must disclose wage and salary information to demonstrate commitment to the principles of affirmative action. Furthermore, a company cannot prohibit employees from discussing salary issues during working hours because this is an abridgement of the constitutional rights of employees.

Compensation Packaging

Because individual employees have individual needs, no compensation program will satisfy everyone. A number of corporations, recognizing this fact, have developed compensation programs commonly referred to as cafeteria plans, which allow each employee to choose a combination of programs most attractive to that person. Thus, employees are informed that their compensation is X dollars, and they then choose a mix of salary and other benefits suited to their particular situation and offered by the corporation. Such benefits might include:

- Major medical and hospitalization insurance
- Pharmaceutical insurance
- Dental insurance
- Optical insurance
- Flexible spending plan
- Life insurance
- Extended care insurance
- Dependent care plan
- Accidental death and dismemberment insurance
- Long-term disability insurance
- Travel accident insurance
- Adoption assistance
- Annuities
- Others limited only by the creativity of human resources administrators

The concept underlying this approach is that an employee will be motivated towards higher performance if such performance carries a dollar value that can then be "spent" by the individual for compensation tailored to meet his or her needs.

Although it is difficult to generalize, younger employees appear to be more concerned with salary and educational reimbursement programs than with life insurance and retirement plans.

Married employees are usually more concerned about life insurance and medical programs than single individuals; older employees are justifiably interested in retirement benefits.

With this type of compensation packaging, a considerable amount of information must be made available to employees for them to have adequate data on which to base decisions. This will obviously increase the administrative costs of the compensation programs. However, the potential benefit in terms of increased performance and the retention of employees could significantly offset the additional costs.

Equity of Pay and Performance

In any organization, employees tend to compare what they get from their job with what they must put into it. At the same time, they are comparing what they make in wages with what coworkers make and how productive their coworkers are. The inevitable outcome of this comparison process is that an individual will see his or her compensation as either equal or unequal to that of fellow employees. Those who feel inequality exists will view themselves as under-rewarded or over-rewarded.

There are heated arguments about the value and legitimacy of performance-based salary and benefits plans. At the top of the list is the question of fairness. Thus, the criteria that are used in a performance-based evaluation model can create heated debate among teachers, administrators, and the general public in a given school district. In turn, this can cause conflicts between employees, which ultimately lead to mistrust of other teachers and administrators. Often mistrust leads to confusion about the requirements of the job responsibilities. At the foundation of equity compensation program is the extent to which the board of education funds the program. Less than adequate funding adds fuel to the fire of the equity issue. These issues are exacerbated in small and medium-sized school districts where all are most employees know each other.[10]

An employee who perceives an inequality may choose unacceptable means of rectifying the situation, which could include avoiding tasks that are not measured by performance standards or criticize the performance of others. In this context, fairness means that the school district compensates employees in an adequate manner that befits the demands and requirements of the position and are recognized, as such, by other employees.[11] Administrators must realize that employees are not only concerned about the absolute amount of money they are paid, but also with the relationship of that dollar amount to what others are paid. When an inequality is perceived, tension is created. The implication for human resources administrators is very clear. Employees are motivated not only by their absolute compensation but also by the relativity of compensation. Where employees perceive inequality, quality of performance may diminish, absenteeism may increase, and resignations may even rise.

Employee Relations in Salary Management

Employees who believe they are unfairly compensated will certainly create a morale problem for the administration. However, low wages alone will not necessarily create a morale problem if employees believe the administration and board of education are doing everything possible to improve wages. Therefore, how salary decisions are presented to the employees is of great importance. The method, of course, will vary with each individual school district because of local traditions and the number of employees. However, most presentation plans must be formulated with sensitivity to the process used in making salary decisions. However, no plan will work if it is not endorsed by the teachers or their representatives. The need to involve teacher representatives may not be necessary in small and some medium-sized school districts where the board of education can talk directly to the teachers.[12]

Thus, the administration should analyze the fiscal condition of the school district; formulate a recommendation that appears reasonable; receive approval from the board of education; and, finally, inform the school district employees of the decision. This method is the most efficient in terms of time spent by the administration, but it is also the most vulnerable in terms of good staff morale because it is basically a "take it or leave it" approach. Although this method is traditional in education, it is also highly suspect even in those school districts where it is used successfully because it has all the markings of a benevolent dictatorship.

In the second process, which is the more defensible, administration and employee representatives work together to develop a mutually acceptable salary and wage package. In over half the states, this process is mandated in varying degrees by state collective negotiations legislation. However, the process is certainly valid even in those states that prohibit collective negotiations by public school employees. Where such a prohibition exists, salary decisions remain with the board of education, but the task of formulating a recommendation becomes a mutual concern of both administrators and employees.

This collaborative process is not without its drawbacks. It can be very time-consuming, and the administration may disagree with the proposals presented by the employee representatives. Chapter 9 discusses in detail the process of collective negotiations as practiced in public school districts.

Whatever process is used, the administration must ultimately present the salary plan and the decision of the board of education to the school district employees. A significant advantage of the bilateral model is that the employees through their representatives have some knowledge of the administration's position. The sensitive nature of salary and wage decisions cannot be overemphasized. Wages affect an individual's ability to support his or her family and maintain an adequate standard of living; a paycheck represents security in a highly materialistic society. Therefore, effective communication is essential in explaining policies and decisions.

There are four basic principles that, if followed, will maximize the effectiveness of presenting salary and wage decisions to the employees: (1) the board of education must place top priority on paying adequate wages when it draws up and approves the school district's budget; (2) the administration must make complete disclosure of the fiscal condition of the school district; (3) the administration must avoid presenting too many technical details of the financial conditions, which could give the semblance of a "snow job"; and (4) the administration should prepare a position statement to distribute to all employees and to the news media. This document may take various forms, but at a minimum it should contain the decision on salary and wages, the process used in reaching the decision, facts about the financial condition of the school district, and data about wages in comparable school districts and the business community.

It is also effective, in minimizing confusion and misrepresentation, to invite employees to call a designated office which will be responsible for answering questions about the salary and wage document. The most obvious central-office component to take this responsibility, of course, is the business and finance office. However, those districts that maintain a public relations office would more properly place this responsibility with the director of community relations.

A final, yet very important, point should be made concerning employee relations in salary management. The building principal is often the last person to be informed about central-office and board of education decisions, but he or she is usually the first person contacted by teachers and other building level employees when they have questions. Therefore, it is both good administrative procedure and good public relations to inform the principals first about salary decisions. This will also help principals identify themselves as members of the school district's administrative team.

Collecting Community Wage Data

A defensible technique in developing cooperation is to establish salary parameters compatible with wages paid by other government agencies and by business and industry in the community served by the school system. In metropolitan areas, this would include more than the immediate vicinity; salaries in the surrounding area would probably give a better indication of the adequacy of salary levels within the district. Thus, a school district located in suburban Chicago should be concerned with the wages paid by private business and industry, municipal governments, and other school districts in the entire metropolitan Chicago area.

If salaries are to be competitive and comparable enough to sustain a reasonable standard of living for school district employees, they must be relative to the salaries received by other individuals living in the same community. Another reason for seeking salary data from other employers in the area is because these corporations and their employees support the school district through taxation; and school district salaries must not be out of proportion with the wages paid and received by these constituents.

A source of information on salaries and wages paid in the community to individuals with occupations similar to non-instructional employees of a school district is the employment agency. Although the quality of such agencies varies, both private and public employment agencies usually have valuable data on wages. The civil service commissions of state and municipal governments also have readily available information on salary systems used in their respective jurisdictions.

The most effective way to gather data on salaries and wages is through a survey. Such a technique has the advantage of clarity and precision. If the survey instrument is accompanied by a cover letter explaining its purpose, most agencies and corporations will cooperate with the school district by supplying the data because they usually view this type of cooperation as a public service.

Surveys dealing with instructional and administrative positions generally follow the guidelines set forth below, but substitute the appropriate position titles, salary, and job descriptions:

- Of course, the most important issue is confidentiality. Corporations and agencies are usually reluctant to answer surveys if there is a possibility that the general public and other corporations and agencies will know who answered the survey. Competition between corporations and agencies to hire the best employees will caution some corporations and agencies to refrain from participation.
- The second most important issue is how the survey questions are formulated. They must be easily understood and elicit, as much as possible, an unbiased response. The typical manner for ensuring objectivity and reliability is to administer the survey to a pilot group in order to analyze the defensibility of the results.
- Wage and salary information is difficult to analyze if it is not reported as the average for a certain job category. This also eliminates the guess work that may be needed to decide equivalency between the corporations and agencies job categories and those in the school district.
- Thus, the information must be requested by job categories. The rationale for the survey is to gather information that is typically used in similar but different enterprises than school districts such as hospitals and not-for-profit organizations.

Examples of job categories that might be used in a survey for non-teaching positions could be skilled craft persons, which could include mechanics, electricians, plumbers, and carpenters. The practice of keeping school district wage and salary rates comparable to the wages paid in the community is becoming imperative not only because of the teacher shortage in some fields, but also because more and more school district employees are attracted to jobs in business and industry. This, of course, is particularly true of craft and clerical positions because of the ease of transferring from public to private sector employment. Administrative assistants, electricians, cooks, and bus drivers are sometimes "in training" with public school districts until an appropriate job becomes available in business or industry. Thus, the principle of like pay for public employees for like work in corporations and other organizations is becoming a necessary human resources policy. Such a policy not only helps a school district to be competitive with the private sector for quality employees, but also helps a school district retain its employees and reduces the expense involved with high turnover.

The salary rates being offered in the private sector are also attracting instructional and administrative personnel. Mathematics, industrial arts, and science teachers are finding many more opportunities in business and industry than ever before. This trend is also reaching into the liberal arts disciplines as corporations recognize that they can train an individual for almost any job if that person is motivated and has a basic college education. Salaries have motivated many teachers to seek employment in the private sector and in jobs where the rewards systems recognize performance. Thus, collecting data about salaries and wages is extremely important. Although school districts individually gather information through the survey method, many cooperative ventures also have emerged with most or all of the school districts in a metropolitan area jointly sponsoring salary and wage surveys.

The following guidelines have been developed as a road map for preparing a wage and salary report that can be used with boards of education, teachers, administrators, staff members, and the general public:

- First, it is important to develop the survey questions in such a manner that data received can easily be fashioned into a report, which can be understood and utilized by people without a background in survey analysis. The ultimate purpose is to have data that will be helpful in establishing wage and salary compensation plans for school districts. Because school districts reflect the values and financial situations of the citizens living in the school district community and businesses that provide goods and services to that community, it is important to establish the wage and salary compensation plans in accordance with the community economic culture. The survey should provide data in such a manner that it can be compared to the categories of jobs in the school districts. Finally, data must reflect the working conditions that impact salary and wage plans such as the length of the work day for staff members such as school bus drivers.
- Second, it is important to minimize the use of technical terms used by statisticians in collating, analyzing, and presenting data. Further, it is also helpful to have the survey available in an online format. This will allow data to be downloaded directly into data analysis software, which permits statistical analysis.[13]

Salary and Wage Review

Since approximately 80 percent of most school districts' budgets are spent on wages, salary planning and review is an essential part of the entire compensation process. Two methods are commonly used by school systems to review compensation programs: continual salary review and annual review.

A continual salary review system is usually tied into a cost of living index. Government agencies use a number of indicators to determine inflation rates, with the Consumer Price Index being the most commonly used. A major problem with such a measure is the fact that this is an average; the actual cost of living in a community may be higher or lower than the average reported.

Under a continual salary review system, adjustments are automatically made on salary schedules as the selected cost of living indicator changes, necessitating a change in the hourly rates for classified employees and the contracts for administrative and instructional personnel. Such a system does not of itself reward performance; it merely adjusts the basic salary of all employees. Merit increases, therefore, are not addressed by the continual review process.

The annual salary review process functions from a much different perspective. Salary schedules are adjusted annually in relation to the prevailing wages in other school districts and businesses in the community. The adjustment may or may not be in keeping with a recognized cost of living indicator; rather, its major focus is on the local community as the appropriate measure. The concern of the annual salary review process is that wages in other school districts and businesses in the community, which continually change, may steal away the more talented employees. As with the continual salary review process, the annual review method does not of itself reward performance. Therefore, merit increases must be viewed as a separate component of the compensation program.

The decision of a school district as to what method best meets the needs of the employees must be tempered with the constraints of the budget. There are two significant differences between public sector and private sector financing. First, school districts are financed primarily by tax revenue, which is usually not received on a consistent monthly basis but rather as taxes are collected; second, in most states, taxes can be raised to meet higher costs only by voter approval, whereas in the private sector, the price of an item can be raised at any time to offset costs. These financial considerations would make the continual salary review process difficult to implement in a school district.

SALARY SCHEDULE CONSTRUCTION In the public sector and particularly in the civil service systems of the state and federal governments, salary schedules are divided into a number of grades, each of which has several step rates. The use of salary schedules can have three distinct disadvantages. First, recruitment of personnel can be adversely affected if the beginning salaries are fixed on a salary schedule that has become traditional in school districts. To move away from that model usually brings concerns of equity by teachers and teacher organizations. Second, teachers are sometimes disheartened when they receive the same rate of increase on a salary schedule as an unproductive teacher. Finally, it has become obvious in some school districts that the single salary schedule in itself has not produced teacher effectiveness as compared with compensation system that provide financial and non-financial rewards for teacher performance.[14]

A major question in establishing such an approach is deciding on the appropriate number of steps to be included within a grade. If the steps are numerous and small, employees will be unhappy because salary increases will also be small. If the steps are large and few, an employee will reach the maximum within a grade in a relatively short time and consequently, will have no place to progress to over the long term. A realistic approach, therefore, could be a compromise setting up six or seven steps within each grade, with each representing a certain percentage increment. Each grade may be further improved by adding longevity steps to the top and expressing these in even dollar amounts rather than percentages. For example, a salary schedule could grant an employee a longevity increase for every two years of service after reaching the last step within a grade.

Each position in the school district is assigned to one of the salary ranges, and each employee is assigned to one of the steps. As new people are hired, they are placed within the range assigned to that position and on a step negotiated with the administration. Advancement from one step to another is based on performance. Consequently, an employee who is performing unsatisfactorily could remain on the same step until termination or resignation. An employee performing satisfactorily could receive a step advancement that would represent a certain percentage salary increase. A meritorious employee could be granted a two- or three-step advancement.

Some school districts have initiated a policy of placing a new employee on the first step for a probationary period, then advancing the employee as he or she demonstrates satisfactory performance. For example, an employee might be moved to the second step after six months. This method is usually effective only with classified employees who, unlike teachers, are not working under an individual contract.

Advancement from one salary range to another is usually based upon either a promotion or an increase in educational qualifications. A teacher who becomes an assistant principal will usually advance to the salary range established for the assistant principalship. In like manner, a teacher who receives a master's degree would be advanced to the salary range established for teachers with master's degrees. This same process is applicable to classified employees. A custodian who is promoted to a head custodial position with supervisory responsibilities over the other custodians in a building would be placed on the appropriate salary level. It is important to note that advancement to a higher salary grade will not necessarily result in a higher wage for an employee. For example, Step 5 of the bachelor's degree teacher salary range may be higher than Step 1 of the master's degree salary range. Consequently, when moving employees to a higher grade, it is important to place them on a step that will ensure an increase in wages for having upgraded their academic qualifications or for taking on greater responsibilities.

Although the types of salary ranges will vary from one school district to another, a few examples of common designations are:

Administrative	**Instructional**	**Classified**
Central Office Director (Example:	Bachelor's degree	Custodian
Director of Federal Programs)	Bachelor's degree plus	Head Custodian
Secondary School Principal	30 graduate hours	Maintenance
Secondary School Assistant Principal	Master's degree	Employee
Elementary School Principal	Master's degree plus 30 graduate hours	Maintenance
Elementary School Assistant Principal	Doctoral degree	Supervisor

Each of these designations would have a salary range with multiple steps.

Exhibit 8.1 is an example of the type of teacher salary schedule to be found in most school districts. There are five categories that correspond to the academic requirement necessary for placement in each category. The categories progress from the "Bachelor's Degree" level on through to the "Doctoral Degree" level. The steps in each category are listed down the left side of the schedule. Those teachers in Category 1 could receive a step increase with satisfactory performance up through ten steps. At that point, they would not receive a step increase until they acquired 15 graduate hours of additional education in their subject area and thus, would move to Step 11 in Category 2. Therefore, this method encourages teachers to upgrade their knowledge and skills. Such is the case with all categories. There are two categories that have experience

EXHIBIT 8.1
Salary Schedule

Step	Category 1 Bachelor's Degree	Category 2 Bachelor's Degree plus 15 graduate hours	Category 3 Master's Degree plus 2 years experience	Category 4 Master's Degree plus 15 graduate hours	Category 5 Doctoral Degree plus 3 years experience
1	35,000	36,575		38,150	
2	36,575	38,150		40,425	
3	38,150	39,725	40,512.50	42,700	
4	39,725	40,300	42,087.50	44,975	46,550
5	41,300	42,875	43,662.50	47,250	48,825
6	42,875	44,450	45,237.50	49,525	51,100
7	44,450	46,025	46,812.50	51,800	53,375
8	46,025	47,600	48,387.50	54,075	55,650
9	47,600	49,175	49,962.50	56,350	57,925
10	49,175	50,750	51,537.50	58,625	60,200
11	52,325		53,112.50	60,900	62,475
12			54,687.50	63,175	64,750
13				65,450	67,025
14					70,000
15					72,275
16					74,550
17					76,825
18					79,100
19					81,375
20					83,650

requirements in addition to the academic ones: the "Master's Degree" level also requires two years of successful teaching experience; the "Doctoral Degree" level requires three years. Thus, a person who is pursuing a master's degree or doctoral degree on a full-time basis without experience in teaching would be placed in the preceding category until completing the successful teaching requirement.

Exhibit 8.2 indicates the percent of increase between categories and steps. Such a salary schedule is commonly referred to as an "index" system. The designation "incremental" system refers to those salary schedules that have an equal dollar amount between steps, such as $500 between Step 1 and Step 2; also, $500 between Steps 2 and 3, etc.

EXHIBIT 8.2

Indices

Step	Index	Index	Index	Index	Index
1	1.0000	1.0450		1.0900	
2	1.0450	1.0900		1.1550	
3	1.0900	1.1350	1.1575	1.2200	
4	1.1350	1.1800	1.2025	1.2850	1.3300
5	1.1800	1.2250	1.2475	1.3500	1.3950
6	1.2250	1.2700	1.2925	1.4150	1.4600
7	1.2700	1.3150	1.3375	1.4800	1.5250
8	1.3150	1.3600	1.3825	1.5450	1.5900
9	1.3600	1.4050	1.4275	1.6100	1.6550
10	1.4050	1.4500	1.4725	1.6750	1.7200
11		1.4950	1.5175	1.7400	1.7850
12			1.5625	1.8050	1.8500
13				1.8700	1.9150
14					2.0000
15					2.0650
16					2.1300
17					2.1950
18					2.2600
19					2.3250
20					2.3900

MULTIPLE SALARY RANGES There will probably be multiple salary ranges in most school districts for administrative and instructional positions. These ranges are necessary to recognize the various levels of academic preparation and responsibility. A secondary school principal with a master's degree, usually a minimum academic qualification, should not receive as much compensation as a secondary school principal with a doctorate. Thus, when a salary plan has multiple ranges, it is usually designated as a "salary schedule." The teachers' salary schedule would usually have a range for each of the following: bachelor's degree, bachelor's degree plus 30 graduate hours, master's degree, master's degree plus 30 graduate hours, and doctorate. Consequently, it is common to find multiple salary schedules with multiple ranges in most school systems. For these professional positions, it is relatively easy to identify appropriate ranges, which is not the case with classified positions.

The use of negotiated contracts is a new phenomenon taking shape in some school districts across the Unites States, and particularly in school districts that are experiencing difficulty finding qualified administrators and teachers. This refers to the practice of providing salary and benefit packages that are tailored to meet the employment demands of desirable candidates. Such candidates might be applying for superintendent, assistant superintendent, principal, or special education positions. For example, there is great demand for secondary school principals with successful experience in large urban school districts, for teachers and administrators experienced in providing quality services to children with autism, and for assistant superintendents with extensive and successful experience in curricular and instructional planning and assessment.

Compensation packaging could include a salary enticement that extends beyond the usual salary schedules or benefits, which might include annuities, professional development financial allowances, extended periods of vacation, use of a school-owned vehicle, or an automobile allowance. However, negotiated contracts could have some limitations because of Internal Revenue Service (IRS) codes. In addition, it is always a good practice to make known the terms of negotiated contracts because they are being financed by taxpayer money. Also, public disclosure militates against exaggerated claims that may accompany agreements that are out of the ordinary.

For classified employees, it is necessary to designate job families based on similarity in duties and responsibilities and similarity in qualifications. From time to time, it might be necessary to reevaluate a position to determine if these criteria are still applicable. An example of a family of jobs with similar responsibilities, duties, and qualifications is the designation: "secretarial-clerical." Not all school district secretaries and clerical personnel have exactly the same working conditions. Therefore, a salary schedule for this designation could be constructed with ranges established to discriminate between the various working conditions. The highest range could be reserved for executive secretaries working for the superintendent and assistant superintendents. Another range would be assigned to building secretarial positions and the lowest range to clerk-typist positions. Similarly, a job family for classified transportation supervisory personnel could include ranges for transportation supervisor, mechanic foreman, and dispatcher, with salary ranges appropriate to these designations.

ESTABLISHING BASE SALARIES There are two processes that can be used to establish the basic wage for each salary schedule range. The preceding discussion of types of salary ranges illustrates the various methods used to calculate step increases, but provides no indication of base salaries.

The first process centers on gathering salary data from other school districts and from the business-industrial community. There is little difficulty in analyzing the data in relation to administrative and teaching positions. Classified positions, on the other hand, present a more challenging situation because of the multitude of job categories with responsibilities unique to the individual organization.

A successful method of setting classified salaries is by designating certain job categories as benchmarks, which include a family of job positions. Thus, a Maintenance Category would include school bus mechanics, carpenters, plumbers, and electricians; an Information Technology Category would include computer programmers, Web designers, and technical assistants. Such benchmark categories allow for comparison with other school districts, business and industry, public agencies, and not-for-profit agencies. Survey data obtained from these other enterprises can be statistically treated in order to obtain measures of central tendency such as means, medians, and dispersion data, which will indicate the relative position of the school district in terms of wage and salary compensation with other institutions and organizations in the community.

The second process involves gathering data from individual employees within the organization concerning the extent of their responsibilities, the tasks they perform, and their qualifications. The data can be analyzed and used to establish salaries as part of the annual review process. The data also provide a vehicle for reevaluating jobs to ascertain if they are properly assigned to the appropriate salary schedule and in the correct range.

In most situations where this procedure is used, the salary review committee is composed of administrators, supervisors, teachers, and non-instructional personnel who are not directly employed in the job categories being evaluated but who have knowledge of the working conditions involved. This gives credibility and objectivity to the process. A committee of three or five people is optimal for the evaluation task. Thus, if a secondary school principal's position is being evaluated, the committee could be composed of one or two elementary school principals, one or two secondary school teachers, and the assistant superintendent for secondary education. In like manner, if a building-level secretarial position is being evaluated; the committee could be composed of one or two central-office executive secretaries, one or two clerk-typists, and the director of staff development.

Each committee member studies the questionnaire completed by the employee and his or her supervisor. Using a scale of one to five with five indicating the highest requirement, each person evaluates the position in terms of the factors indicated on the evaluation form. Finally, a tally sheet summarizing the evaluations is completed. From these data, the assistant superintendent for human resources or another central-office administrator can establish the salary range appropriate to the position.

Payroll Deductions

Making deductions from an employee's salary is such a common practice that most individuals take it for granted. Yet it has significant consequences because of legal and personal considerations. Therefore, the board of education should have a comprehensive payroll deduction policy covering such areas as the minimum and maximum amounts that may be deducted, the number and types of deductions authorized, deduction procedures, and the opening and closing dates for entering deductions on the payroll records.

Pay Periods

The complexity and size of modern school districts has raised a question for education that has been answered in the private sector for many years: *Should salaries be paid on a monthly, semimonthly, biweekly, or weekly schedule?* School districts no longer employ just a few people in simple jobs, and their payrolls can no longer be managed by a hand-worked method. The complexity of multiple deductions for extensive employee classifications has mandated computerization of payroll management, and this in turn has increased the importance of deadlines. The basic principles for determining pay periods are the type of work done by the employee, the amount earned, and the cost to the school district.

Different classifications of employees have different expectations about how often they should be paid. Custodians, bus drivers, and cafeteria workers are more accustomed to being paid on a weekly basis in the business community, and such employees expect a weekly check when working for a school district. Skilled employees such as plumbers, electricians, and carpenters generally receive higher wages than unskilled workers and are more accustomed to being paid on a monthly or biweekly basis. Finally, professional employees such as administrators and teachers are usually paid on a monthly basis; they normally have individual contracts for a set dollar amount, which is divided into equal payments. Some school districts allow teachers to be paid in either nine or twelve payments, at the discretion of the individual teachers. Some building principals, in like manner, work ten months and are given the option of receiving their salary in ten or twelve monthly payments.

The size of the school district will determine the complexity of the payroll process. In larger school systems, of course, more people are employed, which usually increases the number of job classifications having different payroll periods. This will demand more computerization as well as deadlines and specific procedures for handling the payroll. More payroll specialists and equipment will be needed, which will increase the school district's cost in managing the payroll process. In conclusion, the importance of the payroll process to the school system is unquestioned.

Principles for Presenting Recommendations to the School Board

It is assumed that all salary recommendations presented to the board of education will be based upon sound wage and salary practices. The previous sections in this chapter outline defensible procedures that, if followed, will place the administration in such a position. The next objective, then, is to present the recommendations in a manner that will evoke favorable approval by the school board. Of course, the financial condition of the school district along with the agreements with employee unions and associations will have an impact on salary recommendations.

THE FISCAL CONDITION OF THE SCHOOL DISTRICT In the present economy, salary recommendations almost always call for an increase and in some cases a substantial increase, in wages. Salary appropriations account for 80 percent of school district budgets. Clearly, an increase in salaries will create one of the following situations: less money will be available for other categories of school operations, the school district will have enough revenue and/or balances to accommodate the salary increases, or the board of education will have to find additional sources of revenue to meet the increases. In most states, additional revenue can be obtained only through a tax levy increase which, of course, requires voter approval. Inflation has generally created scarcity for most school districts. Therefore, a board of education may be unable to approve a recommendation if the cost is unrealistically high.

THE ADMINISTRATIVE ORGANIZATION OF THE SCHOOL DISTRICT Usually, only two administrative structures affect salary recommendations. If a school district does not engage in collective bargaining, the superintendent of schools, with the advice of the school business administrator, is directly responsible for making the salary recommendations. However, if the school district engages in collective bargaining, the board will be asked to ratify a master contract, which will normally have major sections devoted to salary and wages. The chief negotiator for the school district, with input from the superintendent of schools, will have negotiated within pre-established fiscal considerations. In this latter situation, the salary recommendations along with working conditions and fringe benefits, which also have a dollar value, must be evaluated by the board.

EMPLOYEE UNIONS AND ASSOCIATIONS The American Federation of Teachers, the National Education Association, and many unions representing non-instructional personnel have official positions on salary and wage policies. Most of these unions and associations seek comparability with the private sector and negotiate for their membership along this line. Within recent years, these organizations have come to realize that, because of the large numbers of people they represent, they have a great deal of political influence. This influence has had an effect upon the election not only of school board members, but also of state legislators and even national candidates. An endorsement by a national labor or teacher organization such as the National Education Association is much sought after by all presidential candidates.

SALARY RECOMMENDATION PROCEDURES The procedure for presentation of salary schedules to the board, of course, will vary with the particular needs of the locality. The following set of procedures is a guide for superintendents in formulating salary recommendations to the board of education:

- It is imperative that the recommendations are backed by quantitative or qualitative or both types of evidence, and that they have been presented for analysis and review by the representatives of the teachers, staff members, and the administration team.
- This evidence-based approach and supporting documents must be user friendly and can be fashioned into a PowerPoint presentation along with a CD that should be available to all interested parties, including the general public.
- These data are meaningful only if presented in comparison with previous data, which should clearly identify the differences from previous years and the rationale explaining why it is different.
- It is important to set forth the total salary recommendation that includes all employees at the same time. Thus teacher, administrator, and staff salaries should be packaged together so that the board of education has a complete picture of the salary requirements. This eliminates the criticism that will be leveled against the administration for favoring one group of employees against the others. It also eliminates the speculation that is certain to be a component of the discussion and communication between the various employee groups and their supporters. When needed, secure the services of a consulting firm to compile data regarding prevailing rates in the community. A consulting firm can also be of assistance in establishing classifications of employees and in writing job descriptions.
- All levels of administration should be required to demonstrate through the budget process salary and wage efficiency and effectiveness by having a workflow chart, which will identify the number of employees who are responsible for carrying-out the various functions in the school district.[15]

Small Business Job Protection Act of 1996

This legislation is commonly referred to as the "Minimum Wage Law," because the intent of the legislation was to increase the take-home wages of employees. The passage and signing into law of this Act attracted much attention in the news media. When President Bill Clinton signed the bill in August 1996, the ceremony featured minimum-wage workers and their children, labor union officials, Congressional leaders, and Vice President Al Gore. To sign the bill, President Clinton sat at the desk of President Franklin Roosevelt's Labor Secretary, Frances Perkins.[16]

The minimum wage was increased in two stages, $.50 per hour on October 1, 1996, which raised the total to $4.75; and on September 1, 1997, the minimum wage was increased by $.40 per hour to $5.15. Each increase impacted approximately 10 million workers who received an increase in their pay checks. However, individual states can raise the minimum wage to even higher levels. Further, cities may increase the minimum wage beyond federal and state levels.

Because the law was opposed by many small businesses, Congress included approximately $9 billion in tax breaks for businesses, which took effect over a 7-year period. For example, in the year of purchase the total cost of new equipment that a small business can claim for tax exemption was raised from $17,500 to $25,000. A major implication for school districts, of course, is that budgets must be adjusted to account for the required increase in wages. Custodians, cafeteria workers, and bus drivers are probably the employees most affected by the new law.

Final Comments

A few final comments are appropriate at the end of this section on salary and wage administration. First, executive salaries are usually negotiated on a personal basis and do not fall within the limits of a salary schedule. The executive positions in school districts are relatively few and commonly pertain to the superintendency and associate or assistant superintendencies.

Second, it is extremely important to consider each salary schedule as a separate entity. In some school systems, increases to teacher salary schedules are reflected in an additional percentage increase being applied to administrator schedules. This, of course, defeats the integrity of the salary schedule objective, which is to reward performance within salary limits that are competitive with other school districts and businesses in the community. This can only be done by analyzing each individual salary schedule.

When collective bargaining is involved, such a tied-in procedure also violates the distinction between management and employees. If an administrative salary schedule is affected by an increase to the teacher salary schedule resulting from collective negotiations, the administrators are in actuality being represented by the teachers' bargaining agent.

Third, extra pay for extra duty, which is the common language applied to overtime pay for instructional personnel and overtime pay for classified employees, should be determined by the same procedure used to establish regular salary and wages. The rewards of performance and competitiveness are also primary considerations in overtime compensation.

Fourth, this chapter was written from the viewpoint that salary and wage increases are rewards for performance and are not simply rewards for seniority with the school district. Many districts have developed salary schedules with channels reflecting academic preparation (bachelor's degree, master's degree, and so on) and steps reflecting seniority in the school district. The salary schedules recommended in this chapter provide for ranges reflecting job classification with step increases based on performance.

The practices in most public school districts are not in keeping with the principles set forth in this chapter, which essentially recommend establishing competitive compensation programs that will attract quality personnel.

INDIRECT COMPENSATION: FRINGE BENEFITS ADMINISTRATION

Fringe benefits may be defined as benefits available to all employees resulting from a direct fiscal expenditure. Because fringe benefits are available to all employees and are not contingent upon performance, such services are not motivators but are more properly considered maintenance factors. Nevertheless, fringe benefits are commonly considered to be an important part of an effective compensation program. Retirement programs, medical and hospitalization insurance, and life insurance are only a few of the many fringe benefits offered to employees in school systems.

Because these services are essential in our society, the quality of these and other fringe benefit programs can have a significant effect upon the ability of a school district to attract and retain good employees. Conversely, absenteeism and employee turnover, which are signs of employee dissatisfaction, can possibly be kept to a tolerable level with good fringe benefit and salary programs.

High employee turnover across the nation costs school districts millions of dollars each year. Recruiting, and hiring new employees, which creates direct expenditures of money, should be minimized to a reasonable turnover rate. This factor, however, does not begin to address the problem of meeting the primary objective of the school district to educate students when there is a continual flow of new employees.

Absenteeism costs corporations in the United States an average of $20 billion each year. Although figures on the cost of absenteeism to public education are not readily available, millions of dollars would be a conservative estimate. A substitute teacher must be hired whenever a teacher is absent. The students are still present, and the task of teaching them cannot be passed on to another of the district's regular teachers, nor can it wait until the absent teacher returns.

The key factor in addressing high employee turnover and absenteeism is to establish a positive approach. Attracting individuals with excellent credentials and a desire for excellence in performance, from the outset, will ultimately correct high turnover and absenteeism. Quality fringe benefits attract quality candidates for positions and will maintain employee commitment to the school district.

Types of Fringe Benefits

The cost of fringe benefits in the United States has risen to approximately one third of the total compensation paid to employees. As of the writing of this book, school districts across the country are experiencing severe financial problems. With financial problems continuing to spread, school districts have found that fringe-benefit enrichment is an alternative when large wage and salary increases are not feasible. As more school districts develop elaborate fringe benefit programs, greater pressure has been placed on competing school districts to develop similar programs to attract and keep employees.

There is also a growing recognition that fringe benefits are nontaxable, which has been another major stimulus towards their expansion. If a teacher wants a certain amount of life insurance, there are two advantages in having it purchased by the school district. First, the premium will be lower because the school district will be purchasing a large degree of protection. Second, the teacher would pay the premium for the insurance out of his or her net pay, which is the dollar amount left over after paying taxes. If the school district pays the premium, the teacher has more wages left to pay for other needs and, therefore, this becomes an attractive fringe benefit.

BENEFITS REQUIRED BY LAW Certain benefits must be provided by the school district: Social Security premiums, state retirement insurance, unemployment compensation, and workers' compensation. These benefits provide the employee with financial security and protection at retirement or termination, or when an injury occurs in the workplace; they also provide survivors' benefits to dependents in the event of the employee's death.

The Social Security program usually covers classified employees. Instructional and administrative personnel are normally included in state retirement programs. Social Security is the major source of income for U.S. retirees. This program is financed by the contributions of employees, which are matched by the employer and computed as a percentage of the employee's earnings. Survivors' benefits for the dependents of a deceased employee and disability benefits for an employee who is unable to be gainfully employed are provided through the Social Security Administration.

The Social Security Act is an important aspect of the United States government's attempt to care for and protect the aged by ensuring a minimal standard of living for them. Although Social Security is often referred to as an insurance program, this is a misnomer. Rather, it is a transfer program of a trust fund from one generation to another. We, the currently employed, pay a Social Security tax that is used to support yesterday's retired workers, dependents, and the disabled. It is important for human resources administrators to be cognizant of the fact that Social Security benefits and the program itself are subject to legislation. Thus, changes are certain to occur and must be continually monitored to ensure that adequate budgetary appropriations are available to meet the demands of these potential changes.

Unemployment compensation laws in most states provide benefits to individuals who are without a job. To qualify for these benefits, a person usually submits an application to the State Employment Agency for unemployment benefits and registers with that agency with a willingness to accept suitable employment offered through the agency. In addition, the person must have worked a minimum number of weeks before becoming unemployed.

Unemployment benefits are derived from a tax levied against employers calculated on a percentage of the employer's total salary payroll. Benefits received by unemployed workers are calculated from the individual's previous wage rate plus the length of previous employment. Unemployment benefits are provided on a limited basis, typically for a 26-week period. Unemployment compensation also serves the total economy of our nation because it provides stability in spending power during periods of high unemployment, as when a recession occurs.

Workers' compensation programs provide benefits to individuals injured or disabled while engaged in a job-related activity. Benefits paid to employees for injuries are based on schedules for minimum and maximum payments, depending upon the type of injury sustained. For example, the loss of a hand is compensated with a higher dollar amount than the loss of a finger. In like manner, disability payments are calculated based on the individual's current salary, future earnings, and financial responsibilities.

The funds for workers' compensation programs are borne entirely by the employer. Although the programs are mandated by state laws, the method of obtaining workers' compensation insurance is usually left to the discretion of the employer, who may buy such protection from public or private agencies or provide the protection through a self-insuring program. Like Social Security and unemployment insurance, workers' compensation is subject to the legislative process. Thus, requirements and benefits will certainly change with the passage of time.

Where mandated by state laws, retirement programs for administrators and teachers generally follow the prescriptions of these other protection programs. Contributions are calculated on the basis of an employee's wages and are usually matched by the school district. Benefits based on contributions are paid upon retirement, with survivors benefits being available for the dependents of deceased employees.

In 1986, the United States Congress passed the Consolidated Omnibus Budget Reconciliation Act (COBRA). This federal law requires employers that provide group health plans for their employees and their dependents to offer an extension of the coverage on a temporary basis under certain conditions when coverage would usually end. An employee covered by the group health plan is eligible for continuation of coverage if his or her employment is terminated except in cases of gross misconduct, if he or she is laid off for economic reasons, or if he or she is reduced to part-time employment and thereby would usually lose coverage.

Family members of an employee are entitled to continued coverage under the following qualifying events: death of the employee; divorce or legal separation from the employee; Medicare becoming the employee's primary health care coverage; termination, layoff, or part-time status of the employee; ceasing to be considered a dependent child under the plan.

There are notification requirements under this law and the employee or family members must pay the premiums for the extended group health plan coverage. Extended coverage may last for 18, 29, or 36 months dependent upon certain qualifying conditions.

VOLUNTARY FRINGE BENEFITS This category of benefits may be further divided into insurance programs, time away from the job, and services. Group insurance programs are available for almost every human need. Among the most common are major medical and hospitalization insurance, dental insurance, term life insurance, errors and omissions insurance, and optical insurance. The number of such programs made available to employees depends upon the fiscal condition of the school district and the wishes of the employees. A school district is usually restricted by state statute to paying insurance premiums only for employees. Therefore, an employee who wishes to include dependents under such insurance programs must pay the additional premium for this coverage.

Under federal law and Internal Revenue Service regulations, school districts can design "cafeteria" fringe benefit plans, which will allow individual employees to choose the benefits that most meet their needs. In addition, if the employee is to bear the cost of some of these programs, the premiums he or she pays can be deducted from his or her gross salary or wages before federal income taxes are levied. This tax advantage for employees and the opportunity to choose their benefits from a predetermined list are two reasons why such programs are quite desirable. The administrative expense of such a program and the availability of insurance coverage that does not demand a high percentage of participation are problems. For example, a company may offer a dental insurance program to a school district only if there is 60 percent participation by employees.

Federal tax-qualified plans must not be offered to only highly compensated employees. Beginning in 1997, the definition of a highly compensated employee was changed to include an employee who was compensated for the preceding year in excess of $80,000 and which placed him or her in the category of the 20 percent highest-paid employees. Federal tax-qualified plans are those that are exempt from taxation, such as 401(k) salary deferral plans.[17]

A fringe benefit that is often taken for granted by employees, but creates an additional expense for a school district is time spent away from work. Therefore, sick leave, vacation time, paid holidays, and sabbatical leave are, in fact, benefits provided at the discretion of the school system. In very large school districts, this amounts to a considerable expenditure.

Corporations have long recognized the value of services in a fringe benefit program. Social and recreational events, employee assistance programs, wellness programs, cultural activities, credit unions, company cafeterias, company-provided transportation to and from work, tuition reimbursements, and child care centers are only a few of the services found in many large corporations.

School systems usually provide much more limited services. Services, such as time away from work, are seldom recognized by employees as fringe benefits. Those most commonly found in public education are expenses paid for attendance at workshops, professional meetings, and conventions; tuition reimbursement; and free lunches and coffee. In some districts experiencing a decrease in pupil enrollment and, thus, a reduction in staff, career counseling is provided to teachers in order to help them prepare for jobs outside education. In large school districts, central-office administrators are usually provided with district-owned cars to use when engaged in school business, or they receive mileage reimbursement.

Fringe benefits are certainly an important component of all compensation programs, and they are becoming even more important as alternatives to large salary and wage increases.

MANAGED HEALTH CARE Health care costs continue to increase at an alarming rate. An alternative approach to traditional insurance programs that is meant to maintain a high quality of care ,but at a lower cost and in a more efficient manner is managed health care.

Managed health care coordinates services around the patient and thereby produces a more efficient delivery system. In order to accomplish this, school districts must employ case management specialists who have the job responsibility of evaluating cases that require extensive and/or expensive medical treatment. As an alternative to hiring case management specialists, a school district can contract with a company specializing in third-party health care administration. These case managers or third-party administrators work with patients and physicians in order to identify alternatives that are medically sound, yet cost effective. A common example is developing a plan that incorporates outpatient care after sufficient inpatient hospital care rather than a prolonged hospital stay. Such specialists should also develop employee programs that encourage healthy lifestyles and the prevention of illness. It would probably be cost-effective for a school district to offer mammograms or diabetes testing at a nominal cost to employees.

There are various levels of managed health care. Utilization management attempts to control the cost of a school district's health benefit plan. This is best accomplished through catastrophic case management and utilization review. When an employee suffers a catastrophic illness, the case manager begins the process of assisting the patient and his or her physicians to access the best treatment at the lowest cost. This could include care in a rehabilitation center, nursing home, extended care facility, or outpatient services in the patient's home. The case manager will help negotiate rates with these various facilities.

Utilization review usually includes the reviewing of all inpatient admissions, outpatient surgical procedures, inpatient substance cases, and inpatient psychiatric care. The purpose is to ascertain if such services are medically sound. In addition, before a claim is paid, the case manager will review the charges for accuracy.

An alternative to hiring case management specialists or contracting with a third-party health care administrator is for a school district to join a managed care network. Physicians who are members of the network have agreed to certain fee guidelines and medical facilities that belong to the network have agreed to a certain quality of service and fee guidelines. The network provides the school district with the efficient processing of paperwork and also with cost information that will help the school district in its financial planning.

There are various types of networks. One type is called a preferred provider organization or PPO. Both hospitals and physicians belong to such a network. Physicians treat patients in their own offices. If a school district employee chooses a physician or hospital outside the network, most PPOs will pay a much smaller percentage of the bill. Hospitals and physicians outside the network cannot be monitored to ensure quality care and cost containment.

A second type is a health maintenance organization or HMO. In this arrangement, each patient is provided with a network primary care physician who controls access within the network to care for the employee and his or her dependents. A prepaid fixed monthly fee for all services is another important feature of the HMO. Typically, HMO's are organized around four models: (1) group, (2) staff, (3) individual practice, and (4) point-of-service. In the group model, a group or groups of physicians provide care to patients at one or more locations. In the staff model, physicians are actually employed by an HMO and provide services at one or more locations. In the individual practice association model, an HMO contracts with physicians who practice out of their own offices. In the point-of-service model, an HMO allows school district employees to choose physicians outside the network, but the employee will pay a higher percentage of the cost.

Many PPOs and HMOs have prescription drug plans whereby certain pharmacies within a network offer medication at a reduced cost. This kind of network can also be found outside of PPOs and HMOs.

Health Insurance Portability and Accountability Act of 1996 (HIPAA)

There was little media coverage of this bill until August 21, 1996 when it was signed into law by President Bill Clinton. The law addresses the needs of approximately 25 million Americans who are denied health insurance coverage because of an illness or who cannot change jobs because they, their spouse, or their dependents would be denied insurance coverage because of a preexisting medical condition such as diabetes. The law became effective at the beginning of a new plan year after July 1, 1997. The following are major provisions of HIPAA:

- Immediate coverage for the employee, spouse, and dependents by the new employer if the employee, spouse, and dependents were covered by the previous employer's health care plan for 12 months or 18 months if they enter the new employer's plan late.
- Immediate coverage for pregnant women, newborns, and children placed in the employee's home pending adoption.
- The new employer can deny coverage for up to one year for a preexisting condition, if the employee, spouse, and dependents were not covered by the previous employer for 12 or 18 months respectively. If there was a break in the previous coverage for more than 63 days, the waiting period could start over again.
- Employers can limit a new employee, spouse, and dependents to the same coverage they had with the previous employer even if other employees have additional coverage.
- The health care plan with the new employer could exclude coverage for certain illnesses and could place a cap on benefit coverage.
- Local and state government health care plans may exempt themselves from this law.
- Employers can make premium adjustments to their plans or increase copayments and deductibles in order to offset high claims experience as long as these modifications are applicable to all employees.
- If the new employer does not provide a health care plan, the state in which the school district is located is responsible for providing unrestricted access to a choice of individual health insurance policies to those individuals, their spouses and dependents that were covered by a group health care plan for at least 18 months with a previous employer.

The law does not address the needs of people who are uninsured because they cannot afford to pay insurance premiums. Additionally, individuals who have insurance for long-term care can receive a tax deduction for the cost of the premium and the cost of the care. Finally, the law authorized a pilot program, medical savings accounts, as an alternative to conventional health insurance policies for self-employed people and for employees of small companies. The law also required medical plans to cover illnesses arising from genetic defects. Further, accidents which are caused through participation in recreation activities or hobbies such as skiing must now be covered by health care plans.[18]

School districts must now require their insurance companies to delete provisions from insurance policies that discriminate against employees, employee spouses, and their dependents because of preexisting medical conditions. Small school districts could also be eligible for medical savings accounts.

MEDICAL SAVINGS ACCOUNTS The Health Insurance Portability and Accountability Act of 1996 (HIPAA) established a pilot Medical Savings Accounts (MSAs) program in an attempt to control the rising cost of health care. The program began in 1997 and continued through the year 2000. After the year 2000, employees of school districts that had already established MSAs were allowed to continue with this program. In order to qualify, a school district had to provide a health care plan with a large deductible and had to meet the "small employer" designation. Under this approach, employees can choose the physicians, hospitals, and treatment options they want. Major illnesses are paid for by school districts' insurance companies while money withdrawn from the Medical Savings Accounts is used to pay for minor health care costs. Health insurance coverage with a high deductible creates a much lower costing premium than coverage with a low deductible. A high-deductible plan is one with an annual deductible of at least $1,500, but not more than $2,250 for single coverage or for family coverage with at least a $3,000, but no more than a $4,500 deductible.

Thus, the employer could purchase high-deductible health care insurance and would establish MSAs for each employee. The amount of money saved by the district could then be placed in each employee's medical savings account. Also, the employee can authorize the employer to deduct a certain amount of money from his or her payroll check before taxes are assessed to be placed in the medical savings account to pay for dependent spouse and/or children health care costs that are minor. If the deductible is reached, the health insurance company will pay for the incurred cost.

A small school district is one with no more than 50 employees during the preceding or second preceding year. An employer may continue to establish an MSA for new employees or employees who previously did not have an MSA until the year following the first year when a school district has 200 employees. After reaching this plateau, no new MSAs may be established.

The Medical Savings Account is under the control of the employee, and each year additional contributions could be made to MSAs from the employee through the employer for his or her dependent coverage. The Account should be interest bearing and unspent funds can grow from the contributions and interest. The employee could make withdrawals for nonmedical purposes but such withdrawals would be taxed and penalized.

It is estimated that only 5 to 10 percent of employees would reach the deductible each year. Former employees on Medicare have an option of receiving health insurance and a large contribution to a medical savings account from Medicare funds.

The advantages of MSAs are considerable. Among the most obvious are:

- National reduction of health care costs
- Increased savings for employers
- Increased saving for employees
- Retirement savings for health and non health expenses
- Patients' control of health care choice
- Health care coverage for people and their dependents between jobs (portability)[19]

Procuring Health Care and Related Insurance

In large school districts, the process for procuring fringe benefit insurance is usually the responsibility of the purchasing and procurement departments, along with significant involvement of the director of employee benefits who reports to the assistant superintendent for human resources. In medium-sized districts, an assistant superintendent may be assigned this responsibility; while in small school districts, the superintendent of schools will probably implement the procurement process. Of course, many school districts hire an insurance consultant or broker, who will not be permitted to place a bid, to help in developing the bid specifications and may also oversee the bidding process including the analysis of the bids.[20]

The health care industry has been experiencing a period of significant change and modification; Exhibit 8.3 sets forth categories of coverage in a typical health care program which must be considered when developing such a program.

THE INSURANCE AGENT AND BROKER An insurance policy is a legal contract between an insurance company and the school district. The provisions of insurance policies are usually developed by a third party, an insurance agent, or broker. The majority of insurance companies do business under the American Agency System whereby insurance companies contract with individuals within a given territory. This individual is referred to as an agent because he or she is authorized to issue policies, collect premiums, and solicit renewals. Independent agents represent several insurance companies, whereas exclusive agents only represent a single company.

Insurance brokers are not under contract to any specific insurance company, and they act on a freelance basis. Thus, brokers buy insurance coverage for clients. The broker can purchase

EXHIBIT 8.3

Categories of Coverage in a Typical Health Care Program

Physician and Hospital Selection Annual Deductible Copayment Preventive Care

Routine Physical

Gynecological Exams

Eye Exams

Immunizations

Well-Baby and Pediatric Care

Pediatric Dental Exams

Health Education Home Care Physician Care Diagnostic Services (including X-ray and laboratory tests) Surgery

Outpatient

Consultations and Second Opinions Physical Medicine and Occupational Therapy Hospital Services Maternity Care

Prenatal Care

Postnatal Care

Delivery

Mental Health Benefits Outpatient Inpatient

Chemical Dependency Benefits Outpatient Inpatient

Emergency Care Prescription Drugs and Medications Away from Home Care Maximum Out-of-Pocket Costs to the Employee Maximum Cost Paid in Claims for the Employee insurance directly from an insurance company or may place business through an insurance agent. The major difference, therefore, between an agent and a broker lies in the fact that the agent may act on behalf of the company. If an agent states that the school district is covered by an insurance policy even before the policy is issued, then it is covered. A broker must receive written verification from an insurance company.

SELECTING INSURANCE COMPANIES There are literally thousands of insurance companies selling some form of health care and related insurance in the United States. Companies differ significantly due to their financial capacity to assure timely and accurate processing and payment of claims. In addition, third-party management companies that process claims for school districts that are self-insured also vary depending on their fiscal solvency and performance.

Thus, when bids are received from health care and related services insurance companies or third-party management companies, it is essential to check their performance and financial solvency with well-established rating firms. Among the nationally recognized rating firms are A.M. Best of Oldwick (New Jersey), Duff & Phelps of Chicago, Moody's of New York, and Standard & Poor's of New York. These firms use a letter grade that they award to insurance provider companies based on each company's performance and viability. A.M. Best awards a range of grades from a top grade of A++ to a low grade of F; Duff & Phelps uses AAA to CCC; Moody awards range from a top of AAA to a low grade of C; and Standard & Poor's uses AAA to R. School districts can directly contact at least one of these rating firms with the list of insurance companies that have submitted a bid. The rating firms may charge the school district a fee for their services. Insurance companies desiring a rating must pay an annual fee to the rating firms; thus, many insurance companies may not request a rating from all the rating companies. Consequently, school districts should request in the bidding process that the insurance companies identify the firm or firms by whom they are rated.

The specifications in the request for proposals bid package should be written in such a way that the school district can select a single company to provide all the lines of health care and related insurance or a group of companies with each providing a different benefit. In selecting one or more health care and related insurance companies or third party companies, the following criteria should constitute the minimum required: successful experience in providing coverage or management in at least two other school districts with an equal number of employees and similar benefits; written references from other school districts stating that claims were accurately and promptly processed; useful communication literature for employees concerning the coverage and claims process; evidence that the school district will be required to provide only reasonable administrative assistance; affordable premiums for the district and the employees; and evidence that the insurance companies or management companies will use accurate and appropriate data in establishing future premiums.

Of course, there is a direct relationship between the premium a school district pays for health care and related insurance and the claims experience of the group of employees covered by the insurance. When the sum of money paid in claims is high, premiums are correspondingly higher. Most insurance companies are "for profit," and therefore the premium includes a profit for the company. Premiums also include not only enough money to pay claims but also to build up a reserve for cash flow purposes. In addition, the premium includes a reserve to pay outstanding claims if the school district takes bids and awards a contract to a different insurance company.

There is a significant financial advantage to the school district if the health care and related insurance lines have a deductible that must be paid by the employee before the district's insurance program incurs a claim. There is a direct relationship between the amount of the premium paid by the district and the size of the deductible. For example, if an employee must pay the first $250 in medical costs, the cost of premium paid by the district will be less then if the employee has to pay only the first $100. The reason for this is obvious—a claim is incurred after the $100 rather than after $250.

There are several reasons why a school district should require a deductible for all premium related fringe benefits. The most important reasons are:

- Deductibles encourage employees to retain some responsibility for controlling costs.
- Deductibles avoid nuisance claims.
- Deductibles help to preserve a competitive market for the district's insurance program.
- Deductibles help to reduce administrative costs.

A copayment is an alternative to deductibles that is also a financial benefit to a school district if it is incorporated into the district's health care and related insurance program. For example, a district's program could require a $10 copayment for an office visit to a physician; the insurance program would pay the remainder of the cost for the visit. The copayment approach is more commonly used for prescription drugs and medications. Like deductibles, the copayments would encourage employees to be more responsible in controlling health costs.

Even if a school district has self-funded health care and related insurance programs, deductibles and copayments can bring about the same advantages cited above. The single most important reason why a school district would create a self-funded health care and related benefits program is to save money. There are two ways that a school district can save money if it uses a self-funded approach: first, the premium set aside by the district will not include a profit; second, the money budgeted from the district's revenue for health care and related benefits can be invested, and the interest will help to reduce the cost of the benefits programs during periods of time without large claims.

Self-funding, however, will require a school district to purchase "stop loss" insurance. The purpose of stop loss insurance is to pay a portion of the cost of claims arising from catastrophic illnesses that would significantly deplete the pool of money set aside to pay claims. Insurance should be purchased for individual claims after a certain amount has been paid through the district's self-funded programs and for claims in the aggregate after a certain amount has been paid. For example, the birth of a premature baby will result in a costly hospital bill. Stop loss insurance could pay for that portion of the hospital bill over $100,000, or any other limit set by the school district. In like manner, stop loss insurance could pay for claims from all employees taken together that exceed $3,000,000. The cost of the premium for stop loss insurance depends on the amount of money that the school district pays in claims. Obviously, the more money the school district pays in claims, the less the district will pay in premiums for stop loss insurance.

In those school districts where employee benefits are bargained collectively, these issues are affected by the master agreement. If a school district and its employees do not bargain collectively or do not include these benefits in the negotiations, it is very important for the superintendent to establish an employee advisory committee. This committee should be charged with reviewing the district's health care and related programs, making suggestions for improvements in benefits, making suggestions for containing costs, reviewing specifications for bidding benefit insurance, reviewing the analysis of bids, and for annually making recommendations to the assistant superintendent for human resources through the director of employee benefits.

Health Risks in the Workplace

A major issue facing many school districts across the nation is the rising cost of workers' compensation. In the early years of this century, workers who were injured on the job had to pay for their own medical treatment and probably received no wages during the recovery period. If a worker was seriously injured with an extensive recovery period, he or she most likely would not have a job even when able to return to work. Around 1910 individual states began to adopt various systems of workers' compensation. This approach required employers to compensate workers injured on the job regardless of who was at fault. In return, the workers were not allowed to sue their employers.[21]

However, medical costs associated with workers' compensation have risen over the last ten years. There are probably three major reasons for this dramatic rise in cost. First, in trying to contain general health care costs, employers have initiated cost-cutting measures such as higher deductibles, copayments, case management, utilization reviews, and the establishment of health maintenance and preferred provider organizations. Although these measures contained costs in general health care, employees are now utilizing workers' compensation to receive the same level of benefits prior to initiating the cost-cutting measures. Workers' compensation usually pays the total cost of medical treatment. Second, the original "no fault" approach has deteriorated into a massive legal bureaucracy where lawyers and judges have become the central figures in workers' compensation cases. Finally, the nature of the workplace has dramatically changed with the effect of producing more complicated injuries such as carpal tunnel syndrome.[22]

For school district employees, there are three major categories of health risks. School facility environmental risks are the first. These include: radon gas, lead in the drinking water, asbestos in floor tiles and other building materials, tobacco smoke, fungi, mold and spores, pesticides, cleaning materials, and so on. The second category is violence. Today, teachers and staff members are working with students who have a history of committing violent acts. The emergence of gangs is a contributing factor to the increasing number of violent acts committed against teachers and staff members. Finally, there is the risk of contracting infectious disease that comes with working with children. For special education teachers who work with children who are multiply impaired or physically impaired, there is the risk of back injuries because many of these children must be lifted from one position to another.[23]

Employees need and want health information that will help them manage the work environment in such a way that they can be as health conscious as possible. It is the responsibility of human resources administrators to devise methods for providing this information to employees. Such information could prevent an employee from being injured or from contracting diseases.[24]

As set forth in Chapter 1, fringe benefit management is a component of the human resources function and because workers' compensation is such a complicated and expensive fringe benefit, more and more school districts have established the position of risk manager. This position usually reports to the assistant superintendent for human resources. The responsibilities of this position include identifying and evaluating the school district's exposure to risks. It is possible to seek assistance from the school district's insurance agent or broker or underwriter to help the risk manager conduct an audit in order to ascertain the exposure of the district to injuries on the job. Of course the objective of the audit is the find the potential risk and then to eliminate or minimize the risk.[25] For example, if a school has a problem with gangs, the most appropriate method of dealing with this issue is to develop a comprehensive security program. This plan might include hiring security guards; developing gang prevention or self-esteem curricula; targeting at-risk students for special prevention programs; increasing job opportunities and drug education; strengthening extracurricular and recreational programs, and so on. The development of the strategy which will eventuate into such a security program becomes the responsibility of the director of risk management.[26]

A second example of a method for minimizing or eliminating risk is a comprehensive staff development program. For example, maintenance and custodial staff members are consistently utilizing potentially dangerous equipment and hazardous chemicals. The manufacturer's sales representative or distributor of cleaning chemicals is usually available to train employees in the proper use of equipment and supplies.

Finally, if it is impossible to eliminate or significantly minimize a risk, it will be necessary to develop procedures that will ensure that the workers' compensation program is effective in meeting the needs of the employees.

Crisis Event Management

Crises have been a concern in schools and school districts throughout the history of public education. However, the tragic violence that took place at Columbine High School in Littleton, Colorado, in 1999 brought not only the issue of student violence, but also the issue of crisis event management to the attention of the U.S. public. In terms of risk management, violence is one of an entire range of crises that need to be addressed in all schools and school districts. Crises occur because of a variety of situations, such as the following:

- *Accidents.* Arising out of human error, equipment malfunction, or inadequately maintained facilities
- *Misconduct.* Including bullying of students and staff members, theft, threats, sexual harassment, and immoral public behavior
- *Natural disasters.* Including earthquakes, droughts, floods, landslides, tornadoes and hurricanes, and storms
- *Technology malevolence.* Sabotage of computer equipment and software, unauthorized entry into computer programs, and breaching the confidentiality of computer records
- *Violence.* Ranging from self-inflicted deadly physical injury, as in suicide, to the injuring and killing of others

Of course, these are not the only crises facing neither school administrators nor the full range of possible crises. However, they do represent some of the more common occurrences that require the attention of the director of risk management.

When a crisis occurs, it is usually without warning, and the response that is required to manage the event is time-sensitive. Immediate action is required that could catch off-guard administrators in the unprepared school district. If a school district has a director of risk management, he or she should have the responsibility of managing the entire crisis event. He or she will need the assistance of other administrators including the assistant superintendents and other central office administrators and staff members who should have specific responsibilities in a crisis. For example, the director of maintenance and custodial services could be responsible for notifying public services such as the police and fire departments. The director of community relations could be responsible for contacting the news media and for issuing statements and other communications about the crisis. The director of employee benefits could be responsible for making certain that injured staff members and students are receiving proper medical attention. If the event occurs in a school, the building principal along with the counselor and other professional staff members, will be responsible for communicating with parents and students. The director of transportation could be responsible for evacuating other students and staff members from the crisis scene. Securing the facility and equipment could be the responsibility of the maintenance or custodial supervisors.

TECHNOLOGY AND COMPENSATION

Of course, the first and obvious use of technology in the administration of a school district's compensation programs is providing on-line information about the amount of salary and wage income that is electronically transferred on a payroll schedule into the accounts of employees at financial institution such as banks, savings and loan companies, and credit unions. These data would also include all payroll deductions for fringe benefits and for local, state, and federal withholding tax. This would also provide a history of the amount of income that is usually provided through *pay stubs,* which are still mailed to employees of some school districts.

Further, the intranet of a school district is an avenue through which employees can be reminded of enrollment periods of voluntary fringe benefits such as dental or vision insurance, and money that can be withheld for pre-tax services such as dependent care plans. Email is certainly a method of informing employees of their voluntary and mandatory fringe benefits and explaining the nuances of such plans. In this context, the school district's intranet can ensure transparency and accountability concerning the salary and wage and fringe benefits programs. Employees can access a wealth of information about how such programs are developed and can provide the opportunity for employees to express not only their satisfaction with such programs, but also their dissatisfaction.

Of utmost importance is how technology can be used to orientate employees to the performance-based compensation programs that are tied to the performance-based evaluation programs. This ensures that all increases in salary and wages for individuals and for different categories of employees are equitable. Electronic technology can also be a staff development technique for helping employees know and understand the criteria upon which raises will be awarded.

Finally, it is obvious that all employees can be apprised of the school district's compensation policies and procedures through electronic technology. Thus, the implementation provisions of the Health Insurance Portability and Accountability Act of 1996 (HIPAA) and all other federal and state legislation policies and procedures should be readily available on the school district's Web site. Of course, the obvious state legislation involving compensation is workers compensation for injuries sustained while on the job.

IMPLICATIONS FOR SMALL AND MEDIUM-SIZED SCHOOL DISTRICTS

The implications are tied to the implications for technology and how it supports the compensation programs of a school district because the requirements of all school districts for salary and wage and fringe benefit administration are the same. Of course, what is different is the number of employees but the policies, procedures, and requirements have the same impact.

While a superintendent of schools may have electronic technology skills, he or she will need the assistance of a consultant or consulting firm to set up the computer software that will give compensation information and access to all employees. The access is critical because in small and medium-sized school districts, direct access to payroll and benefit plans will allow employees to exercise direct control over their salary and fringe benefits. For example, if an employee gives birth or adopts a child, adding the new dependent to the medical and hospital insurance program can be readily accomplished by the employee through the school district's intranet.

Knowing and understanding mandatory fringe benefits such as workers' compensation, maternity leave, unemployment compensation, and the Consolidated Omnibus Budget Reconciliation Act (COBRA) are obviously important access requirements for some employees. Thus, employee rights are protected through technology, because the information is readily available.

IMPACT OF GENERATION Y TEACHERS AND ADMINISTRATORS ON COMPENSATION

Generation Y teachers and principals are like other generations in terms of wanting to be justly compensated for their work. However, Generation Y teachers and administrators seem to more often articulate their desire to find purposefulness in their careers. This does not imply that Generation Y teachers and administrators are significantly different than teachers and administrators from other generations, but rather, Generation Y has an intensity of wanting their work activities to be obviously purposeful. This presents somewhat of a challenge because in educating children it is often difficult to see meaningful progress within the immediate future.

As employees of a school district, Generation Y teachers and administrators definitely want financial rewards for their performance and place a high value on salary and fringe benefits. Thus, they tend to compare their salaries and benefits with teachers and administrators in other school districts. If the opportunity arises, they may well be prepared to apply for positions in those wealthier school districts. Salary and fringe benefits can be considered symbolic of the value that a school district has for its employees. Fringe benefits that are most desired are medical, hospitalization, dental, life insurance, and tuition reimbursement.

In hiring and retaining Generation Y teachers and administrators, it is thus important to make use of their desire for purposeful employment to supplement their desire for higher wages and better benefits by developing non-financial rewards. Consequently, Generation Y teachers and administrators will appreciate the opportunity to participate in developing school district policy, and in having more discretion and responsibility as they carry out their professional duties. Also, Generation Y expects to have the opportunity to advance in their careers and places a high value on professional development activities.

Quick Review of Essentials

Psychologists have long recognized that satisfaction of needs is the primary motivation behind all human actions. In satisfying their needs, individuals will act in ways that they perceive to be in their own best interest. A manager who understands human motivation and what employees believe to be in their best interest is able to develop a unique compensation system.

School district administrators should attempt to utilize an "expectancy model" as the vehicle for developing a compensation system. With this model, compensation is linked to employee behaviors that both meet the objectives of the school district and satisfy the needs of the employees.

Five variables must be taken into consideration in a compensation program: (1) employee performance, (2) effort, (3) seniority, (4) skills, and (5) job requirements. The rewarding of performance, however, must be the primary objective of a compensation program.

An effective program must include both intrinsic and extrinsic compensation. Intrinsic compensation consists of those that pertain to the quality of the job situation; they may include participation in the policy-making process, increased responsibility, and greater job discretion. Extrinsic rewards are divided into direct and indirect compensation. Direct compensation is commonly referred to as salary or wages; indirect compensation is frequently referred to as fringe benefits. Nonfinancial compensation has begun to appear in some school districts and is limited only by the imagination of the administration. It is tailored to meet the needs of individual employees. For example, a very status-conscious employee might consider a reserved parking place as a reward for exceptional performance.

Direct compensation, salary and wages, can be effectively administered only if the following principles are incorporated into the pay policy. Skills required in various positions must be recognized; salaries must be competitive; the primary focus of salary increases must be improved performance; and salary schedules must be reviewed annually.

An important question central to all pay policies is, "Does money motivate?" A reasonable conclusion, supported by experience and research, is that money does affect performance if it is clear that performance is rewarded by a salary increase.

There are a number of other issues in salary and wages management that must command the attention of human resources administrators. These issues will have an effect upon pay policy development and include public disclosure of salaries, compensation packaging, equity of pay and performance, techniques for collecting community wage data, methods of making salary recommendations to the school board, payroll deductions, employee reactions to salary decisions, appropriate pay periods, annual wage review, and salary schedule construction.

Indirect compensation, or fringe benefits, may be defined as benefits that are available to all employees and that help a school district to attract and retain good employees. Certain fringe benefits are required by law. These include Social Security, state retirement programs, unemployment insurance, and workers' compensation.

Federal law requires school districts that provide group health plans for their employees and their dependents to offer an extension of the coverage on a temporary basis under certain conditions when coverage would usually end.

Voluntary fringe benefits may be divided into insurance programs, time away from the job, and services. Group insurance programs are available for almost every human need and include medical and hospitalization insurance, dental insurance, term life insurance, errors and omissions insurance, and optical insurance.

A fringe benefit often taken for granted by employees is time away from the job—including sick leave, vacation time, paid holidays, and sabbatical leave. In like manner, certain services offered by school districts are in reality fringe benefits. These include expenses paid for attendance at workshops, professional meetings, and conventions; tuition reimbursement; and free lunches. Central-office administrators are usually given use of a school district car or receive mileage compensation. In districts experiencing decreasing enrollments, teachers are being offered career counseling services in order to help them look for a job outside of education.

Health care costs continue to increase at an alarming rate. Managed health care is an alternative approach to the traditional insurance programs and is meant to maintain a high quality of care, but at a lower cost and in a more efficient manner. Many school districts hire case management specialists who have the job responsibility of helping to contain costs while still providing quality health care to employees of the school district. Two alternatives to this approach are for a district to contract with a third-party health care administration company or to join a managed health care network.

A major issue facing many school districts across the United States is the rising cost of workers' compensation. For school district employees, there are three major categories of health risks: (1) environmental risks; (2) the risk of violence; and (3) the risks, such as contracting infectious disease, that come from working with children. Many school districts have created the position of risk manager. The responsibilities of this position include identifying risks and then developing a plan to minimize risks.

Crises occur because of a variety of situations which include accidents, misconduct, natural disasters, technology malevolence, and violence. Crises are time-sensitive and require immediate action. The director of risk management should be responsible for managing the entire crisis event, but will need the assistance of other administrators.

The director of employee benefits supervises the staff in the fringe benefits department. Of course, the director reports to the assistant superintendent for human resources. Fringe benefits, as an alternative to large salary and wage increases, will continue to play a significant role in compensating employees.

Selected Further Readings

Belfield, Clive R. and John S. Heywood, "Performance Pay for Teachers: Determinants and consequences," *Economics of Education Review*, 27, no. 3 (2008), 243–252.

Cooke, Willa D. and Chris Licciardi, "Principals' Salaries, 2007–2008," *Principal*, 87, no. 5 (May/June 2008), 46–51.

David, Jane L., "Teacher Recruitment Incentives," *Educational Leadership*, 65, no.7 (April 2008), 84–86.

Goldhaber, Dan, Michael DeArmond, Daniel Player, and Hyung-Jai Choi, "Why Do so Few Public School Districts Use Merit Pay?," *Journal of Education Finance*, 33, no. 3 (Winter 2008), 262–289.

Kersten, Thomas A. and Mohsin Dada, "Skyrocketing Healthcare Costs: Is There a Cure?" *School Business Affairs*, www.asbointl.org (2008).

Trainor, Charles K., "Ensuring You're Insured," *American School Board Journal* (January 2008), 40–41.

Taggart, Nina, "A New Competitive Advantage: Connecting the Dots between Employee Health and Productivity," *Benefits & Compensation Digest*, www.ifebp.org (June 2009), 20–23.

CHAPTER

9

Collective Negotiations

FOCUS SCENARIO

You have been the director of employee relations for nine years in a suburban school district with approximately 300 teachers. The state where the school district is located has just passed a strong collective negotiations law for public employees. Furthermore, the Teachers' Association represents the teachers in the district and various other unions represent most other categories of employees.

During the last six years, there have been two teacher work stoppages, which resulted in major changes to the agreement with the Teachers' Association. The school district is experiencing significant financial problems due to the inability of the board of education to convince taxpayers to raise the tax levy. Three referendums have been defeated to raise the levy by $1.25, which is the amount that the board of education claims to be necessary in order to maintain a quality education for the students in the district. Ironically, the school district is composed of many citizens who are members of unions. However, unstable economic conditions have caused major companies to move out of the area, which has resulted in significant unemployment. This situation appears to have worked against the passage of the referendums.

The lack of support by the community has also caused a major shift on the board of education in the recent election. Four of the seven board members are newly elected and are unfamiliar with collective negotiations in school districts and are not members of labor unions. One is a dentist, another is the owner of a floral shop, the third new member is an administrative assistant to the CEO of a medium-sized technology firm, and the fourth member is a pharmacist. It is now time to begin setting goals and developing strategies to begin the collective negotiations process.

The superintendent of schools has asked you to develop a presentation for the board of education that will give members a better idea of how collective negotiations operates in education, the various dimensions of the negotiations process, and what should be done if there is another work stoppage. She has also asked you to organize your presentation around human resources strategies that the board can adopt as its position for the coming negotiations.

Collective negotiations has become an accepted part of American education in 46 states. The first significant collective bargaining contract was negotiated in 1962 with the teachers in New York City. Since that time all but four state legislatures have enacted some form of collective negotiations laws. Personnel considerations such as salaries, fringe benefits, and working conditions constitute the major negotiable items. Membership in teacher organizations has stabilized and because of dues, so have the fiscal resources of these organizations. Because human resources expenditures constitute approximately 80 percent of school budgets, virtually every aspect of education has been influenced either directly or indirectly by the phenomenon of collective negotiations.

Experience indicates that the underlying consideration in collective negotiations is participation in the decision-making process. It is a natural evolution in our democratic society that individuals continually look for more significant ways to participate in governance, whether in the political sphere or in our employing institutions. It is important for teachers, administrators, and school board members to understand that collective negotiations is about fostering workplace democracy and providing a way for people to be heard. Thus, it is a political process.[1] Furthermore, as a process, collective negotiations is working successfully in both the private and public sectors. This chapter deals with the major components of the collective negotiations process as it operates in education.

The attitudes of teachers, administrators, and members of the board of education are critical to the success of collective negotiations because their attitudes affect the relationship between the negotiating parties.[2] If the teachers and representatives of the school district approach the negotiating process with a sense of respect for each other, resentment will be diminished, and the prospect of reaching an acceptable agreement will be enhanced.[3]

As of this publication date, 34 states and the District of Columbia have legislation that requires boards of education to engage in some form of collective negotiations with teachers' unions or organizations. In addition there are 11 states that permit boards of educations to engage in collective negotiations with teachers. Virginia, North Carolina, South Carolina, and Georgia prohibit all forms of collective negotiations for teachers.[4] The terms *collective bargaining* and *collective negotiations* have been used with various shades of meaning when referring to this process in public education. To avoid confusion and because the process is invariable, these terms are used interchangeably in this book.

When representatives of an organized group bargain collectively over salaries, fringe benefits, and working conditions for their membership with management, the group is in essence a labor union. Therefore, the terms *labor union* and *professional association* are also used interchangeably in this book when referring to the involvement that teacher organizations have in the negotiations process. The above definition holds true for administrator associations when they engage in collective negotiations, which appears to be a trend in public education. Collective actions by employees have a history going back to the medieval guilds. These actions have always been influenced by the economic, political, and social conditions of the times. Such influences are even stronger today because the technology of the news media allows daily updating on economic, political, and social trends.[5]

Collective Negotiations in Local and State Governments

Although some professional organizations support passage of a federal teacher collective bargaining law, most educators see this as a state issue. In fact, public school employees are working for a state agency operating at the local level, the school district.

Forty-six states have permissive or mandatory statutes governing the rights of public school employees to organize, negotiate, exercise sanctions, and strike. There are, of course, substantial differences between these state laws. In a number of states, legislation covers all public employees; in others, a specific law covers only school employees.

Model Board of Education Policy on Collective Negotiations

The following is a sample policy on collective negotiations:

> The board of education believes that collaborative decision making is the most effective way to govern a school system. If school district employees have the right to share in the decision-making process affecting salaries, fringe benefits, and working conditions, they become more responsive and better disposed to exchanging ideas and information concerning operations with administrators. Accordingly, management becomes more efficient.
>
> The board of education further declares that harmonious and cooperative relations between itself and school district employees protect the patrons and children of the school district by assuring the orderly operation of the schools.
>
> This position of the board is to be effectuated by:
>
> 1. Recognizing the right of all school district employees to organize for the purpose of collective negotiations.
> 2. Authorizing the director of employee relations to negotiate with the duly elected employee representatives on matters relating to salaries, fringe benefits, and working conditions.
> 3. Requiring the director of employee relations to establish administrative procedures for the effective implementation of the negotiations process. This is to be accomplished under the supervision of the assistant superintendent for human resources who, in turn, is directly responsible to the superintendent of schools.
> 4. Upon successful completion of the negotiations process, the board of education will enter into written agreements with the employee organizations.

Emanating from this board of education policy is the following definition for negotiation: Collective negotiations is the process by which representatives of the school board meet with representatives of the school district employees in order to make proposals and counterproposals for the purpose of mutually agreeing on salaries, fringe benefits, and working conditions covering a specific period of time.

RECOGNITION AND BARGAINING UNIT DETERMINATION

This section is concerned with answering the basic question, *Who represents whom?* In labor history, most of the violence that occurred in the private sector centered on this query. Unions fought each other for the right to represent workers against management. The prize was power. In education, the prize is still the same, but the contest is usually nonviolent.[6]

Recognition is defined as the acceptance by an employer of some group or organization as the authorized representative of two or more employees for the purpose of collective negotiations. Without recognition, each teacher is left to make his or her own arrangements with the school board, which is the antithesis of collective negotiations.

There are two basic types of representation in education—multiple and exclusive. Multiple representation does not occur in many school districts because of the inherent problems when two or more organizations or unions represent a specific bargaining unit. Before collective negotiations elections, it was typical for multiple organizations to be accorded equal representational rights by the boards of education. There are still school districts in which more than one organization claims the right to represent a segment of the professional staff.

In multiple representation, recognition is usually granted by the board of education on the basis of organizational membership. This recognition is operationalized by one of the following methods: The board meets with representatives of each union separately; the board meets in joint sessions with equal numbers of representatives from each union; or the board meets in joint sessions with representatives of the unions proportionally determined. For example, if union A has 500 members and union B has 250 members, A is entitled to twice as many representatives on the negotiating team as B.

Exclusive recognition occurs when a single union represents all members of a bargaining unit. The technical designation for the union in this role is bargaining agent. The bargaining unit consists of all the employees whose salaries, fringe benefits, and working conditions are negotiated by the bargaining agent. The paramount importance of exclusive recognition is that the employer cannot negotiate with anyone in the unit except through the designated bargaining agent.

Exclusive recognition is the most accepted form in education for three reasons: First, it is supported by both the National Education Association and the American Federation of Teachers; second, exclusive recognition is mandated by law for the public sector in many states and widely accepted in most communities even in the absence of state legislation; and finally, private business and industry are witnesses to the fact that this is the most effective form of recognition.

Recognition procedures take various forms in education. The three most commonly used are (1) membership lists, (2) authorization cards, and (3) elections. If a union can demonstrate that it has 51 percent membership of the employees in a bargaining unit, or if 51 percent of the employees in a unit present their signatures on a card authorizing a certain union to represent them, the board may recognize this union as the exclusive bargaining agent.

A more common practice is the representation election which also is necessary in the absence of membership lists or authorization cards that signify majority support. Most school boards prefer an election as a requisite to recognizing a union as exclusive bargaining agent for a number of reasons. Some teachers who join a union may not want that union to represent them in negotiations. Teachers join certain unions for social, professional, or other reasons that have nothing to do with negotiations. In some cases, a teacher may be a member of more than one teacher union.

The representation election poses several questions that must be addressed by both the school board and the unions seeking recognition:

- Who conducts the election?
- Who will pay the costs for the election?
- What are the ground rules for electioneering?
- Who is eligible to vote?
- Who will certify the results?
- What will be the duration of the certification?

There are no correct answers to these questions. Rather, they must be answered within a framework that takes into consideration the variables affecting local situations. A cardinal principle is that the board and unions must maintain credibility and, therefore, a third party is often requested to intervene in finding a workable answer to these questions. The Federal Mediation and Conciliation Service or the League of Women Voters are examples of two independent agencies with the public image necessary to act as the appropriate third party. In many states with collective bargaining laws, recognition procedures and bargaining unit determination are mandated by state legislation. This discussion pertains to those states without legislation and to those states where the law allows latitude on these issues. Some states have public employee relations boards that conduct the elections and make a determination on who belongs to the bargaining unit.

It is necessary to more closely define the term *bargaining unit*. School districts not only employ teachers of many different subjects and levels, but they also employ a wide variety of specialists, such as psychologists, nurses, social workers, and attendance officers. In addition, there are non-certificated employees: cooks, custodians, bus drivers, maintenance workers, administrative assistants, and clerks. To have collective negotiations, there must be a determination on what specific category of employees is represented by the bargaining agent who wins the representation election. In practice, this determination must occur as part of the recognition process, because only those employees in a given bargaining unit will be allowed to vote on which union will represent them. The definition most commonly accepted states that the bargaining unit is composed of all those employees who are covered by the negotiated agreement or master contract.

The fundamental criterion for determining who belongs to the bargaining unit is formulated on the "community of interest" principle. Although it may sound elusive, the principle is not difficult to implement. Employees have a community of interest if they share skills, functions, educational levels, and working conditions. Elementary-school teachers of all levels, secondary-school teachers of all subjects, and guidance counselors clearly have a community of interest and should belong to the same bargaining unit. Clerks and administrative assistants, on the other hand, could not be effectively represented by such a unit and should constitute a separate unit by themselves. It is conceivable that a medium to large school districts might have the following units bargaining separately with the representatives of the school board:

- Certificated educators exclusive of supervisors and administrators
- Building level administrators
- Subject matter coordinators
- Administrative assistants and clerks
- Cooks and cafeteria workers
- Bus drivers
- Custodians
- Maintenance workers

Each of these bargaining units would have a separate agreement or master contract, specifying salaries, fringe benefits, and working conditions, that could be quite different from the others. Besides community of interest, there are two additional considerations determining a bargaining unit. Size of the group is important; an extremely small unit of five or ten employees will have little impact acting alone. In this case, employees would have a more strategic base from which to bargain if they combined with other categories of employees. In a small school district, for example, there might be two bargaining units: a certificated employees' unit including teachers, nurses, psychologists, and so on; and a non-certificated employees' unit including cooks, custodians, maintenance personnel, and others.

A final consideration in determining bargaining units is effective school administration. An unreasonably large number of units would be unworkable. For example, if guidance counselors, classroom teachers, speech therapists, music teachers, physical education teachers, and safety education teachers were each covered by different agreements specifying different working conditions, a building principal would have a difficult job of supervising the staff.

Two other issues have an influence on future negotiations—the agency shop and administrator bargaining units. Agency shop is a term borrowed from industry and is used when referring to a question of equity: An employee who is a member of a given bargaining unit may not be a dues-paying member of the union that is the bargaining agent. If the negotiated agreement with the school board includes an agency shop clause, such an employee would be required to pay a fee, usually the equivalent of dues, to the union. Although the employee would not be allowed to participate in internal union affairs, he or she would be allowed to participate in such unit activities as attending meetings called by the negotiating team and voting on ratification of an agreement.

A growing number of educational administrators, particularly building principals, are organizing into unions and negotiating with school boards. The reasons administrators are turning to collective negotiations include decreasing autonomy and power, and economic concerns. It appears that this trend will continue during the next two decades, and school board representatives will be negotiating with increasing numbers of administrator bargaining units.

THE SCOPE OF NEGOTIATIONS

Scope of negotiations refers to those matters that are negotiable. In some school districts, negotiations are limited to salaries; in other districts, literally hundreds of items are discussed. Negotiations must be focused on those issues that the local board of education and teachers consider to be important, or the process will be considered a failure by both boards and teachers. Behind this last statement must rest a critical perspective concerning the ultimate purpose of the negotiating process, which is student achievement. However, this objective is achieved only through negotiating items that the board of education and teachers consider to be in the best interest of the school district *and* the best interest of the professional concerns of the teachers.[8] Thus, what constitutes an important item, of course, is dictated by local circumstances. A school board might be willing to negotiate only on salaries and refuse to consider such items as a grievance procedure or reduction-in-force policy. Experience indicates that some of these nonmonetary items are just as important to teachers as salaries. Therefore, it is extremely important to place only mandatory limitations on the scope of negotiations. These limitations refer to items that are illegal by reason of state and federal constitutions, state and federal laws, or those items that are contrary to the policies of a given state board of education.[7]

Most state laws on collective negotiations stipulate that negotiations must be confined to "working conditions." However, this phrase usually refers to salaries, fringe benefits, and working conditions. The meaning of salary is self-evident, but there is some confusion over what is meant by the terms *fringe benefits* and *working conditions*. A fringe benefit may be defined as a service made available to employees as a direct result of a fiscal expenditure by the school district. Such services might include major medical insurance, hospitalization insurance, pension benefits, sick pay, dental insurance, and professional liability insurance. Working conditions pertain to the quality of the employment situation. Teaching for a particular school district might be more desirable than teaching in other districts located in the same geographic area because that district has desirable policies concerning class size, duty-free lunch periods, preparation periods, sabbatical leave, and so on.

A major concern in defining the scope of negotiations for a particular situation centers on the concept of educational policy. School boards are required by state law to set educational policy. Although many teachers are deeply interested in educational policy and believe that they should be consulted in formulating such policy, it is commonly understood that such policy is not subject to negotiations.

The following are examples of policy issues:

- Should the school district provide a foreign language program in the elementary grades?
- Should statistics be offered in the high school mathematics program?
- Should extracurricular activities be sponsored or supported by district funds?

The obvious problem is that virtually all educational policy decisions have implications affecting working conditions. For example, funds expended to introduce a foreign language program in the elementary grades could leave less money available to lower class size. Therefore, it is often impossible to decide issues pertaining to policy apart from those pertaining to working conditions.

THE BARGAINING PROCESS

The Negotiating Team

The purpose of this section is to analyze those factors that influence the "at-the-table" process of negotiations. Within this purpose, it is critical for the negotiating teams to understand and appreciate the necessity of developing a collaborative attitude towards the negotiating process.[10] The first issue that must be addressed is the composition of the school board's negotiating team. There is no universally accepted practice in forming a negotiating team; however, the size of a school district appears to have a significant influence on the makeup of the team. In small school districts, a committee of school board members usually negotiates directly with a team of teachers. In medium to large districts, the assistant superintendent for human resources along with other central-office or building-level administrators might be designated by the superintendent to negotiate with the teachers union. In some large districts, a chief negotiator is employed on a full-time or *ad hoc* basis.[9]

In keeping with the model presented in Chapter 1, medium to large school districts should employ a director of employee relations who has responsibility for managing the entire process of collective negotiations and who acts as the chief negotiator on the board's team. The size of the team is relative, but it should have an odd number of members to avoid a deadlock in making strategy decisions. Therefore, a team of three, five, or seven members would be appropriate. Experience also dictates that a team composed of more than seven members impedes decision making.

Membership on the team may be by job description, appointment, or election. The author of this book prefers a team of five members. The chairperson and chief negotiator, of course, is the director of employee relations, by virtue of job position. Additional membership on the team should include building-level principals, because they are the first-line supervisors who will be managing the master agreement. Also, many principals have been critical of school boards for "negotiating away" their authority. On a five-member team, one principal from each level (elementary school, junior or middle school, high school) elected by the other principals would give the team high credibility among building administrators. The final member of the team should have some specific expertise and knowledge of the district's financial condition. Thus, the assistant superintendent for administrative services or the business manager would be an appropriate appointee.

This team must function as an entity over the entire academic year. As will be pointed out later in this section, the development of strategies and the construction of proposal packages cannot be accomplished only during a few months of the year. Although a major portion of work will fall to the director of employee relations, the team will be required to expend a great deal of time. However, it is helpful to the collaboration that is necessary for teachers' and board's teams to meet throughout the year. Consequently, it is advisable to provide those principals who serve on the team with some compensation such as a stipend or with additional administrative assistance in their buildings.

The negotiating team for the teachers, of course, is composed of teachers. Sometimes, the officers of the local association or union act as the team; in other situations, a negotiating team is appointed by the union officers or elected by the teachers. If the local is affiliated with a national union, experts in the bargaining process are made available to advise union officers.

A final issue concerning the board's negotiating team must be addressed. What if the building administrators organize, form a bargaining unit, and elect a bargaining agent to represent them concerning salaries, fringe benefits, and working conditions? This, of course, is the current trend, especially in large urban school districts. In this case, the same structure for the board's negotiating team may be maintained with the substitution of assistant superintendents for principals. Because each bargaining unit negotiates a separate master agreement, which reflects salaries, fringe benefits, and working conditions for employees in a given job category, it is not inconsistent with good administration for principals to negotiate for the board on the one hand and against the board on the other hand.

Developing Strategies

The negotiating team is responsible for the entire bargaining process, which must begin with strategy development. This entails two activities, (1) assessing the needs of the school district and (2) establishing goals for negotiations. It is always important to enter into negotiations from the perspective that there must be give-and-take on both sides.[11]

Needs assessment may take various forms, but certain tasks must be completed:

- Review the current master agreement to determine if its provisions meet the goals of the district and if they allow for effective administration.
- Study the previous negotiating sessions to determine if the ground rules provide for effective negotiations.
- Analyze the formal grievances filed by both the union and administration.
- Study the arbitration decisions rendered on these grievances.
- Meet with school district administrators to gather input concerning the provisions of the current master agreement.
- Meet informally with the union to ascertain their concerns over the current agreement.
- Confer with the board of education and superintendent to learn their concerns and to establish fiscal parameters.

From this information the team sets the goals and objectives for negotiations, which are formulated into operational language in the proposal package.

SETTING THE GROUND RULES

With the advice and consent of the negotiating team, the chairperson should meet with the union negotiators to determine rules for the "at-the-table" process. A significant perspective in setting the ground rules is that no two school districts are alike and that holds true for the teachers and staff members that will be engaged in the negotiating process. Attention to the culture or cultures operating in the schools are important perspectives to keep in mind on both sides of the table.[12] Key points that must be determined include:

- The time and place for the sessions
- The number of participants who will sit at the table
- The role of each participant
- The manner in which each side will present its proposals
- The target date for completing negotiations
- The kinds of school district data that will be needed by each side
- The conditions governing caucuses

- The provisions for recording the sessions
- The method to be used in recording counterproposals and agreements
- The policy on press releases
- The types of impasse procedures that will be employed and when
- The format for the written agreement
- The procedure for agreement approval by the school board and union membership
- The procedure that will be used in publishing the ratified agreement

At-the-Table Sessions

There are two objectives for being "at the table." First, through making proposals and counterproposals, the negotiating teams should be able to ascertain what issues are critically important to each side. Second, each team should be able to assess the other side's bargaining power. This is the ability to get the other team to agree on an item or the entire proposal package based on your terms.

Thus, the bargaining power of the school board's team can be viewed in terms of what would be the cost to the teachers' team of disagreeing with the terms of the school board in contrast to what would be the cost of agreeing with the terms. In like manner, the bargaining power of the teachers' team can be viewed in terms of what would be the cost to the board's team of disagreeing with the terms of the teachers in contrast to what would be the cost of agreeing with the terms.

Political pressures, negotiating skill, and psychological elements are important sources of bargaining power. Although it is impossible to measure bargaining power exactly, it is apparent that, at some time, the overall advantages of agreement outweigh the overall disadvantages of agreement. During the bargaining sessions, it is very important to keep the board and entire administrative staff informed as to the progress being made. If this is not effectively accomplished, rumors may adversely affect the bargaining power of the board's team.

When an agreement is reached by the negotiating teams, ratification by the respective governing bodies is the final step in the process. The board's team meets with the superintendent and board of education to explain and recommend the agreement. In like manner, the union's team meets with the bargaining unit membership to explain and recommend the agreement. Formal ratification occurs when a majority of school board members vote to accept the agreement and when a majority of the bargaining unit membership similarly votes approval.

Because negotiating is an art rather than a science, it is extremely difficult to develop a formula for success. Nevertheless, a number of practical hints may be in order. The following are recommendations made to local boards of education by the Ohio School Board Association:

- *Keep calm—don't lose control of yourself.* Negotiation sessions can be exasperating. The temptation may come to get angry and fight back when intemperate accusations are made or when "the straw that broke the camel's back" is hurled on the table.
- *Avoid "off the record" comments.* Nothing is "off the record." Innocently made remarks have a way of coming back to haunt those who said them. Be careful to say only what you are willing to have quoted.
- *Don't be overly-candid.* Inexperienced negotiators may, with the best of intentions, desire to "lay the cards on the table face up." This may be done in the mistaken notion that everybody fully understands the other and utter frankness is desired. Complete candor does not always serve the best interests of productive negotiations. This is not a plea for duplicity; rather, it is a recommendation for prudent and discriminating utterances.

- *Be long on listening.* Usually a good listener makes a good negotiator. It is wise to let your "adversaries" do the talking—at least in the beginning.
- *Do not be afraid of a "little heat."* Discussions sometimes generate quite a bit of heat. Do not be afraid of it. It never hurts to let the "opposition" sound off even when you may be tempted to "sound" back.
- *Watch the voice level.* A wise practice is to keep the pitch of the voice down even though the temptation may be strong to let it rise under the excitement of emotional stress.
- *Keep flexible.* One of the skills of good negotiators is the ability to shift position a bit if a positive gain can thus be accomplished. An obstinate adherence to one position or point of view, regardless of the ultimate consequences of that rigidity, may be more of a deterrent than an advantage.
- *Refrain from a flat "no."* Especially in the earlier stages of a negotiation it is best to avoid giving a flat "no" to a proposition. It doesn't help to work yourself into a box by being totally negative too early.
- *Give to get.* Negotiation is the art of giving and getting. Concede a point to gain a concession. This is the name of the game.
- *Work on the easier items first.* Settle first those things that generate the least controversy. Leave the tougher items until later in order to avoid an early deadlock.
- *Respect your adversary.* Respect those who are seated on the opposite side of the table. Assume that their motives are as sincere as your own, at least until proven otherwise.
- *Be patient.* If necessary, be willing to sit out tiresome tirades. Time has a way of being on the side of the patient negotiator.
- *Avoid waving red flags.* There are some statements that irritate teachers and merely heighten their antipathies. Find out what these are and avoid their use. Needless waving of red flags only infuriates. For example, nothing agitates teachers more than stating that they only work nine months for their salaries while taxpayers work twelve months.
- *Let the other side win some victories.* Each team has to win some victories. A "shut out" may be a hollow gain in negotiation.
- *Negotiation is a way of life.* Obvious resentment of the fact that negotiation is here to stay weakens the effectiveness of the negotiator. The better part of wisdom is to adjust to it and become better prepared to use it as a tool of inter-staff relations.

IMPASSE PROCEDURES

In considering impasse procedures, it is important to understand what could be the root case of an impasse. The most common cause is a lack of "good faith" in the bargaining process, which is the product of a closed mindset before the process begins.[13]

It is extremely difficult to define the term *impasse*. Negotiators often have trouble knowing when an impasse has been reached. However, for this discussion, an impasse will be considered as a persistent disagreement that continues after normal negotiation procedures have been exhausted.

An impasse must be expected to occur from time to time, even when both parties are negotiating in good faith. There are, unfortunately, no procedures that are guaranteed to resolve an impasse. Some procedures have been more successful than others, and the objective of this section is to outline these procedures. Also, it must be kept in mind that improperly used impasse procedures can aggravate rather than resolve a disagreement. Therefore, a working knowledge of procedures is essential to all participants in the negotiating process.

Twenty-two of the states that have passed collective negotiations laws also have established public employee relations boards. Each board is charged with implementing the law and, in most cases, with administering impasse procedures, including mediation, fact finding, and arbitration.

Mediation

Mediation is usually the first procedure used when an impasse has been reached. The negotiators for both labor and management must agree on the need for third-party assistance. The role of the mediator is advisory, and consequently, the mediator has no authority to dictate a settlement. Some mediators use the tactic of first meeting with both parties separately and thereby, attempt to ascertain what concessions each party might be willing to make in order to reach an agreement. This procedure has been most effective when one or both parties consider making concessions to be a sign of weakness. Meeting jointly with both parties is helpful, particularly in assessing the actual status of negotiations and in obtaining agreement from the parties on the importance assigned to each unresolved issue. Most mediators will use a combination of separate and joint meetings to facilitate an agreement.[14]

Mediators usually refrain from recommending a settlement until they are sure that their recommendations will be acceptable to both parties. Up until the time of recommendation, the mediator acts only as a clarifier of issues and through the process attempts to defuse the antagonism between the parties, which is frequently the cause of the impasse. A mediator may be called into a dispute at any time. In some cases, the mediator may even practice preventive mediation by making suggestions useful to the parties early in the negotiations. Because mediation is a voluntary process, in the stages preparatory to the actual negotiations, the parties must decide who will mediate and what the mediator's role will be. In approximately one-third of the states, this issue is settled by statute and a formal declaration of "impasse" is all that is required to put the process in motion. Often a master agreement will contain provisions outlining impasse procedures to be followed in negotiating the agreement. When mediator services are not provided by a governmental agency, the fee for a private mediator is borne equally by both parties to the dispute.

Fact Finding

Fact finding is the procedure by which an individual or a panel holds hearings to review evidence and make recommendations for settling the dispute. Like mediation, the fact-finding process is governed by a state statute, provided for in a master agreement, or established by both parties before negotiations begin.

The formal hearing is usually open to the public. Parties having a vested interest in the dispute are given the opportunity to offer evidence and arguments in their own behalf. Fact finders are sometimes requested by both parties to mediate the dispute and avoid the formal hearings.

The fact-finding report and recommendations are usually made public. The process is voluntary, and the parties may reject all or part of the report. To a certain extent, the action of the parties will depend on the public's reactions, which in turn depend partly on the prestige of the fact finders.

Arbitration

Arbitration is the process by which the parties submit their dispute to an impartial third person or panel of persons that issues an award the parties are required to accept. Arbitration can be either compulsory or voluntary. Compulsory arbitration must be established by statute; 19 states have such legislation. The voluntary use of arbitration has gained some acceptance in the public sector for handling grievances arising from the interpretation of master agreements.[15]

The Federal Mediation and Conciliation Service

The Federal Mediation and Conciliation Service (FMCS) works annually to resolve disagreements arising out of collective negotiations in the public sector, which amounted to approximately 8 percent of the agency's caseload. The Federal Mediation and Conciliation Service is an independent agency of the federal government created by Congress in 1974 with a director appointed by the President of the United States. The primary purpose of the FMCS is to promote labor-management peace. To more effectively carry out this mission, the agency has established regional offices and field offices staffed by professional mediators.

Federal labor laws do not cover employees of state and local governments. However, if state legislatures fail to establish mediation services for public employees, the FMCS may voluntarily enter a dispute. The FMCS also has an Office of Arbitration Services in Washington, D.C. This office maintains a roster of arbitrators located in all parts of the country. On request, FMCS will furnish a randomly selected list of arbitrators from which the parties to a dispute may choose a mutually acceptable arbitrator to hear the dispute and make a decision.

In summary, it is too difficult to promote one impasse procedure as the most effective approach to handling all persistent disputes that arise at the bargaining table or in grievances over master agreement interpretation. It is more appropriate to think in terms of sequence. Mediation should be utilized first, followed by fact-finding, and then, where it is permitted by law, arbitration. This sequence places the responsibility for resolving the dispute first on the parties themselves. Experience teaches that better and more effective agreements are reached when the parties can resolve their own disputes. Yet, when disputes cannot be resolved and when it is mandated by law, arbitration curtails strikes, which always have a devastating effect upon school districts.

WORK STOPPAGE STRATEGIES

The Scope of Strikes

Nothing is more disruptive to a school district than a strike. As board members, administrators, teachers, and support personnel engage in heated and public argument, schisms occur that often last for years. Community groups also become divided over who is right and who is wrong. When a strike occurs, the administrative team has the responsibility to keep the schools open; to protect students who report to school; to protect school property; and to maintain communications with parents, teachers, and the public.

Work stoppages by public school employees are illegal or, at least, limited by most state laws. However, this has not prevented strikes from occurring each year in many states. The news media daily remind us of the magnitude of this issue. There is also no indication that strikes will go away as school employees, administrators, and teachers become more proficient in the negotiations process.

In past decades, most teachers felt that strikes were not in keeping with their professional status. This thinking has vanished, and the personal traumas once associated with this type of action also are gone. Today, teachers engage in strikes over many issues, including recognition of their unions, salary increases, curriculum control, reduction in force, and lack of community support. Teachers also have honored strikes by nonteaching personnel and have attempted to get their unions to support them in their work stoppages.

School Employee Strike Tactics

A strike by school employees is usually the result of failure at the bargaining table. The objective of all strikes is to gain as favorable a settlement as possible from the board of education within the shortest period of time.

A few key issues have been used by teacher unions to rally support for a strike. These include the pupil/teacher ratio; planning time, particularly for elementary school teachers; and, extra pay for extra duty, particularly for secondary-school teachers. With the onslaught of the accountability reform movement, the rallying call centers on job security and compensation issues.

Teacher unions have almost unlimited resources from their state and national affiliates at their disposal in a strike. In very sensitive strikes, as many as a 100 field staff members may be available to help the local union. A careful examination of several strikes will verify the following tactics as some of the most commonly used by teacher unions:

- Inundating the community with the reasons for the strike. Handbills, advertisements in the local press, and news coverage are the main vehicles usually employed.
- Placing the blame on a specific person such as the superintendent of schools or board president, thus channeling the pressure exerted by parents and the community.
- Encouraging local and state politicians to become involved in the dispute. School employee groups represent a sizable number of votes.
- Working diligently to gain support from other unions in the community.
- Staging a strike in the late spring because this will interfere not only with graduation but also with state aid, which is usually calculated on a certain number of days in attendance before the end of the school year.

Although some strikes do occur spontaneously because of unexpected developments, most teacher work stoppages are well-orchestrated. Teacher unions generally are aware weeks or even months in advance that certain negotiation demands are strike-producing issues.

Administrative Strategies

If a school system finds itself in the middle of a strike without an adequate plan of action, the administration and the board of education have not been paying attention to the tenor of the times or to the situation in their own school district. In fact, the superintendent and his or her cabinet should have a carefully developed strike plan even in the most tranquil of school settings. The strike plan should operate at both the district and building levels. Exhibit 9.1 contains a series of steps that can serve as a guide for administrators in establishing their own individual district plans. The exhibit has been fashioned after a plan that was developed by the American Association of School Administrators.

When the administrative control center set forth in Exhibit 9.1 is established at the central office, duties are assigned by the superintendent of schools with the advice of his or her cabinet. Central-office administrators are assigned specific tasks to be performed during a strike. The director of labor relations could be given the task of notifying staff members of the state law and board policy concerning strikes. The director of community relations would have the responsibility of notifying the news media of the manner for providing daily information concerning a strike. In like manner, the building principal and, if it is a large school, his or her administrative team are responsible for implementing the building-level provisions.

EXHIBIT 9.1

Sample Strike Plan

Before a Strike

District Level

The Board of Education should develop an overall district plan well in advance of an anticipated strike. Such a plan should include the following provisions:

- Notifying the news media, parents, teachers, and staff of the likelihood of a strike
- Notifying teachers and staff members of applicable state law and school board policy concerning a strike
- Establishing provisions for an administrative control center where administrators will have the capability of dealing with issues that arise in a strike
- Contacting emergency responders such as the police and fire department about the possibility of a strike and establishing a method of contact in an emergency
- Developing electronic emergency communication systems for on-going information to all constituencies
- Having the board of education pass necessary legal resolutions required to deal with a strike such as restraining orders and injunctions

Building Level

The principal should develop an overall building plan in conformity with the district plan well in advance of an anticipated strike. Such a plan should include the following provisions:

- Securing back-up personnel for each building principal to act in his or her stead during the strike
- Making provision for a daily, early-morning report to the administrative control center setting forth the names of teachers and staff members who reported for duty and the number of students in attendance at the school
- Making provision for continuity of communications if the usual means of communication are disrupted in the school
- Making provision for each building principal to have specific guidelines and authority to close the school when the safety and health of the students are threatened, or when it is impossible to carry on an educational program
- Making provision for building security

After a Strike

District Level

The board of education should develop an overall district plan that includes the following provisions:

- Notifying all constituencies that the strike has ended
- Holding information sessions for all administrators and board members.
- Holding information sessions for building principals in preparation for the return of teachers
- Providing information to all other constituents about the details of the strike settlement
- Developing a plan to defuse "anti-climactic" emotions

Building Level

The principal should develop an overall building plan in conformity with the district plan containing the following provisions:

- Making plans to not allow teachers who participate in the strike to return to the classrooms until all substitute teachers are out of the school
- Making plans to focus major attention on the educational program and learning environment for students

ADMINISTRATION OF THE MASTER AGREEMENT

Collective negotiations is ineffective unless the agreement reached by a board of education and a union or organization is codified in writing. Thus, a detailed written master agreement becomes the policy statement governing the board and union or organization in relation to the issues and rights of the parties that were agreed to. If the agreement is not reduced to writing, there is a likely possibility and even a probability that controversies will arise concerning what was agreed to. Also, the master agreement becomes a tool to be used in communicating with all constituents in the school district, which is so critical because of the focus on transparency in the collective negotiating process.[16]

Most master agreements include the salaries, fringe benefits, and working conditions that were negotiated. The following articles are universal and should be included in all master agreements:

- General Purpose and Duration of the Agreement
- Recognition
- Description of Employees in the Bargaining Unit
- Fair Practices Provisions
- Redirection of the Agreement
- Ratification and Final Disposition
- Grievance Procedure
- Description of Employees in the Bargaining Unit
- Impasse Procedures

The style and format of the master agreement will sometimes be dictated by state statutes; but in the absence of legislation, school boards and unions must look elsewhere for help. In many cases, teacher associations affiliated with national unions have access to model master agreements that can be adapted to local situations. In fact, some models are complete in every detail except for filling in the blanks with the proper data.

Implementing the Master Agreement

It is the responsibility of the administration to implement and interpret the provisions of the agreement. Furthermore, the administration is limited only by the specifics of the master agreement, which is commonly referred to as "management prerogative."

In the day-to-day interpretations of the agreement, it is certainly possible for violations to occur. Most written agreements, therefore, provide for a grievance procedure by which individuals or the union can allege that the master agreement is being violated or misinterpreted. Most grievance procedures contain the following elements:

- A detailed descriptive definition of the term grievance
- The purpose of the grievance procedure
- A clause stating that a person alleging a grievance or testifying in a grievance will not face prejudicial treatment by the other party
- A clear outline of the appropriate steps to be taken in a grievance and the time allotments between each step
- In the case of arbitration, who will bear the costs of arbitration and the qualifications required for an arbitrator

Labor-Management Relations Committee

In an attempt to diffuse the adversarial relationship that sometimes exists between the board of education/administration and unions, labor-management committees have been organized in some school districts. The charge to these committees is to work through concerns, problems, and issues before they appear at the table in the next round of negotiations. In a large school district, the director of employee relations will have the responsibility of chairing the board/administration team, which should include first-line supervisors. In smaller districts, an assistant superintendent or even the superintendent may wish to assume this responsibility. Shop stewards or other representatives of a given union will constitute labor's membership on the committee.

The approach to labor-management committee meetings should be informal with the emphasis upon mutual interests and collaboration. Compromise is the key to a successful relationship as is true in at-the-table negotiations. A win-win strategy should also prevail, with each party attempting to come away with something that it wants. Whatever is agreed to at these sessions should be put into writing, which, in turn, will help avoid confusion at a later time. Of course, a labor-management committee should not deal with monetary and fringe benefits issues but, rather, with working conditions. If this committee is to be successful, it must meet throughout the term of the master agreement.

Alternative Approaches to Collective Negotiations

In the mid-1980s, a movement began with the hope of defusing the hostility that sometimes accompanies collective negotiations. This has resulted in a derivation of the collective negotiations model presented in this chapter. In collaborative bargaining there are not two teams, but just one and it is composed of teachers, board members, and administrators. This team's mission is to problem-solve rather than to engage in bargaining.

The collaborative model was operationalized in the Ashland, Oregon School District in 1986. As part of the process, their team went through a seven-part training program that included communication skills; problem-solving skills; creative-thinking skills; orientation to collaborative bargaining; development of group agreements; development of super ordinate goals; and group recorder, convener, and process observer roles.

Super ordinate goals, such as "enhancing teaching and learning," are highly valued, attainable, and commonly sought after by the group members. These goals provide the framework within which the various issues are addressed and solved. Consensus is the essence of the decision-making process. However, collaborative negotiations usually requires more time than the more traditional model. It can be a very effective approach especially if the traditional model has resulted in overt hostility. However, it is important to approach collaborative negotiations with caution; it is not a panacea.

TECHNOLOGY AND COLLECTIVE NEGOTIATIONS

In keeping with what has been stated in the preceding chapters, the amount of information that is available because of technology has changed the negotiations-planning process for boards of education, the administration, and teachers unions and organizations. Furthermore, the scope and analysis of data has also changed the at-the-table negotiating process. These dimensions of collective negotiations have moved the process into a more complete and focused evidence-based approach to decision making.

In many school districts, the skepticism of faulty data or incomplete data that dominated many negotiating sessions has ceased to exist. Of course, this evidence-based approach to decision making can only be successful if two demonstrated board of education or administrative policies are firmly operationalized. First, there must be a culture in the school district that values and uses data in all decision making. Second, there must be complete transparency in terms of the school district's budgeting process. Revenue and expenditures must be available on the district's Web site for all to review.

For example, salary information should be available that sets forth the number of teachers that fall on the various categories and levels of the salary schedule. Administrator salaries, in like manner, should be available. This does not mean that an individual's salary should be on-line except for that of the superintendent of schools and, in some districts, the salaries of the assistant superintendents.

School districts that have a computer network, which captures data from all administrative functions into databases, can make available data that will give a complete picture of the school district's financial situation. This is critical in all collective negotiations. For example, it is possible to generate reports on fringe benefit usage such as medical and hospital insurances usage, sick day leave, and extra-curricular compensation. The Internet and school district Web sites permit a school district and teachers union or organization to garner comparative data from other school districts on all aspects of budgeting not only in terms of salaries and fringe benefits, but also on expenditures that impinge upon working conditions such as class size and the number of teacher assistants.

Technology also provides the boards of education, the administration, and teachers unions and organizations with the opportunity to keep all constituents apprised of progress in the negotiations process through emails, iPods, and other electronic devices.

IMPLICATIONS FOR SMALL AND MEDIUM-SIZED SCHOOL DISTRICTS

Of course, there are many school districts that do not have full-time directors or assistant superintendents for human resources administration nor for employee relations. In fact, the superintendent of schools and members of the board of education may be the negotiators for the school district designated to meet with the teachers' representatives. There may be only one bargaining unit that represents both teachers and staff members. There may be no formal ground rules for the negotiating process. Impasse procedures may be limited to time away from the negotiating table waiting for parents to demand that the board of education and teachers' organization or union return to the table. There may be no requirement in the state where the school district is located to formalize the final agreement with the teachers into a master agreement. However, boards of education, administrators, and teachers are engaged in collective negotiations in 46 states across the United States.

Thus, the purpose in organizing the material in this chapter is to provide the reader with the maximum amount of information on the most advantageous manner to engage in collective negotiation. It is understood that each person will take from this chapter the material that will be most helpful given his or her current situation.

However, regardless of the individual size of the school district or the legal requirement to engage in some form of collective negotiations, the following elements of the negotiations process should be adhered to:

- The teachers and staff members should be represented by the union or organization that they designate through a formal process of selection.
- Negotiations should be centered on salaries, fringe benefits, and working conditions.
- Those charged with representing the board of education and the teachers and staff should agree upon a set of ground rules on how the at-the-table meetings will take place.

- The representatives of the board and teachers and staff should agree upon data that the district should provide for the negotiating process.
- The final agreement must be ratified by the board of education and the teachers and staff members in the aggregate through a formal vote.
- Work stoppage should be avoided at all costs.

THE IMPACT OF GENERATION Y TEACHERS AND ADMINISTRATORS ON COLLECTIVE NEGOTIATIONS

As set forth in Chapter 8, Compensation, Generation Y teachers and administrators are concerned about equity and fairness, financially supporting themselves and their families, saving money for retirement, and participating in governance to the extent that they can affect policy.

All of these characteristics are addressed in the collective negotiations process, which typically includes bargaining for improved working conditions, better fringe benefits, and higher salaries. At the foundation of all these characteristics is the search for security that is usually manifested in having a good job with an adequate salary accompanied by good fringe benefits and with an opportunity for career advancement. It is what Samuel Gompers always answered when asked about what he wanted from management, which is *more.* Thus, Generation Y teachers and administrators are usually very supportive of professional associations like the National Education Association (NEA) and the American Federation of Teachers (AFT) because these associations are supportive of participation in the policy making process, which is the ultimate purpose for engaging in collective negotiations.

They also tend to be activists in the political process at all levels, which certainly would include supporting candidates for boards of education who are supportive of teachers and administrators to the extent that they need and deserve better working conditions, fringe benefits, and salaries. Working conditions that would very likely be of interest to Generation Y teachers include those that recognize the importance of balancing professional and personal responsibilities such as job sharing and daycare services in the school district for teachers and administrators with very young children. Like other younger teachers and administrator, Generation Y employees are greatly concerned about having a salary that will help them as they start their families, while teachers and administrators from other generations are probably concerned about better fringe benefits.

A final characteristic about Generation Y employees is their desire to get ahead faster than teachers and administrators from other generations. Thus staff development opportunities and assistance with tuition for graduate education are also concerns of Generation Y.

Quick Review of Essentials

Collective negotiation has become an accepted part of American education, as evidenced by the fact that over three-fourths of the states have enacted collective negotiations laws affecting teachers. The underlying consideration in collective negotiations is participation in the decision-making process, which is a natural extension of our democratic life style.

Teachers and administrators want to have input into the priorities established by school boards when these affect their salaries, fringe benefits, and working conditions. Collective negotiations may be defined as the process by which representatives of the school board meet with representatives of the school district employees in order to make proposals and counterproposals for the purpose of agreeing on salaries, fringe benefits, and working conditions for a specific period of time. To operationalize this process, it is necessary for the board of education to adopt a policy that will give the administration authority to implement negotiations.

There are six aspects to the collective negotiations process: (1) recognition and bargaining unit determination, (2) the scope of negotiations, (3) the bargaining process, (4) impasse procedures, (5) work stoppages, and (6) the administration of the master agreement.

Recognition and bargaining unit determination answer the question, *Who represents whom?* Recognition is the acceptance by an employer of a bargaining agent as the authorized representative of a bargaining unit. There are two types of recognition, multiple and exclusive. Experience indicates that exclusive recognition is the most effective. The three most commonly used recognition procedures are (1) membership lists, (2) authorization cards, and (3) elections. In an election, a third party, such as the Federal Mediation and Conciliation Service, should be engaged to handle the mechanics of the election process.

The bargaining unit is composed of all employees to be covered by the negotiated master agreement. The criteria for deciding who belongs to the unit include a community of interest among the members, effective bargaining power, and effective school administration.

The scope of what is negotiable usually includes salaries, fringe benefits, and working conditions. A major problem in defining the scope is the fine line between educational policy, which is the prerogative of the school board, and working conditions, which are negotiable.

The at-the-table bargaining process must begin with the formation of a negotiations team. An odd-numbered team composed of the director of employee relations, building principals, and a central-office fiscal administrator has the greatest potential for being effective. This team is responsible for developing strategies, formulating goals, setting the ground rules, preparing proposals, and participating in negotiating sessions. Once an agreement is reached, the team makes a recommendation to the superintendent and school board members, who formally ratify the agreement.

If there is persistent disagreement at the table after normal negotiations procedures are exhausted, an impasse has been reached. The three procedures usually employed in an impasse are (1) mediation, (2) fact finding, and, where permitted by law, (3) arbitration. Mediation is the voluntary process of bringing in a third party who intervenes for the purpose of ending the disagreement. Fact finding is a procedure by which an individual or panel holds hearings for the purpose of reviewing evidence and making a recommendation for settling the dispute. Arbitration occurs when both sides submit the dispute to an impartial third person or panel that issues an award which the parties are required to accept.

Nothing is more disruptive to a school district than a strike, a tactic that is sometimes used by unions when negotiations reach an impasse. Although strikes by teachers are illegal in most states, a number of strikes occur each year throughout the country. It is extremely important, therefore, for the administration to develop a strike plan, even in the most tranquil of school settings.

The process of collective negotiations is usually ineffective unless the agreements reached are put in writing, thus formalizing the basic rights governing the parties and reducing potential controversy. It is the responsibility of the administration to implement and interpret the master agreement. Furthermore, the administration is limited only by the specifics of the agreement, which is commonly referred to as "management prerogative."

In the day-to-day interpretation of the master agreement, it is certainly possible for violations to occur. Most written agreements, therefore, provide for a grievance procedure by which individuals or the union may allege that the agreement is being violated. In some school districts, labor-management relations committees have been formed for the purpose of working through concerns, problems, and issues before they appear at-the-table when the existing master contract is renegotiated.

Innovative approaches arose in the mid-1980s. The purposes of these approaches were to defuse hostilities that sometimes accompany the traditional negotiations process. In this process, there is one team composed of teachers or other categories of employees reflecting the bargaining unit, administrators, and board members. The goal is to problem-solve issues, and the essence of the process is consensus.

The amount of information that is available because of technology has changed the negotiations planning process for boards of education, the administration, and teachers unions and organizations. Furthermore, the scope and analysis of data has also changed the at-the-table negotiating process. These dimensions of collective negotiations have moved the process into a more complete and focused evidence-based approach to decision making.

Selected Further Readings

Bennett, Ron, & John Gray, "Principal-Centered Negotiations," *Leadership*, 36, no. 5 (May/June 2007), 22–24.

Department of Labor. www.dol.gov, 2007.

Hewitt, Paul, "Bargaining within the School Culture," *Leadership*, 36, no. 5 (May/June 2007), 26–30.

Holley, William H., Kenneth M. Jennings, and Roger S. Wolters. *The Labor Relations Process*. Winfield, Kansas: Southwestern College Publication, 2007.

Kerchner, Charles Taylor, & Julia E. Koppich, "Negotiating What Matters Most: Collective Bargaining and Student Achievement," *American Journal of Education*, 113 (Electronically Published, March 2007), 349–365.

Martinez-Pecino, Roberto, Lourdes Munduate, Francisco J. Medina, and Martin C. Euwema, "Effectiveness of Mediation Strategies in Collective Bargaining," *Industrial Relations*, 47, no. 3 (July 2008), 480–495.

Stover, Del, "State of the Unions," *American School Board Journal* (April 2008).

CHAPTER

10

Legal and Ethical Issues in the Administration of Human Resources

FOCUS SCENARIO

You are the director of risk management in a large metropolitan school district serving approximately 30,000 students. You and your staff have conducted the yearly safety and security audit and have found a number of safety hazards and security needs in many of the district's schools. The audit report is a written document that is presented to the assistant superintendent for human relations. However, she has informed you that the facilities budget has been reduced by 10 percent due to a shortfall in state aid again for a second year, which will keep many of your safety and security recommendations from being implemented.

Shortly after you were told that the money was not available for building repairs, a loose ceiling tile fell on a student causing a laceration to her head that required plastic surgery. The parents of the student have retained an attorney who has filed a lawsuit alleging negligence by the school district. The assistant superintendent for human resources talked with you about the incident and reminded you that the employee responsible for the maintenance of the building where the accident occurred is an at-will employee without a contract and that he can be terminated for neglecting the necessary repairs. She further indicated that the audit reports are internal documents that do not need to be made available to the public.

You set forth in writing to the assistant superintendent that the policy of the school district requires a thorough investigation by the school district's attorney when a lawsuit is filed in order to determine the material facts before a defense strategy can be formulated. This is the second year that the annual audit report has included the identification of loose ceiling tiles. You have the distinct impression from the assistant superintendent that she wants you to find a way to minimize the potential for the district to lose the case in court.

This final chapter is concerned with legal and ethical issues in the administration of human resources. An understanding by current and future human resources administration of litigation has become more important within the last decade because of the ever-increasing societal emphasis on legal rights and responsibilities. Human resources administrators are as vulnerable to litigation as teachers and principals. In fact, with the multitude of federal and state laws, regulations, and procedures that impinge upon human resources functions, defensibility and accountability must be continuing concerns in the human resources department.

Relevant, concise, and clear personnel policies become the foundation upon which the eight human resources functions rest. Administrative processes and procedures operationalize these policies and provide the internal structure necessary to accomplish the school district's primary mandate, to educate children. Consequently, this chapter has been written with these issues in mind and should provide direction to all persons concerned with human resources administration including boards of education, superintendents, assistant superintendents, and human resources managers.

CONTRACT MANAGEMENT

Teachers and administrators usually work under the provisions of an individual contract; classified personnel such as clerks, bus drivers, and custodians are employed at an hourly rate or for an annual salary. In school districts where a master contract has been negotiated by a union, teachers and/or administrators belonging to the bargaining unit do not have individual contracts, but rather work under the provisions of the master agreement. There are exceptions to these general statements; however, for all practical purposes these are the alternative methods by which employees are hired to work in a school system.[1]

The question may legitimately be asked, "What is the purpose of issuing individual contracts to teachers and administrators?" While the purpose will vary in different states, the most accurate response is tradition. As professionals, teachers and administrators are employed to perform a service for which they receive a certain amount of financial compensation. The performance of the service may require a teacher to take student projects home to be graded or may require a teacher to remain after the school day to talk with the parents of a student having problems. The time it takes to perform the service and the amount of work involved are not considerations under the contract method of employment.

Classified employees also are paid to perform a service, but the time and work involved does make a difference in the amount of money received. When such employees are required to work after the regular eight-hour day, they receive overtime pay. If they are required to perform a task not specified by the categories outlined in their job descriptions, they receive additional compensation.

Those professional employees who are covered by the terms of a master agreement have a closer identity to classified employees than to teachers and administrators with individual contracts. Their working conditions are spelled out in the master agreement.

Board of education policies sometimes address working conditions, but these policies are usually not as specific as the terms of a master agreement. Teacher and administrator handbooks also may contain references to working conditions, but these are usually more concerned with internal procedures.

Although using individual contracts for teachers and administrators is a matter of tradition, it is also mandated in some states such as Missouri. Individual contracts also distinguish an individual's working conditions from those termed "classified." A teacher's or administrator's contract must meet the requirements of general contract law. Because school districts are legal entities with a corporate character, they may sue and be sued; purchase, receive, or sell real and personal property; make contracts and be contracted with. The contracts entered into by a school district must conform not only to contract law, but also to state statutes governing contracts and to the precedents established through case law. An individual contract is an agreement that must possess five basic components in order for it to be valid. The components are (1) offer and acceptance, (2) competent persons, (3) consideration, (4) legal subject matter, and (5) proper form.

Offer and Acceptance

A valid contract must contain an offer and an acceptance. In the selection process, therefore, it is poor procedure to notify unsuccessful candidates for a position that the job has been filled until after the prospective employee has accepted the offer of employment. For example, if the board of education approves a contract for a specific person to teach high school English, there is no agreement until the contract is executed, which constitutes acceptance.

A few other facts about the legal nature of an agreement must be kept in mind. First, an offer can be accepted only by the person to whom it was made. For example, the husband of a candidate for a teaching position cannot accept the offer for his wife. Second, an offer must be accepted within a reasonable time after it is made. If an individual does not sign and return a contract within a few weeks in the hope that another job offer will be made by a different school district, the board of education may offer the contract to another candidate. Finally, a newspaper advertisement is not an offer of a position, but rather an invitation to become a candidate for a job.

Competent Persons

A contract is not valid unless it is entered into by two or more competent parties. This means that the persons have the legal capacity to enter into a contract. As a corporate entity, a school district has the power, through the legal action of the school board, to enter into a contract. Certain classes of individuals, however, have a limited capacity to contract. The most commonly identified classes include minors, mentally ill persons, and individuals who are intoxicated. If a person was mentally ill or intoxicated to the extent that he or she did not understand the significance of the action at the time of entering into a contract, he or she may have the contract set aside because there was no agreement, which is essential to the validity of every contract.

Consideration

For a contract to be valid, it must be supported by a consideration, which is usually defined as something of value. The type of consideration found in an employment contract is referred to as "a promise for an act." For example, in a teacher's contract the board of education promises to pay an individual $40,000 to teach third grade for one year. The teacher fulfills the act by teaching during the designated time period.

Legal Subject Matter

In all 50 states an individual may teach only if he or she possesses a license to teach issued by the respective state department of education. Consequently, if a board of education enters into a contract with a person who does not possess a license to teach the third grade, such a contract would involve illegal subject matter and would be invalid.

Proper Form

For a contract to be enforceable, it must be in the form required by law. The courts recognize both oral and written contracts. However, most states have statutory provisions that require teachers' and administrators' contracts to be in writing and even specify the proper wording for the contracts.

LITIGATION IN HUMAN RESOURCES MANAGEMENT

School districts have experienced an increase in litigation partially due to the fact that sovereign immunity has been abrogated to varying degrees by 19 states' legislatures and the District of Columbia. Sovereign immunity is the common law principle that protects government officials from lawsuits resulting from the performance of their duties. School districts are governmental subdivisions of the state operating on the local level, and thus, school board members have been protected from such lawsuits. However, many states have taken away this "cloak" of immunity.

The ripple effect from this situation has caused human resources administrators to become more vulnerable to judicial review of their decisions and actions. Even if human resources administrators act in good faith and with reasonable deliberation, they may find themselves defending their actions in court. Therefore, it is imperative that all administrators have a rudimentary understanding of the U.S. judicial system and are capable of carrying out their daily responsibilities in such a manner that they can legally defend themselves if they are sued. The following discussion is meant to provide future human resources administrators with a better understanding of their potential liabilities.

The U.S. Judicial System

There are two systems of law. The first, known as "civil law," is descended from Roman law; the rule of law in this system is established through statutes enacted by a legislative body. The second system, known as "common law," is the basis of law in England. Under this system, the decisions rendered by a court become a guide or precedent to be followed by the court in dealing with future cases. The system of law found in the United States is a mixed system, using both civil and common law principles.[2]

Sources of Law

There are three major sources of law that form the foundation of the U.S. judicial system: (1) constitutions, (2) statutes, and (3) case law. There are two additional sources of law that affect education even though they are not primary sources: (1) administrative law and (2) attorney general opinions.[3]

CONSTITUTIONS Constitutions are bodies of precepts that provide the framework within which government carries out its duties. The federal and state constitutions contain provisions that secure the personal, property, and political rights of citizens. School districts have been continually confronted with constitutional issues, many of which have resulted in lawsuits. Some of these issues have dealt with racial discrimination in hiring practices, due process rights for individuals faced with employment termination, and the privacy right of employees in relation to their personnel records.

STATUTES Statutes, more commonly called "laws," are the enactments of legislative bodies. Thus, the U.S. Congress or a given state legislature may enact a new law or change an old law by the passage of legislation. A statute is subject to review by the respective state or federal court to determine if it is in violation of the precepts set forth in a state or federal constitution.

The presumption is that laws enacted by legislative bodies are constitutional, and the burden of proving otherwise is determined only through litigation. Thus, if a state legislature passes a law that allows school administrators the right to terminate tenured teachers without a hearing before the school board, a teacher or group of teachers could initiate a lawsuit asking the state's Supreme Court to consider the constitutionality of the new law. The basis for the lawsuit might be a provision in the state constitution dealing with the permanent employment status of tenured teachers.

Because public schools are state agencies, the legislature of every state has created statutes governing school districts. School operation, therefore, must be in compliance with such state statutes, and it is the responsibility of the board of education and the superintendent of schools to ensure compliance. Furthermore, the board of education cannot establish policies that are in conflict with state statutes or the acts of the U.S. Congress; in addition, the policies must not be in conflict with either the federal or state constitutions. If a school board, for example, creates a policy prohibiting the employment of individuals with disabilities as teachers, this policy would be in violation of federal law—in particular, the Rehabilitation Act of 1973—and probably violates the due process guaranteed by the Fourteenth Amendment to the U.S. Constitution; it might also violate a given state constitutional provision stipulating that all citizens have a right to employment opportunities.

CASE LAW The third source, common law, is more properly called "case law" because it is derived from court decisions rather than from legislative acts. Past court decisions are considered to be binding on subsequent cases if the material facts are similar. This is the doctrine of precedent. Lower courts usually adhere to the precedent (rule of law) established by higher courts in the same jurisdiction. The U.S. Supreme Court and state supreme courts can reverse their own previous decisions and thereby, change the rule of law. Thus, a state circuit court may apply a rule of law established by a state supreme court as to what constitutes due process in the termination of a tenured teacher. In a later case, the U.S. Supreme Court may redefine what constitutes due process and thus, change the rule of law.

ADMINISTRATIVE LAW AND ATTORNEY GENERAL OPINIONS Administrative law has developed through the creation of state and federal boards and commissions charged with administering certain federal and state laws. In carrying out their responsibilities, these boards and commissions establish rules and regulations. For example, school employees are likely to be affected by the regulations of the Social Security Administration, the Employment Security Administration, or the Workers' Compensation Commission. Of course, the actions of these boards and commissions are subject to review by the courts.

A second and frequently initiated legal procedure is the requesting of an opinion from a state attorney general on the interpretation of a certain statute. In the absence of case law, this opinion can be used by educators in addressing legal issues.

Human resources administrators must continually research professional journals that speak to significant court decisions and legislation. Most state departments of education also notify school administrators concerning recent state court decisions and laws that affect school district human resources practices and policies. The agencies of the federal government are very diligent in notifying school districts across the country about regulations with which they are required to be in compliance.

Major Divisions of Law

There are two broad classifications of law: criminal and civil. Criminal law is concerned with protecting the rights of society; and as such, the state, representing the people, is responsible for prosecuting wrongs committed against society by individuals or corporate entities. Civil law is concerned with protecting the rights that exist between individuals, between an individual and a corporate entity, or between two corporate entities. Most of the litigation that arises out of human resources management, of course, will deal with civil law. Civil law embraces many areas including contracts, wills and estates, corporate law, divorce, and torts. Human resources administrators are most vulnerable in lawsuits dealing with contracts and torts.

The Court Structure

The municipal court structure is of little or no concern to human resources administrators. These courts are usually concerned with enforcing the ordinances of municipal governments, which include housing and building codes and traffic ordinances.[4]

The federal court structure, of course, is divided into three levels: (1) the federal district courts, (2) the courts of appeal, and (3) the U.S. Supreme Court. The district courts are courts of original jurisdiction where all suits involving federal law will be filed. Civil suits that involve agencies of the U.S. government also are heard in the federal district courts. Thus, *Grutter* v. *Bollinger* (2003) originated in the respective federal district courts. The case was eventually appealed to the U.S. Supreme Court and has become landmark decisions. Human resources administrators should be familiar with the nuances of the federal court system due to the multitude of federal employment laws, which are potential areas of litigation.

The state court structure is analogous to the federal system. The court of original jurisdiction in most states is termed the circuit court and is where all civil lawsuits are filed. Cases involving tenure and contract management will be heard in the circuit court. The decisions of the circuit court may be appealed, usually to an appellate court and, finally, to the state supreme court. Once again, it must be stated that human resources administrators should become very familiar with the workings of the state court system because of the high incidence of litigation involving state laws as they relate to human resources management.

There is a distinction in the manner by which certain courts can hear cases, which is an important distinction for human resources administration. Certain issues are traditionally tried in "equity" by the state circuit courts and federal district courts. The most familiar to human resources administrators are injunctions. For example, a school district may go to a state circuit court to ask for an injunction directing a group of teachers to leave the picket lines and to return to their classrooms, if there is a state statute prohibiting strikes by teachers. Obviously, if the parties named in an injunction fail to obey the court order, they are in contempt of court and may be punished by a fine or by a jail sentence.

The Role of the Attorney in Human Resources Management

A common misconception about the role that a school district's attorney fulfills in a lawsuit against a school district is that he or she will entirely handle the litigation. An attorney's expertise centers on his or her ability to take the material facts in a case and research the statutes and the precedents of other court cases for the purpose of organizing a reasonable defense. An attorney must begin with what you, the human resources administrator, can offer by way of documentation. The defense will only be as strong as the level of accountability that has been demonstrated through human resources procedures and policies. Consequently, a good indication of the workability of procedures and policies is whether they were helpful or a hindrance in previous lawsuits.

The Anatomy of a Lawsuit

Although lawsuits do not follow a set pattern, there is enough commonality in litigation to make a few general observations (see Figure 10.1). The plaintiff files a petition with the appropriate court of jurisdiction, setting forth the cause of action, which is the allegation. A summons is then delivered by the court to the defendant, who is required to appear in court on a given date for the purpose of pleading to the petition.

The next step involves clarifying the allegation and the material facts supporting it. This may be accomplished by the taking of depositions, a formal procedure in which the parties to the lawsuit answer questions posed by the respective attorneys. Also, written queries may be required by the attorneys in lieu of or in addition to the depositions.

If the material facts do not support the allegation, then the school district's attorney will probably enter a motion to have the petition dismissed. If the judge does not dismiss the petition, a trial date will be set. In civil cases involving tenure, a contract, or a tort, the defendant usually has the option of a jury trial or may rely on the judge to make a decision. Who the defendant is in a civil lawsuit is determined by the nature of the petition and the material facts. In a tenure or contract dispute, the board of education as a corporate body is usually the defendant because the board approves all personnel contracts. If it is a tort, an individual or a group of individuals may be named as the defendant because the petition may allege that a civil wrong has been committed against the plaintiff by one person or a group of persons. In a judgment favoring the plaintiff, damages are assessed in dollar amounts to be paid by the defendant.

Plaintiff Files a Petition

Court Serves a Summons on the Defendant

Defendant Pleads the Petition

Depositions and/or Written Queries Are Taken by Both Parties

Defendant May File a Motion for Dismissal or Plaintiff May Drop the Lawsuit

Trial Is Held if the Lawsuit Is Not Dismissed or Dropped

Decision of the Judge or Jury Is Rendered

If the Decision Is in Favor of the Defendant, the Case Is Dismissed

If the Decision Is in Favor of the Plaintiff, a Remedy Is Addressed

Appeal by the Defendant to a Higher Court

FIGURE 10.1 Anatomy of a Lawsuit

Tort Liability in Human Resources Administration

There is a tendency to take a "shotgun" approach in some types of civil lawsuits, particularly torts, when identifying defendants in litigation. For example, if a student is injured as a consequence of using gymnastics equipment, the teacher might be sued for being negligent in supervising the student or for not properly instructing the student on how to use the equipment. The building principal might be sued for neglecting to properly evaluate and remove the teacher who allegedly did a poor job of supervising the student. The superintendent might be brought into the lawsuit because he neglected to remove the principal who inadequately supervised the teacher. The board of education might be sued because the members neglected to supervise and monitor the superintendent in evaluating the performance of the principal. This path then follows the chain-of-command in a school district and ensures that the responsible party or parties will be identified by the court.[5]

This same type of situation is applicable to human resources management. A case could be made alleging that a given teacher's references were not properly investigated by the assistant superintendent for human resources, which eventuated in the hiring of an unqualified applicant.

It goes without saying that employment situations may carry more vulnerability than those involved with instruction. Therefore, it is important for human resources managers to be well-informed about tort liability. With this knowledge, they will be able to establish human resources processes and procedures that will accomplish the objectives of the human resources department and also will be easy to defend in court. A tort is a civil wrong, other than a breach of contract, committed against a person or a person's property.

Tort law emanates from common law, which is composed of those principles established through court cases that are usually referred to as precedent. The acts of legislatures have either broadened or narrowed these common law principles. For example, at common law, an individual wrongfully causing the death of another person incurs no civil liability; however, Florida, Georgia, Missouri, New Jersey, New York, and other state legislatures have enacted statutes that impose civil liabilities in favor of certain persons, including a surviving spouse and children.

There are two major types of torts: intentional torts and negligence. Intentional torts are further classified as to whether the action interfered with a person or with the person's property. Assault, battery, and defamation are the most common types associated with personal interference; malicious trespassing is the most common interference with respect to property rights.

In human resources management, defamation of character is a potential area of litigation with regard to the giving of references and communicating the contents of an individual's personnel file. Defamation occurs when false information is communicated either by word of mouth (slander) or in writing (libel), brings hatred or ridicule on a person, and produces some type of harm to the person. With regard to the human resources function, the harm produced by defamation might be the loss of an employment opportunity or a job promotion.

To protect against such litigation, established procedures should outline who is responsible for writing references and under what circumstances the contents of an individual's personnel file can be released. Although each situation will vary, the following guidelines should be observed:

1. The employee has a right to review the contents of his or her personnel file in the presence of a human resources administrator.
2. The supervisor of an employee has a right to review the contents of an employee's file in the presence of a human resources administrator.
3. Only official and approved documents may be added to an employee's file (for example, attendance records, payroll records, performance evaluation forms).

4. No document may be removed from an individual's personnel file without notification to the employee, who has the right to question the removal.
5. The contents or partial contents of an employee's personnel file may not be released to other parties without the written permission of the employee (for example, attendance records being requested by a potential employer).
6. Under no circumstances should a human resources administrator discuss over the telephone information in an employee's file.

Negligence is that type of tort which involves some form of injury to another person as a result of conduct that falls below an established standard. It is the duty of an assistant superintendent for human resources and other human resources administrators to establish processes and procedures that do not violate federal and state laws and that accomplish the objectives of the human resources function. Therefore, in the recruitment and selection of new employees, affirmative action procedures must be followed so that the rights of protected groups are not violated. A human resources administrator who neglected to properly initiate or follow such procedures could be guilty of a tort if a minority applicant was denied an opportunity to be interviewed for a position and, as a result, lost a job opportunity. Even though a charge of discrimination would probably be filed in this case with the Equal Employment Opportunity Commission (EEOC), there is also the possibility of a civil lawsuit being brought against an individual administrator.

In a tort liability lawsuit that involves a question of negligence, the court will apply the principle of the reasonable person, which has some limitations in a pluralistic society.[6] This concept has a very specific application and definition. The reasonable person is someone who:

1. Possesses average intelligence, normal perception, and memory
2. Possesses such superior skill and knowledge as the defendant has or purports to have
3. Possesses the same level of experience that the defendant has
4. Possesses the same physical attributes that the defendant has

Thus, the conduct of a human resources administrator involved in a lawsuit is compared against the conduct of a mythical reasonable person. If a reasonable person could have prevented the consequence, the administrator will be found negligent by the jury. The moral of the example is that all administrators should examine their professional responsibilities to determine if their conduct in fulfilling these responsibilities can withstand the test of the reasonable person.

In a civil lawsuit resulting in a judgment favoring the plaintiff, the defendant usually will be required to pay actual damages, which is the amount of money that the injury cost. The loss of a job opportunity has a potential for costing the defendant a considerable amount of money, which could conceivably reach into the hundreds of thousands of dollars. If it can be demonstrated in court that the defendant deliberately caused the injury, punitive damages may also be levied. This dollar amount is a punishment for intentionally bringing about a civil wrong. In some cases, punitive damages may equal or supersede the actual damages assessed by the court. A human resources administrator who publicly disagrees with the concept of affirmative action and who tells ethnic jokes to fellow employees might be laying the foundation for the allegation that he or she deliberately neglects to follow affirmative action procedures.

Errors and Omissions Liability Insurance

It should be clear from this presentation that every human resources administrator should be protected by errors and omissions liability insurance. Sources for obtaining such coverage include professional organizations and the school district's insurance carrier.

Many professional educator associations offer this type of insurance as a part of the regular membership benefits. Many of the large insurance companies will be happy to provide such protection under a group policy for all central-office administrators or for any other group of employees. The members of the board of education also may be included in this coverage and should be covered, particularly in those states where sovereign immunity has been abrogated. Finally, it should be remembered that most errors and omissions liability insurance policies do not cover punitive damages, because this would amount to condoning an act that was deliberately perpetrated.

ETHICAL CONSIDERATIONS IN HUMAN RESOURCES ADMINISTRATION

People in the United States have become increasingly aware of the vulnerability of those who occupy leadership positions in private business, government, churches, and in public education. It is a topic that is on everyone's mind because of the major scandals that have plagued our American society and culture. A pervasive attitude of the American people is mistrust of leaders in all segments of our society.[7] The news media constantly reveal crimes committed even by those who hold not only leadership positions, but also positions of significant trust. However, nothing is more disheartening than to read about a member of the clergy or teacher who sexually abuses a child. These occurrences are easily judged as being immoral or unethical.

The central issue in this treatment is the fact that all people must make decisions on a daily basis where the lines of appropriate behavior are somewhat blurred, the grey area. Human resources administrators are particularly vulnerable because their decisions affect people in that most important area of life, employment. Students are also affected because the quality of their education depends on the quality of the people employed by a school district.

The basis for making ethically sound decisions is usually grounded in religious beliefs or philosophical assumptions. The Judeo-Christian-Islamic tradition sets forth norms of appropriate conduct that are accepted by most U.S. citizens. Many of these religious beliefs and philosophical assumptions are contained in the documents upon which the United States, as a nation, was founded. However, espousing the principles found in these religious traditions and documents does not guarantee that the practices of a school district will support human development. Thus, the proof is in the development of strategies and procedures that ensure social justice.[8]

The American Association of School Personnel Administrators has adopted the Statement of Ethics for School Administrators, which was developed by the American Association of School Administrators. Although this statement is appropriate, it is intended for all categories of administrators and does not go far enough to provide guidance in the many diverse and complicated situations that face contemporary school human resources administrators. There are three principles that have been gleaned from the above sources and that constitute the foundation upon which the responsibilities in Exhibit 10.1 have been developed.

First, the exercise of these responsibilities in making judgments for decisions, over time, will help an individual to determine the sort of person and human resources professional he or she wants to become. Any given decision usually does not determine an individual's central ethical orientation unless it is a decision of monumental significance such as deliberately committing a felony. Rather, a person is constantly in the state of becoming either a better person and professional or a person who gradually loses his or her integrity. Even inappropriate decisions about issues that might appear to be rather insignificant can chip away at the edges surrounding a person's central core of integrity.

EXHIBIT 10.1

Responsibilities for the Ethical Administration of the Human Resources Function

School districts have an ethical and legal obligation to provide children and young adults with the best education possible given the human and financial resources available to them. The quality of education depends on the quality of personnel who directly or indirectly provide the educational service. Consequently, boards of education and superintendents of schools must be diligent in the selection of human resources administrators. Once employed, human resources administrators will be held accountable for the following responsibilities.

Responsibilities to the School District and Its Staff:

- Support and implement the policies of the board of education in a positive and effective manner
- Support and implement administrative procedures in a positive and effective manner
- Through appropriate means, pursue changing board polices and administrative processes and procedures that are not consistent with sound practice
- Project a positive image of the school district to the community-at-large and the education community
- Treat colleagues and subordinates with dignity and fairness
- Help colleagues and subordinates fulfill their obligations and aspirations
- Help subordinates achieve their maximum potential
- Maintain confidentiality in carrying out the obligations of a school human resources administrator
- Promote adherence to all local, state, and national ordinances and laws
- Promote the equitable treatment of individuals, groups, and companies

Responsibilities to the School Human Resources Profession:

- Promote membership in the activities of school human resources professional associations at the local, state, and national levels
- Accept leadership roles in school human resources professional associations
- Promote research in school human resources administration that will enhance the effectiveness of the profession
- Promote professional development activities that will enhance the performance of school human resources administrators

Personal Responsibilities:

- Fulfill the obligations of a school human resources administrator in an open manner
- Seek consultation from colleagues or other professionals when faced with an ethical or professional problem for which there appears to be no appropriate solution
- Continue to grow as a person and as a school human resources professional through attendance at conventions, seminars, conferences, or through university coursework
- Develop the virtues of prudence, honesty, and justice so your behavior will enhance not only your integrity as a person, but also the integrity of the school district in which you work and the school human resources profession that you represent

Second, the decisions of school human resources administrators have a definite effect upon school districts as institutions. This effect will be either positive or negative depending upon the motivation for the decision and its magnitude. For example, an assistant superintendent for human resources who attempts to influence the hiring of a candidate solely because that person is his or her friend has made a decision that will have a negative effect on the school district for which he or she is employed. If this type of action is repeated over time, the school district could take on a negative image that would affect morale among other employees and among other educators in the surrounding school districts. In a similar manner, the decisions of human resources administrators will have a positive or negative effect upon the school human resources professional associations in which the administrator is a member or has a position of leadership. Human experience indicates that it is virtually impossible to keep inappropriate actions from becoming common knowledge.

The third principle is taken from the Declaration of Independence. "All men are created equal. . . . they are endowed by their creator with certain unalienable rights, that among these are life, liberty, and the pursuit of happiness." Any action by a school human resources administrator to show preferential treatment to certain people, groups, or companies is contrary to this principle. The human resources administrator has a duty to ensure that such rights are manifested not only in the daily actions of employees, but also in the policy and procedural processes of the school district.

ETHICAL RESPONSIBILITIES OF HUMAN RESOURCES ADMINISTRATORS

The responsibilities set forth in Exhibit 10.1 are grouped under three separate headings: (1) those pertaining to the school district and its staff, (2) those pertaining to the school human resources profession, and (3) those pertaining to the human resources administrator as a person. This approach has been selected over the more traditional approach wherein a list of prohibitions is presented as a code of ethics. The emphasis here is on carrying out responsibilities that will have a positive effect on the school district, the human resources profession, and the human resources administrator. Also, because each human being is constantly in the state of becoming either a better person or a person of decreasing integrity, just avoiding certain types of actions is not enough to steer the process in a positive direction. Each person must be proactive. This is the reason why, in this presentation, the ethical administrator is portrayed as a person who seeks to fulfill responsibilities.

Responsibilities to the School District and Its Staff

This first group of ten responsibilities clearly addresses the communal aspect of public school administration and, in particular, the communal aspect of school human resources management. School human resources administrators have obligations to the institution for which they work, the school district. Furthermore, they have obligations to their colleagues and subordinates. Thus, loyalty to the board of education, superintendent of schools, colleagues, and subordinates becomes the vehicle for fulfilling these responsibilities. Sometimes, it happens that a certain human resources administrator cannot ethically accept the policies or practices of the school district for which he or she works, and must seek other employment. However, in practice the overarching responsibility is to help establish an ethical culture in the school district through implementing ethical human resource systems. Thus in marketing, recruitment, selection, placement, induction, staff development, performance evaluation, compensation, and collective negotiations, the goals should be publicly defensible processes and procedures that ensure social justice. In this manner, the human resources function becomes a vehicle for promoting ethical sensitivity in all dimensions of the school district.[9]

Responsibilities to the School Human Resources Profession

The next group of responsibilities defines the professional obligations of the human resources administrator. Emphasis is placed on participation in professional associations and working within these associations to enhance the profession. This is particularly important in the areas of research and professional development.

Personal Responsibilities

The final group of responsibilities is concerned with the personal growth of the human resources administrator. This growth is nurtured through professional development activities. The practice of certain virtues, particularly the virtue of honesty, should help administrators avoid conflict of interest situations and the virtue of prudence should help them to avoid even the appearance of such a conflict. Thus, accepting gifts, services, or anything of value because of an act performed or withheld certainly violates the virtue of honesty. Accepting gifts, services, or something of value even though "no strings" were attached violates the virtue of prudence. Honesty is also violated when administrators use their position in a professional association for personal gain. When an employee receives preferential treatment simply because of friendship with a certain administrator, the virtue of justice is violated.

All people need help at times. Seeking consultation from other professionals when the need arises is viewed here as an obligation. Therefore, to continue an inappropriate practice or to persist in behavior that could bring derision upon the school district, the human resources profession, or the administrator is a violation of this obligation. Thus, ethical literacy should be a focus of all staff development programs in school districts, and the case study approach is appropriate for practicing human resources administrators and staff members.[10]

LEGAL AND ETHICAL TECHNOLOGY ISSUES

The advent of information technology and the Internet changed forever the way school districts carry out the administration of human resources. On a daily basis, human resources administrators and staff members access, analyze, create, and distribute information throughout schools and school districts. These administrators and staff members have an obligation not to abuse technology resources and to respect the rights of teachers, other administrators, and other staff members in the school district community.

With this caveat in mind, it is recommended that every school district create a policy covering the proper use of technology. Such a policy should identify what technological components are covered by the policy. What follows is a model policy that incorporates those provisions that the author of this book deems necessary in order to safeguard the legal and ethical dimensions of the proper use of technology:

> The Board of Education, Superintendent of Schools, and the administration and staff of the Human Resources Department recognize that the effective administration of human resources functions depends upon the full and proper utilization of technology in formulating human resources procedures and policies. This policy is applicable to all human resources employees of the Goodville School District regardless of their authorization to use or not to use certain technologies owned by the School District. Those technological components that are covered

by this policy are computers, databases, data storage, networks, printers, related equipment, and software. This policy is also applicable if such employees engage technological systems owned by the School District on a privately owned computer.

This policy is being enacted in order to ensure that the School District's technology systems are available, reliable, and used only for the human resources purposes for which they were created and made available. Thus, the following activities by authorized human resources administrators and staff members are prohibited:

- Accessing and modifying elements of the system for which they are not authorized
- Accumulating information for unauthorized purposes
- Impeding or interfering with the authorized use by other employees of technological systems
- Using the technological systems for purposes that violate the public status of school districts such as political activities
- Attempting to override the security component of the systems
- Using the systems for illegal purposes such as sexual harassment, racial and ethnic harassment, or promiscuity
- Impersonating others in technological communication
- Modifying the technological equipment
- Violating the licenses agreements of hardware or software

In like manner, the following basic employee rights are ensured for human resources administrators and staff members:

- The right of free inquiry and expression in relation to carrying out employment responsibilities
- Maintaining and securing personal passwords
- The proper registration of equipment
- Minor personal use of the systems when such usage does not impede the performance of responsibilities such as receiving emails of a personal nature

The Board of Education recognizes that the Superintendent of Schools may authorize accessing the systems without the consent of the authorized users for the following purposes:

- To diagnose and repair systems
- When required by federal, state, and local courts and agencies
- When there is reasonable evidence that there has been a violation of policy or law
- To protect public health and safety

Each employee of the Human Resources Department has certain responsibilities that are associated with the improper use of the School District's technological systems that should be reported to the Superintendent of Schools:

- If an employee believes that his or her personal integrity has been compromised
- If an employee observes that others are violating policy or law

> Penalties for such infractions may include temporary or permanent suspension of access or termination of employment. Of course, the employee so penalized has the right to appeal such penalties to the Board of Education.

Certainly school districts will modify the above model policy based upon the culture and board policies of individual districts. Furthermore, job descriptions should clearly set forth the technological responsibilities of each employee required to use such technology.

IMPLICATIONS FOR SMALL AND MEDIUM-SIZED SCHOOL DISTRICTS

Only large-sized school districts can afford to have a legal department staffed by attorneys specializing in school law. However, every school district has no choice but to hire an attorney to represent the school district when the district is involved in a law suit. Thus, when a law suit arises in relation to the human resources function, obviously it is imperative to hire an attorney who has expertise in the legal dimension of human resources administration. The vetting process for hiring the attorney will depend upon a number of variables, and the most important is to have sufficient financial resources in the school district's budget to hire the best qualified attorney.

Other considerations include the following:

- It is better to hire a legal firm rather than a single attorney because other attorneys from the firm can take over a case, if the lead attorney is unable to continue with his or her responsibilities because of illness or other obligations that might spontaneously arise.
- It is better to hire a firm which has had experience in school law cases.
- It is better to hire a firm that has attorneys who have handled other human resources-related cases.
- It is better to hire a firm which has a fee structure that is in keeping with the financial constraints of the school district's budget.
- It is better to hire a law firm on a retainer basis for a set period of time, perhaps one to three years. This will make it easier and quicker for the school district to respond to a law suit rather than attempting to find legal counsel on an immediate need basis.
- The law firm should also have the capability to provide the administrative staff with counsel in terms of administrative practices and policies that will provide the school district with a proactive, rather than a reactive response to carrying-out administrative responsibilities.
- Obviously, it is not a good practice to hire a firm only on the basis of its fee structure, but rather on the success of representing clients in law suits. Thus, rather than "taking bids," the school district should seek portfolios from interested law firms that include the types of cases the firms have been involved with, the success of the firms, and the fee structures.

The location of the school district is another consideration in seeking portfolios, because there may not be attorneys practicing law in the vicinity of the school district who have experience in the law suit facing the district. Experience of the law firm is of paramount importance.

Obviously, the size of a school district has no bearing on the ethical responsibilities of the administrators who are responsible for the human resources functions. Thus, the material presented in this chapter on ethics is applicable to all administrators and staff members. Finally, the responsibility of the school district to develop policies that are defensible, appropriate, and proactive is also a responsibility of all human resources administrators regardless of the size of the districts. There are significant resources available to school districts from state and national professional associations such as the National School Boards Association.

THE IMPACT OF GENERATION Y TEACHERS AND ADMINISTRATORS ON LEGAL AND ETHICAL INTEGRITY

Generation Y teachers and administrators tend to be rather conservative in their approach to legal and ethical issues. In order to understand this conservatism, it is important to remember the signs of the times in which they have moved into adulthood with significant responsibilities to themselves and their families. Rightfully so, the news media has brought to their attention many concerns that include the following: misconduct of religious leaders, business leaders, government and military leaders, and law enforcement leaders; fiscal instability of business and financial institutions; life issues including cloning human organs and other genetic engineering issues; safeguarding civil rights in dangerous times; universal access to medical and pharmaceutical services and products; environmental deterioration, and terrorism.

Perhaps, the ultimate issue for Generation Y teachers and administrators is that of trust. Who can they trust? Of course, the above issues are not the only concerns, but they are all ethical issues and most have legal ramifications. Furthermore, there are implications for school district and particularly human resources policy development. Most Generation Y employees want some voice in the governance function manifested in policy development, which is witnessed in the collective negotiations process. Also, they want supervisors whom they can trust and admire and who are professional in their conduct. Generation Y teachers and administrators expect transparency, accountability, and equity as the hallmarks of the human resources policies and procedures.

Quick Review of Essentials

This chapter is concerned with legal and ethical issues in human resources administration. These issues have become important within the last decade because of the increased emphasis on legal rights and responsibilities.

Teachers and administrators usually work under the provisions of an individual contract; classified personnel are employed at an hourly rate or for an annual salary. Using individual contracts for teachers and administrators is a matter of tradition that also is mandated by law in some states and that distinguishes a professional employee's working conditions from those of classified employees. Teachers' and administrators' contracts must meet the requirements of general contract law, state statutes, and the precedents established through case law. A contract is an agreement between two or more competent persons for a legal consideration on a legal subject matter in the form required by law. The five basic components, therefore, to every valid contract are (1) offer and acceptance, (2) competent persons, (3) a consideration, (4) legal subject matter, and (5) proper form.

School districts have experienced an increase in litigation. In addition, human resources administrators are far more vulnerable today than previously to judicial review of their actions. It is imperative, therefore, that administrators have a rudimentary understanding of the American judicial system and are capable of making decisions that are legally defensible.

There are basically two systems of law. The first, called a civil law system, attempts to establish all laws in the form of statutes enacted by a legislative body. The second is referred to as a common law system. It is the basic approach used in England and was adopted in theory by most of the states in our country. Under this system, the decisions rendered by a court become a precedent to be followed by the court in dealing with future cases. The system of law in the United States is a mixture of both civil and common law.

There are three major sources of law that form the foundation of the American judicial system: (1) constitutions, (2) statutes, and (3) court cases. Constitutions are bodies of precepts that provide the framework within which government carries out its duties. Statutes are the enactments of legislative bodies; they are more commonly called "laws." As stated above, common law emanates from the decisions of courts rather than from legislative bodies. There are two additional sources of law that affect education even though they are not traditionally considered primary sources: administrative law and attorney general opinions. Administrative law consists of those regulations set forth by agencies established by the U.S. Congress and state legislatures. In the absence of case law, the state attorney general may be requested to render an opinion on the interpretation of a certain statute.

The two broad classifications of law are criminal and civil. Civil law is concerned with protecting the rights of individuals and corporate entities; criminal law is concerned with protecting the rights of society.

The judicial system is composed of municipal, state, and federal courts. Most states have three categories of courts: (1) circuit courts, (2) courts of appeal, and (3)supreme courts. In like manner, there are three categories of federal courts: (1) district courts, (2) the U.S. Courts of Appeals, and (3) the U.S. Supreme Court.

The U.S. judicial system also preserves the concept of equity. The state circuit and U.S. district courts may handle both law and equity issues. Certain issues are traditionally tried in equity, the most common being injunctions.

Human resources administrators should become familiar with the nuances of the state and federal court systems because of the great number of laws affecting employment and because of the potentiality for tort liability lawsuits.

In human resources management it is also extremely important to understand the role of the attorney. The attorney takes the material facts in a case and researches the statutes or laws and precedents of court cases for the purpose of organizing a reasonable defense. The defense will be only as strong as the level of accountability that has been demonstrated through human resources procedures and policies.

A lawsuit begins with the filing of a petition, setting forth the allegation in the appropriate court of jurisdiction. The next step is clarifying the allegation and the material facts. The final step is the trial.

A tort is a civil wrong, other than a breach of contract, committed against a person or a person's property. The two major types of torts are classified as intentional torts and negligence. Assault, battery, defamation, and trespassing are the most common types of intentional torts. In human resources management, defamation is a potential area of litigation with regard to the giving of references and the communicating of the contents of an individual's personnel file.

Negligence is a tort that involves conduct falling below an established standard that result in some type of injury to another person. Negligence, therefore, implies neglect of a duty. The duty of human resources administrators is to establish processes and procedures that do not violate federal and state laws and that meet the objectives of the human resources department. For example, a human resources administrator who neglected to initiate or follow such procedures could be guilty of a tort if a minority applicant was denied an opportunity to be interviewed for a position and, as a result, lost a job opportunity.

In a civil lawsuit resulting in a judgment favoring the plaintiff, the defendant may be assessed actual damages and even punitive damages, if the injury was deliberately perpetrated. Each and every human resources administrator, therefore, should be protected by an errors and omissions liability insurance program.

People in the United States have become increasingly aware of the vulnerability of those who occupy leadership positions. The central issue is that all people must make decisions on a daily basis when the lines of appropriate behavior are somewhat blurred. Human resources administrators are particularly vulnerable because their decisions affect people in that most important area of life, employment.

The basis for making ethically sound decisions is usually grounded in religious beliefs or philosophical assumptions. There are three principles that have been gleaned from these beliefs and assumptions. First, the exercise of responsibilities in making judgments for decisions, over time, will help an individual to determine the sort of person and human resources professional he or she wants to become. Second, the decisions of school human resources administrators have a definite effect upon school districts as institutions. The third principle comes from the Declaration of Independence, which sets forth that all people are created equal and have certain unalienable rights among which are "life, liberty, and the pursuit of happiness."

The ethical responsibilities of school human resources administrators are grouped around the following: responsibilities to the school district and its staff; responsibilities to the school human resources profession; and personal responsibilities.

Effective policies are the key to successful human resources management. Boards of education should take a deliberate approach to policy development that will ensure defensible human resources operations.

Selected Further Readings

Buckley, M. Ronald, Danielle S. Beu, Dwight D. Frink, Jack L. Howard, Howard Berkson, Tommie A. Mobbs, & Darden, Edwin C., "School Law: Responsibility and Obligation," *American School Board Journal,* August 2007, 42–43.

Dutton, Marcy, "A Good Contract Only Starts with the Signing," *School Administrator*, 64, no. 6, June 2007, www.hwwilson.com.

Essex, Nathan L., *School Law and the Public Schools: A Practical Guide for Educational Leaders*, 3rd ed. Boston: Allyn & Bacon, 2005.

Miller, Paul, "Strategy and the Ethical Management of Human Resources," *ProQuest LLC*, 2008, www.proquest.umi.com.

Schimmel, David, and Matthew Militello, "Legal Literacy for Teachers: A Neglected Responsibility," *Harvard Educational Review*, 77, no. 3, Fall 2007, 1–14.

GLOSSARY OF TERMS

This glossary is divided by chapters in order to provide easy reference to selected terms, phrases, and acronyms that will help readers understand the terms used in each chapter as well as other terms and acronyms that are not used in the chapters, but which contribute to a grasp of its concepts and ideas.

Chapter 1: Organizational Dimensions

Assistant superintendent for human resources The chief human resources administrator in a school district who is charged with developing the strategies and implementing the policies, processes, and procedures necessary to the effective management of the human resources function. Alternative titles are director of personnel or director of human resources.

Asynchronous Refers to the experience of using technology independent of real-time constraints. Thus, a person can log on to a school district's Web site and process a medical claim after normal working hours.

Automatic patch management software Computer security software patches for programs and systems. The most promising patches detect unidentified viruses by recognizing virus-like patterns.

Board of education Elected or appointed policy-making body of a school district.

Cyberethics The study of how technology has affected public policy through computing and communicative electronic techniques.

Datamart Technological term that refers to a specialized depository of data created from a school district-wide data warehouse and used only by specific departments such as the human resources and the business departments.

Data mining Refers to an array of analytical applications used to identify patterns in a database.

Data warehouse School district-wide database designed to support the activities of an entire district. It is usually batch-updated and provides rapid on-line information and summaries.

Decision support system An interactive computer based system that allows a user to solve problems through databased modeling.

Employee relations Strategies, policies, processes, and procedures used in collective negotiations that implement the preparatory phase for negotiations, at-the-table bargaining, managing the master agreement, and grievance management.

Generation Y Often referred to as the *Millennial Generation*, and composed of people born in or after 1980, who are old enough to be seeking post-collegial professional employment as teachers and administrators in school districts.

Human resources administration Management of the processes, procedures, and techniques necessary to implement the following dimensions of the human resources function in a school district: planning, recruitment, selection, placement and induction, staff development, performance evaluation, compensation, and collective negotiations.

Management approach Approach to human resources administration that centers on developing strategies and carrying out processes, procedures, and techniques.

Metadata A summary and directory of the kinds of data that are stored in a warehouse.

National Council of Chief State School Officials The professional organization that supports the role and function of state commissions and superintendents of education.

No Child Left Behind Act (NCLB) Federal legislation signed into law by President George W. Bush in 2002. The law requires all children to be proficient in reading and mathematics by 2014. Other provisions mandate improved communications with parents and improved safety at school for children.

On-line analytical processing An interactive computer-based system that allows a user to reframe multidimensional data gathered from various sources and stored in a warehouse; allows data to be organized into many different representations.

Personnel administration Alternative designation for human resources administration.

Relational database A database that permits the sharing of information from multiple files, which can be linked or related.

Risk management The strategies, policies, processes, and procedures necessary for implementing a health and safety program for a school district that includes safety and security audits, training and education, monitoring, and crisis event management.

Synchronous Refers to the experience of interacting with another person through technology in real time. Thus, a retiree may be communicating through email with a staff member in a school district's benefits office during normal working hours.

Transcendental leadership A leadership theory that is predicated upon the premise that a person acts from the totality of who he or she is as a human being. The theory requires administrators to reflect upon the fact that their decisions are prompted by more than just the immediate circumstances and have an effect that goes beyond the present situation.

TQM An approach to administration based on the philosophy of W. Edwards Deming that views all employees as stakeholders and empowers them to make strategic decisions about how to meet the goals and objectives of an organization.

Workflow The technological capability to initiate multiple transactions through a single data entry.

Chapter 2: Human Resources Planning

Acquired Immune Deficiency Syndrome (AIDS) A viral infectious disease; those who contract it are protected under Section 504 of the Rehabilitation Act of 1973. Fear of contagion by itself does not permit federal agencies and federally assisted employers to discriminate against employees infected with the AIDS virus.

Affirmative action This refers to detailed and results-oriented programs whose objective is compliance with the equal employment clauses found in most civil rights legislation.

Age Discrimination in Employment Act of 1967 A federal law, as amended, that promotes the employment of workers between the ages of 40 and 70 based on ability rather than age. It makes it illegal to discriminate against older workers in all areas of employment.

Americans with Disabilities Act of 1990 (ADA) The most comprehensive legislation ever passed protecting the rights of individuals with disabilities. This legislation extends the Rehabilitation Act of 1973 in that it pertains to the private sector and to local and state governmental agencies that receive no federal monies. Both the United States Department of Justice and the Equal Employment Opportunity Commission (EEOC) have been given jurisdiction for the enforcement of ADA.

Civil Rights Act of 1964 Title VII of this federal law, as amended, provides that a person cannot be denied a job or fair treatment on a job because of race, color, religion, sex, or national origin.

Civil Rights Act of 1991 A federal law that extends compensatory and punitive damages and jury trials to employees who have been discriminated against because of race, national origin, sex, disability, or religion.

Enrollment prediction An estimate of the number of students who will attend specific schools at specific grade levels over a five- to ten-year period of time. The cohort-survival method is commonly used in many school districts.

Equal Employment Opportunity Commission (EEOC) Established by Title VII of the Civil Rights Act of 1964 and strengthened by the passage of the Equal Employment Opportunity Act of 1972, this agency investigates charges of discrimination, attempts conciliation, and can litigate cases.

Equal Pay Act of 1963 A federal law that requires employers to pay males and females the same salary or wage for equal work.

Executive orders In the federal government, the presidential orders that have the force of law. They have been issued by several presidents to address issues of employment discrimination.

Family and Medical Leave Act of 1993 A federal law, the fundamental purpose of which is to provide eligible employees with the right to take 12 weeks of unpaid leave per year because of personal or family health reasons and for first-year parenting purposes.

Hostile environment sexual harassment Occurs when unwelcome sexual conduct interferes with an employee's job performance.

Human resources forecasting Estimating future human resources needs, usually established through expert estimates, historical comparison, task analysis, correlation, and modeling.

Human resources inventories A human resources profile of the employees of a school district that includes age, job title, education and/or training, placement, sex, special skills, and certification.

Human resources planning The process whereby a school district ensures that it has the right number of people, with the right skills, in the right place, and at the right time in order to effectively carry out the goals and objectives of the district.

Pregnancy Disability Amendment An amendment to Title VII of the Civil Rights Act of 1964 that makes it illegal to discriminate against pregnant women in all employment-related situations including hiring, promoting, assigning, the granting of medical benefits, and receiving seniority credit.

***Quid pro quo* sexual harassment** Occurs when personnel decisions are made because of an employee's submission to an employer's or supervisor's sexual advances.

Reduction in Force (RIF) A process required when decreasing student enrollments produce a surplus of teachers in a given school district. The reduction can be humanely carried out through attrition, early retirement incentive programs, enhancing curricular programs, and helping employees acquire new skills or find other positions.

Rehabilitation Act of 1973 Title V of the Rehabilitation Act contains five sections, four of which relate to affirmative action for people with disabilities and one which deals with voluntary actions, remedial actions, and evaluation criteria for compliance with the law.

Sexual harassment In 1980, the Equal Employment Opportunity Commission (EEOC) declared sexual harassment to be a violation of Title VII of the Civil Rights Act of 1964. There are two types of sexual harassment: *Quid pro quo* and hostile environment harassment.

Social justice The concept that people have certain rights and responsibilities simply because they are members of a given society.

The Omnibus Transportation Employee Testing Act of 1991 The provisions of this federal law allow certain employers to conduct preemployment, postaccident, random, reasonable suspicion, and return-to-duty alcohol and controlled substances testing on persons in safety-sensitive jobs.

Title IX Title IX of the Education Amendments of 1972 prohibits discrimination against women in educational programs and activities, including employment, when an educational agency receives federal financial assistance.

TRICARE The Department of Defense's health insurance plan for military personnel and their families (formerly CHAMPUS, the Civilian Health and Medical Program of the Uniformed Services). When employees are called up for active military service, they are immediately covered by this military health care system. Their dependents may be covered by TRICARE under certain conditions, including length of mobilization.

Vietnam Era Veterans Readjustment Assistance Act of 1974 The purpose of this federal law is affirmative action for veterans with disabilities, especially those who served in the Vietnam Conflict.

Chapter 3: Recruitment

Advertisement The techniques used to communicate position vacancies; also important verification of a school district's efforts to promote affirmative action and equal employment opportunity.

Alternative certification programs College and university programs designed for people with bachelor's degrees that give them the opportunity to become licensed as teachers in a relatively short period of time. These programs have been designed in many states where there is a shortage of teachers.

Employment agency Private companies that help clients search for employment opportunities and charge either the client or the hiring school district a fee for this service.

On-line recruitment Use of the Internet by school districts to post job vacancies, provide information about the districts, provide information about a given job, and indicate how to apply for positions.

Recruitment Process used to ensure that a school district has qualified candidates for positions which become vacant because of retirements, resignations, terminations, and enrollment growth.

Recruitment brochure Specialized type of advertisement commonly used to recruit principals and superintendents that provides extensive information about the school district, the position, the community, and the application process.

Theories of occupational choice Set of theories concerning the interaction between a person's psychological makeup, his or her vocational and occupational choices, the availability of appropriate jobs, and the culture of various communities.

U.S. Training and Employment Service Federal government agency that supervises state employment agencies which provide services to people who are without employment, including the management of unemployment benefits and job searches.

Chapter 4: Selection

Assessment center Places where candidates for jobs can be observed as they work through a series of simulations, usually taking the form of case studies and decision-making exercises—dealing with administrative problems.

Criminal-background investigation Process used by school districts to check both the references and credentials, and the records of law-enforcement agencies to identify candidates who might have been convicted of a criminal act.

Employment test Intelligence, aptitude, ability, and interest tests constitute the usual battery of tests that are used in the selection process for certain types of jobs.

Immigration Reform and Control Act of 1996 Federal law that makes it unlawful to knowingly hire an unauthorized alien, to continue the employment of one who becomes an unauthorized alien, or to hire any individual without first verifying his or her employability and identity.

Job analysis Process of gathering information about a given job that centers on that job's parameters; how tasks are carried out; skills, education, and training requirements; physical and environmental conditions that affect it; and its relationship to other jobs.

Job description Formal job designation that includes the job title, duties, authority and responsibility, and specific qualifications.

Job vacancy announcement Based upon the job description; provides potential candidates with sufficient information to decide whether to apply for a position.

National Association of State Directors of Teacher Education and Certification (NASDTEC) A professional organization that promotes the role and function of state certification officials and maintains the Teacher Identification Clearinghouse.

On-line application The use of the Internet by school districts to receive applications and resumes via email and to post job vacancies on a school district's Web page. Through the intranet, an administrator can check the status of an applicant in relation to the selection process, or can search the human resources database to find a candidate whose profile fits a certain job description.

Open-ended interview Type of interview that encourages the candidate to talk freely and at length about the topics introduced by the interviewer(s).

Organizational change An organizational learning theory that is implemented in school districts under two rubrics. First, all stakeholders are identified with the organization; second, an organization must be focused on a vision that gives it direction.

Selection criteria Those ideal characteristics that if possessed by a person to a minimal degree would ensure successful performance of a given job.

Selection interview Structured conversation with direction and format between one or more interviewers and a candidate for a job in order to generate information about the person being interviewed; to learn about the candidate's opinions, beliefs, and attitudes; and to experience the candidate as a person.

Selection process Process designed to hire people who will be successful on the job; includes developing a job description, establishing selection criteria, advertising the job vacancy, interviewing candidates, checking reference and credentials, making the job offer, and notifying unsuccessful candidates.

Teacher Identification Clearinghouse National database of all teachers who have been denied certification and whose certification has been revoked or suspended for moral reasons.

Chapter 5: Placement and Induction

Induction Process designed to acquaint both newly employed and newly assigned employees with their job positions, the community, and their colleagues. With newly employed individuals an orientation to the school district is most beneficial.

Mentoring Practice of pairing newly employed teachers, staff members, and administrators with experienced colleagues to provide support and encouragement.

Personal adjustment The aspect of an induction program which focuses on helping a new employee establish professional relationships with colleagues and others with whom he or she is required to interact. It also refers to helping the employee acquire a sense of job satisfaction.

Placement Job assignment of an employee based upon the best judgment of the superintendent of schools or a designee in relation to the school district's programming, staff balancing, and the welfare of the students.

Chapter 6: Staff Development

Apprenticeship training Oldest form of training whereby a person understudies a master worker for a given period of time or until the trainee acquires the necessary skills.

Conditions of learning In order to facilitate learning, which is a change in human capability, the instructor must utilize stimulus, response, reinforcement, and motivation techniques.

Education Process of helping an individual understand and interpret knowledge through the development of reasoning processes that allow him or her to analyze the relationship between variables.

Off-the-job training Refers to various kinds of training techniques such as lectures, seminars, workshops, case studies, programmed instruction, and simulations.

On-the-job training Refers to training in which employees are placed in the actual work situation in order for them to learn by doing but are monitored by a supervisor.

Professional learning community A school or school district that has four focuses: (1) on learning rather than teaching, (2) on collaboration, (3) on viewing all members of the community as learners, and (4) on self accountability.

Program design Process of matching needs with available resources through an effective delivery method.

Staff development Because of knowledge expansion and advances in technology, every employee is in need of acquiring new information, understanding, and skills in order to meet the goals and objectives of a school district. The staff development dimension consists of conducting needs assessments, establishing staff development goals and objectives, designing programs, implementing delivery plans, and evaluating the programs.

Teacher centers Places where teachers determine their own staff development needs and, on their own initiative, implement staff development programs.

Training Process of learning a sequence of programmed behaviors that can be broken down and analyzed in order to determine the best way to perform certain tasks. Training is most effective in learning routine tasks.

Chapter 7: Performance Evaluation

Drug-Free Workplace Act of 1989 Federal law that gives employers the choice of rehabilitating or dismissing employees working in federal grant programs who are convicted of drug abuse offenses in the workplace.

Due process Procedures enacted to safeguard the rights of an employee, including the right to a fair and impartial hearing on allegations of noncompliance, with the policies, goals, objectives, rules, and regulations of a school district.

Employment termination Cessation of a person's employment for a cause based upon documentation that can stand up against legal scrutiny.

Evaluation instrument Formal document used by supervisors in evaluating the performance of personnel in relation to behavior traits and/or goals and objectives.

Evaluation process In human resources administration from a central-office perspective, refers to the development of policies, procedures, methods, and instruments used in evaluating the performance of personnel with emphasis on legal and due process considerations.

Interstate New Teacher Assessment and Support Consortium (INTASC) A national consortium that developed standards considered to be best practice for the licensure of teachers in many states.

Progressive discipline Corrective action taken by a supervisor when an employee does not meet socially acceptable standards or comply with the rules and regulations of a school district. The severity of such corrective measures depends upon the type of behavior exhibited by the employee and the number of incidences.

Results evaluation Method of evaluating the performance of an employee based upon objectives that were developed by the employee and agreed to by his or her supervisor.

Trials evaluation Method of evaluating the performance of an employee against a predetermined set of performance indicators.

Chapter 8: Compensation

Administrative Service Organization (ASO) Refers to a third-party administrator under contract to a school district and responsible for monitoring and processing claims when a school district is self-insured.

Career ladder Advancement to a higher level of recognition and financial rewards because of attaining a higher level of professional proficiency.

Catastrophic case management When an employee, his or her spouse, or his or her dependent suffers a catastrophic illness and a case manager assists the patient and his or her physician to access the best treatment at the lowest cost.

Consolidated Omnibus Budget Reconciliation Act of 1986 (COBRA) Federal law that permits an employee, employee's spouse, and dependents to continue health care coverage through the school district's group insurance programs under certain conditions when the employee is no longer employed by the district.

Compensation packaging The distribution of an individual employee's compensation into a certain amount of salary and into certain fringe benefits based on his or her expressed desire and needs.

Copayment Amount of money an employee pays for medical services in addition to that paid by the school district's medical plan; usually, a significantly smaller amount than the district's portion.

Deductibles Amount of money, usually within a calendar year, that an employee must pay for medical and hospital services before a school district's insurance programs begin to pay the remaining cost of the services.

Direct compensation That part of a compensation program that comprises salary, overtime pay, holiday pay, and merit pay.

Expectancy model Model for compensating employees by which they can readily understand that when they act in the best interest of the school district, they are acting in their own best interests.

Extrinsic compensation Usually divided into direct and indirect compensation.

Fringe benefits Benefits available to all employees resulting from a direct fiscal expenditure; usually classified as insurance programs, paid time away from work, and services.

Garnishment Legal summons to deduct a certain amount of money from an employee's salary for remission to a court in order to satisfy a creditor.

Health Insurance Portability and Accountability Act of 1996 A federal law guaranteeing certain health insurance coverage to employees, their spouses, and their dependents, even if they have preexisting medical conditions.

Health Maintenance Organization (HMO) In this approach to health care management, health insurance and the delivery of health care are combined. Physicians receive a salary for providing services or, through a contract, the physicians receive a fixed per-patient payment regardless of the number of visits.

Indemnity health care plan Traditional health care insurance plan that allows the employee, employee's spouse, and dependents to choose any physician and hospital in order to receive services.

Independent Practice Association (IPA) Groups or networks of physicians in which physicians remain independent while contracting with HMOs.

Indirect compensation That part of a compensation program which includes protection programs, pay for time away from work, and services.

Insurance company ratings Nationally recognized independent rating companies like A.M. Best of Oldwick, Duff & Phelps of Chicago, Moody's of New York, and Standard & Poor's of

New York rate insurance companies according to their performance and financial solvency.

Intrinsic compensation Satisfaction that accompanies the successful performance of job responsibilities through participation in the policy-making process, job discretion, responsibility, and opportunities for staff development.

Managed health care Approach to coordinating services around the patient and thereby producing a more efficient health care delivery system which also will be more cost-effective.

Mandatory fringe benefits Benefits which are required by law and constitute a direct cost to a school district. All states require districts to contribute to employee retirement, unemployment, and workers' compensation programs.

Medical Savings Accounts (MSA) Established by the Health Insurance Portability and Accountability Act (HIPAA), this program is an attempt to manage the rising cost of health care. Under certain conditions employers can place the savings that are realized through establishing high medical deductibles into an employee savings account which can be supplemented by employee contributions in order to pay minor health care expenses.

Merit pay Financial compensation in addition to a person's salary as a reward for above-average job performance.

Negotiated agreements A practice that is used by school districts that have difficulty in recruiting and hiring highly qualified administrators and teachers. Such districts are designing compensation packages that are tailormade to meet the employment demands of desirable candidates.

Out-of-network If an employee, spouse, or dependent accesses the services of a physician or hospital that is not under contract to an HMO or a PPO network, the health care plan pays a smaller portion of the costs that result from receiving the services.

Point of Service (POS) An HMO plan that permits a member to access health care services outside the HMO. However, the HMO plan usually imposes a high deductible for such services and will pay a much smaller portion of the cost after the deductible is reached.

Preferred Provider Organization (PPO) Individual health care professionals, hospitals, health care organizations, or groups of health care organizations that provide services to employees, their spouses, or dependents at a discount.

Primary care physician Health care professional who acts as a gatekeeper, making the referrals that are required by the managed care plan for the patient to receive health care services.

Salary and wage administration The management of direct compensation, which includes compensation research and development, payroll management, position control, and salary determination.

Salary schedule Method of calculating an individual teacher's salary based upon either an incremental or an index schedule that credits seniority, number of graduate course hours, and academic degrees.

Service Component of indirect compensation that provides a benefit to employees, such as a wellness program, tuition reimbursement, employee assistance program, and paid attendance at workshops or conventions.

Small Business Job Protection Act of 1996 Commonly referred to as the "Minimum Wage Law" because it increased the take-home wages of employees.

Social Security The U.S. government's attempt to care for and protect the aged by ensuring them a minimum standard of living through a monthly allottment of money resulting from a trust fund that is transferred from one generation to the next.

Third-party health care A company hired by a school district to manage its health care program, including cost analysis, cost projection, case management, catastrophic case management, utilization review, and claims management.

Unemployment compensation State laws that provide benefits to individuals who are without a job, if they comply with certain regulations.

Voluntary fringe benefits Indirect compensation programs provided to employees by a board of education, usually in the form of insurance programs, time away from work, and services.

Workers' compensation State programs that provide benefits to an individual injured or disabled because of a job-related activity.

Chapter 9: Collective Negotiations

Agency shop Situation in a school district in which certain employees are not members of the union that is the bargaining agent for the bargaining unit to which they belong and, thus, are required to pay a fee to the union.

Arbitration An impasse procedure by which a board of education and an employees' union agree to be bound by the decision of a third party in the bargaining process or in a grievance.

Bargaining power The favorable balance of influence to compel the other party's agreement with a proposal or entire proposal package because of the consequences accompanying disagreement.

Bargaining process At-the-table engagement of representatives from the board of education and an employees' union concerning salary, fringe benefits, and working conditions.

Bargaining unit Those employees who are organized into a category by reason of the fact that they have a community of interest in order for them to be represented in collective negotiations.

Bargaining unit determination Process of determining which employees have a community of interest so they can be organized into a category for the purposes of collective negotiations. Size of the group and effective administration are additional considerations.

Certification of bargaining agent Designation by an authorized state agency or the board of education that a certain organization or union is representing a bargaining unit as its exclusive bargaining agent.

Collaborative bargaining The entire process of negotiations that includes recognition and bargaining unit determination, the bargaining process, impasse procedures, and master agreement administration.

Community of interest Designation that a certain group of employees share common skills, functions, levels of education, and working conditions.

Court injunction Order from a court of jurisdiction to perform or to cease performance of an activity. A court order requiring a group of striking employees to return to work is an example of an injunction.

Dues checkoff Deduction of membership dues from an employee's paycheck remitted to the union or organization.

Employee organization Organization or union that represents employees in the collective negotiations process concerning salary, fringe benefits, and working conditions.

Exclusive representation Designation that refers to an organization or union that is the exclusive representative of a bargaining unit. Such designation is usually given by a state agency or the board of education after a recognition procedure has been carried out.

Fact finding An impasse procedure under which testimony from interested parties is taken, and information is gathered and analyzed, to formulate a recommendation for resolving a grievance or an impasse in the bargaining process.

Fair share fee Usually the equivalent of dues proportioned to cover the service that is rendered by a union or organization in the collective negotiations process. This fee is paid by nonorganization or nonunion members because they are benefitting from the representation.

Federal Mediation and Conciliation Service (FMCS) An independent agency of the federal government created by Congress in 1974 for the purpose of promoting labor-management peace. The agency is staffed by professional mediators.

Grievance procedures Process for resolving an allegation by an employee or an employee organization or union that a school district or an administrator of the district misapplied, misinterpreted, or violated a provision of a master agreement.

Impasse Formal designation by the representatives of the board of education and the representatives of the employees that agreement cannot be reached on an issue or issues in the at-the-table bargaining process. Initiates predetermined impasse procedures.

Labor-management relations committee Committee composed of administrators and employees from a school district who meet on a regular basis in order to resolve concerns, problems, and issues related to working conditions.

Management rights Those responsibilities that are endemic and necessary to the administration of a school district.

Master agreement Provisions arising out of the collective negotiations process that have been approved by both the board of education and the employees and have been put into writing. The provisions set forth in the master agreement have the force of board policy.

Mediation An impasse procedure whereby a third party meets together or separately with the representatives of the board of education and the employees in order to help them resolve an issue arising during collective negotiations or from a grievance. Mediation is always a voluntary measure.

National Labor Relations Board (NLRB) Federal agency created by Congress in 1935 through enactment of the National Labor Relations Act, that has jurisdiction to conduct union representation elections and to apply this Act against unfair labor practices in the private sector.

Recognition Acceptance by the board of education of an organization or union as the authorized representative of certain employees for the purpose of collective negotiations.

Representation election Recognition procedure that identifies an employee organization or union as the exclusive representative of a defined bargaining unit. The organization or union receiving a majority of the votes is the exclusive representative.

Scope of negotiations The subject matter of collective negotiations, usually consisting of salary, fringe benefits, and working conditions. The scope is commonly a bargained issue.

Union Organized employee group whose representatives meet with the representatives of the board of education for the purpose of collectively negotiating salaries, fringe benefits, and working conditions.

Union shop Agreement between the board of education and a union whereby an employee is required to become a member of a bargain unit as a condition of employment and to remain a member during the term of the bargained agreement.

Win-win bargaining Approach to collective negotiations having the goal of producing a nonadversarial climate that will allow both sides to form consensus on issues related to salary, fringe benefits, and working conditions.

Work stoppage Commonly referred to as a strike; occurs when employees of a school district refuse to perform their responsibilities as a protest against the actions of the board of education, usually in relation to the collective negotiations process.

Chapter 10: Legal and Ethical Issues in the Administration of Human Resources

Civil law Law that is concerned with protecting the rights that exist between individuals, between an individual and a corporate entity, or between two corporate entities. Most of the litigation that arises out of human resources management concerns civil law.

Common law Also called "case law" because it is derived from court decisions rather than from legislative acts. Past court decisions are considered to be binding on subsequent cases if the material facts are similar, which is the doctrine of precedent.

Constitutions Bodies of precepts that provide the framework within which government carries out its duties. The federal and state constitutions contain provisions that secure the personal, property, and political rights of citizens, which is a concern in developing human resources processes and procedures.

Contract An agreement between a school district and an employee that consists of an offer and acceptance, a competent person, consideration, legal subject matter, and proper form.

Criminal law Concerned with protecting the rights of society and thus, local, state, and federal governments representing the people are responsible for prosecuting wrongs committed against society by individuals or corporate entities.

Errors and omissions liability insurance Insurance that pays for the defense of an employee and actual damages arising out of a civil lawsuit.

Ethics Human conduct norms that provide a guide for administrators in the practice of human resources management.

Lawsuit A petition filed with an appropriate court of jurisdiction setting forth a cause of action.

Libel Defamation committed through communicating false information in writing that brings hatred or ridicule on a person and produces some type of harm to him or her.

Policy Guidelines setting forth the authority and general means of attaining the goals and objectives of a school district or a division, department, or other administrative component of a district.

Reasonable person concept Criterion in liability litigation against which the actions of the defendant will be compared. The reasonable person is someone who possesses average intelligence; normal perception and memory; and the same level of skills, knowledge, experience, and physical characteristics as the defendant.

Role of attorney An attorney's expertise centers around his or her ability to analyze the material facts in a case, research the statutes and precedents of other court cases, and set forth the position of the plaintiff or defendant in a reasonable manner.

Slander Defamation committed through communicating false information by word of mouth that brings hatred or ridicule on a person and produces some type of harm to him or her.

Tort A civil wrong, other than a breach of contract, committed against a person or a person's property. Libel and slander are types of torts committed against a person.

U.S. judicial system A mixed system that utilizes principles of both civil and common law.

ENDNOTES

Chapter 1

1. Iowa Association of School Boards, *School Board Member Handbook* (Des Moines, IA, 2009), 37–40.
2. Ronald W. Rebore, *A Human Relations Approach to the Practice of Educational Leadership,* (Boston: Allyn & Bacon, 2004), 75–85, 153–155.
3. Herman T. Tavani, *Ethics and Technology: Ethical Issues in an Age of Information and Communication Technology* (Hoboken: NJ, 2007), pp. 5–7.
4. William G. Cunningham and Paula A. Cordeiro, *Educational Leadership: A Bridge to Improved Practice,* 4th ed. (Boston: Allyn & Bacon, 2009), pp. 81–88.
5. Vern Brimley, Jr. and Rulon R. Garfield, *Financing Education in a Climate of Change* (Boston: Allyn & Bacon, 2008), pp. 358–359.
6. Barbara Kiviat, "Jobs Are the New Assets," *Time* Magazine Annual Special Issue, 173, no. 11 (March 23, 2009), 46–47.

Chapter 2

1. David A. DeCenzo and Stephen P. Robbins, *Fundamentals of Human Resource Management*, 9th ed. (Hoboken, NJ: John Wiley & Sons, Inc., 2007), pp. 124–126.
2. American Association of School Administrators, www.aasa.org (as of 2009).
3. David A. DeCenzo and Stephen P. Robbins, *Fundamentals of Human Resources Management*, pp. 126–131, 138.
4. Ronald W. Rebore, *The Ethics of Educational Leadership* (Upper Saddle River, New Jersey: Merrill/Prentice Hall, 2001), pp. 227–238.
5. John Rawls, University of Stanford Encyclopedia of Philosophy. plato.stanford.edu/ (as of 2009).
6. U.S. Constitution, Bill of Rights, and Declaration of Independence. www.archives.gov/ (as of 2009).
7. Labor Law Reports—Employment Practices, Office of Federal Contract Compliance Manual, 2nd ed., Report 86, No. 580. www.dol.gov/esa/ofccp/regs/compliance/fccm/fccmanul.htm (as of 2009).
8. The eight steps are a composite of those found in the Equal Employment Opportunity Commission's Web site, www.eeoc.gov (as of 2009).
9. Federal Equal Employment Opportunity Commission's Web site, www.eeoc.gov (as of 2009).
10. Federal Equal Employment Opportunity Commission, Administrative Process. www.eeoc.gov/charge/overview_charge_processing.html (as of 2009).
11. Federal Equal Employment Opportunity Commission, Bona Fide Occupational Qualification. www.eeoc.gov/policy/vii.html (as of 2009).
12. Equal Employment Opportunity Commission. www.eeoc.gov (as of 2009).
13. Peter Schmidt, "Affirmative Action Survives, and So Does the Debate," *The Chronicle of Higher Education*, Special Report (July 4, 2003), S1–S7.
14. Civil Rights Act of 1991. www.eeoc.gov/policy/cra91.html (as of 2009).
15. Department of Health, Education, and Welfare, *Nondiscrimination on the Basis of Handicap*, Federal Register, 41, no. 96, May 17, 1976. www.gpoaccess.gov/fr/ (as of 2009).
16. Department of Health, Education, and Welfare, *Nondiscrimination on the Basis of Handicap,* paragraph 87.4 of the Federal Register. www.gpoaccess.gov/fr/ (as of 2009).
17. Federal Equal Employment Opportunity Commission, *The Americans with Disabilities Act of 1990: Your Responsibilities as an Employer.* www.eeoc.gov/types/ada.html (as of 2009).
18. Equal Employment Opportunity Commission, *Final Rule: Equal Employment Opportunity for Individuals with Disabilities*, Federal Register, 56, no. 144. www.gpoaccess.gov/fr/ (as of 2009).

19. Equal Employment Opportunity Commission, *Final Rule, 35735*. www.gpoaccess.gov/fr/ (as of 2009).
20. Ibid., *35735–35736*. www.gpoaccess.gov/fr/ (as of 2009).
21. Federal Equal Employment Opportunity Commission. www.eeoc.gov (as of 2009).
22. Federal Equal Employment Opportunity Commission, *Accessibility*. www.eeoc.gov/facts/fs-disab.html (as of 2009).
23. Federal Equal Employment Opportunity Commission, *Noncompliance*. www.eeoc.gov/policy/docs/chap10.html (as of 2009).
24. American Civil Liberties Organization, *AIDS and Employment Discrimination*. www.aclu.org (as of 2009). Department of Justice, *AIDS and Employment Discrimination*. www.usdoj.gov/crt/ (as of 2009).
25. Vietnam Era Veterans Readjustment Assistance Act of 1974. www.dol.gov/compliance/laws/compvevraa.htm (as of 2009).
26. Civilian Health and Medical Program of the Uniformed Services, TRICARE. www.tricare.mil/ (as of 2009)
27. Omnibus Transportation Employee Testing Act of 1991. www.dot.gov/ost/dapc/ (as of 2009).
28. Family and Medical Leave Act of 1993. www.dol.gov/esa/whd/fmla/ (as of 2009).
29. Federal Equal Employment Opportunity Commission, *Equality for Women*. www.eeoc.gov/epa/index.html (as of 2009).
30. Sara Lipka, "High Court Expands Protections of Title IX," *The Chronicle of Higher Education* LI, no. 31 (April 8, 2005), A1, A36.
31. Equal Employment Opportunity Commission, *Retaliation*. www.eeoc.gov/types/retaliation.html (as of 2009).
32. Pregnancy Disability Amendment of Title VII, Civil Rights Act of 1964. eeoc.com/guidance/discrimination/pregnancy-discrimination/ (as of 2009).
33. Equal Employment Opportunity Commission, *Guidelines on Sexual Harassment in the Workplace*. www.eeoc.gov/types/sexual_harassment.html (as of 2009).
34. Equal Pay Act of 1963. www.eeoc.gov/policy/epa.html (as of 2009).
35. Department of Justice, *Equal Pay*. www.usdoj.gov (as of 2009).
36. Age Discrimination in Employment Act of 1967. www.eeoc.gov/policy/adea.html (as of 2009).
37. Robert Half, "Attracting and Retaining Millennial Workers," *Information Executive*, 10920374, 11, no. 7 (July 2008), 4, 9, 11–13.

Chapter 3

1a. National Center for Educational Statistics, *Teacher Career Choices* (April 2008).
1b. National Center for Educational Statistics, *Mobility in the Teacher Workforce* (2005).
1c. National Center for Educational Statistics, *Projections of Education Statistics to 2017* (September 2008). http://nces.ed.gov/
2. National Center for Educational Statistics, *National Indian Education Study* (2007). http://nces.ed.gov/
3. Kathryn H. Au and Karen M. Blake, "Cultural Identity and Learning to Teach in a Diverse Community: Findings from a Collective Case Study," *Journal of Teacher Education*, 54, no. 3 (May/June 2003), 192–205.
4. David A. Decenzo and Stephen P. Robbins, *Human Resource Management*, 7th ed. (New York: John Wiley & Sons, Inc., 2002), pp. 150–153.
5a. Sheila J. Henderson, "Follow Your Bliss: A Process for Career Happiness," *Journal of Counseling and Development* (Summer 2000), 305–315.
5b. Sherry E. Sullivan and Lisa Mainiero, "Using the Kaleidoscope Career Model to Understand the Changing Patterns of Women's Careers: Designing HRD Programs That Attract and Retain Women," *Advances in Developing Human Resources*, 10, no. 1 (February 2008), 32–49.
5c. Shelley M. MacDermid and Andrea K. Wittenborn, "Lessons From Work-Life Research for Developing Human Resources," *Advances in Developing Human Resources*, 9, no. 4 (2007), 556–568.
5d. Roni Reiter-Palmon, Marcy Young, Jill Strange, Renae Manning, and Joseph James, "Occupationally Specific Skills: Using Skills to Define and Understand Jobs and Their

Requirements," *Human Resource Management Review* 16 (2006), 356–375.
6. David A. Decenzo and Stephen P. Robbins, *Human Resource Management*, 154–162.
7. Coomes, Michael D. and Robert DeBard, eds., "Serving the Millennial Generation." *New Directions for Student Services.* (San Francisco: Jossey-Bass, 2004), pp. 52–56.
8. Half, Robert, "Attracting and Retaining Millennial Workers," *Information Executive*, 10920374, ll, no. 7 (July 2008), 2, 3, 5.
9. Ibid.

Chapter 4

1. David A. DeCenzo and Stephen P. Robins, *Human Resources Management*, 7th ed. (New York: John Wiley & Sons, Inc., 2002), p. 191.
2. Ibid., pp. 136–143.
3. H. B. Polansky and M. Semmel, "Hiring the Best and Retaining Them," *School Administrator*, 63, no. 8 (2006), 46–47.
4. M. Yate, *Hiring the Best: A Manager's Guide to Effective Interviewing and Recruiting,* (Avon, MA: Adams Media, 2006), 109.
5. S. M. Koenigsknecht, "Stacking the Deck During Interviews," *School Administrator*, 63, no. 3 (2006), 55.
6. W. G. Cunningham and P. A. Cordeivo, *Educational Leadership: A Problem-Based Approach* (Boston: Pearson, 2006), 286–287.
7. L. Davila and L. Kursmark, *How to Choose the Right Person for the Right Job Every Time,* (New York: McGraw-Hill, 2005), p. 44.
8. Equal Employment Opportunity Commission (www.eeoc.gov).
9. N. L. Essex, "The Legal Toll of Candor in Personnel Recommendations," *School Administrator*, 62, no. 9 (2005), 47.
10. C. Garvey, "Outsourcing Background Checks," *HR Magazine*, 46, no. 3 (2001), 95–104.
11. Robert Half, "Attracting and Retaining Millennial Workers," *Information Executive,* 10920374, ll, no. 7 (July 2008), 2, 3, 5.
12. Michael D. Coomes and Robert DeBard, eds., *Serving the Millennial Generation: New Directions for Student Services* (San Francisco: Jossey-Bass, 2004), 52–56.

Chapter 5

1. Linda Molner Kelley, "Why Induction Matters," *Journal of Teacher Education*, 55, no. 5 (November/December 2004), 438.
2. Synthia Simon Millinger, "Helping New Teachers Cope," *Educational Leadership*, 61, no. 8 (May 2004), 66–69.
3. Pamela Grossman and Clarissa Thompson, "District Policy and Beginning Teachers: A Lens on Teacher Learning," *Educational Evaluation and Policy Analysis*, 26, no. 4 (Winter 2004), 298.
4. Elizabeth Useem and Ruth Curran Neild, "Supporting New Teachers in the City," *Educational Leadership* (May 2005), 46.
5. Linda Gilbert, "What Helps Beginning Teachers?" *Educational Leadership* (May 2005), 38.
6. C. R. Wanberg, E. T. Welsh, and S. A. Hezlett, "Mentoring Research: A Review and Dynamic Process Model." In J. J. Martocchio & G. R. Ferris (Eds.), *Research in Personnel and Human Resources Management,* vol. 22 (Oxford, UK: Elsevier Science LTD, 2003), pp. 39–124.
7. Manda H. Rosser, "Mentoring From the Top: CEO Perspectives," *Advances in Developing Human Resources,* 7, no. 4 (November 2005), 527, 530–537.
8. A. Darwin, "Critical Reflection on Mentoring in Work Settings," *Adult Education Quarterly*, 50 (2000), 197–211.
9. Kimberly S. McDonald and Linda M. Hite, "Ethical Issues in Mentoring: The Role of HRD," *Advances in Developing Human Resources*, 7, no. 4 (November 2005), 571–572.
10. L. T. Eby and S. E. McManus, "The Protégé's Perspective Regarding Negative Mentoring Experiences: The Development of a Taxonomy," *Journal of Vocational Behavior*, 65 (2004), 255–275.
11. Rick Allen, "Supporting New Educators," *Educational Leadership* (May 2005), 96.
12. Robert Half, "Attracting and Retaining Millennial Workers," *Information Executive,* 10920374, ll, no. 7 (July 2008), 4–5.
13. Michael D. Coomes and Robert DeBard, eds., *Serving the Millennial Generation: New Directions for Student Services.* (San Francisco: Jossey-Bass, 2004), 34–43.

Chapter 6

1. William A. Firestone, Melinda M. Mangin, M. Cecilia Martinez, and Terrie Polovsky, "Leading Coherent Professional Development: A Comparison of Three Districts," *Educational Administration Quarterly*, 41, no. 3 (August 2005), 415–416.
2. Richard DuFour, "What Is Professional Learning Community?" *Educational Leadership*, 61, no. 8 (May 2004), 6–11.
3. Husby, Vicki R., *Individualizing Professional Development: A Framework for Meeting School and District Goals* (Thousand Oaks, California: Corwin Press, 2005), pp. 3–4.
4. David A. DeCenzo and Stephen P. Robbins, *Fundamentals of Human Resource Management*, 9th ed. (Hoboken, NJ: John Wiley & Sons, Inc., 2007), p. 211.
5. Husby, *Individualizing Professional Development* (2004), pp. 6–7.
6. Peter Earley and Sara Bubb, *Leading and Managing Continuing Professional Development: Developing People, Developing Schools* (England, London: Paul Chapman Publishing, 2004), pp. 39–46.
7. William A. Firestone, et al., *Leading Coherent Professional Development* (2005), p. 417.
8. Ibid.
9. Peter Earley, *Leading and Managing Continuing Professional Development* (2004), pp. 47–52.
10. William G. Cunningham and Paula A. Cordeiro, Educational *Leadership: A Bridge to Improved Practice*, 4th ed. (Allyn & Bacon, 2009), pp. 315–319.
11. William Penuel, R., Barry J. Fishman, Ryoko Yamaguchi, and Lawrence P. Gallagher, "What Makes Professional Development Effective? Strategies That Foster Curriculum Implementation," *American Educational Research Journal*, 44, no. 4 (December 2007), 928–932, 949–952.
12. Earley, Peter, *Leading and Managing Continuing Professional Development* (2004), pp. 77–84.
13. Thomas R. Guskey, "Does it Make a Difference? Evaluating Professional Development," *Educational Leadership*, 59, no. 6 (March 2002), 45–51.
14. Gabriel Diaz-Maggioli, *Teacher-Centered Professional Development*. Alexandria, Virginia: Association for Supervision and Curriculum Development, (Alexandria, Virginia: Association for Supervision and Curriculum Development 2004). pp. 1–18.
15. Stephen P. Gordon, *Professional Development for School Improvement: Empowering Learning Communities* (Boston: Pearson Education, Inc., 2004). pp. 138–140, 145–153.
16. David A. DeCenzo and Stephen P. Robbins, *Fundamentals of Human Resource Management*, 9th ed. (2007), pp. 211–212.
17. Ibid., pp. 211–213.
18. Ibid., p. 212.
19. Stephen P. Gordon, *Professional Development for School Improvement* (2004), pp. 129–130.
20. Lovely, Suzette and Austin G. Buffum, *Generations at School: Building an Age-Friendly Learning Community* (Thousand Oaks, CA: Corwin Press, 2007), pp. 75–88.

Chapter 7

1. Marilyn Cochran-Smith, "Teaching Quality Matters," *The Journal of Policy, Practice, and Research in Teacher Education*, 54, no. 2 (March/April 2003), 95.
2. David A. DeCenzo and Stephen P. Robins, *Fundamentals of Human Resource Management*, 9th ed. (Hoboken, NJ: John Wiley & Sons, Inc., 2007), pp. 291–293.
3. Carolyn J. Kelley and Kara Finnigan, "The Effects of Organizational Context on Teacher Expectancy," *Educational Administration Quarterly*, XXXIX, no. 5 (December 2003), 618–620.
4. Charlotte Danielson and Thomas L. McGreal, *Teacher Evaluation: To Enhance Professional Practice* (Princeton, New Jersey: Educational Testing Service, 2000), 110–114.
5. Council of Chief State School Officers, New Teacher Assessment and Support Consortium (INTASC) (May 2005), www.ccsso.org.
6. Ibid.
7. North Carolina State Board of Education and Department of Public Instruction, The INTASC Standards (May 2005), www.dpi.state.nc.us/pbl/pblintasc.htm (as of 2009).

8. David A. DeCenzo and Stephen P. Robins, *Fundamentals of Human Resource Management*, pp. 100–106.
9. Drug-Free Workplace Act of 1988, www.dolgov/asp/programs/drugs/workingpartners/regs/dfwp1988asp (as of 2009).
10. Equal Employment Opportunity Commission, www.eeoc.gov (as of 2009).
11. Lovely, Suzette and Austin G. Buffum, *Generations at School: Building an Age-Friendly Learning Community.* (Thousand Oaks, CA: Corwin Press, 2007), pp. 75–88.

Chapter 8

1. Pamela Babcock, *Find What Workers Want*, HR Magazine, 50, no. 4 (April 2005), 50–57.
2. David A. DeCenzo and Stephen P. Robbins, *Fundamentals of Human Resource Management*, 9th ed. (Hoboken, NJ: John Wiley & Sons, Inc., 2007), 286–300.
3. Koppich, Julia E., "All Teachers Are Not the Same: A Multiple Approach to Teacher Compensation," *Education Next*, 5, no. 1 (Winter 2005), 13–15.
4. Ackerman, Arlene, "Do the Math: Rethinking Teacher Compensation: Can We Afford Not To Change the Way Pay Them?," *The College Board Review*, no. 208 (Spring 2006), 34–37.
5. William C. Cunningham and Paula A. Cordeiro, *Educational Administration: A Problem-Based Approach* (Boston: Allyn & Bacon, 2000), 307.
6. Zhang, Zhijuan, Deborah A Verstegen, and Hoe Ryoung Kim, "Teacher Compensation and School Quality: New Findings from National and International Data," *Educational Considerations*, 35, no. 2 (Spring 2008), 25–26.
7. Kelor, Eileen M., "Catching Up with the Vaugn Express: Six Years of Standards-Based Teacher Evaluation and Performance Pay," *Education Policy Analysis Archives*, 13, no. 7 (January 23, 2005), 3–17.
8. David A. DeCenzo and Stephen P. Robbins, Fundamentals of Human Resource Management, 9th ed., 296–297.
9. Stites, Janet, "Equal Pay for the Sexes," *HR Magazine*, 50, no. 5 (May 2005), 65–69.
10. Amey Marilyn J. and Kim E VanDerLinden, "Merit Pay, Market Conditions, Equity, and Faculty Compensation," *The NEA 2002 Alamanac of Higher Education*, www.NEA.org. (2002), 22.
11. David A. DeCenzo and Stephen P. Robbins, *Fundamentals of Human Resource Management*, 9th ed., 288, 297.
12. McElroy, Edward J., "Teacher Compensation: What Can Be Done to Maintain (and Improve) Teachers' Wages and Benefits?" *Teaching K–8*, www.Teachingk-8.com. (August/September 2005), 8.
13. Susan E. Morgan, Tom Reichert, and Tyler R. Harrison, *From Numbers to Words: Reporting Statistical Results for the Social Sciences* (Boston: Allyn & Bacon, 2002), pp. 1–4.
14. Hanushek, Eric A., "The Single Salary Schedule and Other Issues of Teacher Pay," *Peabody Journal of Education*, 82, no. 4 (2007), 579–584.
15. Ronald W. Rebore and Angela L. E. Walmsley, *An Evidence-Based Approach to the Practice of Educational Leadership* (New York: Pearson Education, Inc., 2007), pp. 6–12.
16. Small Business Regulatory Enforcement Fairness Act of 1996, www.sba.gov/advo/laws/sbrefa (as of 2009).
17. Internal Revenue Service, Nondiscrimination in 401(k), www.irs.gov/nondiscrimination401(k) (as of 2009). Newkirk Products, Inc., "Nondiscrimination Provisions," 1996 Tax Law Summary, 1996, 13.
18. Health Insurance Portability and Accountability Act of 1996, www.hhs.gov/hipaa (as of 2009).
19. Health Insurance Portability and Accountability Act of 1996, Medical Saving Accounts, www.hhs.gov/hipaa/msa (as of 2009).
20. Ronald W. Rebore and Angela L.E. Walmsley, *An Evidence-Based Approach to the Practice of Educational Leadership*, pp. 218–223.
21. David A. DeCenzo and Stephen P. Robbins, *Fundamentals of Human Resource Management*, 9th ed., pp. 318–319.
22. New York State Workers' Compensation Board, www.wcb/nys.gov (as of 2009).
23. Vern Brimley, Jr., and Rulon R. Garfield, *Financing Education in a Climate of Change*,

10th ed. (Boston: Pearson Education, Inc., 2008), pp. 341–343.

24. Lin Grensing-Pophas, "Health Education Turns Proactive," *HR Magazine*, 50, no. 4 (April 2005), 101–104.
25. William G. Cunningham and Paula A. Cordeiro, *Educational Leadership: A Bridge to Improved Practice*, 4th ed. (Boston: Pearson Education, Inc., 2009), p. 346.
26. Vern Brimley, Jr. and Rulon R. Garfield, *Financing Education in a Climate of Change*, pp. 351–353.

Chapter 9

1. Kathryn Tyles, "Good Faith Bargaining," *HR Magazine*, 50, no. 1 (2005), 51.
2. P. D. V. Marsh, *Contract Negotiation Handbook*, 3rd ed. (Burlington, VA: Gower, 2001), 224.
3. Ibid.
4. North Carolina School Boards Association. www.ncsba.org/advocacy/Advocacy.htm (as of 2008).
5. David A. Decenzo & Stephen P. Robbins, *Human Resource Management*, 7th ed. (New York: John Wiley & Sons, 2002), pp. 418–422.
6. Ibid., pp. 422–426.
7. Emily Cohen, Kate Walsh, and RiShawn Biddle, "Invisible Ink in Collective Bargaining: Why Key Issues Are Not Addressed," *National Council on Teacher Quality* (Washington, D.C.: The Council, 2008), pp. 1–24.
8. Kerchner, Charles Taylor & Julia E. Koppich, "Negotiating What Matters Most: Collective Bargaining and Student Achievement," *American Journal of Education*, 113 (Electronically Published, March 2007), 349–365.
9. C. Daniel Raisch & Charles J. Russo, "How to Succeed at Collective Bargaining,"*School Business Affairs,* (www.asbointl.org, December 2005), pp. 8–10.
10. Linda Kaboolian, "Table Talk," *Education Next*, 6, no. 3 (Summer 2006), pp. 14–17.
11. Susan Black, "Bargaining: It's in Your Best Interest," *American School Board Journal* (Electronically produced 2008), 52–53.
12. Hewitt, Paul, "Bargaining within the School Culture," *Leadership*, 36, no. 5 (May/June 2007), 26–30.
13. Todd A. DeMitchell, "Unions, Collective Bargaining, and the Challenges of Leading," *The Sage Handbook of Educational Leadership: Advances in Theory, Research, and Practice* (Thousand Oaks, California: Sage Publications, 2005), pp. 545–546.
14. Martinez-Pecino, Roberto, Lourdes Munduate, Francisco J. Medina, and Martin C. Euwema, "Effectiveness of Mediation Strategies in Collective Bargaining," *Industrial Relations*, 47, no. 3 (July 2008), 480–495.
15. Brady, Kevin P., "Bargaining," *Yearbook of Education Law* (2007), 100–107.
16. Fuller, Howard & George A. Mitchell, "A Culture of Complaint," *Education Next*, 6, no. 3 (Summer 2006), 18–22.

Chapter 10

1. Charles J. Russo, *Reutter's the Law of Public Education*, 6th ed. (New York: Foundation Press, 2006), 434–436.
2. Ibid., pp. 1–2.
3. Ibid., pp. 2–14.
4. Ibid., pp. 15–24.
5. Ibid., pp. 375–408.
6. Moran Mayo, *Rethinking the Reasonable Person: An Egalitarian Reconstruction of the Objective Standard* (New York: Oxford University Press, 2003), 315–316.
7. Fulmer, Robert M., "The Challenge of Ethical Leadership," *Organizational Dynamics*, 33, no. 3, 2004, 303–317.
8. Miller, Paul, "Strategy and the Ethical Management of Human Resources," *ProQuest LLC*, 2008, www.proquest.umi.com.
9. Buckley, M. Ronald, Danielle S. Beu, Dwight D. Frink, Jack L. Howard, Howard Berkson, Tommie A. Mobbs, Gerald R. Ferris, "Ethical Issues in Human Resources Systems," *Human Resources Management Review*, 11, 2001, 11–29, www.HRmanagementreview.com.
10. Winstanley, Diana, and Jean Woodall, "The Ethical Dimension of Human Resource Management," *Human Resource Management Journal*, 10, no. 2, 2000, 5–20.

INDEX

H

I

J

K

L

T

U

V

W

Y

Z